The Writers, Artists, Singers, and Musicians of the National Hungarian Jewish Cultural Association (OMIKE), 1939–1944

Shofar Supplements in Jewish Studies

Zev Garber, Editor
Los Angeles Valley College

The Writers, Artists, Singers, and Musicians of the National Hungarian Jewish Cultural Association (OMIKE), 1939–1944

Edited by Jenő Lévai

Expanded English edition edited by Frederick Bondy

Translated by Anna Etawo

Purdue University Press
West Lafayette, Indiana

Printed in the United States of America.

First edition published 1943 by Jenő Lévai.
Originally published as *Írók, színészek, énekesek és zenészek regényes életútja a Goldmark-teremig: Az OMIKE színháza és művészei* (The Illustrious Careers of Writers, Artists, Singers and Musicians Associated with Goldmark Hall: The Theater and Artists of the OMIKE [Orszagos Magyar Izraelita Kozmuvelodesi Egyesulet; National Hungarian Jewish Cultural Society]).

Cataloging-in-Publication Data on file at the Library of Congress

ISBN 9781557537645 (pbk.: alk. paper)
ISBN 9781612494807 (epdf)
ISBN 9781612494814 (epub)

Cover image: Photo of 1941 performance of *A Denevér* (The Bat). Courtesy of the Hungarian Theater Museum and Institute, Budapest.

Dedicated to the artists of the OMIKE Művészakció, their martyrs, members of the Bondy, Ráfáel (Raphael), Katona (Klein), Erényi, and Váradi families, and all of the 565,000 Hungarian Jews who perished in the Holocaust.

Also dedicated to my dear, kind, lovely, and recently departed wife, Joan M. Bondy, z"l, who patiently stood beside me with encouragement over the many years spent to create this book.

—Frederick Bondy, editor of the English edition

Contents

Foreword to the English Edition xi
Magda Horák

Foreword to the Hungarian Edition xvii
Jenő Lévai

Editor's Note to the English Edition xix
Frederick Bondy

Introduction to the English Edition 1
István Deák

Chapter 1. The OMIKE Theater in Goldmark Hall 21

Samu Stern, President of the Jewish Religious Community of Pest
"The Cultural Mission of Hungarian Jewry Is to Ensure the Existence of the Artistic Enterprise" *22*
Géza Ribáry
"About Those Who Fulfill and Those Who Fail to Fulfill Their Obligations" *24*
Hugó Csergő
Quoting Géza Ribáry *25*

Chapter 2. The OMIKE Artistic Enterprise 29

The Leadership *29*
The Director *30*
Economic Structure of the Artistic Enterprise *31*
Official Duties and Regulations *31*
Artistic Duties *32*
Programming *32*
The OMIKE's Company *33*
Casting *34*

Chapter 3. The Drama Company 37

The Artistic Director and Dramaturgist (Playwright) *37*
OMIKE's Most Successful Writers: Hugó Csergő, Dezső Kellér, Jenő Mohácsi, Ferenc Molnár, and Ernő Szép *39*
The Artists Associated with the OMIKE Artistic Enterprise and Others Involved in Theatrical Operations *53*
The Main Director of the Drama Company *56*
Notable Members of the Drama Ensemble:
Gyula Bartos, Lajos Gárdonyi, Lajos Gellért, József Gonda, Klári Lakos, Béla Lénárd, György Nagy and Kató Bán, Béla Ormos, Erzsi Palotai, Judit Párdányi, Sándor Radó, Alíz Rajna, Imre Rádai (Ráday), Magda Rosti (Rosty), Sándor Rott, Béla Salamon, Aladár Sarkadi, Zsuzsa Simon, Ibolya Solt, Dr. Dezső Szabó, Kálmán Szentiványi, Vilmos Szirmai, Ferike Vidor, and Kálmán Zátony *57*

Chapter 4. Musical Life in the OMIKE Artistic Enterprise 97

The List of Artists Performing in Musical Events (Opera, Concert, Operetta) *97*
The Musical Direction of the OMIKE *98*
Conductors of the OMIKE *100*
The Vocal Artists of the OMIKE Artistic Enterprise:
Dezső Ernster, Sándor Farkas, Pál Fehér, Kató Gergely, Manci Herendi, Oszkár Kálmán, Ilona Ladányi, Andor Lendvay, The Ney Family, Erzsi Radnai, Gabriella Relle, Vera Rózsa, and Annie Spiegel *103*
Known and Unknown Heroes of the Orchestra *122*

Chapter 5. The Technical Operation of the OMIKE Artistic Enterprise 125

The Auditorium *125*
The Stage *126*
The Invisible Actors *128*
Preparing for the Show *130*

Chapter 6. A Few Interesting Statistical Data 135

Afterword to the English Edition 137
Péter Bársony

Acknowledgments to the English Edition 149
Frederick Bondy

Appendix 1. Photographs of Goldmark Hall, Performances, and OMIKE Artists 153

Appendix 2. Programs of *Művészakció* Plays, Concerts, Operas, Cabaret, and Operettas 183

Appendix 3. Announcements of Fine Arts Expositions for Painters, Graphic Artists, and Sculptors 207

Appendix 4. OMIKE *Művészakció* Victims of the Holocaust 213

Glossary to the English Edition 217
Zvi Erenyi

Contributors to the Hungarian Edition 231

Contributors to the English Edition 233

Bibliography 237

Index 241

Foreword to the English Edition

The writers of the book entitled *Írók, színészek, énekesek és zenészek regényes életűtja a Goldmark-teremig: Az OMIKE színháza és művészei* (The Illustrious Careers of Writers, Artists, Singers, and Musicians Associated with Goldmark Hall: The Theater and Artists of the OMIKE), edited by Jenő Lévai and published in the fall of 1943, couldn't have known that only a few months later, on March 19, 1944, at the main rehearsal of one of Molière's comedies, a few German soldiers led by a young director from Szeged, István Horváth, would end the almost five-year-long activity of the OMIKE *Művészakció* (Artistic Enterprise). This meant the end of Europe's probably most significant Artistic Enterprise, working with the most people and consisting of different genres and which was operating during the fascist period in Budapest.

The writing of what would become a memorial book by Lévai and his companions was done partially by the necessity for the artists to earn a living and partially with the aim of encouraging people to attend the "ghettoized" theater. Thus, because of the theater's abrupt end, Lévai's book cannot be expected to give a full picture of its subject, the OMIKE (*Országos Magyar Izraelita Közművelődési Egyesület*; National Hungarian Jewish Cultural Society), or of its versatile activities. In spite of this, the work is of great importance from a cultural and a historical point of view.

Lipót Lőw (Leopold Low, 1811–1875), a rabbi and a scholar, who called for the emancipation of the Jews, was the first to urge the establishment of a Jewish cultural society in 1865. Despite several attempts, however, the society was only organized in 1909, following the emancipation of the Jews as individuals by the Habsburgs (1867), the Hungarian Law of Reception of Judaism (1895), and finally the firm intervention by the rabbi and philosopher of religion, Simon Hevesi. Wealthier Jews took an active part in establishing and running the OMIKE. It was also supported morally, and even financially, by numerous non-Jews in Budapest such as Mari Jászai, a prominent personality from Hungarian theater.

The OMIKE, mainly meant to serve a cultural purpose, had to also put significant efforts into social activity because of compelling circumstances (e.g., WWI, Numerus Clausus, anti-Jewish Laws). During its 35-year history, it ran language courses, a library, a cultural institution, a cafeteria, an army kitchen, a free school of fine arts, and summer holidays for children.

From the beginning of Admiral Miklós Horthy's regency in the spring of 1920, the development of Hungarian culture was soon affected by the government's intentions to divide intellectuals based on their political views and their origins, and by the forced exile of a part of the intelligentsia. Although the best of the Christian intelligentsia, for example, Béla Bartók, Zoltán Kodály, and other Hungarian writers and painters, protested against the First Jewish Law (1938), their protests proved futile. Hungarian cultural life was already influenced by the irredentism of official politics, racism, and the extreme right's violent rallies. With politics shifting more and more to the right, individual protests against segregation also proved to be pointless (Pál Jávor, one of the most popular and best-known actors of all time, was arrested by the Gestapo in 1944 and taken to Sopronkőhida because he protested at the *Theater and Film Chamber* [Actors' Guild] against the denigration of his colleagues and fellow actors). Members of the press, who took action against fascism, were also silenced and often imprisoned. Following the German occupation, anti-Nazi newspapers were banned.

The new government cultural policy in the declared interest of "enforcing and ensuring the requirements of national spirit and Christian morality," in other words, "the elimination of Jews," was carried out within a short period of time. At the same time, the quality of theatrical programs and public interest in them kept declining.

From 1938, theatrical programs, especially performances of lighter genre pieces, were characterized by avoidance of social problems. The audience sought entertainment and not intellectual stimulation. For example, certain Church celebrations and the twenty-year anniversary of Horthy's ascendance became theatrical programs. In spite of the avoidance of social issues, the extreme right and the Catholic press felt that the performances of the pieces expressed decadence and blasphemy, even in the most harmless comedy. The country's number one theater, the *Nemzeti Színház* (National Theater), was also affected by daily politics.

The situation of the opera was more complicated than that of the theaters. Not only were excellent artists affected by the anti-Jewish laws, but so were lesser-known persons, as were the previously solid guarantees of quality. While the *Nemzeti Színház* had already started to dismiss "half-Jews" on its staff, the then director of the opera, László Márkus, was able to protect the jobs of 21 Jewish staffers, until the German occupation, by inviting the Arrow Cross leader Ferenc Szálasi to his home for coffee. By doing so, he managed to take Szalasi's mind off the artists of the opera for a while.

As a result of the First (1938) and Second (1939) Jewish Laws, hundreds of people from all cultural areas lost their jobs. The majority of painters and sculptors of Jewish origin were totally excluded from purchases of their work by state and local authorities. Thus, the writer and dramaturgist, Lajos Bálint, and the attorney, Géza Ribáry, a prestigious person who served in the management of the religious community, arrived at a solution to the problem of the work and living needs of a growing number of jobless actors, musicians, writers, and journalists. They received authorization to operate a theater from the Hungarian authorities and the leadership of the Jewish religious community by making reference to the Jewish theater in Berlin, which was still functioning in Nazi Germany. The Jewish religious community in Budapest agreed to organize the Artistic Enterprise, provided that it would be under the aegis of the OMIKE, and the civil authorities stipulated that only private performances could be held, attended exclusively by members of the Jewish religious community.

The objective of the Artistic Enterprise was to maintain Hungarian Jews at their current cultural level, to provide job opportunities to the artists and performers excluded from the Theater Chamber and from performing before the general public, and to ensure a modest living for them. However, it did not include any apostate artists, no matter how talented they were.

The OMIKE Artistic Enterprise began its theatrical operation with miscellaneous programs on November 11, 1939 in a number of buildings owned by the Budapest religious community (Goldmark Hall, Cultural Hall on Hollán Street, Bethlen Square synagogue and its community hall, and the synagogue on Öntőház Street). The miscellaneous programs were soon replaced by theatrical performances, cabarets, concerts, operas, performances for children, and so on.

The selection of programs, apart from providing for the necessary employment of artists, music compositions, piece writing, and the translation of operas, was determined by merit and not on the basis of the author's origin. Mozart, Verdi, and Beethoven were on the programs as much as, or even more than J. Offenbach or Leó Weiner, who were of Jewish origin. In addition, a Kodály evening was held on the composer's sixtieth birthday, with the composer present, despite all prohibitions. The *Divertimento* composed by Béla Bartók, living already in the US in 1939, was first introduced in Hungary by Frigyes Sándor of the Artistic Enterprise in 1942.

In programming, things taken into account were: (1) the fact that Goldmark Hall was located right next to the great Dohány Utcai (Street) synagogue, (2) the oversight and control of the program by the civil authorities, and (3) the necessity of achieving employment for the large group of artists working in various genres. For example, from 1942 on, because of the growing number of draft call-ups for labor service, actors had to be selected in such a way that they could be replaced at any time. The limited size of the stage, lack of dressing rooms, lack of wind instruments, and the limited number of costumes, decorations, and procurement of scores raised difficulties. The need for wind instruments was partly solved at orchestral concerts by having Christian musicians unofficially perform as well. Similarly, musicians who had been laid off as a result of the anti-Jewish laws performed with other orchestras.

Advertisements to the Jewish community, who had been banned from attending public theaters and cinemas, had to be properly organized. Public posters were not permitted, but program booklets and flyers were allowed by the authorities. Besides, plenty of information was available about cultural life in the Jewish papers, for example, *A Magyar Zsidók Lapja* (Hungarian Jews' Paper), *Mult és Jövő* (Past and Present), *Libanon* (Lebanon) (especially about exhibitions of fine arts), and *Évforduló November* (November Anniversary) (reviews about composers, directing, and so on). The audience could read the reviews of performances in these publications.

In order to help painters, graphic artists, and sculptors, a fine arts exhibition was organized at least once a year in one of the rooms of the OMIKE or in the Jewish Museum. Beginning in 1942, in many cases, one of the relatives of the artist doing forced labor service brought their allotted artistic work to the exhibition. A catalogue with prices was prepared for the exhibitions (see appendix 3).

An annually published anthology was issued by the press group of the OMIKE and served to employ 325 writers and journalists. One of the designers of the volumes was László Reiter, murdered in 1945, who was an internationally known and renowned illustrator.

While Mihály Kolosváry-Borcsa, president of the now-fascist *Press Chamber* (Guild), was working on his book, *A zsidókérdés magyarországi irodalma—A zsidóság szerepe a magyar szellemi életben* (Hungarian Literature on the Jewish Question: The Role of Jews in Hungarian Intellectual Life), before he had Jewish writers' books pulped; Mihály András Rónai compiled *Antologia Coacta—Nyugateurópai költők és irok gyűjteménye-t* (Anthology Coacta—The Collection of Western European Poets and Writers), between his two forced labor service terms. Rónai also selected the best non-Jewish poets' and writers' translations of literary works for the volume.

The activity of the OMIKE Artistic Enterprise hasn't become widely known over the last 70 years since the Holocaust, neither abroad nor in Hungary. One reason is linguistic isolation, but another is misinterpretation of the functioning of the Artistic Enterprise. Articles, writings, and films published in recent years have judged the Artistic Enterprise merely on the basis of certain prosaic performances as a denominational theater. In reality, OMIKE was created by artists banned because of their Jewishness. Yet, while continuing to work, these dedicated artists served international and Hungarian culture by staging the works of Jewish writers which have consequently stayed part of these cultures before and after the fascist and Nazi laws.

Finally, in memoriam, a few of the many members of the Artistic Enterprise who were murdered during the Holocaust, after Lévai wrote his book, are listed below. Others are listed or denoted in later sections of this volume.

Imre Ámos, painter (1907–1944). He reported shocking visions about his tragic experiences during WWII (Dark Times series; *Fugitive, War and others*).

István Bondy, actor (1905–1944). He acted at the *Vígszínház* (Comedy Theater) for many years and earlier at the *Új Színház* (New Theater), *Magyar Színház* (Hungarian Theater), and several others.

Hugó Csergő, journalist, writer (1877–1944). He was editor of the anthology *Száz év zsidó magyar költől* (Jewish Hungarian Poets of a Hundred Years).

Lajos Gárdonyi, actor (1896–1945). He was a major star at the *Vígszínház.*

György Goldmann, sculptor (1904–1945).

Bertalan Göndör, painter, graphic artist (1908–1945).

Zoltán Hirsch (aka Zoli the Clown), world-famous acrobat (1885–1945). Most of the time, he performed at the famous Circus Olympia in London, where he was a star.

Sándor Kuti, composer, conductor (1908–1945).

Artúr Lakner, writer, film dramaturgist (1893–1944). He was the founder of the *Gyermekszínház* (Children's Theater).

Miklós Lőrincz, cabaret composer, journalist, critic (1899–1944).

Jenő Mohácsi, poet, writer, translator (1886–1944). Most of his literary work served to strengthen ties between Hungarian and German cultures.

György Nagy, actor, writer (1905–1945).

Dávid Ney, Jr., opera singer (1905–1944).

Károly Pap, author of short stories, novelist (1897–1944).

László Reiter, book publisher, graphic artist, writer (1894–1945). He was the founder and a member of the management of the Hungarian Bibliophile Society, honorary teacher of the School of Applied Arts in New York, and had an exhibition at the Brooklyn Gallery in New York in 1933.

Sándor Rott, actor (1868–1942). He was one of the most popular artists of Budapest.

Géza Steinhardt, comedian (1873–1944).

Endre Vadász, painter, graphic artist (1901–1944).

László Weiner, composer (1916–1944).

Below are a few artists of the hundreds of artists of OMIKE who survived the Holocaust:

Lajos Bálint, writer, dramaturgist, translator (1886–1974). He was the stage manager of the OMIKE artistic enterprise.

Oszkár Beregi, actor (1876–1965). He was made a life member of *Nemzeti Színház* (1946).

Dezső Ernster, opera singer, basso profundo (1898–1981). After the war, he performed again in Basel and at the Metropolitan in New York.

Annie Fischer, pianist (1914–1995). She made her debut in the US in 1961. She performed all Beethoven piano concertos with Otto Klemperer at the Royal Festival Hall in London.

Róbert Gerle, violinist, conductor, music professor (1924–2005). He immigrated to the US after WWII and became a noted professor of music at the University of Maryland, Baltimore County.

Oszkár Kálmán, opera singer (1887–1971). He was made a life member of the Opera House in Budapest (1947). He also had successful guest performances in Germany, Vienna, Prague, and Barcelona (at the premiere of Stravinsky and Hindemith works).

Vilmos Komor, conductor (1895–1971) He was an Artist of Merit (1953), Franz Liszt Prize-winner (1963), and music director of the OMIKE artistic enterprise.

Alfréd Márkus, composer, conductor (1888–1946). His musical work has become an integral part of film history.

Anna Pallay, dancer, prima ballerina, teacher (1890–1970).

Vera Rózsa, singer, music teacher (1921–2010). She was awarded the Order of the British Empire (1991) and Honorary Citizen of London (1999).

János Starker, cellist (1924–2013). He immigrated to the US in 1948 and was considered one of the greatest cellists in the world.

Magda Horák
OMIKE *Művészakció* historian and writer
May 2013

Foreword to the Hungarian Edition

This past fourth season of the Hungarian Jewish Theater, which was limited to the less convenient OMIKE Artistic Enterprise (*Művészakció*) compared to the freedom once enjoyed on the general artistic stage, has reached a level that can now satisfy higher artistic demands. The goal of the Artistic Enterprise for this next season is to achieve a higher level of performance than ever before on the stage of the Goldmark Hall. We believe that this goal can be achieved and that the OMIKE audience will also appreciate and be able to follow, with its artistic taste, this enthusiastic thirst for development. History shows that the skilled artists of the OMIKE and the interest in art demonstrated by the audience of the Goldmark Hall are also inspired by an eighteen-hundred-year-old Jewish theatrical culture.

This book strives for perfection but, as we all well know, cannot reach it due to our limited resources. It was prepared for the jubilant fifth anniversary season of the present Hungarian Jewish Theatre, the OMIKE Artistic Enterprise. There were several technical problems as well. Still, we feel that we broke new ground and that in founding the Hungarian Jewish Theater our work was not in vain. Its detailed story will certainly be recorded one day.

Jenő Lévai
September 1943

Editor's Note to the English Edition

A large portion of the pages that follow comprise the complete English translation of the original 1943 book, by Jenő Lévai, on the OMIKE *Művészakció* (Artistic Enterprise), entitled *Írók, színészek, énekesek és zenészek regényes életútja a Goldmark-teremig: Az OMIKE színház és művészei* (The Illustrious Careers of Writers, Artists, Singers, and Musicians Associated with Goldmark Hall: The Theater and Artists of the OMIKE). This unique Artistic Enterprise was created in response to the anti-Jewish laws of 1938 and 1939, which resulted in Hungarian Jewish artists losing their jobs and no longer being allowed to perform in front of the general public.

My interest in the history of the OMIKE *Művészakció* and its achievements, which led to the creation of this new, expanded book (with an added foreword, historical introduction, photos, playbills, afterword, bibliography, glossary, and index) was due to my uncle, István Bondy, who was an actor with this artistic group. Earlier, he had performed at the *Vígszínház* (Comedy Theater) for many years as well as at the *Új Színház, Magyar Színház* and other theaters in Budapest. He subsequently perished in the Holocaust with some 170 other *Művészakció* members, including singers, musicians, writers, composers, conductors, painters, graphic artists, poets, and sculptors.

Years ago, I visited Goldmark Hall with Péter Mura (aka Mandl) who had been a young pianist and opera repetiteur with the *Művészakció*. He showed me the OMIKE *Művészakció* Martyrs plaque containing my uncle's name and I wondered about who these other artists were, exactly what they did, how old they were, and how they looked. This curiosity and a desire to share this information further propelled me to create this book.

This new English-language edition is meant to further record the memorable history, operations, and contributions of this courageous artistic enterprise and its artists, giving the book an expanded readership of academics, art history students, aspiring artists, others interested in the losses to culture and Hungarian Jewry due to the Holocaust, and those interested in Judaica. This edition also adds the history of the final year of the OMIKE *Művészakció* since Lévai's original book appeared in 1943. (The *Művészakció* continued to function under the most adverse conditions of the Horthy anti-Jewish regime until the entry of the Nazi army into Hungary on Sunday morning, March 19, 1944.)

This book is also meant to place faces to the names of these artists (actors, actresses, singers, musicians, playwrights, composers, writers, painters, graphic artists, sculptors, and others) through photographs and to recall their performances (plays, concerts, operas, cabaret and operettas) through playbills and photos (see the appendices).

Names of plays and theaters are shown in Hungarian in italics, followed by their equivalent English names unitalicized and in parentheses. Names of individuals follow English-language practice, with the given name first and the surname second. Their names have not been translated into English and I have kept their diacritical marks. For example, the name of the opera singer "Pál Fehér" has not been translated into "Paul White."

Frequently Hungarian surnames of artists appear with either an "i" or "y" ending, such as Imre Rádai (Ráday) and Magda Rosti (Rosty). Such discrepancies sometimes appear between the Lévai text and the playbills. When this occurs, the spelling of the artist's name as it appears in the playbills (programs) has been used from appendix 2, Programs of Művészakció Plays, Concerts, Operas, Cabaret, and Operettas.

The new foreword to the translation, the introduction, and the afterword place the OMIKE *Művészakció* in a historical context, both before and after the Holocaust.

Lists of names of OMIKE *Művészakció* artists who perished during the Holocaust are given in both the foreword to the translation and the afterword. The martyred artists are also denoted, as such, in their portrait photos. Appendix 4 gives a most comprehensive listing of all the identifiable victims, as derived from several sources.

The afterword provides many further details on the group's musicians not covered in the original Lévai book. Finally, in addition to listing the *Művészakció*'s musicians, the afterword briefly covers the history of other courageous Jewish theatrical and musical endeavors during this period, such as those in Berlin, the Lodz and Riga ghettoes, and Theresienstadt.

Frederick Bondy
New York, 2016

Introduction to the English Edition

The Hungarian-Jewish Historical Context Leading to the Creation of the OMIKE *Művészakció* and Its Aftermath, 1848–1945

This introductory chapter which has been written for the expanded, English-language version of Jenő Lévai's 1943 book, *Irók, szinészek, énekesek, regényes, életútuja a Goldmark teremig.Az OMIKE szinháza és művészei* (The Illustrious Careers of Writers, Artists, Singers, and Musicians Associated with Goldmark Hall: The Theater and the Artists of the OMIKE), is based to a large extent on my essay that appeared in Randolph Braham's book, *Auschwitz Reports and the Holocaust in Hungary* (1–27). I, Fred Bondy, and others, who have labored so diligently on this book, extend our profound gratitude to Dr. Braham for allowing us to use significant parts of this essay.

The Age of Hope

The history of the Jews in Hungary is complex with many twists and turns. So where did it all begin? What is the historical context that led to the formation of the OMIKE *Művészakció* which functioned so admirably, under great difficulty, during the 1939–1944 anti-Jewish period, as described in the foreword of this book by Magda Horák? Historians agree that the unfolding of the intensive Hungarian-Jewish relationship must be sought in early nineteenth-century history. Jews had long been living in the area of what is today Hungary when the conquering Magyar tribes arrived from the East in the ninth century, but originally theirs was a traditionalist and isolated existence. When persecution did occur, it was generally milder than in medieval and early modern Western Europe. The story becomes more exciting and more complex with the step-by-step integration of Jews into Hungarian society that began late in the eighteenth century as an integral part of a nationwide drive for modernization. Because the landowning nobility that, until the mid-nineteenth century, counted as the embodiment of the nation was loath to engage in commerce and industry, it needed the services of the Jews. Also, once the ideas of nation and nationality took root, the same nobility became painfully aware that the Hungarian speakers formed a minority in the country. It was another reason for them to foster the acceptance of the Jews, who combined their economic usefulness with a willingness to become patriots and to exchange their German or Yiddish speech for Hungarian.

Understandably, the story was not simple, and one meets with as many signs of antisemitism among the reforming nobility as one meets with signs of reluctance on the part of Jews to give up their ancient way of life. Still, one can state with confidence that, in nineteenth-century Europe, no country was more hospitable to Jewish immigration and assimilation and no country won more enthusiastic support from its Jews than the Hungarian kingdom. One might say even that there existed, at least since the liberal, nationalist revolutions of 1848–1849, a tacit agreement between the ruling gentry and the enlightened, educated, and patriotic segment of Jewry for a division of labor in modernizing Hungary. The Jews would contribute the investment capital, supplied by some great Western banking houses, and their own business acumen, dynamism, and diligence. The non-Jewish political elite would provide the legislative and administrative assistance necessary for economic expansion.[1]

The resulting success of Jews was dazzling. Although they constituted less than five percent of the pre-World War I population, Jews created, owned, and managed the majority of Hungarian heavy industry and mining, and nearly every one of the great banks. They were hardly less successful in commerce, small entrepreneurship, crafts, the liberal professions, and all aspects of culture and the arts. By the beginning of the twentieth century they had also made significant inroads into state service, the judiciary, the officer corps, and large landownership. Assimilation for the Jewish elite increasingly took the form of intermarriage.

Hungarian Jews were, as a whole, very patriotic; they supported both Emperor-King Francis Joseph and the governing conservative-liberal parties in Hungary. Of course, not all Christian inhabitants of the country were happy with these developments; those who did not profit from the economic boom, or profited less than others (for instance, members of the ethnic minorities, impoverished gentry, the clergy, small shopkeepers, artisans, and peasants) tended to blame the Jews for their own misfortune. In 1882–1883, there was a wave of wild antisemitic outbursts in connection with the so-called Tiszaeszlár blood-libel trial, but the government and the dominant liberal press firmly rejected what they considered a return to medieval obscurantism.[2] The antisemitic political party that was set up on that occasion disappeared from the scene within a few years. Meanwhile, the Jewish elite would not even consider creating a separate Jewish political organization. Although Theodor Herzl was born in Budapest, his calls for a Jewish state met with categorical rejection among Hungarian Jewish leaders and in the press. For educated Jews, Judaism was but a religious denomination; therefore, Zionist nationalism amounted to treason. Few people paid attention to Herzl's warning, in 1903, to a Hungarian Jewish politician: "The hand of fate shall also seize Hungarian Jewry. And the later this occurs, and the stronger this Jewry becomes, the more cruel and hard shall be the blow, which shall be delivered with greater savagery. There is no escape."[3]

If Zionism made no inroads in Hungarian Jewish life, political radicalism and socialist ideology did, and mostly among the sons and daughters of assimilated and successful bourgeois, who turned with messianic zeal against the Hungarian ruling elite, which they identified with both retrograde feudalism and oppressive capitalism.[4] Truly, for a young intellectual imbued with the ideas of Marx, Nietzsche, and Kautsky, it must have been hard to stomach such a surreal spectacle as the celebration of the 1,000th anniversary of Hungary at the new and beautiful Dohány Street Synagogue in Budapest. Here is the scene as described in a Neolog Jewish newspaper.

> In front of the temple, which was decorated with flags, there stood . . . an entire barricade of coaches that had brought the ladies and the gentlemen in white tie. In some of the more decorative private coaches arrived [Jewish] coreligionists sporting splendid Hungarian national gala costumes, complete with sword, clasps, egret feathers [on their high fur hats], cocky, with pelisses thrown on one shoulder, frogs and loops laden with jewels, as well as gold or silver spurs attached to long and dashing cordovan boots. . . . The most dazzling Hungarian national gala costumes were worn by Berthold Weiss, Sándor Deutsch de Hatvan, and Lajos Krausz de Megyer.[5]

Then came World War I, in which Jews participated en masse, providing, among other things, more than one-fifth of the Dual Monarchy's reserve officer corps.[6] But whereas in the armed forces antisemitism was not tolerated, in politics, the press, and public opinion, it experienced a quick revival. Very simply, scapegoats had to be found for the suffering of the population and the death of half a million Hungarian citizen-soldiers. The defeat of the Central Powers in the fall of 1918 came as a terrible shock to a misinformed public, yet also as a welcome relief from what was perceived to be Habsburg-Austrian oppression. The fact that, in the eyes of the other peoples of the monarchy, the Hungarians were the quintessentially dominant nationality did not in the least influence the Hungarians' perception of themselves as oppressed victims. Thus, the end of the war was celebrated as the beginning of an independent and more progressive Hungary; celebration turned to despair, however, when the terrible costs of war became more visible, and when the armies of Hungary's old and new neighbors occupied much of what in prewar times had been officially known as the "Hungarian Empire" within Austria-Hungary. For the Jews, World War I had marked the apogee of their success; in 1944, nothing would symbolize more their fall from grace than the wartime decorations they had to leave on the walls of the houses and flats from which they had been deported.

Counterrevolution and the End of the Christian-Jewish Symbiosis

The collapse at the front brought two successive revolutions, one democratic, the other Bolshevik: in both, the youngish Jewish reformers and social critics played a crucial role. In fact, they made up almost the entire leadership of the Republic of Soviets, which functioned for 133 days in 1919.[7] This regime was terminated by the invading Romanian army acting under French guidance; the ensuing power vacuum allowed a small band of White counterrevolutionary officers to seize power in the same year. For this, they enjoyed the support of the French and British governments.

Post-World War I Hungary was not only impoverished but was inundated by refugees from the newly lost territories. Many of the refugees were civil servants and professionals, who now engaged in a desperate competition with the Jews for even the lowliest positions in commerce and the professions. This, combined with the country's dismemberment and the frightening experience with the revolutionary Republic of Soviets, led to a deepening of middle-class antisemitism.[8]

Interwar Hungary represented a mass of contradictions, and so did its Jewish policy. The country was a kingdom without a king; its head of state was Regent Miklós Horthy, a former Austro-Hungarian admiral without a fleet. The system of government was constitutional but the counterrevolutionary movement that had brought Horthy to power was one of violence and terror. Hungary had a parliament in which, as late as March 1944, sat a few social democratic and other progressive deputies, but the majority of deputies heralded fascist ideas. In the upper house of the parliament two of the highest representatives of the Jewish community had the right to sit, but both lower house and upper house were obsessed with the "Jewish question." In fact, preoccupation with the Jews was akin to a sickness that afflicted all strata of society, but especially the educated classes.[9]

In 1920, the Hungarian parliament adopted a law (Numerus Clausus) meant to reduce the presence of Jewish students at the universities to something approximating their presence in the general population, which was a little less than six percent, but this law was suspended eight years later. What counts is that the old silent contract between gentry and Jews had come to an end. Now even the most moderate counterrevolutionaries expected the majority of Jews eventually to leave the country.

The Horthy regime was desperate to open jobs, especially in industry, commerce, and the liberal professions to gentiles, yet as late as 1935, the proportion in Hungary of Jewish lawyers, medical doctors, journalists, and engineers was higher than even in the pre-World War I period, often approaching one-half.

The proportion of Jews among the professionals practicing in the capital and among those with the biggest income was higher still.[10] And now just one more fact: as late as 1941, the absolute majority of the biggest taxpayers and those with the greatest personal wealth were Jews or converts of Jewish origin.[11] These and similar statistics were constantly belabored by the press and the politicians, but what they failed to say was that the absolute number of Jews was steadily declining because of emigration, a low birth rate, and conversions, and that once the economy began to improve, as it did in the late 1930s, there would be ample space in lucrative positions for the newly educated Christian middle class as well.

The counterrevolutionary regime advocated a militant Christian ideology, which meant that it was opposed to free masonry, liberalism, democracy, atheism, secularism, Jewish influence, Marxism, bolshevism, cosmopolitanism, modernity, abortion, homosexuality, divorce, and avant-garde art; yet many of these "sinful" activities and ideologies flourished in Horthy's Hungary, creating, among other things, a new golden age of literature and the arts. Despite the government's incessant anti-urban and unsophisticated propaganda, Budapest remained a most sophisticated place in a much poorer and much less developed countryside. In the capital, Jews made up nearly one-fourth of the inhabitants and nearly one-half of those with the right to vote. The press was infinitely freer than in the Soviet Union, Nazi Germany, and fascist Italy, and the judiciary, although certainly class based, often ruled in defiance of government interests. The ruling elite was badly divided between those who cultivated old-fashioned conservative values and those with fascistic inclinations, between defenders and critics of the rigid social hierarchy, between moderate and radical antisemites, between Anglophiles and the admirers of Nazi Germany. Nor are the history books correct which claim that, in the late 1930s and early 1940s, the radical right was steadily gaining ground at the expense of the moderate rightists. Rather, things changed all the time; the fascist Arrow Cross Party, for instance, had three times as many members in 1939 than in the fall of 1944 when the Germans put it in power. Also, to give another example, the conservative, Anglophile elite operating under the guidance of former prime minister Count István Bethlen almost completely regained power in 1943 as well as in the several weeks preceding the Arrow Cross takeover in October 1944.[12]

The Horthy regime's main domestic policy goal was to avoid such fundamental social reforms as the distribution of the enormous landed estates among the millions of landless; its main foreign political goal was to recover some, if not all, the territories that Hungary had lost after World War I. At stake were two-thirds of the old kingdom and more than three million Magyar speakers now living under foreign rule. The government's policy goals were tightly intertwined with the "Jewish question"; after all, the anti-Jewish economic measures represented the beginnings of a most unfair but still genuine redistribution of wealth.[13] Also, the recovery of the lost territories required the support of Nazi Germany; Hitler's insistence on drastic anti-Jewish measures was one reason for a series of Hungarian anti-Jewish laws that began in 1938. However, ideology and greed played their part as well.

With the advent of the First and Second anti-Jewish Laws of May 29, 1938 and May 5, 1939, passed under the Horthy regime, the percentage of Jews allowed in the professions were reduced to 20% and then 6%, respectively. It is estimated that over 200,000 Jews lost their livelihoods, including actors, musicians, and other artists. For example, Jews were ultimately not allowed to be members of the Theater Guild and as such were unable to perform in theaters.

In response to this, Géza Ribáry, a lawyer and amateur pianist, and others petitioned the government to allow Jewish artists to continue in their professions and earn a living. An agreement was reached with Balint Hóman, Minister of Cults and Public Education, and Ferenc Keresztes-Fischer, Minister of Interior, which would allow Jews to perform in Goldmark Hall, as well as a few other Jewish venues, but the audience could only be Jews and they could not publicize their performances to the general public via posters and flyers. Hence Ferenc Keresztes-Fischer issued a permit on September 12, 1938 and the OMIKE *Művészakció* (Artistic Enterprise) began.

Again at War

The adoption of the first anti-Jewish law coincided with the recovery, thanks to Hitler and Mussolini, of a part of what used to be northern and northeast Hungary. From then on territorial recovery and anti-Jewish measures intertwined until nearly one-half of the lost lands had been regained and the country's antisemitic laws had become at least as drastic in their definition of race as those of Germany. But, unlike in Germany, these laws were often respected in their breach and, strange as it may sound, until March 1944, most Jews still worked in their professions, if often at a reduced salary.

In June 1941, Hungary entered the military campaign against the Soviet Union, which gradually brought it into war with Great Britain and the United States. But while the Soviet Union and bolshevism were seen as true enemies, the conservative Horthy regime went out of its way to show admiration and friendship toward the British and the Americans.[14]

In the winter of 1942–1943, a great Soviet offensive destroyed the Hungarian army at the front; among the dead, the frozen, and the POWs were thousands of Jews whom the army high command had drafted for labor service. By then, even highly decorated Jewish reserve officers had been deprived of their ranks, and those who had been drafted had to dig ditches or pick up mines at the front. It was as if the army found a particular delight in torturing and killing the decorated heroes as well as the intellectuals among the Jewish labor service men. One of the victims tortured to death in Ukraine was the Olympic gold medalist and reserve officer Attila Petschauer, whose cruel death inspired a horrifying scene in István Szabó's celebrated film, *Sunshine*. But, again, by far not all Jewish labor service men were mistreated by their guards, and the Jewish forced laborers suffered fewer casualties due to combat, the atrocious winter weather, and the sadism of their Hungarian guards than because of hunger and epidemics in the Soviet POW camps. The Red Army treated the captured labor servicemen no better than it treated the captured Hungarian soldiers.[15]

The government of Miklós Kállay that Regent Horthy installed in March 1942, with the mission of cautiously counterbalancing the German and local fascist influences, at first adopted a few more antisemitic measures but, following the defeat of the Hungarian Second Army at the Don River and the German defeat at Stalingrad, changed its policy toward the Jews. The lot of the Jewish labor service men was considerably alleviated, and the anti-Jewish laws were not always put into effect. Moreover, British and American bombers flying over the country were not fired upon, and Prime Minister Miklós Kállay attempted to reach a secret agreement with the Western Allies. But the British and US land forces were nowhere to be seen.[16] Fully informed through his spies of Hungarian machinations and alarmed by the approach of the Red Army, Hitler ordered the German armed forces into Hungary on March 19, 1944. There was no resistance and, within a few days, Regent Horthy was caused to appoint a new, strongly pro-Nazi government.

As noted, in Magda Horák's foreword to this book, March 19 also marked an end to the OMIKE *Művészakció*. In the months that followed, some 170 of its actors, musicians, writers, poets, playwrights, composers, conductors, directors, painters, and sculptors would fall victim to the Holocaust. These losses are further covered in the afterword, appendix 4, and other parts of this book.

From March to October

Because the German occupation of Hungary was followed by the Holocaust of Hungarian Jewry, the mobilization of the non-Jewish population for total war, the Soviet invasion, and the country's destruction, Hungarians have been asking themselves ever since what could have been done to avoid it. During the first thirty years after the war, the unanimous judgment of both communist and democratic authors was that Horthy and Prime Minister Kállay should have turned against the Germans and ordered armed resistance, at least on the day of the German invasion. Yet such a move was scarcely possible in a country whose pro-German elements, especially within the military, wielded enormous influence and power. A more sophisticated view is that of Randolph L. Braham, the foremost historian of the Hungarian Jewish Holocaust, who writes: "Ironically, it appears in retrospect that had Hungary continued to remain a militarily passive but politically vocal ally of the Third Reich instead of provocatively engaging in essentially fruitless, if not merely alibi-establishing, diplomatic maneuvers, the Jews of Hungary might possibly have survived the war relatively unscathed."[17] Unfortunately, it is highly unlikely that had the Kállay government collaborated more vocally, the Hungarian Jews would have escaped relatively unscathed. The approaching front line and the Final Solution were too important for the Germans to let nearly a million Jews stay alive in Central Europe. Still, Braham's statement makes clear that, in 1944 at least, Jews and non-Jews did not have the same immediate interests, and that the meaning and consequences of resistance and collaboration cannot be given a uniform interpretation. For the Jews, every new day improved their chances of ultimate survival; therefore, it was not in their interest for the government to provoke German aggression. But it was very much in the interest of Hungary as a whole to show, no matter how symbolically, that it was not a German satellite.[18]

When General Döme Sztójay's puppet government took over, late in March 1944, 60,000-odd Hungarian Jews were already dead. Among them, 15,000 to 20,000 had been killed by the SS and the Ukrainian militia in the spring of 1942, following the deportation of those Jews from northeastern Hungary to Galicia who had been unable to prove their Hungarian citizenship; another thousand or fewer were massacred by the Hungarian military during a "cleansing" operation in northern Yugoslavia, and the rest died, as already shown, either at the front, in 1942–1943, or in Soviet POW camps. Now the operation began in earnest against the remaining 760,000, about 100,000 of whom were Christians by religion. Within a few weeks, those whom the law regarded as Jews were excluded from all skilled employment and their food and clothing rations were drastically reduced. They were subjected to the authority of the newly created Jewish Councils, who were then ordered to help confiscate Jewish telephones, typewriters, radios, autos, bicycles, dogs, horses, stamp collections, art works, jewelry, and bank accounts. In addition, huge bribes had to be paid to Adolf Eichmann's Gestapo, which arrived in Hungary with the German troops.

On April 5, all Jews were made to wear a yellow star and two days later the first secret directives were issued concerning the ghettoization of Hungarian Jewry. The transfer of Jews into the newly created ghettos began late in April; systematic mass deportation started on May 15 and ended only in July; in that short period 437,000 persons were dispatched to Auschwitz, of whom the great majority were gassed immediately without anyone bothering to register their names. The suffering of the deportees has been described innumerable times: the sudden departure from home, the move from a small ghetto to a larger ghetto and from there to some brick factory outside a city with no shelter, hardly any food or drinkable water, and no sanitary facilities. There was the incredible brutality of the gendarmes and many of the city police who, in their ravenous hunger for silver and gold, indiscriminately tortured man, woman, and child. Finally came the march to the railroad station and the slow, tortured voyage in frightfully overcrowded freight cars to the ramp in Auschwitz-Birkenau. Note, however, that some 20,000 of the deportees were diverted for industrial and agricultural labor at Strasshof in Austria, where the great majority of them survived. Note also that those who were not gassed immediately at Auschwitz-Birkenau, meaning the relatively healthy and the relatively young, had a fair chance of surviving the periodic "selections" as well as slave labor in German factories and mines.[19]

One of the many insoluble dilemmas of these mind-boggling events is why Regent Horthy allowed them to happen. True, he was a confessed antisemite but he also had some Jewish friends; he often claimed to prefer the patriotic and assimilated sector of the Jews to the Arrow Cross "hoodlums and traitors," and a year before the German invasion he categorically rejected Nazi demands for the deportation of the Jews.

The event occurred in April 1943, at a meeting at Klessheim, where Hitler demanded that Hungary finally solve the Jewish question. According to a German report on the meeting, Horthy's reply to Hitler's comment on the matter was, "What, then, should [I] do with the Jews after they have essentially been denied almost every opportunity to earn a living. Why, [I] couldn't kill them."

Thereupon Goebbels wrote in his diary on May 8, 1943: "The Jewish Question is solved least satisfactorily by the Hungarians. The Hungarian state is permeated by Jews, and the Fuhrer did not succeed during his talk with Horthy to convince the latter of the necessity of more stringent measures. . . . He [Horthy] gave a number of humanitarian counterarguments which of course do not apply at all to this situation."[20] And now the same old-fashioned gentleman, who claimed to follow in the footsteps of Francis Joseph, his famously tolerant former master, informed the council of ministers that he was leaving Jewish matters entirely in their hands. Horthy also quietly assured his visitors that the Jews were simply taken to Germany for useful labor; as a humanitarian gesture, the Germans allowed their families to go with them. He said this knowing full well that, aside from the Jews of Budapest, the only other Jews not deported abroad were men of working age; by June 1944, all Jewish men between the ages of 18 and 48 had been drafted into military labor service, and therefore those who went to the gas chambers were mostly women, children, the old, and the infirm. There is really no other answer to the Horthy dilemma than that he was weak and easily influenced, a type of behavior by which he certainly did not stand out alone in Europe.

And what about those serving under the regent? It has been calculated that 200,000 persons in public service participated in the swift and amazingly efficient execution of the deportations. They included everyone, from Prime Minister Sztójay through Andor Jaross, László Endre, and László Baky, that trio in the cabinet who were directly in charge of the Hungarian Final Solution, down to county prefects and subprefects, the mayors, the entire administrative machinery, including the gendarmes, the police, the railroad men, and such teachers who had been drafted into assisting the bureaucrats. Even doctors and midwives were called upon to search the intimate parts of Jewish women for hidden jewelry. History does not record a single instance of a public servant openly refusing to cooperate, yet the punishment would have been minimal. It is true, however, that dozens were dismissed from the higher echelons of service and dozens of others chose retirement. Their deputies took over immediately and completed the process of deportations.

In many places people cried when watching the sorry parade of their former neighbors, but then the lure of abandoned goods proved to be irresistible, and there was wholesale looting.[21] A few church leaders tried to intervene in order to alleviate the condition of the baptized Jews in the camps, but basically no one publicly protested the deportations. Nor did anyone attempt to sabotage the trains that departed almost incessantly.

It was indeed a smooth operation, in which the Jewish Councils, too, performed their assigned role. The Central Council in Budapest and the local councils have been the subject of much debate with, for instance, both Hannah Arendt and Randolph Braham strongly condemning the councils' collaborationist attitudes.[22] And it is true that these Jewish dignitaries, formerly with good governmental connections and often highly decorated by the Horthy regime, could think of no other action but dutiful obedience. They were patriots who remained confident that the regent and their other gentile patrons would not abandon them and their flock. There is no doubt, however, that some council leaders and many council employees were overzealous in trying to please the Germans and the Hungarian authorities: witness the contemporary anecdote: "There is violent banging on the door of a Jewish family early in the morning. All are terrified; finally, the wife gathers enough courage to open the door. She returns much relieved and smiling: 'Relax, it is not the Jewish Council, only the Gestapo.'" What would have happened if the councils had refused to obey orders and instead tried to encourage their flock to flee for their lives? It is not clear how such a message could have been communicated and where the hundreds of thousands would have been able to hide. Also, the chaos created by massive disobedience would have benefited primarily the most enterprising, the wealthy, the secularized, and the assimilated who were, in any case, often able to fend for themselves. Finally, to ask the council members to engage in a massive disobedience or to commit suicide, as Hannah Arendt has suggested, is to demand that they get out of their skin.

But why did the Hungarian authorities obey Eichmann and his minuscule crew of a few dozen specialists? Clearly, there remained only a few months before the arrival of the Red Army when those who had collaborated with the Germans were likely to be punished. The answer can only be that those who participated in the Final Solution found the threat of eventual punishment less compelling than the immediate satisfaction of seeing the Jews go away and of being able to acquire houses, apartments, shops, and well-paying positions—or for a shoeless poor peasant to acquire a pair of good boots. One thing is certain: even those who bemoaned the fate of the Jews did not expect them ever to return. There is a shattering passage in Imre Kertész's Nobel Prize-winning novel, *Fateless,* on the last encounter between the deported Jews and a gentile Hungarian. Kertész's hero, the boy George Köves, reaches the Polish border in a crowded railroad car when a Hungarian gendarme appears at the entrance, offering to relieve the suffocating passengers of their hidden jewels, gold, and money:

> "Men," he said to us, "you've reached the Hungarian border." He wanted to use this occasion to make an appeal to us . . . it was his opinion that we had no need of these where we were going . . . everything we might still hold onto would be taken from us by the Germans anyway . . . why shouldn't these things find their final resting place in Hungarian, rather than German, hands?
>
> The gendarme's appeal got him nowhere because the inmates of the car demanded water first and only then would they give up their valuables; he, on the other hand, insisted on a reverse order of proceedings. "After all, you are still Hungarians," the gendarme exclaimed.
>
> Finally the furious military policeman concluded: "Stinking Jews, you make a business out of even the holiest of things!" And in a voice choking with outrage and disgust, he added this wish: "Die of thirst, then!"[23]

The deportations did not remain a secret, and Horthy soon began to receive messages from István Bethlen, who was in hiding, as well from other such conservative, mostly aristocratic, politicians whom the Gestapo had not been able to arrest. Now, at last, Pope Pius XII, King Gustav VII of Sweden, President Roosevelt, and other world leaders also began to send messages, urging the regent to act to protect the remaining Jews in Hungary. Deeply impressed by Allied successes in Normandy, Horthy on July 7, 1944, forbade further deportations. The interdiction came when the gendarmes gathered in Budapest to begin deporting the 200,000-odd Jews in the capital. Persuaded by his conservative friends that the gendarmes and some far right politicians were planning a coup d'état against him, the regent ordered some armored units to Budapest.

The smoothness and speed of the deportation of the Hungarian Jews from the countryside was unique in the history of the Holocaust; but so was Horthy's decision to order military forces to prevent the deportation of Jews. Although Eichmann subsequently managed to smuggle a few thousand more Jews to Auschwitz, in July the deportations came to an end, not to be renewed until after Horthy's overthrow in October.[24]

Now came another surreal period in wartime Jewish history when those in Budapest were quartered in so-called Yellow Star houses and suffered from many humiliating restrictions but were also able to make plans for the opening of schools for Jewish children in September, and when it was relatively easy to obtain a certificate from the regent's office exempting one from the anti-Jewish laws. Also, the Swedish, Swiss, Portuguese, and Vatican consulates began to hand out affidavits, which offered a degree of personal protection with the vague promise of postwar immigration to their country or else emigration to Palestine. Moreover, those in labor service were generally decently fed and could feel quite safe; at the time of the deportations to Auschwitz, many of the men of military age had been saved literally in the last minute by the military authorities. Considering that, before March 1944, the army was notoriously more antisemitic and more pro-German than the civilian leadership, its relatively lenient behavior in the spring and summer of 1944 belongs to the many unsolved mysteries of the period.

Early in September 1944, following Romania's sudden defection to the Allied side, the Red Army invaded Hungary. Horthy had already dismissed his pro-Nazi prime minister and he now began to negotiate an armistice with the Soviet Union—hoping for an agreement which would allow the German troops to withdraw unmolested—but discussions proceeded slowly. The Germans knew about these plans; they began to prepare for a coup d'état and as a first step, on October 15 they kidnapped Miklós Horthy, Jr., the regent's only surviving son, whose older brother had been killed at the front. Horthy announced his intention to surrender to the Red Army that same day, but the army high command, imbued with the fanatical anticommunism which Horthy himself had encouraged, refused to follow his instructions and the surrender attempt failed. German SS and paratroopers arrested Horthy and, in order to secure his son's safety, the old man signed a piece of paper which made his archrival, the Arrow Cross leader Ferenc Szálasi, his successor. Horthy and his family were then put on a train to Bavaria where they were held under house arrest. A few military commanders went over to the Soviets; the army as a whole, however, swore loyalty to Szálasi—not that its fighting ability was of high quality.

Arrow Cross Rule

The pre-March and post-March 1944 political leadership did not differ socially from one another; they were all products of the counterrevolution and had their origins in the old aristocracy, gentry, and the civil service; they differed only in their conflicting views on Hungary, its Jews, and the war. Even the conservative and liberal critics of the Horthy regime originated from the same counterrevolutionary elite. But those whom the SS now entrusted with mobilizing the country for a last-ditch defense were different, not because they had only a handful of titled aristocrats and old gentry among them (in Hungary nothing ever happened without a few counts and other noblemen), but because their majority came from the less exalted classes of society, even from the lumpen proletariat.

The Arrow Cross has been judged harshly; for instance, while the people's courts tried members of the Horthy regime as individuals, members of the Szálasi regime were branded collectively as traitors and war criminals. The politics of the group was described as one of hare-brained ideas and extreme violence; today, Hungarian nationalist circles routinely blame the Arrow Cross for all the crimes of the period; indeed, Szálasi has become the supreme alibi of Regent Horthy and his cohorts. It is currently quite common to hear younger generations of

Hungarians, even some confused Jewish survivors, stating that Szálasi had come to power in March 1944 and that the Arrow Cross militia were at least partly responsible for the brutalities of the deportation to Auschwitz. In reality, the latter was the work exclusively of the old administration under Regent Horthy.[25]

Following Horthy's overthrow, Eichmann came back to Hungary to complete his deportation project, but things had changed substantially. The *SS-Reichsführer* Heinrich Himmler no longer allowed deportations to Auschwitz and in any case, the Red Army was approaching. So late in November, 50,000 Budapest Jews, mostly women, as well as nearly the same number of labor service men, were marched off to the Austrian border, there to build fortifications. The monstrosity of the Arrow Cross militia and army soldiers who guarded the deportees was surpassed only by the monstrosity of the Austrian *Hitlerjugend* and other local uniformed formations that took over the deportees at the border.[26] The behavior of the peasant population ranged from the helpful through to the indifferent to the murderously hostile in both countries.

Amazingly, thousands of Jews, especially among the old, were turned around and brought back to Budapest by the decision of Himmler and through the efforts, especially, of Raoul Wallenberg, who was a delegate of the American War Refugee Board, acting under the protection of the Swedish Legation in Hungary. The activities of Wallenberg, the Swiss Consul Carl Lutz, the Vatican Nuncio Angelo Rotta, the pseudo-Spanish Consul (in reality Italian anti-Nazi) Giorgio (Jorge) Perlasca, and the International Red Cross representative Friedrich Born constitute perhaps the best-known chapter of the Hungarian Holocaust.[27] These courageous men used mainly the promise of diplomatic recognition by their own governments to impress the Arrow Cross leaders. As a result, they were able to distribute affidavits, also called protective passes, to thousands of Jews as well as to bring back others from the road to Austria. Most importantly, the consuls caused the creation of a number of so-called protected buildings in a once heavily Jewish upper-middle class area of Budapest. But before we accept the claims of the enthusiasts that Wallenberg, for instance, saved the lives of 100,000 Jews, we have to consider that were all the claims true, the consuls would have saved more lives than there were Jews left in Budapest. We must also consider that Wallenberg and company owned at best a few pistols among them, and that they would have been powerless to save any lives had some Arrow Cross leaders, for instance, the Foreign Minister Baron Gábor Kemény, not been willing to cooperate with them. Ultimately, the decision not to have all the Jews of Budapest killed was that of the Szálasi government. Of course, there is no particular merit in not committing even more murders, but the fact of Arrow Cross cooperation with the consuls must be registered.[28]

The most important of the regime's decisions was to set up a ghetto in Budapest, late in November, which ended up housing nearly 100,000 Jews. This was at that time a unique institution in Europe.[29] Conditions inside the wooden-board walls were atrocious, but the Budapest municipality fed the inhabitants so long as any food could be found, and a mixed crew of policemen and Arrow Cross militiamen offered some degree of protection against roving bands of other Arrow Cross militiamen and SS men; such protection was something sorely missing at the Swedish, Swiss, and other protected buildings. As conditions in Budapest worsened and the Szálasi government took off to western Hungary, toward the end of December, the capital remained in the hands of local Arrow Cross leaders who terrorized the entire population and, among other things, regularly took inhabitants out of the protected buildings to shoot them into the nearby Danube River. Meanwhile, however, small units of Zionist organizations had installed themselves under the protection of especially the Swiss Consulate and forged thousands of affidavits, birth certificates, and whatever one needed to hide in the city. This, of course, often devalued the real affidavits, and Arrow Cross authorities tore up such papers as often as they accepted them. The Zionists had long concluded that there was no point in trying to offer armed resistance; this was left to a handful of communists and other armed partisans. Nevertheless, the Zionists' efforts were invaluable.[30]

The Red Army reached the southeastern outskirts of Budapest at the end of November 1944 and, on December 24, in a dashing move, Soviet tanks surrounded the entire capital. The chaos and the hardships in the place are impossible to describe in a few sentences. Before the siege began, the Arrow Cross regime attempted to mobilize the entire population, or at least to force everyone to move to the west. Ever more bloodthirsty proclamations threatened the recalcitrant people with immediate extermination. Because almost no one obeyed the mad orders, the city was now hiding thousands of military deserters and draft dodgers, which meant that the population at large had become accomplices, in a way, with the Jews in the ghetto and, even more, with those in hiding. It seems that about 25,000 Jews and baptized Jews survived the war and the siege disguised as gentiles. Considering, however, that in Budapest most everyone was capable of detecting a Jew and also that most of those in hiding were not denounced, it is likely that at least 100,000 gentiles gave active assistance to the Jews, while many more simply looked the other way.[31] The tragedy is that such popular solidarity had been all but inconceivable in the spring when the deportations to Auschwitz were taking place.

Because of the furious madness of roving Arrow Cross bands, it was now truly risky to hide a Jew. In this connection, let me name only three of the saviors, the Catholic Grey Sister Margit Schlachta, the evangelical minister Gábor Sztehló, and the journalist Béla Stollár. The first repeatedly intervened on behalf of the Slovak Jews during the war and journeyed to see the Pope on their behalf; in 1944, she mobilized her entire order to assist the Hungarian Jews. The second harbored hundreds of Jewish children in different homes. The third hid many Jews and provided others with forged papers; he also set up a small resistance group made up of military deserters and Jewish escapees from labor service. On Christmas Day 1944, Béla Stollár and his companions were killed in a gunfight with the gendarmes and the Arrow Cross militia. That there were many others equally brave is shown by the hundreds of Hungarian names among the righteous gentiles listed at the Yad Vashem Institute in Jerusalem.

Liberation and Postwar Trauma

The siege of Budapest led to enormous destruction and the death of about 20,000 civilians, maybe half of whom were Jews. The Red Army freed the starving Jews in the ghetto and in the protected buildings between January 16 and 18, 1945. Many of those hiding on the Buda side of the city had to wait until February 13 to be free. No doubt, most were painfully aware that what was liberation for them appeared as enemy occupation to their gentile neighbors. In any case, both Jews and gentiles suffered from the rapaciousness and unpredictability of the Red Army soldiers. The classic picture is that of the recently freed Jewish survivor being taken into a Soviet POW camp and ending up in Siberia simply because the Soviets needed workers to help rebuild their country.

The Jews who had been dragged to the west from Budapest in Arrow Cross times were liberated only in the last days of the war in places like Dachau and Mauthausen, where they often met with the survivors of the death marches from Auschwitz and other concentration camps in the east. The death rate among the deportees was enormous both before and following liberation by the US army. Many died after liberation because of the sudden availability and large consumption of nourishing food. This caused refeeding syndrome. Their bodies lacked the required phosphate (ATP, adenosine triphosphate) and potassium. The ATP was needed for their metabolism to handle the energy supplied by their large intake of food and the potassium was required for digestion.

Soon, the majority of survivors made their way home, often in the same group with Hungarian soldiers, right-wing refugees, students, and others who had been ordered abroad by the Arrow Cross regime. Many among these people returned not to Hungary but to areas that now again belonged, respectively, to Romania, Yugoslavia, and Czechoslovakia, or to a land that had been part of Czechoslovakia then became Hungary but was now in Soviet Ukraine. Thousands of Jewish survivors as well as fugitive war criminals and other gentile refugees remained in Germany, many Jews hoping to get to Palestine, others, whether Jewish or non-Jewish, eventually moving to the US, Canada, Australia, and in the case of the war criminals, mainly to Argentina.

The postwar fate of the survivors and of the perpetrators, the memory of the Holocaust or rather, how both communists and nationalists attempted to play down its memory, deserve a separate essay. Here it should be enough to say that retribution under the aegis of a democratic coalition regime was more severe than in most other countries and that, despite many grave shortcomings, the proceedings of the newly constituted people's courts were adequate. Certainly, these were no show trials, and every defendant had his day in court. Many of the guilty escaped justice, especially those who had fled west with the German troops, but more than 300 of the principal war criminals were sent back by the US Army in 1945–1946. As a result, four prime ministers, including, of course, Döme Sztójay and Ferenc Szálasi, were executed, together with nearly 200 other generals, politicians, high-ranking civil servants, ordinary sadists, and the murderers of Jews. Prime Minister László Bárdossy was shot for the debatable crime of having waged war on the Soviet Union, but crimes against the Jews figured in almost every trial. Regent Horthy was never tried, in part because the Americans refused to send him back from his German exile, and in part because Stalin appreciated Horthy's effort, in October 1944, to secede from the war. He died in Portugal in 1957, having been supported, as a penniless refugee, by a few American diplomats and by his Jewish friends. If anyone should ever have been both decorated for valor and executed for the vilest of crimes against humanity, it was this dignified, charming, rather dim-witted former Austro-Hungarian admiral.[32]

The reconstruction of ruined Hungary proceeded at an amazing pace in which Jewish entrepreneurs and engineers played a crucial role. Moreover, because the Jews alone were absolutely reliable and untainted by fascist crimes, the Soviet occupation authorities, and the first democratic coalition governments, entrusted the Jewish survivors with key positions in the police and administration.

Unfortunately, many of the artists of the OMIKE *Művészakció* were not alive to see the liberation of Hungary.

After the war, the OMIKE continued to hold musical concerts, poetry readings and a few other cultural events. (Goldmark Hall had suffered significant damage from an Allied bomb, as shown in a photo in appendix 1, and was not restored for many years). After the hall's restoration in the 1970s, cultural programs were once again held in Goldmark Hall, as shown in the appendix photos of an August 1993 Israeli dance performance. However, the *Művészakció* as it once existed never returned, and soon in the 1950s the OMIKE, itself, essentially ceased to exist.

In 2011, Goldmark Hall was further renovated and modernized by the Jewish community, with a new stage, lighting and sound technology, seating, and so on. In the lobby, leading to the performance hall, a touch-screen video display of Jewish and Holocaust history in Hungary has been added.

Notes

1. The best work on the history of Hungarian Jews in English is Raphael Patai, *The Jews of Hungary: History, Culture and Psychology* (Detroit: Wayne State University Press, 1996).
2. See Andrew Handler, *Blood Libel at Tiszaeszlár*, East European Monographs 68 (New York: Columbia University Press, 1980).

3. Theodor Herzl to Ernö Mezei, who was a member of the Hungarian parliament, on March 10, 1903. Quoted in T. D. Kramer, *From Emancipation to Catastrophe: The Rise and Holocaust of the Hungarian Jewry* (Lanham, MD: University Press of America, 2000), xii.
4. On the much debated subject of Jewish participation in the Hungarian radical movements before World War I see, for instance, John Lukacs, *Budapest 1900: A Historical Portrait of a City and Its Culture* (New York: Weidenfels and Nicolson, 1988), especially chapter 6.
5. *Egyenlöség* (Budapest), May 15, 1896. Quoted in Gábor Schweitzer, "Miért (nem) kellett Herzl a magyar zsidóknak? A politikai cionizmus kezdetei és a magyarországizsidó közvélemény," [Why the Hungarian Jews did (not) need Herzl. The beginnings of Hungarian Zionism and Jewish public opinion in Hungary], *Budapesti Negyed* (Summer 1994), 42.

   Note that the splendid and frightfully expensive national gala costumes were the creation of nineteenth-century Hungarian nationalist imagination. Their wearers, all members of the Hungarian political, social, economic, and cultural elite, dressed the way they thought the ninth-century Chieftain Árpád or the sixteenth-century Hungarian aristocratic warriors were dressed. Needless to say, the great tailors who created the rather theatrical outfits were mostly of Czech, Austrian, or Jewish origin.
6. On Jews in the Habsburg Army before and after World War I, see István Deák, *Beyond Nationalism: A Social and Political History of the Habsburg Officer Corps, 1848–1918* (Princeton: Princeton University Press, 1990), 172–78; Erwin A. Schmidl, *Jews in the Habsburg Armed Forces, 1788–1918*, Studia Judaica Austriaca XI (Eisenstadt: Österreichisches Jüdisches Museum, 1989).
7. On the role of Jews in the Hungarian Soviet Republic, see Charles Gati, *Hungary and the Soviet Bloc* (Durham, NC: University of North Carolina Press, 1986), 100–07; Rudolf L. Tökés, *Béla Kun and the Hungarian Soviet Republic; The Origins and Role of the Communist Party of Hungary in the Revolutions of 1918–1919* (Stanford, CA: Praeger, 1967).
8. On the overproduction or better, the underemployment of the Hungarian intelligentsia in the interwar period, see Mária M. Kovács, *Liberal Professions and Illiberal Politics: Hungary from the Habsburgs to the Holocaust* (New York: Oxford University Press, 1994).
9. A very fine work on Regent Miklós Horthy is Thomas Sakmyster, *Hungary's Admiral on Horseback: Miklós Horthy, 1918–1944*, East European Monographs 396 (New York: Columbia University Press, 1994). For an essay on Sakmyster's book, see István Deák, *Essays on Hitler's Europe* (Lincoln: University of Nebraska Press, 2001), 148–58. On twentieth-century Hungarian politics and society, in English, see László Kontler, *A History of Hungary: Millenium in Central Europe* (New York: Palgrave, 2003), chapter 7; Paul Lendvai, *The Hungarians: 1000 Years of Victory in Defeat* (Princeton: Princeton University Press, 2003), chapters 30–33; and, especially, Ignác Romsics, *Hungary in the Twentieth Century* (Budapest: Corvina, 1999).
10. For all further information on the role of Jews in the professions, business, and industry as well as on the wartime spoliation of the Jews, the reader is referred to Gábor Kádár, "Rationality or Irrationality? The Annihilation of Hungarian Jews," *The Hungarian Quarterly* 45, no. 174 (2004): 32–54. Please note that converts to Christianity, often the best educated among the Jews, were heavily represented in business and the liberal professions, adding substantially to the proportion of unconverted Jews.
11. Dezsö Zentay, *Beszélö számok* [Talking numbers] (Budapest: Globus, 1941), 102–03.

12. On Bethlen see, Ignác Romsics, *István Bethlen: A Great Conservative Statesman of Hungary, 1874–1946,* translated from the Hungarian by Mario D. Fenyo (New York: Columbia University Press, 1995).
13. It has been calculated that, in 1938, Jews owned up to one-fourth of the national wealth. For all further details, see again, Kádár, "Rationality or Irrationality?"
14. A characteristic victim of this charm attack was the US minister to Hungary, John Flournoy Montgomery, whose *Hungary: The Unwilling Satellite* (New York: Devin-Adair, 1947), exculpates the regent and his advisers for collaboration with Nazi Germany and for the anti-Jewish laws. See also Horthy's apologetic *Memoirs* (New York: R. Speller, 1957).
15. On the Jewish labor service system, see Randolph Braham, *The Politics of Genocide* (Detroit: Wayne State University Press, 2000), chapter 10; the tragic fate of the captured labor service men is well analyzed in George Barany,"Jewish Prisoners of War in the Soviet Union During World War II," *Jahrbücher für Geschichte Osteuropas* 31 (1983): 161–209. It seems that 80 percent of the Jewish POWs did not survive Soviet captivity.
16. On all this, see Nicholas Kállay's *Hungarian Premier: a Personal Account of a Nation's Struggle in the Second World War* (Westport, CT: Greenwood Press, 1954); and Mario D. Fenyo, *Hitler, Horthy and Hungary: German-Hungarian Relations, 1941–1944* (New Haven: Yale University Press, 1972).
17. Braham, *The Politics of Genocide*, 233–34.
18. On the question of Hungarian behavior toward the Germans see, among others, István Deák, "A Fatal Compromise? The Debate Over Collaboration and Resistance in Hungary," in István Deák, Jan T. Gross, and Tony Judt, eds., *The Politics of Retribution in Europe: World War II and Its Aftermath* (Princeton, NJ: Princeton University Press, 2000), 39–73.
19. There are only a few memoirs, in English, on the process of deportation. For instance, Judith Magyar Isaacson, *Seed of Sarah: Memoirs of a Survivor* (Urbana: University of Illinois Press, 1990). Christian Gerlach and Götz Aly, *Das letzte Kapitel. Der Mord an den ungarischen Juden 1944/1945* (Stuttgart: Deutsche Verlags-Anstalt, 2002) analyzes the Final Solution on the basis of German documentary sources.
20. The Horthy statement is cited in, among others, Lani Yahil, *The Holocaust: The Fate of European Jewry* (New York: Oxford University Press, 1992), 501. The Goebbels diary entry is in Louis Lochner, ed., *The Goebbels Diaries, 1942–1943* (Garden City, NY: Doubleday, 1948), 357.
21. On the wasteful dissipation of Jewish goods and, in general, on the catastrophic economic effect of the anti-Jewish measures, see Kádár, "Rationality or Irrationality?"
22. Hannah Arendt, *Eichmann in Jerusalem: On the Banality of Evil* (New York: Viking, 1963), 104; and Randolph L. Braham, "The Holocaust in Hungary: A Retrospective Analysis," in David Cesarani, ed., *Genocide and Rescue: The Holocaust in Hungary 1944* (Oxford: Berg, 1997), 42–43. For a review of this book, see Deák, *Essays on Hitler's Europe*, 159–62.
23. Imre Kertész, *Fateless,* translated from the Hungarian by Christopher C. Wilson and Katharina M. Wilson (Evanston, IL: Northwestern University Press, 1992), 54–55. On Kertész, see István Deák, "Stranger in Hell," *The New York Review of Books*, Sept. 25, 2003, 65–68.
24. It must be stated that some other Jews, besides those in Budapest and those in labor service, also escaped deportation. One small but important group consisted of the members of the Baron Jenö Weiss and related great capitalist families who, behind

the back of the Sztójay government, negotiated their transportation to Portugal with representatives of the SS. In exchange, they handed over much of Hungary's heavy and armaments industry to the SS. Himmler allowed another, much larger group, consisting of 1,684 individuals, to be transported out of Hungary and all eventually reached Switzerland. The release of the group was negotiated by Rudolf (Rezső) Kasztner and other Hungarian Zionists in exchange for money. Himmler and other SS leaders also hoped thereby to escape the hangman's noose if Allies won the war. Both the Weiss and the Kasztner cases provoked an enormous literature, which should constitute the basis for another essay. For an introduction to the subject, see Yehuda Bauer, *Jews for Sale? Nazi-Jewish Negotiations, 1933–1945* (New Haven: Yale University Press, 1994), 145–251; and Gábor Kádár and Zoltán Vági, *Self-Financing Genocide: The Gold Train, the Becher Case and the Wealth of Hungarian Jews* (Budapest: Central European University Press, 2004), esp. 175–278, which discuss the case of the SS officer Kurt Becher, who was deeply involved in negotiations regarding the fate of the great capitalist families and the so-called Kasztner train.

25. Nicholas Nagy-Talavera, *The Green Shirts and Others: A History of Fascism in Hungary and Romania*, 2nd ed. (Portland, OR: Center for Romanian Studies, 2001), usefully compares the Hungarian Arrow Cross movement with the Romanian Iron Guard.
26. Note that, after the war, most of the Austrian people's court trials dealt with the case of such Austrian soldiers and *Hitlerjugend,* who had beaten Hungarian Jews to death. Several of the defendants were hanged.
27. Of the many works on Wallenberg, see especially Kati Marton, *Wallenberg* (New York: Random House, 1982); Danny Smith, *Lost Hero: Raoul Wallenberg's Dramatic Quest to Save the Jews of Hungary* (London: HarperCollins, 2001); and Per Anger, *With Raoul Wallenberg in Budapest*, translated by David Paul and Margareta Paul (New York: Holocaust Library, 1981). The Swiss consul's extraordinary achievements are lovingly presented in Theo Tschuy, *Dangerous Diplomacy: The Story of Carl Lutz, Rescuer of 62,000 Jews* (Grand Rapids, MI: William B. Eerdmans, 2000).
28. The activities of the neutral consuls are convincingly discussed in Robert Rozett, "International Intervention: The Role of Diplomats in Attempts to Rescue Jews in Hungary," in Randolph L. Braham and Scott Miller, eds., *The Nazis' Last Victims; the Holocaust in Hungary* (Detroit, MI: Wayne State University Press, 1998), 137–52.
29. On the Jewish policy of the Szálasi regime see, among others, László Karsai, "The Last Phase of the Hungarian Holocaust: The Szálasi Regime and the Jews," in Braham and Miller, *The Nazis' Last Victims*, 105–16.
30. On Zionist activities in Budapest see, among others, Asher Cohen, "The Dilemma of Rescue and Revolt," in Braham and Miller, *The Nazis' Last Victims*, 117–36. Also, by the same author, *The Halutz Resistance in Hungary, 1942–1944*, Social Science Monographs (New York: Columbia University Press, 1986).
31. A characteristic case of a Jewish family in hiding is that of the financier and philanthropist George Soros, who was then fourteen. Their adventures in Budapest in 1944–1945 are entertainingly described in the memoirs of his father, Tivadar Soros, in *Masquerade: Dancing Around Death in Nazi-Occupied Hungary* (New York: Arcade Publishing, 2000). The book was translated into English from the original 1965 edition in Esperanto. Not uncharacteristically, the Soros family in disguise had regular access to swimming pools, restaurants, and opera performances in Budapest and, not uncharacteristically, the author fails to recognize how many gentiles had assisted him or, at least, how many had failed to denounce him, his mother, his wife, his sons,

and other relatives in hiding. For a critique of the Soros memoirs, see István Deák, "Artful Dodger," *The New York Review of Books*, November 15, 2001.

32. Retribution in post-World War II Hungary is well discussed in László Karsai's essay, "The People's Courts and Revolutionary Justice in Hungary, 1945–46," in Deák, Gross, and Judt, *The Politics of Retribution in Europe*, 233–51.

István Deák
Columbia University
October 2013

1

The OMIKE Theater in Goldmark Hall

When we talk about the OMIKE Artistic Enterprise (*Művészakció*), we should remember the birth of the Goldmark Hall, where Jewish artists, having been forbidden to perform elsewhere, found a home and a chance to perform.

In the last decades of the nineteenth century, the Jewish primary school located in the wing of the present headquarters of the Jewish Religious Community of Pest on Wesselényi Street also served cultural purposes. Until the foundation of this school, at the corner of Wesselényi Street and Nagyatádi Szabó István Street, little school boys and girls studied at its predecessor. In 1920, the community started a large construction program. It included the restoration of the beautiful synagogue on Dohány Street and the construction of the Temple of Heroes to serve as an eternal memorial. Behind its archway, the Jewish Museum was also established. The old school's site on Wesselényi Street was now devoted to a cultural center. The rabbinate office was established on the ground floor, the communal tax office on the first floor, and the huge cultural hall on the second floor was devoted to larger meetings, festive gatherings, free university presentations, and cultural performances. The name of the artistically designed ceremonial hall commemorates the world renowned Jewish composer, Károly Goldmark.

The cradle of the youth movements rocked in Goldmark Hall. Within its walls, cultural performances were held in succession, which were followed by others in the city's districts. Later, youth groups presented plays here.

When Jewish artists were not allowed to perform anymore in theaters, an idea emerged that Goldmark Hall could serve as a home and a stage for them. In 1939, definite steps were taken by the Social Working Committee to implement the plan. Subsequently, the realization of the OMIKE Artistic Enterprise can be attached to the name of Dr. Géza Ribáry. He put an enormous amount of energy into this matter of high importance. He created this refuge for Jewish artists literally overnight.

The leadership of the Jewish Religious Community of Pest recognized the great significance of the intiative and gave its full support for the realization of the project. In November 1939, authorization was granted to the OMIKE Artistic Enterprise by the Minister of Education, Bálint Hóman; the Home Secretary, Ferenc Keresztes-Fischer; and by the police, as well, to start its activities.

Samu Stern, President of the Jewish Religious Community of Pest

"The cultural mission of Hungarian Jewry is to ensure the existence of the Artistic Enterprise"

The ceremonial speech of the President of the Jewish Religious Community of Pest, Samu Stern, at the opening ceremony of the fourth season of OMIKE:

> Ladies and Gentlemen,
>
> The task that I have undertaken by giving an introductory speech at the opening evening of this year's season of the Artistic Enterprise is unusual for me and might not even suit me. It is unusual because I normally give speeches on other matters such as religious, public, or economic life. Here, on this stage, the artist has the right to speak, while the place for us, the audience, is down there in the auditorium. Our voice can only be the echo that resonates in our hearts, expressed externally in applause for the performances of the artists. It is us, the audience, who should be grateful and thank the Artistic Enterprise for making us forget our daily sorrows and enjoy the art—even if it's only through acting—by making us smile or even cry with a good feeling in these dark times.
>
> This Artistic Enterprise was regarded by many, especially at the beginning, as one of the charities that are unfortunately so needed these days. They thought that since so many writers, actors, singers, and musicians had lost their jobs, through which they could express their art and could make a living, they needed to be assisted. Which hurts more: losing earnings or the ability for self-expression? In my opinion: for real artists art is above all. They would rather face hardship and put up with less in order to pursue their artistic ambitions.
>
> Therefore, this Artistic Enterprise achieves the most beautiful and noble mission for our unemployed artists by not only giving them a chance to earn their modest bread but also by providing a place for them to perform. It makes it possible for them to express and demonstrate their God-given talents and to spice up the piece of bread thus acquired with our applause. The Artistic Enterprise in this sense is about art rather than charity, although it is charitable to the extent that it is beneficial for us when we fly away on the wings of art from our everyday problems. It is not we who give to our art-

ists, rather the artists are the ones giving to us, because we can never offer as much as they can, since they give the greatest gift: the beauty of art. Let's accept this gift with love and be grateful for it.

I believe that in supporting this Artistic Enterprise, providing a place for it and generously making it possible for a growing audience to benefit from its beauty and goodness, the community of Pest fulfills a spiritual mission for its members. By offering the Goldmark Hall to the Artistic Enterprise we give a place to Hungarian Jewish culture and I declare that it is the cultural duty and obligation of the community of Pest, of all Hungarian Jewry, to ensure its existence and development, not only to provide a livelihood for our artists, but also to offer a spiritual experience for us, the cultured Hungarian Jewish audience, who can enjoy performances which live up to our high expectations. I hope that the example of the community of Pest will influence the communities in the countryside. They also have cultural obligations: to welcome this Artistic Enterprise as often as possible and to launch similar actions.

The experiences and the results of past artistic seasons speak for themselves. We can all be proud of the performances at this place. And you, ladies and gentlemen, are on a cultural mission by embracing this Artistic Enterprise. Spread the news of this initiative and get new patrons for Hungarian Jewish art, since this project is not able to sustain itself from the regular membership fees because of the limited seating capacity of the hall. Just like the large national opera houses which maintain their standards thanks to the sacrifices of the friends of the opera, we also need more and more friends so that a growing audience can benefit from the artistic beauty provided by this Artistic Enterprise.

I expect and demand from the leading classes of our society to set a good example in this regard. I expect all those who have kept aloof from the Artistic Enterprise to join us, as friends, since the performances have reached such a high level of artistic quality. It cannot be accepted as an excuse if someone says that he doesn't go out at all. Even if you don't go out in general, you must come here and even if you have a regular place to go to, then you must also try this one.

Come and see for yourselves that, although we cannot offer plush armchairs, sumptuous decoration and pomp, or a revolving stage and complete stagecraft, our theatrical culture is still of high standards and, in this modest setting, the pearl of art shines.

That's all I wanted to say, ladies and gentlemen. This is why I was ready to give a season-opening speech: to be able to share with you, as the head of your community, the President of the Jewish Religious Community of Pest, my commitment to the moral and spiritual value of this enterprise.

Géza Ribáry

"About those who fulfill and those who fail to fulfill their obligations"

Dr. Géza Ribáry, the first president of the Cultural Committee of the OMIKE, said the following shortly before his sudden tragic death:

> Let's see how our artists and society have complied with their obligations concerning this Artistic Enterprise. It is up to the audience to decide whether our artists have done their best in serving the Artistic Enterprise with their God-given talents. The answer is generally "yes," for my part, to the other question: regarding whether Jewish Hungarian society has fulfilled its obligation towards the Artistic Enterprise, since it is thanks to the society that we are here. However, I have to mention that, although many fulfilled their duty well, and some much more than expected, there were and still are those who, completely and incomprehensibly and despite belonging to the spiritual or financial aristocracy, refrain from supporting our cultural aspirations and from aiding us.
>
> I read the following truth in the text of a recently given speech by Dr. Kálmán Molnár, an academic professor at the Royal University of Pécs:
>
>> Everything is interconnected. The dazzling light that shines in our eyes from one of the stars or from the stage—the sound wave emanating from the stage to us or the one that is breathed into the air on the other side of this space; thoughts and acts, and not only great acts, but ordinary manifestations as well, all have lasting effects.
>>
>> A bright smile, an encouraging word, a supportive act, making a sacrifice; all have effects, all excite and strengthen, stimulate, vibrate in the souls touched and determine walks of life. In this way, it can happen that they concentrate as a factor to shape history.
>
> For this reason, I would like to thank all the patrons and friends of this Artistic Enterprise and our kind audience for their friendship and support by refering to the fact that while you are enjoying yourselves here, satisfying your cultural needs, supporting our artists, your sacrifice and applause also have an effect. They excite and strengthen, stimulate and vibrate in the souls touched, thus they concentrate as a factor to shaping our future and hopes.
>
> I must cite another truth from the speech of this outstanding professor at the University of Pécs. It goes like this:
>
>> Everybody's responsible, responsible for the never-ending series of events that he initiated with his words, movements or actions, even for those which he failed to initiate because he was too lazy or too idle to do good.

I draw the attention to its responsibility of that segment of Jewish Hungarian society which has failed to support our cultural aspirations and to aid us, to its responsibility, in the hope that recognition of its responsibility will be enough incentive to make it comply with its obligation in the future—hopefully already in this season.

When I talk about those who haven't fulfilled their obligations, I also have to mention someone who stands out by having done more than expected. From the first moment, he has appreciated our efforts more than anyone else. He has supported us with great enthusiasm and put all his energy into the realization and development of the Artistic Enterprise. I speak about the president of an association called The Friends of the OMIKE Artistic Enterprise, who is also the President of the Jewish Religious Community of Pest and leader of Hungarian Jewry.

Thanks to Samu Stern, we managed to overcome the financial and legal hurdles to realize the Artistic Enterprise. He gave a venue to the Artistic Enterprise, and we thank him for its artistic restoration. He was the one who convinced the board of the community that the foremost community of the country must support the Artistic Enterprise. He was the one who made Hungarian Jewish society feel responsible for the Artistic Enterprise, through his active involvement in acquiring financial assistance from patrons, founding members and friends. Through his regular visits to our performances and through his encouragement of the leading segment of Jewish society to come and see the performances. Not only are the performances of the Artistic Enterprise on a high standard today, but its audience is as well.

Hugó Csergő

Quoting Géza Ribáry

It's been a year since he left us.[1] But as the far sky shines purple long after the sun has already set, so the spirit of our deceased friend keeps on radiating warmth and light in this hall. Everything is filled with him. The diversity of colors on the posters in the lobby, the portraits of artists on the staircase, the gold monogram of Goldmark above the door, the warm burgundy tone of the walls and windows, the arrangement of the chairs as they are lined up behind one another, the worn cyclorama of the stage and the painted canvas of the coulisse—all, all remind us of him, all, all are impregnated with his memory.

In the limelight, which illuminates his portrait, he comes to life again—he is alive and speaks. He speaks in a slightly mocking, slightly teasing way that hides his deep empathy, with a little skeptical smile on his lips, which suggests his worries inside him. Whether or not the feeling flowing towards him is real, his eyes still glisten with fever, inflamed by his seething spirit, which heated the forge of his mind till the last flicker. He says the following: "Thank you for thinking of me. Thank you for still remembering me." And we answer: "Géza Rébáry, all of us here and elsewhere are and will be one with you in spirit and in our memories":

> We thank you, Géza Ribáry, that you existed. Thank you for your creative works in which you put of yourself, in such a way that they survive you and you, yourself, survive in them and live on through them. Thank you for the thoughts and beauty you gave us—the thought which you realized in the idea of the OMZSA and the beauty which you passed on to us in the form of the Artistic Enterprise.[2]
>
> The solidarity, the thought of sharing our fate: the idea of the OMZSA which you planted in our hearts and memories then turned into action so that they are followed by good deeds in these dark times and value is created in bleak circumstances.
>
> And the beauty of the illusion: the beauty that you left us in the OMIKE Artistic Enterprise—the beauty of the illusion which weaves a veil of imagination around reality and which through play makes us forget about our lives and which by the magic of art takes us to a world we wish for, far from the one from which reality now excludes us.
>
> He gave us the most beautiful thing which creative imagination can give: a toy for the child that we are and we will be, till we die. When we are on the verge of bursting into tears, we begin to smile, even today, when we hear the jingle of the fool's cap which you shook and which continues to ring even now when your arm is already stiff. Just as in olden days when we heard our mother's lullaby chase away lurking monsters of the night, so we now are relieved of the nightmare when we hear the sublime majesty of Beethoven in this hall or when Verdi's sentimentality softens into a deep low voice or when the melting silver of Puccini's arias flows in all directions or when we hear Offenbach's naughty rhythms bouncing. Thus through this sonorous flow of sounds and colors the disharmony of our lives melts into balsamic harmonies. All that is bad outside vanishes inside in this Goldmark Hall, the cradle of which you, Géza Ribáry, rocked and in which we now rock in a musical cradle and dream of a life that reality can never replace.
>
> You established a stage for our artists, for whom the stage is everything, and you created a stage for us for whom only performance can give the illusion of life.
>
> Who says that you died when the rhymes of the dead poet can be heard on this stage just as much as those of the live poet? How could Bach's fugues, Mozart's melodies, which you also brought to life so many times, become silent while there is a stage and a musician to play the piano? Only the tran-

sient part is lost of the man, but the spirit which created something timeless will last and lives on in his work.

Your spirit, Géza Ribáry, lives in the ideals of thought and beauty. When we pay tribute to you on this stage with our modest, quiet words, we do not mourn but glorify your everlasting memory. In honor of your glorified memory we perform a masterpiece of the immortal Beethoven, instead of singing funeral hymns, to unite in the endless beauty of music so that your spirit finds its way to our heart and doesn't enclose your memory in a coffin but rocks it as a cradle into the nicer future of our life-giving dreams, where the radiant bridge of your works leads us.

We answer this to you, Géza Ribáry, when you smile thankfully at us from your picture for remembering you.

And we just add:—"Good"—We remember you. "Good," we think of you. Artists, authors, painters, sculptors, the audience; we are with you and we will always remember you.

Ladies and gentlemen, let's rise for a moment and think of him, in silence, without a word. Only for a few moments. And now let us fondly and quietly whisper his name like this: Géza Ribáry, Géza Ribáry, we will follow you till we die, stay with us, stay with us . . . !"

Notes on the Translation

1. Speech given at the Ribáry Memorial Evening of the OMIKE Artistic Enterprise, circa May 1943. Dr. Géza Ribáry died of natural causes on May 9, 1942.
2. OMZSA–Országos Magyar Zsidó Segítő Akció (National Hungarian Jewish Aid Organization).

2

The OMIKE Artistic Enterprise

The OMIKE Artistic Enterprise was one of the branches of the National Hungarian Jewish Cultural Society. The OMIKE charter states that the society's responsibilities include "to stage performances." This stipulation made it legally possible to establish this branch, to develop it appropriately, and to hold meaningful activities. Since the society can only stage performances for its members, tickets can only be purchased by ordinary and supporting members of the OMIKE.

The Leadership

The leadership of the Artistic Enterprise is headed by the OMIKE Cultural Committee. Its first chairman was Dr. Géza Ribáry. After his death, it was of great aid to the Artistic Enterprise that Samu Stern, the current chairman, accepted the post. Since the beginning, the vice-chairman has been Hugó Csergő. The chairman and the vice-chairman served as managers. At the same time they liaised the OMIKE with the Jewish Community of Pest, which gave a venue for the Artistic Enterprise. The chairman has the right to veto the pieces selected for performance.

At this time, the cultural committee consists of 46 members and has the following subcommittees: OMIKE management (five members), Jewish Religious Community of Pest (six members), financial committee, audit committee, and artists committees (actors, musicians, authors, journalists, fine art artists). Since money makes the world and its institutions go round, the financial committee is very active. It supervises the financial management of the Artistic Enterprise, which is also controlled by the accountancy department of the Pest community.

The Director

The director of the Artistic Enterprise in Goldmark Hall is Dr. László Bánóczi. We will try to give an objective, illustrative picture of his work, duties, and problems. The statement that "one man can direct many theaters, but one theater cannot be directed by more than one man," is not new, but is still quite correct. It is true about the Artistic Enterprise, which functions in a relatively small space. However, as we will see, it has a huge number of staff and thus has many visible, invisible, and indescribable problems.

Bánóczi's Theatrical Past in a Nutshell

Dr. László Bánóczi founded the Thalia Society at the age of eighteen and directed it since then with his colleagues, especially with Sándor Hevesi. In its program and acting style, the society supported the revival of Hungarian acting. It has the same art historical importance as Antoine's Théâtre Libre in France, or the Freie Bühne Movement led by Otto Brahm in Germany. This initiative included in its program D'Annunzio, Ibsen , Gorky, Heyermans, Hebbel , and Hauptmann, and it discovered György Szemere and Menyhért Lengyel as playwrights. It created ensemble art and broke with the pathetic reciting style.

Later, he was the director of the *Vígszínház* (Comedy Theater), the stage manager of the *Magyar Színház* (Hungarian Theater), the dramaturgist of the *Új Színház* (New Theater) and he directed the *Tragedy of Man* at the *Városi Színház* (City Theater). He translated numerous plays from German, French, and Italian. He was the drama critic at several daily newspapers and periodicals. His study, *Shakespeare on the Modern Stage*, was published by the Kisfaludy Society.

As a member of the capital committee, he dealt with many cultural issues. It is thanks to his suggestion that, even today, there is a scholarship for acting awarded annually in the capital.

He is one of the founders of the OMIKE Artistic Enterprise and its director from the beginning.

Duties of the Director

Dr. László Bánóczi is the financial, administrative, and artistic head of the Artistic Enterprise. His financial duties include taking care of the finances and their appropriate distribution. He deals with procurement. The director releases checks under the supervision of the management, the financial committee, and the accountancy department. One important task is to set the price of seats from time to time. He is supported in his administrative duties by an office consisting of a number of employees. In this field his deputy is Dr. Sándor Zoltán, an outstanding expert who was Secretary General of the Actors' Alliance for a long time. Among the artistic duties of the director, the most important ones are programming and casting. The director periodically reports on artistic plans to the cultural council and on the financial situation to the management.

Economic Structure of the Artistic Enterprise

The director prepares a budget at the end of each season for the following year and, on the basis of realistic circumstances, he estimates the huge deficit that is inevitable. If the Artistic Enterprise worked only as a normal theatrical company, then it could even be profitable. However, at this institution social aspects take precedence over economic ones. The chairman approves the estimate of the huge deficit, which is highly important, as he must cover the deficit through social connections. On the revenue side of the budget there are two cumulative items: the charitable contributions meant for the elimination of the deficit and the membership fees because, as mentioned earlier, tickets are only available to members. The seating capacity of the theater is 382. The price of seats for opera is higher, thus the potential receipts for opera performances are about 30% higher than those for regular performances.

Costs vary according to the type of performance. Opera performances are the most expensive because they require a 36-member orchestra and a 12- to 24-member choir. In addition, there are the royalties. The fees for score rental and stage setting are usually more costly. Opera members usually earn more per performance than play actors. Most of the time, a full house doesn't cover all the costs.

Concerts are quite expensive because the orchestra has more than 40 members plus soloists. It is surprising that concerts have, so far, only aroused modest interest.

Dramas are usually cheaper. Cabaret is more expensive, as there is a small orchestra and also because for social reasons they try to employ more people. Apart from the company, the theater employs six permanent, stage technical staff and fourteen ushers and cleaners. Renting out the bar and the cloakroom brings extra earnings for the Artistic Enterprise.

Official Duties and Regulations

A series of police and fire safety measures must be followed, and compliance with these measures is taken very seriously. The spaces in Goldmark Hall—two cloakrooms, a consulting room, a scenery and property room—are very small. At each performance there are two firefighters, two detectives, an adequate number of police and, for their supervision, a fire chief and a police commander. There is a doctor on duty at each performance. In accordance with fire safety measures, all components of decoration and stage are impregnated with fire retardants. The place is equipped with a modern sprinkler system. There is a separate water hydrant at the stage and a direct telephone connection to the fire brigade. In accordance with official regulations, a bomb shelter was built in the basement under the building.

Each play must be presented to the authorities before being performed for prior authorization and censorship. Once authorization is granted, it is valid henceforth.

Artistic Duties

The director's duties include programming and the casting. (The two visible links between the two main departments of the Artistic Enterprise, the regular and the musical, are Lajos Bálint and Vilmos Komor, who will inform our readers about their duties later in this book.)

Programming

The most striking feature of the programming is that it has to be done one month in advance. The reason is that the OMIKE cannot disseminate public posters. It has to provide its services to only its members. It must send programs to its members (about 5000 supporting members) by post. This is quite costly and for this reason cannot be repeated weekly. The new program has to be composed in the middle of the month, then sent to the press and finally to the members. Members receive the program around the 20th, and then the advanced booking starts.

It is easy to understand that this way of programming is reliable since certain pieces or plays are always included in the program depending on the interest they attract. It is a little bit more difficult to decide the schedule of performances for a longer time in advance, although—as is usual in theaters—a precise tally is made at each performance of the number of spectators and tickets sold.

There are official rules which make it necessary to compose a mixed program. This is why there is often a drama or a comedy combined with a shorter, one-act opera (Giovanni Battista Pergolese [1710–1736], Mendelsohn, Mozart, Offenbach, etc.) in the framework of one show.

The regular pieces are selected on the basis of three theoretical considerations:

1. The works of Jewish authors (Ferenc Molnár, Dezső Szomory, Hugó Csergő, Ernő Szép, etc.).
2. Pieces of world literature about Jews (*Judit* [Judith] by Friedrich Hebbel, 1813–1863), *Eszter* [Esther] by Jean Racine, 1639–1699).
3. Classical plays (Shakespeare, Molière [1622–1673], Henrik Ibsen [1828–1906]).

In this respect, the management is convinced that these classical plays are necessary in order to develop the program and the company and also because the Artistic Enterprise must serve the needs of the audience as well. Ibsen is still one of the most important authors for actor training and company formation and performing his works also ensures prestige.

The considerations governing the selection of plays are varied and more circumstantial than at theaters. First is the fact that performances are held at the headquarters of the community, in the same building as the offices of the rabbinate, with a synagogue next door. Attention must be paid to the small size of the stage and to the number of actors available. It always has to be considered whether the staging of a play would not be too costly. One of the objectives is to employ as many artists as possible. Thus, pieces calling for only a few actors are avoided.

Apart from the performance of current and well-known pieces, management focuses on premieres. They don't want the OMIKE to become a so-called "second-run theater." Several times, they called for plays from about forty Hungarian Jewish authors. These calls were partly successful and ensured the performance of works by Hugó Csergő, Jenő Mohácsi, and others. However, the Artistic Enterprise doesn't have its own composers. There were only a few cases when certain pieces needed setting to music. There were two operas in the program, the translation of which turned out to be too outdated. Sándor Fischer was entrusted with producing a modern, new translation of *Don Pasquale* and *Windsori víg nők* (The Merry Wives of Windsor).

It doesn't even need to be mentioned that a lot of unknown, dilettante authors came to see us with their works, as at the theaters. In four years, we received about 300 such pieces. Most of them were useless artifacts, but there were some which were worthwhile. An author, surely talented, from Újpest, dramatized the story of Joseph by Thomas Mann. The only problem was that there were 30 actors in his play, and this was too many for our small stage.

The ratio between regular and musical programs was 50:50. This means that drama, comedy, cabaret, and light opera were in one group, and opera and concert in the other group. The cabaret shows mostly consist of old, never-failing items. In the comic programs, the most important social consideration was to involve as many artists as possible. A 90-minute-long light opera type evolved, beside which cabaret could also be performed.

The OMIKE's Company

This group of artists, available to the audience at Goldmark Hall, is one of the most diverse in the world. The booklet with the typed list of the company members is thick: there are 432 names altogether. However, this doesn't mean the actual number of individual persons, because there are actors registered as directors as well and there are many, especially among the musicians, who play different instruments and, moreover, have their names listed as solo performers and as members of the orchestra. (However, it must also be noted that aside from the artists, the Artistic Enterprise employs many other people.)

It's worth taking a look at this list. So many European and Hungarian celebrities! There are so many solo artists among the members of the orchestra that, with their solo concerts, they could fill the programs of several stages for a long time.

Let's see some figures. There are 75 ordinary actors, 59 actresses, 3 child actors, 3 male dancers, and 10 female dancers. Solo singers: 22 sopranos, 5 contraltos and mezzos, 10 tenors, 8 baritones, and 4 bass singers. There are 40 solo musicians, among them 22 pianists. There are 111 orchestra members, grouped according to instruments, 41 choir members, 11 conducting conductors, and 15 accompanying conductors.

There is a strict rule that only artists belonging to the Jewish Community may perform. This rule must be obeyed at all times. However, once, during an emergency, when one of the leading actors of an opera became sick on the day of the show and the performance and the earnings of the performers for that day were at risk, they were saved by a kind, noble, non-Jewish artist, who performed as an understudy.

In principle, in the Artistic Enterprise, only those artists who worked before the promulgation of the Jewish laws can perform. Because of this, we cannot talk about the education of a new generation of artists (a separate acting school), even less so, since the present circumstances don't seem to make it possible to ensure their future. There are only two exceptions to the mentioned rule—in very rare cases; if a young artist graduated later than the promulgation of the Jewish laws or if a beginner shows extraordinary talent. Due to the religious and cultural nature of the institution, the law doesn't hinder the employment of nonchamber (guild) members.

No one has a contract. Thus the number of appearances is not regulated. It is only the performance which is "supported." The OMIKE Artistic Enterprise cannot distribute charity, no matter how highly renowned an artist may be.

Casting

Casting is the most sensitive and complicated duty. Its most important aspect is that the role should suit the artist. However, this can only be realized in theory. In practice, it cannot be the sole determinant. Besides aptitude, a person's neediness must also be taken into account. If there are two artists with similar talent and character, a role will first be assigned to the one with a larger family. As a result, it sometimes happens that the most competent person doesn't get a middle-sized role. Attention must be paid to distribute duties as evenly as possible among all persons during the year. For instance, if a dramatic actor has a huge success in a major role, he might not be assigned to another important dramatic role because others must be considered as well. This rule cannot be departed from, no matter how profitable it may be for the theater. One person cannot be privileged because others are waiting for roles, too. It is just natural that everybody should be dissatisfied when it comes to acting: those who get too much to do and also those who don't.

The Artistic Enterprise doesn't award contracts to its artist members. Pay is given per show, but this—in accordance with official regulations—is not considered remuneration for the appearance, but "support."

Concerning the premieres, the role of directing is assigned to different persons for each piece. The dramatic directors of the Artistic Enterprise are: Lajos Bálint, Oszkár Beregi, Lajos Gellért, György Nagy, and Imre Ráday. The opera directors are: Lajos Bálint, Dezső Gál, and Ernő Szabolcs. Light opera and cabaret directors are: Dezső Gál, Miklós Harsányi, and Ernő Szabolcs.

It often happens that if the director is an actor as well, he also performs in the play which he directs. In theory, this is not preferable since the director is not always able to adapt to the roles he performs as an actor. An outsider can judge the role and the actors better. In a repertoire theater, this problem very rarely results in concrete complaints since it is not possible to leave the huge amount of directing work of a whole program to the few nonactor directors.

3

The Drama Company

The Artistic Director and Dramaturgist (Playwright)

In the OMIKE Theater the old and renowned expert is Lajos Bálint, the artistic director and dramaturgist. When asked to talk about himself, he was at first guardedly reluctant. Then he replied, attentively, with the sentences of an essayist:

Interviewer: In your career, how did you get to the OMIKE Artistic Enterprise?

Lajos Bálint: Following a long break of many years with OMIKE's leadership, we worked together again with László Bánóczi, with whom we had started our theatrical career. The Thália Company was founded in 1904. This was our first experience with theater and, at the same time, our first collaboration. I was Secretary of the Thália Company. This was the first attempt at a modern, free stage, which meant a theatrical revolution and it brought new literature and acting styles. Following this, I partly stayed abroad, partly worked as a critic until 1915, and then for 21 years as Dramaturgist-Secretary General at the *Nemzeti Színház* (National Theater). After that, I worked for three years as Dramaturgist-Manager at the *Magyar Színház* (Hungarian Theater) and at the *Andrássy úti Színház* (Andrássy Avenue Theater).

My involvement in the shows here started earlier than the OMIKE Artistic Enterprise. While working at the *Magyar Színház*, at the request of the secretary general of the community, I undertook to work with the problems of the artists, writers, and actors who were threatened by the law being prepared. I came here every afternoon. We tried different campaigns, for example, mailing postcards for the fine arts expositions, which produced results, and we also directed theatrical plays on a few occasions. These attempts then combined with Géza Ribáry's idea, which led to the emergence of the OMIKE Artistic Enterprise and, of course, I also got involved in it. When the Artistic Enterprise began, I was no longer at the *Magyar Színház*.

I am now the artistic director and dramaturgist here. This activity and my directing work have extended to a new field for me: the direction of operas. This meant that I had to do preparatory work, by myself, to enter into this totally new field alongside the excellent conductors of the OMIKE.

Interviewer: What are your directing duties?

Lajos Bálint: Every year, I direct a maximum of two ordinary plays and two operas. I wouldn't want to do more, because my artistic conviction is that the direction of three or four pieces with the appropriate preparation is enough for a director. Here, this work is more difficult than in any other theater because these operas were composed for the so-called large stages and their sizes must be reduced to fit our small stage. For example, singers who are used to a stage of 18 meters, and all of a sudden find themselves on a six-meter stage, must change their acting style completely. Instead of wide, large gestures and large movements, they will have to reduce them and shift to small ones. The director has the same problems concerning the acting style of the whole piece. Drama must be stylized for this small stage just like the opera. This also includes, of course, the scenery because here we can only work with stylized props instead of large structures and instead of great designs we must rather search for scenic effects. It is not an easy thing to do for a director, an actor, or a singer if they were originally used to the great dimensions of a large theater.

Interviewer: What is the scope of your duties as dramaturgist (playwright)?

Lajos Bálint: The duties of a dramaturgist are, on the one hand, to read pieces and to express an opinion about them and on the other hand, to be available to the authors and the theaters for occasional correction and adaptation of pieces.

Interviewer: Are there any new submissions by writers? What considerations decide if a piece is to be selected for performance?

Lajos Bálint: The structure of the OMIKE program, the fact that we have to work with four to five types of programs, makes it impossible that individual pieces reach a high number of performances. Thus, it's understandable that this doesn't really inspire the writing of new pieces, which takes many months. Despite this, during the three-year OMIKE program, there have been a few world premieres in every theatrical year.

Apart from these, there have been many new pieces by writers and non-professionals alike. Unfortunately, there are many considerations which limit the chances for a piece to be performed, apart from its merits. Thus, in spite of all the good qualities of the pieces received, we often cannot stage a good play by a good writer because it exceeds our stage options or because it doesn't fit into the artistic program that we, in the framework of this Artistic Enterprise and in the building of the community, must accomplish or because other considerations don't allow its performance in the present conditions. You can imagine what a serious task it is for the leadership to select pieces and what difficulties they have to overcome.

Interviewer: How is the program of the Artistic Enterprise prepared, in detail?

Lajos Bálint: The manager involves the artistic directors in the preparation of the one-year program, which determines more or less the pieces to be staged and their order. Of course, as usual at theaters, it is still not the final version. There are often changes. The selection of the pieces and the casting are done by the manager on the basis of discussions with the artistic directors.

Interviewer: Are there disputes, jealousy, intrigues here, too?

Lajos Bálint: Where there is a stage and there are actors: it's a theater. Theater has its own nature which doesn't change from the north pole to the south pole. It's possible that the famous dictum of the excellent German theater manager, Laube, that has become a maxim, "Beim Theater kommt immer alles anders" ("In theater, everything always works in a different way"), is true for all the other areas of the theater—but not for this one.

Interviewer: Is there patronage here, too?

Lajos Bálint: The comforting experience of my past thirty years of working in theaters and as a critic is that the patrons have always used their influence on behalf of untalented people. I can't remember any talented person being recommended to me. It seems that patrons have an excellent sense with which to recognize the lack of talent. On the basis of all that was mentioned above, the OMIKE is a theater, too, and there are a lot of patrons—on the same basis—with very little result.

OMIKE's Most Successful Writers

Let us review the case of a few interesting writers who are the most successful ones in the OMIKE Artistic Enterprise.

Hugó Csergő

"Since primary school, we were dreaming of literary successes"

We conducted an interview with the popular writer, Hugó Csergő. The questions were banal. We asked him about the details of his writing career. However, most of the *answers* should become part of the history of literature. We felt as if the prehistory of Hungarian journalism and the most brilliant pages of our literary history came to life while he spoke:

> I started a little bit too early. I was in third grade in primary school when I wrote my poem *Tavasz* (Spring). When I was in my first year in high school, my poem was published in *Előre* (Forward), the school newspaper, which

> we edited and distributed ourselves. We were infected with literature since our early school years. In the Markó Street High School, we dreamed of poems and literary successes. We edited a newspaper, we wrote poems, short stories, and literary studies. We attended the meetings of the Petőfi and Kisfaludy Societies, while we adored Klára Küry, the star of the *Népszínház* (Popular Theater). Later they remembered us as an artistic class. Gyula Szini, Árpád Odry, Román Maleczky, Alfréd Németh, Pál Páriss, Árpád Pásztor, Géza Tormay, and Róbert Bednárz went to the same class with me, all of whom became prominent figures in art, literature, and public life. Gyula Szini's father was already a writer. Károly Szini, the first Hungarian national socialist, who led an illustrious life, was not, of course, a national socialist in today's sense. He was an enthusiastic Hungarian of 1848 and Mihály Táncsics's best friend. He wrote his work *Új evangélium* (New Gospel) in hexameters. In it, he proclaimed his doctrines and recorded the uncommon adventures of his outspoken paper called *Lámpás* (Lantern). He was even jailed because of the paper, but Emperor Francis Joseph I pardoned him.

"Our first plan was to write a geography book"

Hugó Csergő and Gyula Szini decided already in the first year of high school that they would become writers. Not being satisfied with the fact that their more minor works had already been published in their hand-written paper *Szivárvány* (Rainbow), which had a circulation of one copy, they wanted to surprise the world with something great. Following botanical and geological preliminary studies in Zugliget,[1] they decided to write a geography book as a result of their affection for their geography teacher, Dr. Brunó Schwicker. However, not a kind that any Hungarian "writer" could write, but one in the German language. That they could hardly speak the language of Heine didn't really bother the two candidate writers. The old Károly Szini was working at his desk in his rented flat on Váci Street, when the two little pupils began the foreword to their work. He turned his attention to them: "You want to write in German?" he shouted and he suddenly pulled out his cherry wood pipe.

After this, the "great work" miscarried; however, Hugó Csergő didn't become unfaithful to the muse. When he was in fifth grade, his poem, "*A muzsahoz*" ("To the Muse"), was published in the newspaper *Ifjú Magyarország* (Young Hungary), whose editor was Lajos Bartók and in which Gyula Pekár, Géza Lampérth, and Géza Szilágyi began their careers. This poem placed fifth by the readers' votes. When he was in eighth grade in high school, he could already introduce himself as a poet on the pages of the *Magyar Géniusz* (Hungarian Genius) and the *Ország-Világ* (Country-World) and even of *A Hét* (The Week). Szini, Csergő, Árpád Pásztor, Alfréd Németh, and Pál Páriss also formed a writers' society: their slogan was "WW," that is, "The World is Wicked." Hidden in corners of cafés, they "studied" literature.

How He Became a Journalist

High school graduation arrived. Pásztor and Németh declared that they wanted to be journalists. Szini and Csergő longed to work in an editorial office as well. Their dream didn't come true immediately. Szini became a clerk at Register of Births Office, while Csergő enrolled in the faculty of law.

"In 1896," Csergő continued "I was finally able to join the staff of a paper. Lajos Mikes, then already an excellent writer, who was otherwise the police reporter for *Fővárosi Lapok* (Metropolitan Papers), went abroad. This was how I started working for the paper, with Németh's recommendation, as a volunteer police reporter."

Kálmán Porzsolt was the chief editor, Emil Makai the assistant editor, and Ádám Lipcsey, László Buday, and Géza Molnár were the main staff. In such company it was difficult to excel. Still, he managed to stand out. When news about the writer Károly Szini's death arrived at the editorial office, Csergő presented himself to the editor, saying that he knew well the interesting life story of the deceased writer.

"Then you can write about it."

His first, great, independent article was written. The following day, the volunteer proudly read the article, the end of which was adorned by his full name. The editor had put the name of the young journalist beneath the well-done report. In the afternoon, there were two new surprises for the reporter. The *Nemzet* (Nation), Mór Jókai's paper, and the *Pester Lloyd* adapted his article adding that "Hugó Csergő wrote about it in *Fővárosi Lapok*." Adolf Ágai, who was an old friend of Károly Szini, was curious to find out who this Csergő could be, who wrote such interesting, personal data about Károly Szini. He was really surprised when, instead of somebody of his generation, he was introduced to a six-foot-tall, bearded, young "new dandy."

The Two "Transdanubian Critics"

Csergő got to know Ferenc Molnár the same year he began his work and, as "Transdanubian critics," they became friends for life. The "Transdanubian critics" only meant that they were entitled to write about performances at the Kisfaludy Theater in Óbuda in their papers; for Csergő, in *Fővárosi Lapok* and for Molnár, in *Budapesti Napló* (Budapest Journal).

And now we quote, word by word, what the subject of our interview said, because it should be part of the history of literature:

> A wonderful coincidence! On a day in December 1896, the first essay of Ferenc Molnár was published in the *Budapesti Napló* at the same time as my first light poem appeared in *Fővárosi Lapok*. Intoxicated with my first success, I happily accepted the assignment to go to the Royal Great Hall for the Hubay-Popper string quartet concert, brilliant concert hall; ladies in evening dresses, gentlemen in tuxedos. I met Ferenc Molnár in such a milieu.

"Hello, colleague" we greeted each other.

There was shushing to be quiet, so we two reporters left the hall. Both 18-year-old Molnár and I spoke:

"I heard that you wrote an article for *Budapesti Napló* and that it will be published."

"It will be?" Molnár pulled out the newspaper triumphantly from his pocket. "It has already been published. I give this one to you as a complimentary copy."

Naturally, by chance, I also had a copy of *Fővárosi Lapok*, in which my light poem was published and I immediately reciprocated Molnár's kindness.

"Your first article was published today, too?!" Molnár was excited. "Moreover, as a poem! Well, this is great. We're going to celebrate. We are going to organize a 'public dinner' in your honor. The question is whether we have enough money."

We counted our money. In total, we had two forints sixty pennies.[2] We went to the nearest food store. Molnár bought smoked fish, dried sausage, salami, baloney, an orange, Malaga grapes, and bread. He even got an 80-penny *libapezsgő*.[3] We went out to the street. Molnár shouted to the crowded boulevard:

"Public dinner in the honor of our first published article."

On the boulevard we had an eleven-course dinner. The great meal was finished with drinking *libapezsgő*. This is how I celebrated with Ferenc Molnár, all along the boulevard, in the manner of a public dinner, the publication of our first articles.

Interview with General Arthur Görgey

In 1897 Makai left and signed a contract with *Pesti Napló* (Pest Journal), taking along with him Csergő, who had a 30-forint salary and received the catchy "court columnist" title. At the paper, he became friends with Gyula Krúdy and Viktor Cholnoky and he joined the Writers' Society, which formed around Sándor Bródy and Jenő Heltai. The first book of the young journalist, entitled *Utolsó felvonás* (Last Act), was published in 1900. In it, Csergő, the writer, who had just started his career, published his court-related articles. Also, his poems appeared quite often in *A Hét* (The Week) and in other literary journals. He was already the assistant editor of *Pesti Napló*, when poems of his, from a volume entitled *Versek* (Poems) were displayed in windows of bookstores. The critics accorded great acclaim to both books.

However, something came up. They wanted to entrust Csergő with responsibility for the political column and he asked for a raise. He didn't get it, so he quit.

"We were sitting once, at dawn, with Molnár in the New York Café, at dawn," Csergő says. "I was not working for any paper and was in a bitter mood. Molnár gave me the following advice: 'Go to Visegrád and get an interview with General Arthur Görgey: Ask him of his opinion on the Russo-Japanese war.'

I went to see Görgey, who had been silent since 1849. The general received me and answered my questions. This was his very first interview. The article appeared in *Pesti Napló* and this helped me later to join this paper."

Vilmos Vázsonyi launched a paper called *Polgár* (Citizen) in 1905 and the 26-year-old Csergő became its executive editor. A year later, both of them left the editorial office. Then the former executive editor passed his comprehensive examination and obtained his PhD.

He Who Doesn't Believe in His Own Success

A little bit later, Imre Kálmán asked the young writer to write a light libretto opera. In complete seclusion in Bikszád, he wrote a half-verse, half-prose comedy called *A lovag úr* (Mr. Knight), instead of the planned light opera.

"When I finished the last scene in Pest," Csergő recalls, "I went to Miklós Faludi, the Dramaturgist Manager of the *Vígszínház*. There were many people in his office and because of this I didn't dare to talk about my piece, but asked for two free tickets instead.

'I thought you brought a piece.'

'I have that with me too.'

'Come here Tuesday afternoon and then we'll talk about it.'

To be honest," Csergő continued, "on that Tuesday afternoon Miklós Faludi was sprawled out on his comfortable armchair and, since he had been with company until morning, he was trying to nap while I was reading my piece out loud. However, he suddenly looked up and started to pay attention. When I finished reading the second act he asked me: 'When do you want to have the premiere of *A lovag úr* (Mr. Knight)?' and he immediately gave me an advance of 1000 crowns.

The piece was performed with great success on November 17, 1906, starring Varsányi, Hegedűs, Tanay, Tapolczay, Sarkadi and Vendrey.

The premiere was the saddest evening in my life," Csergő admits. "I heard the applause; friends and acquaintances kept shaking my hand. I can't tell how many times they called me in front of the curtain, but I was convinced that this must have been done by friends and patrons. The following morning, I started to believe in my success. Valentin, the theatrical agent, came to my flat and reserved the piece, for the rural stages, with an advance of 1000 crowns."

The following year, in 1907, the success of *Mr. Knight* was proven by receipt of the capital's 2000-crown Francis Joseph Award. In 1908, the *Vígszínház* staged Csergő's play *Félszerelem* (Almost Love). Not much later, his slim lyrical novel, *Levelek, amelyeket meg nem írunk* (Letters That We Never Write), was published.

Hugó Csergő's career came to a turning point. The mayor, István Bárczy, invited the writer to the capital at the beginning of the First World War, to organize public assistance during the war. He formed the Center for Social Welfare and appointed Csergő its director. However, Csergő continued to commit himself to writing. At the request of Bárczy, he edited the city's *Népjóléti Közlöny* (Social Journal). He also wrote a novel, *A mi szivünk asszonya* (The Lady of Our Hearts), which garnered much success and is considered to be among the best novels written in Budapest according to Lajos Mikes, Aurél Kárpáti, and Béla Zsolt.

In 1923, Hugó Csergő came up with a new theatrical piece. The *Renaissance* presented *Első hajnal* (The First Dawn). "A work with poetic beauty," they said of the piece. It, too, garnered huge literary and public success and was even performed in the United States.

In 1926, the *Otthon Kör* (Home Circle) organized a celebration on the occasion of the thirtieth anniversary of Csergő's literary activity. His collected works were published at this time, too.

Three Series of Articles

In 1928, the Jewish Community of Pest invited the writer to join in its service. Thus Csergő was able to prove his organizational talent in the capital. He became the first town clerk of the community. The "literate town clerk" promoted literature and arts in every respect. In addition to his responsibilities, he wrote a series of sensational articles at his desk, at home. Among these, the five most important articles were those which unfolded the behind the scenes history of the First World War. The first article was entitled: *Ferenc Ferdinánd meggyilkolásától–a világháború kitöréséig* (From the Assassination of Franz Ferdinand until the Outbreak of the World War). Its continuation was published under the title, *Ami a Hóferből kimaradt* (All That Was Left Out of Hófer). *Hogyan vesztettük el a békét?* (How Did We Lose the Peace?) was third in the series, followed by the fourth, *Sixtus-féle békekísérlet* (Sixtus Peace Attempt).[4] Then, *Összeomlás* (Disintegration) concluded the series, serving as a historical resource (on the military collapse in WWI) and consisting of more than 300 references. His series of articles, *Hogyan lett Molnár Feriből Molnár Ferenc?* (How Feri Molnár became Ferenc Molnár?),[5] which captured the beginning of the world-renowned writer's career in light of a lifelong friendship, is well known. The time will come when this work and its related manuscripts, with autographic marginal notes made by Molnár, will be kept in a museum. Among Csergő's many works, the novelistic biography of Gyula Krúdy stands out. It was published under the title *Regényes utazás Krúdy Gyulával Szinbád vörös postakocsiján* (Novelistic Journey with Gyula Krúdy on Sindbad's Red Post Coach).

Csergő also edited the speeches of Vilmos Vázsonyi, the great Jewish politician, after his death, in order to keep alive forever the memory of the man by whose side he had stood from the beginning of his political career to the last day of his life.

The publication of hundreds of writings in daily papers and in the religious press shows how the time has passed by since then. In 1942, the OMIKE Artistic Enterprise included in its program Hugó Csergő's worthwhile literary work, *Őszi szonáta* (Autumn Sonata), which was one of the outstanding successes in Goldmark Hall.

In this interview we could only vaguely outline the milestones in Hugó Csergő's literary career. One more thing, which may be added as an honest confession: "Many things wouldn't have happened the way they did," Csergő says, "had it not been for my spouse, who has been my support in good and bad times alike. She has been the inspiration for my writing."

His wife, poet-writer, Mária Csergő, is a known writer, too. The author of many children's plays, her light opera for children, *Kis hercegnő kis huszárja* (The Little Hussar of the Little Princess), was performed at the *Városi Színház* (City Theater). Her children's play, *Mátyás király ifjúsága* (The Childhood of King Mathias), is yet to be performed in better times. Among Mária Csergő's many works, there is one called *Rokokó* (Rococo), the verse-scene of which, was performed at the OMIKE in 1943 and received great acclaim by the press and audience.

Hugó Csergő concluded his statement with a cheerful story: "In past years, being busy with my office work, I could only devote a limited amount of time to literature. At the same time, my wife could work without interruption. Recently I was at a party with my wife. I arrived later and when I introduced myself to one of the persons, he exclaimed: 'How's that? Are you the husband of the famous authoress?!'"

How Did I Become a Playwright?

Written by Dezső Kellér

Everything in life depends on chance. I must give thanks to a fireman that I became a playwright.

I was in the junior year of high school, when I walked out with a classmate of mine, Árpád Neumann, to the city park on a summer afternoon. Opposite the present Széchenyi Baths, there was then a theater called *Kornél Sziklay Kis Színházköre*.[6] It was a wooden summer theater, where performances started at 4 pm and finished at 9 pm. That day, a play called *Lulu, a tánc-király* (Lulu, the Dancing King) was performed. It's about the life of a scoundrel in thirty scenes. The first scene was set in an amusement park, the second in the Folies Bergère in Paris and the thirtieth again in the amusement park. I remember as if it were today. A young man at the gate of the theater rang a bell to attract the audience. I was standing there with my friend, both of us longing to go inside, but we didn't have a penny.

This time, an angel sent from above arrived in the uniform of a fireman.

As we were standing there staring, the fireman on duty at the theater came and asked us: "What is it, kids? Would you like to go inside?"

"Yes," we answered at once.

"Come with me, I will take you in. We are going to say that you are my sons."

We really liked the idea. Neumann's father was a grocer in Verseny Street; mine was a picture-dealer. Neither of us had a fireman father so far.

In no time we were behind the scenes. The fireman asked the stage manager for two chairs for his children and he made us sit down at the foot of a painted wall.

What a wonderful world it was.

We had never seen such a thing.

What happened on stage was no longer interesting to us. We were exclusively focused on the life that was going on there in the back, where there was "no entry except for authorized persons." We were watching bustling property men, who were toting furniture; actors, smelling of mastic as they were waiting for their last call, restlessly; and pretty young girls, who danced in to the sound of music.

All these were nothing yet.

Suddenly the prima donna stopped by us: the beautiful Gizi Bogár. Without any comment she starts undressing. She had to move fast, she didn't have time to go to her dressing room . . . The dress fell off from her the same way, as a horse-chestnut falls off a tree in the autumn wind.

I and Árpád Neumann were staring so hard that our eyes almost dropped out.

I know, I feel, I declare that I decided then, that I would choose a profession that makes it possible to stay close to the scenes. This is how I became a playwright.

There is only one thing I don't understand: Why did Árpád Neumann become a wooden spoon manufacturer?

Jenő Mohácsi, the Poet of Legends

If we could make Dr. Jenő Mohácsi appear—suitably—in an imaginary environment, the way we would commemorate him would be to say that he was kissed by the muse of poetry twice. This is how he became a bilingual poet. He translated *Az ember tragédiájá* (The Tragedy of Man), *Csongor és Tünde* (Csongor and Tünde), and *Bánk bán* (Bank Ban) into German. We can read and hear that these translations, whose purpose was to show the world representative pieces of Hungarian literature, are masterpieces in themselves. We will now only select one field within his works as a Hungarian writer and poet: we will discuss his works about Jews. The OMIKE audience derived a lot of pleasure from his legendary tale *A gyermek és a Messiás* (The Child and the Messiah). Primarily, we would like to hear about it from him:

Jenő Mohácsi: My legendary tale, in verse, *The Child and the Messiah,* for which Hugó Kelen composed beautiful music, is part of a series of legendary tales, in verse. Originally, my idea was to write short pieces in verse which could be performed anywhere, on a large or a small stage or even outdoors. I imagined that in these tales there would always be a storyteller, who would be almost like a master of ceremonies on the subject and that the characters would speak. These small dramas could even be performed without a stage and told without declamation. The performers sit down next to each other: the person whose turn it is, stands up; he or she speaks his or her verse part, and then sits down again. With dialogues, obviously both actors stand. It is the storyteller who links the various events. *The Child and the Messiah* was first performed in its simplest form by members of the youth religious community led by Dr. Zoltán Kohn, and I can tell you that it had the greatest impact. This piece had a similarly great effect when set to Hugó Kelen's music. It has been performed during the week of Passover on the OMIKE stage for three years. Most recently, it was also performed at the Inner City Religious Community in Budapest.

Interviewer: You were talking about a series of legendary tales a short while ago. What are the other parts of the series?

Jenő Mohácsi: I have written five such tales so far. Several of them have already been performed, especially in the countryside. Four of them have been published in different Jewish yearbooks. The first one was *The Child and the Messiah*, which is about the Passover feast. I really like the one called *Legenda* (Legend). I found its subject in a German book of legends. It is about a terminally ill rabbi for whom days are collected so that his life lasts longer. Then a young girl donates her whole life. The rabbi recovers, the girl dies. The rabbi now lives internally through the girl's life. He goes through all the important moments of the girl's life. All his contemporaries die around him, only he remains. He can only die at the moment when the girl's life was supposed to come to an end. This piece of mine will also be set to music by Hugó Kelen. I found the subject of another legend in a book about the history of Hungarian Jewry by Sámuel Kohn. It is set in Nagyszombat in the age of King Sigismund, in the fifteenth century. I would be really pleased if these tales, whose subjects are the collective property of Jewish people, were performed at more and more places, even in their simplest form.

Interviewer: What are your other works about Jews?

Jenő Mohácsi: One of them is my little book about Judah Halevi. It is a brief biography about the greatest Hebrew poet. My novel, *Hegedű és koldusbot* (Violin and Misery), published last year, is about the life of Márk Rózsavölgyi, the great Hungarian Jewish musician and Petőfi's friend.

Interviewer: How long have you been dealing with Jewish literary themes?

Jenő Mohácsi: I have been dealing with Jewish themes for about 30 years. My short stories and poems were already published in Jewish journals during the First World War. My serialized short story, *Jetti* (Jetti), was published in 1918. It is about a Jewish woman living in a small Slovak village. This short story of mine appeared in the pro-Jewish *Morgenzeitung* daily newspaper in Vienna in 1920 and in a Jewish journal in Swedish, in Finland, in the same year.

Ferenc Molnár

It would be most interesting to interview Ferenc Molnár now. However, the world-famous writer lives in America and, this time around, he wouldn't even be able to answer our questions by letter.

Even though he cannot speak to us now, his books, plays and articles are here. Reports written about him are available, even in the encyclopedias. Let's assemble the story of his life, until he came to the OMIKE here.

He Wanted to Be a Lawyer

His father, a doctor, thought that his son, Feri, would become the most famous lawyer. Perhaps even Ferenc Molnár hoped so, when he was studying at the University of Geneva. However, he was destined for something else.

He started his career at the *Budapesti Napló* in 1896. His unique contributions soon drew attention. His chronicles on Sunday inventively mocked the oddities of life in Budapest. He analyzed social issues sharply and intelligently.

One day, the editor of *Budapesti Napló*, Sándor Braun, was embarrassed because he had no proper essay for the following day's paper.

"Write something," he told Molnár.

The young journalist ran home and pulled out his essays from his drawer.

"This is good!" Sándor Braun concluded of the first.

Actually, he began his literary work with his novels, called *Magdolna* (Magdalena) and *A csókok éjszakája* (The Night of Kisses). His first original works didn't attract any particular attention. He started to become famous following the publication of his novel *Éhes város* (Hungry City). Critics acknowledged that his portrayal of the sometimes cruel image of the capital at the end of the nineteenth century was powerfully painted with dark colors. The public thought that he was a writer with special talent.

Premiere at the Vígszínház

November 1902. Posters advertise that the *Vígszínház* will present the three-act burlesque of Ferenc Molnár, *Doktor úr* (Mr. Doctor), on the 28th. The director, Sándor Góth, will also star in the title role. The other performers were to be: Irén Varsányi, Gyula Hegedűs, Zoltán Szerémy, Nina Nikó, and Emil Fenyvesi.

A slim young man with a black mustache took his bows at the premiere in front of the velvet curtain. He didn't even know how many times the audience called him back with its applause.

Success without any doubt, but not the real one yet. It came with *Ördög* (Devil), presented five years later. This lyrical poem, written in dramatic form, brought him his first laurels and showed him the way to worldwide success.

"You just became part of world literature, Feri," the successful playwright of *Vígszínház*, Gyula Komor, said at dress rehearsal, as his prophecy was fulfilled.

And indeed, this is how it turned out. *Devil*, that profound symbol, was performed even abroad. It happened through its unforgettable interpretation by the world-famous Italian dramatic actor, Zaccini.

Suburban Legend in Three Acts

Ferenc Molnár wrote his most renowned literary play, *Liliom, egy csirkefogó élete és halála* (Lily, a Scoundrel's Life and Death), on the basis of his beautiful, fantastic short story, *Altatómese* (Lullaby Tale). The story of a barker in the *Városliget* (City Park) and a little servant girl presents an extraordinary effect, in which the author travels not only all over the earth, but in heaven as well. "It is not the work of a virtuoso, who writes according to the tastes of the audience, but the work of a poet, who professes love and the brotherhood of all," concludes an authoritative critic.

On the evening of December 7, 1909, in the parlor of the *Vígszínház*, the author, wearing a monocle and in the tails which he wore to the premiere of *Ördög* (Devil), would take out his legendary Princess[7] tin box (cigarette case) more and more often to light a new cigarette. He wrote his three-act suburban piece with all his heart and soul. How did the audience receive it?

To tell the truth, His Highness, the spectator, gave the tale a very cool reception at the premiere. Budapest only discovered the piece with its poetic beauty (in which Irén Varsányi as Julika and Gyula Hegedűs as Lily gave their most amazing performances) when it was later performed in the best theaters of Vienna, Berlin, Rome, Paris, and even New York, thus making the author's name known worldwide.

Lily was restaged again in 1937 in Budapest. Here are a theatrical reporter's notes:

> We wanted to write a report asking how many performances of the revived *Liliom* (Lily) have there been in the *Művész Színház* (Artist Theater). The report could not be completed because the career of *Liliom* cannot be expressed in statistics. Perhaps there is no theater in the world where this great play from Budapest hasn't been performed with success. Even Molnár's own representatives can't say exactly where and how many times the play has been performed. This is why we gave up. Instead, we asked the manager, the director, the actors, and a few illustrious guests to write a few words in a Ferenc Molnár album. They wrote:
>
> "I was at the original premiere and now at the revival. On the earlier occasion, the piece reflected a revolutionary spirit; now it has been refined into a classic. Its genre dominated then; now its human depth. It was not only an artistic experience, but the revival of this beautiful play with this beautiful performance was also really enlightening for me." —Kálmán Csathó

> "In your world-renowned career, our *Liliom* (Lily) performance can only be an insignificant episode. However, for us, it is a great, memorable experience, as the old words came to life in a new glitter and with a new charm at the rehearsals . . . Certainly, we don't often have the opportunity to enjoy something, on the realization of which we worked so hard. I don't know if it's possible to thank you for something like this, but we thank you, Feri!" —Artúr Bárdos
>
> "I love him, appreciate him. I am grateful for the good times." —Sándor Hunyadi
>
> "It is a great pleasure for me that I can participate in the present revival of *Lily*. Fifteen years ago, I acted in *Lily* (in the title role) in New York; now I'm playing in the role of Ficsúr.[8] I guess there will be another revival in 15 years and—I already announce my request now—I want to be in it! If there is nothing else, I am even willing to play Mrs. Muskát or Mrs. Hollunder." —Márton Rátkai
>
> "When the weekly program plan is published in the manager's office, I go home and paint the weekdays of the calendar red because every day is a red-letter day when I can play in *Lily*." —Antal Práger
>
> "I always had the feeling when I saw or read *Lily* that Ferenc Molnár wrote Julika's role for me. And each time the play ended, I imagined Ferenc Molnár standing in front of me and I would say to him, 'Thank you.'" —Margit Dayka
>
> "*Lily* is the God-given pure soul behind our dirty lives. *Lily* is the flower of young Budapest. We meet young Budapest, with our old age and beautiful youth, and with the eternal youth of poetry, when we see *Lily* flourishing again in Artúr Bárdos's theater." —Ernő Szép
>
> Finally a few sentences from the director's report:
>
> "*Lily* has reached the height of its series of victories. It has triumphed over the span of 30 years, which is more wondrous and greater than the distance of legendary centuries, which makes everything look nice. Its deep poetic worth moved everybody, primarily the actors, who rejoiced humbly in that they had a chance to act in this masterpiece. The only problem at the gala evening was that the master was not there and couldn't see that the younger generation is fascinated by the legend he wrote for their predecessors." —Andor Pünkösti

This is what they wrote about the master and his play in 1937. In 1943, the OMIKE Artistic Enterprise decorated its program with *Lily*. Imre Rádai acted in the title role.

Cross of the Legion of Honor

There is a large amount of data piled up on our desk. Let's select a few of them.

In Molnár's novels *Egy gazdátlan csónak története* (The Story of an Ownerless Boat), *Andor* (Andor), and *Gőzgép* (Steam Engine), the reader is fascinated by the freshness of observation, the shrewd knowledge of mankind, the correctness of composition, and the directness of the narrative voice. His children's novel, *A Pál-utcai fiúk* (The Paul Street Boys) deserves a special place. It has been translated into most of the languages of the world and chosen as compulsory reading in schools in the United States of America. The author of this beautiful novel shows how exceptionally he knows children's souls and the book is a real hymn of love.

Then there were the great Molnár premieres, *Testőr* (Bodyguard), *A farkas* (The Wolf), and *A fehér felhő* (The White Cloud) at the Nemzeti Színház.

1914. Ferenc Molnár wrote colorful, vivid, impressive articles as a war correspondent during the First World War.

1917. The famous writer became a member of the Kisfaludy Society. In 1908, the Petőfi Society honored him with membership.

Success and recognition were meant for Molnár as a playwright. Thanks to his worldwide successes, modern Hungarian dramatic literature began its victorious career in the world.

One of the encyclopedias states: "He began the series of triumphs which Hungarian dramas earned, from then on, in the theaters abroad."

Géza Szilágyi writes about him, "Ferenc Molnár knows how to use his writing skills. He is very clever at seducing the naive and the refined segments of the audience alike. He incomparably plays all the instruments of the theatrical technique. He is also a man of feeling, a fine writer, and a gifted artist—beyond technique, stunning wit, and with a desperate search for success. He is the grand master of the stage. He's not stiff, he doesn't like following the same path, imitating himself; his last work is never a continuation of the preceding one, rather, he aims at variety in his subjects, novelty in form, and surprise in technique."

The premiere of *Hattyú* (Swan) in Paris helped the world-famous writer to obtain the Cross of the Legion of Honor. *Égi és földi szerelem* (Heavenly and Earthly Love), *Vörös-malom* (Red Mill), *Riviera* (Riviera), *Olimpia* (Olympics), *Üvegcipő* (Glass Shoe), *Egy, kettő, három* (One, Two, Three), *Csoda a hegyek között* (Magic in the Mountains), *Harmónia* (Harmony), *Valaki* (Somebody), *Jo tündér* (Fairy), *Ismeretlen lány* (Unknown Girl), and *Játék a kastélyban* (Playing in the Castle) are Ferenc Molnár's newer dramas. Many of them have not only been performed on stage, but also have gone around the world as films.

In 1935, the celebrated master, who proudly referred to his Hungarian nationality everywhere, was awarded a Corvin Wreath.

Ferenc Molnár traveled to America before the new World War, where many of his plays are staged and many of his works have been filmed. He still lives in America.

The wheel of the time machine has turned a lot. In our days, only the OMIKE Artistic Enterprise includes one of Molnár's plays in its program.

Ernő Szép

The poet, who chooses his words well and is the author of so many lovely writings, told us at our request how his poetic career began. Also note the way he talks, sometimes he jokes, sometimes he becomes emotional:

> You want to know how my glorious career began? I didn't become a so-called poet right away, because I only started to write poetry when I was about 14. As a matter of fact, I was a painter until the age of 14. I had already started painting, or rather first just drawing, in primary school. I passionately imitated, copied every illustration in my exercise book, spelling book, and the storybooks lent to me. It is a pity that I didn't stick to painting because I would surely have become a bad painter and there is no happier person in the world than a bad painter. Because all bad painters think that they are the greatest artists.
>
> So at the age of 14, as a senior in the Piarist High School in Debrecen, I suddenly started to be a poet. I was a small boy. I was sitting in the front row between two other small boys, János B. and Sándor B., who were students from the orphanage whom I envied a lot for their institutional uniforms. Neither of them, poor boys, got any pocket money. However, they were really smart. Since I wrote most of my poems on my lap during algebra and geometry classes, they already knew me as a poet and convinced me to publish my poems. They offered to reproduce my poems on the orphanage's lithograph machine: let's make a booklet that we will—rather they will as my publishers—sell for ten fillér.[9] As a matter of fact, perhaps a week later, they brought the first publication to school.
>
> In another week's time, the most embarrassing thing happened. An overzealous lawyer guy—later it was revealed that he was the culprit—took the thin lithographed booklet which he bought to the editorial office of *Ellenőr* (Inspector) in Debrecen. The editor, Dr. Péter Király, wrote a one-page article about the poet and within the framework of the article he published eight of his poems. I snuck around for weeks, because all the students of Debrecen would point at me. I was even afraid that I would be expelled from school. My fear vanished only when the instructor of Hungarian at the high school, a lovely, nice, fine soul who could have been a most typical eighteenth-century French abbot, named József Láng, suddenly called me to his room after class. Ernő Szép's poems were lying on the table. The teacher caressed my hair and praised the poems. Then—as spring was coming—he took me to Nagyerdő[10] every Saturday afternoon. Both of us carried books of poetry with us under our arms, Csokonai, Petőfi, Arany, Berzsenyi,

István Gyöngyösi, and Bálint Balassi. He made me read aloud the poems of the great Hungarians on every Saturday. That's how he taught me about the beauty of Hungarian metrical structure and Hungarian rhythm. As a matter of fact, almost all of the poems in my booklet were in hexameters.

Concerning my publishers, their pockets were always full of licorice, Saint John's Bread (carob), Turkish delight, even chocolate. I didn't get as much as they did, although we had agreed to a 50-50 split between us. At the age of 14, I should have already concluded that the publisher is always better off than the writer. Nevertheless, on the one hand, I enjoyed enough sweets. On the other hand, the sweetness that poetry gave my soul was more special than any sweet taste of summer fruits, even that at the Gerbeaud.[11] Not having been forced to feel the ugly obligation to make a living, I can thus tell you that the start of my career gave me a feeling of glory and happiness that I haven't tasted ever since.

Ernő Szép fell silent. After minutes of silence I looked at the poet like someone waiting for a sequel. But he raised his hand and waving it he said: "The rest is not interesting anymore."

The Artists Associated with the OMIKE Artistic Enterprise and Others Involved in Theatrical Operations

Stage Manager

Oszkár Beregi

Directors

Marcell Bálint, Péter Földes, Dezső Gál, Lajos Gellért, Miklós Harsányi, György Nagy, Ernő Szabolcs, Tibor Váradi

Artists

Rózsi Ács, Jolán Bernáth, Ida Boross, Klári Bóth, Zsuzsa Elek, Panni Faragó, Erzsébet Faragó, Ágnes Ferenczi, Zsuzsa Földi, Erzsi Gerő, Matild Győri, Hédy Hidas, Mädy Horváth, Luci Igaz, Dóra Kelen, Ági Komor, Kató Kornis, Klári Lakos, Erzsi Palotai, Blanka Pálffy, Judith Párdány, Erzsi Pártos, Irén Pór, Alice Rajna, Mária Rajna, Magda Rosthy, Mária Róbert, Mária Rózsa, Zsuzsa Simon, Ibolya Solt, Klára Szántó, Hédy Szécsi, Bea Szilágyi, Ágnes Szilárd, Judith Tordai, Valéria Vándor, Kató Váradi, Ilona Vécsey, Éva Vágó, Ferike Vidor, Vera Zágon, György Aczél, Pál Ádám, István Balázs, Gyula Bartos, Oszkár Beregi, Róbert Békeffy, István Bondy, Harry Brenner, Benő Csillag, Ernő Darvas, István Dózsa, István Fabinyi, István Fellegi, Tivadar Fehér, György Fehér, Árpád Fenyő, Róbert Füzesi, Lajos Gárdonyi, György Gáti, Pál Gáti, Sándor Gelléri, Lajos Gellért, Jenő Gonda, József Gonda, Péter Hajós, Ferenc Horváth, Gyula Justh, Gyula Kárpáti, Károly Kürti, Dezső Lányi, Tivadar László, István Major,

Lajos Mányai, József Molnár, György Nagy, Béla Ormos, Sándor Peti, Ernő Poprádi, István Rab, Imre Rádai, Tibor Rákos, Géza Rónai, Sándor Rott, Béla Salamon, Aladár Sarkadi, Imre Sas, József Sándor, Ede Simai, Zsigmond Somlár, Dr. Dezső Szabó, Kálmán Szentiványi, Jenő Szigeti, Vilmos Szirmai, István Ujfalusi, Jenő Várnai, Kálmán Zátony

The Stage Manager of the OMIKE

First of all, we asked Oszkár Beregi, the stage manager of the OMIKE, about the excellence of the drama company and about his life. He answered as follows:

> I often turn pages of the picture book of my life:
>
> In the grassless yard, a mock (make-believe) garden playground in Pest, among many students, an indomitable little boy frisks about, plays soldier, drills his pals and is only disciplined when he has to sing children's songs.
>
> Another page: from his father's factory, he goes to an elementary school in Pest on a steamer departing from the Franz Joseph Bridge, and with his mother's embroidery scissors he cuts his hair and makes a mask.
>
> The little high school student goes to a fight at Fa Square and at Gyár Street. Policemen disperse the gang. It's only because he can recite his lessons well that he doesn't have to repeat the school year. The teacher of Hungarian saved him. Today a student who is a good sportsman is given privileges. Then a student who could recite well was forgiven a few things at school. Knowledge of math is satisfactory, but that of Hungarian literature is excellent. Awarded an honorary certificate by the school literary and debating society. Knows Petőfi: *Az őrult* (The Lunatic) and Coppée: *A hajőtörés* (Shipwreck).[12] Knowledge of natural science is weak, but he knows about 100 poems by heart.
>
> Another page: he is 16, but looks 19. The family decision: if that most highly regarded person, Ujházi, says he has talent, then he can go to drama school. He can go. And he grows up. Paulay says to Ujházi at the exam: this one didn't need your patronage.
>
> Other pages: after drama school, comes the *Nemzeti Színház* (National Theater) of Kolozsvár. Ditrói is the manager. A year later, the *Vígszínház* (Comedy Theater) is opened. In *Prológ* (Prologue) by Andor Kozma, he plays Kisfaludy. At one of the first performances, the emperor is present and he—at the age of 20—recites the opening lines turning towards the emperor. However, he has not much to do in the program at the *Vígszínház,* which is made up mostly of French burlesques. He is discovered in the drama, *Katonák* (Soldiers) by Zoltán Thury, in which he plays a Hungarian squire, and, as a result, intendant (general director) Count Keglevich and manager Count Festetich offer him a contract at the *Nemzeti Színház*. However,

> before that, Count Keglevich helped him to obtain, without a final exam, a one-year voluntary right on the basis of the so-called artist provision.[13] No actor before him had obtained this. He was the "precedent." He's 22 years old and a member of the *Nemzeti Színház* of Budapest. His first role is Francis Rákóczi II. Happiness!
>
> More: I am turning pages of the picture book of my life. On which page should I stop? Here's a funny picture. Our friend is already a lieutenant and he sits again at a high school desk. Latin, Greek: graduation exam! Eight semesters at the University of Budapest. Dissertation about the actor's state of mind. New roles at the same time. Student in the daytime, actor in the evening. The characters in my imagination come to life. They enter reality: Romeo and Ferdinand, Troilus and Antonius, Constantine, László Árva, Hamlet, Faust, and Adam. They accompany me throughout my life. They take me to Berlin, Vienna, and America. My imagination turns to renewing, enriching paintings: naive drawings of my picture books evolve. Behind the pictures, I notice, with grateful love, the fine silhouettes of László Beőthy, Sándor Somló, Imre Tóth, and Zoltán Ambrus. From the new pages of the picture book, modern pictures look at me. Zilahy's drawing of His Excellency, another minister by Fodor, a foreign envoy, a wigged English lawyer. And my picture book—to use a film expression—is slowly recopied onto the theatrical pages of the OMIKE. The rest is known.

We also ask him about his roles at the OMIKE. His answer is extraordinary. He talks about the Bible:

> My first public performance (bar mitzvah) was at the age of 13, in front of the audience in a full house, listening devoutly. Great success. Compliments. They also gave generous gifts. I received a Bible in the synagogue on Dohány Street. I stayed loyal to the Bible since then and the Bible to me as well. We have done a lot to bring joy to each other. We have brought success to each other and made each other popular. It didn't matter to me whether it was private company, small hall, large hall, small synagogue, large synagogue. The only thing that mattered was having a Bible. In it, you will find lyrical poetry, elegies, drama, tragedy, comedy, naturalism, realism, and expressionism. He who searches can find everything in it, if he searches properly. Even if they clap their hands at my readings outside the synagogue—since it is, of course, forbidden to clap at my performances inside the synagogue—I still prefer reading the Bible in the synagogue. I always hold the book up high and point at it to indicate that the applause is not for me, but for the Bible. I told the audience several times that if they liked what they heard, then I would regard it as my greatest success if they would read the Bible again and again and be entirely taken up with it just as I am. The Bible will be like other pleasures. The greatest physical and spiritual joy is nothing if we enjoy it superficially. The best bits, the most beautiful

artistic creations, the wonders made by nature or man can only be enjoyed if we are fully open to receive them.

I'm not afraid of the truth and I admit that it happened to me several times that a few days after my reading, I was asked by someone from the audience who stopped me on the street to ask if the way I read it is really in the Bible? Last time, as well, when I read the law of the Holy One for a few evenings at Goldmark Hall, despite mentioning the title, the following morning a man, who lived in South Africa for years and was the owner of many apartment houses in Budapest, stopped me on the street and asked me what it was that I was reading last night. "The law of the Holy One." "And in which book can it be found?" "In the Bible." "What Bible?" "In our Bible." "And where can it be found?" "At the book store." "In which one?" "In any of them, if it's not sold out." He didn't believe me. I went to a book store with him, where there were still a few Bibles (books of the Torah) left. He still didn't believe me. I had to turn to the page and show him. Finally, he believed me. However, he was really surprised. And this man owns so many apartment houses in Budapest.

Poor rich!

Poor rich people!

The Main Director of the Drama Company

We talked to Ernő Szabolcs. He said that he wrote a book entitled, *Nem a nap süt, csak a reflektor* (It's Not the Sun That's Shining, but the Reflector), but that it will never be published because he wrote it for his own enjoyment and to educate his son. With his approval, the first chapter of the book which he wrote on March 25, 1941, on the 30th anniversary of the beginning of his career, is specially published here:

I REMEMBER . . .

Nessun maggior dolore
che ricordarsi del tempo felice
nella miseria.
Inferno, Canto V

there is nothing sadder,
than remembering old good times
in misery.
Mihály Babits's translation

It seems that I'm not miserable enough yet, because I don't feel the truth of the above-mentioned Dante quotation.

My wound doesn't hurt if memories stir it up. I go to the site of my old successes, where everything is one with me, like a traveler going abroad.

Images pass before me, but they cannot catch me. They are only shadows and memories.

The memories are quiet. They seem to be quiet even though they are not real.

The memories give me strength.

I counterbalance the bad *present* with the good *past* in the hope of a better future.

I acknowledge that there was a different world that is now lost to me. In these past years, a lot of maximum was reduced to minimum and in the present political situation the more artists love their profession, the more they suffer.

And I really loved it.

If I look back on the past three decades, I can safely say that even if I don't have too many reasons to show off, I definitely don't have to be ashamed of anything.

The value of my work was defined by my intention not by the result.

All the things which I took responsibility for, or which I undertook, I regarded as the aim of my life. I worked accordingly and was busy doing my work thoroughly, precisely and with all my soul. This is why I always had credibility in the eyes of actors, success in front of audiences, and honor in the presence of the leadership.

I was not upset if I received hostile reviews and I didn't thank the friendly ones. I respected artistic freedom in this as well: everybody can write as they feel and think.

It is said that remembering means that one is getting old.

I don't argue with that, I just counterbalance it.

The past: I just look back at it; the future: I look into it.

Because I know that the day will come when the sun will shine on me, too, and the reflector will brighten up my work again.

Notable Members of the Drama Ensemble

Gyula Bartos

He has served the nation for more than 50 years.

We went to see Gyula Bartos, a permanent member of the *Nemzeti Színház*, in his small, but lovely villa on Svábhegy.[14] We found him holding garden shears in his hands, seriously working. Every square meter of the garden had already been economically used, even before the mayor's order to cultivate all usable land.

We are sitting on the airy, glass-fronted terrace. His homegrown fruits are on the table. Gyula Bartos starts to talk about the very early memories from his long and pleasant acting career:

When I was a senior in high school, I ran away from home and wandered for twenty months with actors. When they learned at home what I had become, my mother expressed the family's opinion with these words: "I have five sons, one of whom has gone astray. I feel as if I had a daughter who had changed for the worse." I joined Aladár Szabadhegyi's company. The Actors' Association revoked its permit to Szabadhegyi to operate and the company became a consortium under Gábor Szabó's leadership. The company would travel from village to village. Already then, I played mostly old men. The casting was determined by special considerations. In one of Gergely Csíki's plays, for example, there is a baron. I was the one playing him because I had the nicest trousers. The lead actress could have been my grandmother. I would distribute playbills, too, which were written by me.

It happened in Majsa that a parson said to me: "My son, whose son are you? How did you become an actor? You are still a child. Well, if you really want to be an actor, go home, continue your studies; afterward you can still be an actor." He appealed to my feelings and he influenced me so much that I listened to him and went home to Szeged. I met my classmates and envied them because they were ahead of me. To catch up with part of the time lost, I decided to enroll in a commercial school where I could obtain a high school diploma a year earlier. Through private classes with the assistance of a teacher, István Hegedűs, I finished the senior year and passed the exam. In the meantime, I worked at the law office of a relative for 15 forints per month and spent the money earned there on my studies. I was a good student at the commercial school. I was exempted from payment of school fees and even received a scholarship. However, in the third year I couldn't overcome my old passion and started to attend the theater, neglected my work and failed my German course exam. I passed the repeat exam, but didn't pass the graduation (Regents) exam. I thought that if I could obtain the final certificate, then I'd have the voluntary right, which was the main thing. Then I wouldn't need to take the graduation exam. I enrolled in acting school in Budapest. When I went home for a holiday, after the first year, my mother told me: "My dear son, for my sake, please pass the graduation exam." I fulfilled her wish. I still know a lot of what I learned then. For example, the Bill of Exchange Act.

After acting school, my first contract was with the Albert Kövesy Ensemble. We performed at Sátoraljaújhely, Nyitra, Eperjes, and Vác. The next contract was with a company in Kolozsvár. Mór Ditrói went to Budapest to the *Vígszínház* and Dezső Megyery became the theater manager in Kolozsvár. He wrote a letter to me to let him know about my terms. I answered him that I would join without any precondition. He should just let me perform. Then he will be able to decide what I am worth and pay me accordingly. I spent three years in Kolozsvár. I loved Kolozsvár and I was also loved.

> But I wanted to get ahead, in the capital. This is why I signed a contract with Ignác Krecsányi, the theater manager in Timisoara, whose summer base was in Buda. However, in the meantime, Krecsányi got the theater at Szeged and I lost Buda as a summer base. Finally, when Krecsányi returned to Timisoara again, my wish came true. I could play in the capital. I appeared as Emperor Nero at the *Budai Színkör* (Buda Round Theater) in a play entitled *A kereszt jéleben* (Under the Sign of the Cross), adapted from the novel *Quo Vadis*. Mór Ditrói and József Márkus came up to the stage to congratulate me. One paper wrote this: "On the stage of the *Budai Színkör*, a young actor appeared whose journey will lead him to the number one stage in the country."
>
> When Sándor Somló, manager of the *Nemzeti Színház*, asked me to tell him my terms, I answered as I had told Megyery before. So he asked me to appear as a guest artist. I appeared at the *Nemzeti Színház*, where I played Tiborc and Don Justo in *Folt, amely tisztit* (Stain, Which Cleans) by Echegaray. This was done so that they could see how I move and speak in a social theatrical play, not only in a classic one. I received the contract on May 1, 1907. I have been at the *Nemzeti Színház* since then.

He related this with such devotion, as if he was a priest doing his sacred service at a shrine. He has been doing it, indeed, for decades. His relationship with the *Nemzeti Színház* is unbreakable: on the occasion of the twenty-fifth anniversary of his career there, he was appointed a permanent member. He also was an honorary performer at the larger OMIKE celebrations.

Lajos Gárdonyi

"For years I was a civil servant during the day and an actor in the evening"

On the stage of the *Vígszínház*, the last part of the play was on. The actors had gotten to the last sentence and then arrived, after which the author had written: "The end, the curtain goes down."

Lajos Gárdonyi, the great comedian, who was sitting at a small table in his dressing room, didn't hear the applause this evening. He was occupied with something else. He was saying good-bye. Without words, silently . . .

He turned to his dressing person, "Please have this package sent to my flat."

The little package was already prepared. In it, there was paint, a towel, a little coat, a mirror, and trifles needed in an actor's dressing room. Gárdonyi didn't go to the neighboring dressing rooms where his colleagues turned into civilians. He started going home at a slow pace. On the way, pictures must have flashed before him which later resulted in his book *Véletlenül történt* (It Happened Accidentally), in which he wrote about some stages of his acting career from the beginning to the last performance in the *Vígszínház*. We turn the pages of the book while the artist talks about his life.

"My first dramatic role, while I was a student, had a huge effect. I played Lucifer then. 'No problem,' I thought, 'if I demonstrate talent in this, then I will be a comedian.' Not much later, I performed as a singer. I was promised a salary of two crowns, but I haven't received this sum till today."

The "Circle of Friends" formed when he was 15 years old. In the first program, Gárdonyi's name was included and next to it was written "Saloon Comedian."

Following high school graduation, he started working at a wheat supply firm. When the call for applications to the Actors' Association appeared in the papers, a friend asked him to escort him. Gárdonyi escorted his pal on the day of the entrance exam. The junior clerk called for the next person in line to go in front of the commission:

"Lajos Gárdonyi!"

The young man was shocked. He didn't register for the entrance exam. He only learned later that his friend had registered him.

"Recite something!"

"*A fülemüle* (The Nightingale) . . . János Arany's poem."

The involuntary candidate actor recited it.

"Thank you . . . you can leave."

He was admitted. From then on, the civil servant led a double life: he was doing his internship industriously during the day and studying to be an actor in the evening. He was already the head of the packaging department and the owner of his own desk when he was forced to leave acting school. He continued in Szidi Rákosi's school. At the first exam, he played Sergeant Loriot in *Nebántsvirág* (Touch-Me-Not). Márton Rátkai drew the attention of the *Belvárosi Színház* (City Center Theater) to the young actor.

He received his first contract. He didn't dare leave his job and he didn't dare admit that he was an actor either. He continued to play both roles in his life.

Before receiving a new contract at the *Vígszínház*, György Dénes revealed to Gárdonyi that he would not play the role assigned to him in *Bárонő levelei* (Letters of the Baroness).

The newest member then got his role at the *Belvárosi Színház* and started his success story in the next play, *Gazdag lány* (Rich Girl) by Béla Szenes, as the clumsy Mr. Kovács.

He'd been an actor for four years. He obtained better and better roles in succession.

He became one of the best known artists with his performance as George Dandin and with other performances. Then he decided to leave his office, his "safe foundation." He invited his dearly loved mother to the theater where he performed.

"What is your opinion, Mom?" he asked her after the performance.

"Kabos is a great actor," his mother replied cautiously, because she wanted her son to keep his job at the wheat supply firm.

Gárdonyi was one of the stars of the *Terézkörúti Színpad* (Teréz Boulevard Stage). He was making the audience laugh in Endre Nagy's musical satires, in the evenings, when Béla Salamon decided to get him a contract at the *Vígszínház* (Comedy Theater). So he invited Dániel Jób and Imre Roboz.

"What kind of actor do I suggest?" Salamon asked beaming with joy.

"Terrible!" the managers of the Comedy Theater said.

Gárdonyi didn't know anything about this and was surprised one morning when Salamon took him to the office of the Comedy Theater. They gave him a contract very reluctantly.

Following the premiere of *Noszti fiú esete Tóth Marival* (Young Noszty's Affair with Mary Tóth), the managers realized that the new contract would be profitable for the leading private theater of the country.

The big roles came. The monkey leader at the *Majomszínház* (Monkey Theater), the clumsy financial officer in *Templom egere* (Church Mouse), the post office clerk in *Vörös malom* (Red Mill). The papers reviewed Lajos Gárdonyi's artistic performances with the utmost praise.

Following his successes in theater, cabarets, and films, this excellent actor raised his reputation on stage with the role of an old clown in the revue entitled *Cirkusz csillaga* (Star of the Circus).

Certainly a contract abroad would have been possible, but 1939 arrived.

The stages in the capital were out of question as well.

Lajos Gárdonyi gathered and packed his belongings in the dressing room in the Comedy Theater and was without job for a short period of time.

To perform in front of an audience became possible again in the framework of the OMIKE Artistic Enterprise for the divinely inspired actor, who does the most that an artist can do today, to play and make the spectators forget their everyday problems. He makes them laugh.

Lajos Gellért

Jedermann, Timosa, Dybuk . . .

Do you remember the last open-air performance as Jedermann? Do you remember the leading character of Ibsen's drama *Kisértetek* (Ghosts), the painter Osváth? Or Saint Paul in *Missa Solemnis*? Or the *Dybuk's* Mesulah? You certainly do because these plays and the roles, as performed by one of Hungary's greatest dramatic actors, Lajos Gellért, can never be forgotten. These were experiences—a series of experiences for life—where the artist gave his entire soul in each of his roles to bring to life to all those that the writer dreamed about.

Far from the noise of the streets, separated from the present, we silently speak to Lajos Gellért, who was the first to play Ibsen in Hungarian in Hungary. The second thing is that he has never denied and never rejected his Jewishness.

His first performance was in 1907. After graduating from the Academy of Dramatic Art, Gellért was offered two contracts. One by Sándor Hevesi, the manager of the Thália Society, and the other one by the management of the National Theater of Pécs. He accepted the latter one, which kept him busy at this rural cultural center for two years. He chose the National Theater of Pécs because there was a performance each day, whereas the Thália opened its doors to art fans only once a week. Lajos Gellért signed a contract at Pécs as a comic actor. However, this didn't suit his personality, and when Sándor Hevesi told him in a letter that he was going to ensure a place for him at the Thália if he decided to terminate the contract at Pécs, Gellért asked for a holiday and went to Budapest. Sándor Hevesi gave the then twenty-year-old Gellért a copy of Ibsen's drama *Ghosts* to read and select his role.

He wanted to play Osváth, the crazy painter, who has a sad fate because of his parents' sin. Hevesi was surprised by his choice, but accepted it. Here is what happened, afterwards, in Lajos Gellért's own words:

> I prepared for this role for weeks. Thoroughly, as with the plays, I studied medical books. I knew Moravcsik's book *Psychiatry* almost by heart. For six weeks I would go to the mental hospital in Angyalföld[15] each day and study the unforunate inmates, whose life I put on stage. We had 70 rehearsals until I played Osváth, the painter, in front of an audience. In the mental hospital, I got to know the director-head physician, Dr. Károly Nyéki. He asked me, while we were talking, where I graduated and whose psychiatric classes I attended. "I am not a doctor," I told the head of the mental hospital, "just an actor." He didn't want to believe it.

His last performance before the enforcement of the Jewish law was as Jedermann, which he performed on an open-air stage. His performance reflected an entirely new concept. He appeared in tails, under the light of the reflectors. Then a Viennese paper attacked him. Gellért defended himself by saying that the author didn't specify the time and place of the events. The attack stopped, but a month later the Viennese theaters presented Jedermann in tails according to Gellért's concept.

It is interesting that it was Gellért who wrote the first radio play that was performed in the Budapest Studio under the title *A nagy riport* (The Big Report). His second radio play was *Texasi vakáció* (Vacation in Texas), which was broadcast to radio listeners in Vienna, Basel, and Warsaw, in that order. He translated several pieces, among them the *Dybuk* (Dybbuk) the legend of S. An-ski;[16] he wrote a play, *Timosa*, which was performed in Budapest 450 times. Nevertheless, he is proudest of his open-air performance at Pécs in the role of Saint Paul in *Missa Solemnis*, by György Ujházi, in which he told the audience about love. His performance was preceded by attacks in the press. The papers of the extreme right objected to having this role performed by a Jew. However, the directors couldn't be dissuaded from their original concept, and when the author gave the laurel wreath to Lajos Gellért at the dinner, after the performance, he even said: "To my Jewish brother, Lajos Gellért."

Gellért is a great artist, a great Hungarian and a Jew who firmly sticks to his religion. He is one of the notable figures on the OMIKE staff.

József Gonda

There was a young student attending the high school in Barcsay street, who was one of the worst students. He would take the admonitions home quarterly, so punctually, as if he wanted to contribute to the house rent with them. This boy wasn't just a bad student, but—believe it or not—was also "deadly" in love by the age of thirteen. The lady of his choice was a milliner girl, who, if she was sent somewhere, always made it possible to wait for her "suitor" at 1 pm at the gate, when classes were over at the high school. Once, however, as the boy and the girl were walking on the boulevard arm in arm, like bolt from the blue, the boy's father appeared unnoticed and slapped his son's face to express his disapproval of his courting.

The strict father, being fed up with his only child's "issues," went to the boy's form-master[17] the following day to find out about the progress of his son's studies. Although the answer he received was not unexpected, it was devastating. The form-master talked very favorably about the boy's activity in the school literary and debating society and about his performing skills. However, he had a very bad opinion about the progress of the student in his studies.

"What can I do with my child?"—the father asked desperately.

"Nothing," the teacher answered. "Give me your word of honor that you will send the boy to drama school and then I promise that the boy will pass."

The father agreed. The star of the performances of the literary and debating society was transferred from the high school to a commercial school, where he passed the graduation exam with great difficulty. The father kept his promise. After graduation the promising young man went to the Academy of Dramatic Art, where he passed the entrance exam in front of Imre Pethes with success.

"You were born in Little Cumania weren't you?[18] Your pronunciation is so nice."

This boy with the nice pronunciation grew up on the asphalt of Budapest, and nobody would have believed that he was a Jew. His name is József Gonda.

He can look back on a colorful and highly successful past. He won two scholarships: one from the cultural minister, József Vass, the other from the capital city, Budapest. Following the graduation from the Academy of Dramatic Art, he received a contract from the *Belvárosi Színház* (Central City Theater). Later he worked at the Renaissance Theater. Then he had success in Szeged and Győr. This is when the *Új Színház* (New Theater) was founded, and he was a member for five years. He had huge success performing in *Béla, aki 26 éves* (Béla, Who Is 26 Years Old), *Dybuk* and *Tüzek az éjszakában* (Fires in the Night). He received a contract from the *Magyar Színház* (Hungarian Theater) and was a member until the end of 1939. His brilliant performances in *Az Úr katonáiban* (In the Lord's Soldiers) and in *III. Richard* (Richard III) had sweeping success. Then there was the Theater Chamber (Guild), which didn't grant a membership to the Jewish actor with the "most beautiful Hungarian pronunciation." József Gonda lost his job but didn't lose his talent and his enthusiasm for creativity, which can now be used in the service of the OMIKE artistic theater.

Soubrette—Of a Swimmer

Klári Lakos didn't choose her profession voluntarily. She had to be lured in a tricky, almost forceful way. And how much she, nevertheless, came to love her calling is best shown, even thoroughly explained, by the circumstance that just a few months later the youngsters in a college town fought fierce, if bloodless, battles against those who questioned the precocious maid's sole rule on her favorite throne.

Klári Lakos, who is a girl from Budapest, performed in the countryside for a few years. During this time, she lived under constant, caring "supervision." Her theatrical mother, who was her older sister, was a piano teacher. The bodyguard-sister, who is present at our current conversation as well, and just like an experienced manager, she thoroughly complements what is missing from the chatter of the giddy artist. Certainly, the perfect collection of clippings containing news of the young artist in the daily, weekly papers and theatrical journals in the capital, the countryside and the reclaimed area, also shows her care. In a few short years, accumulated heaps of articles, news items, interviews and photos have been piled up in albums, boxes and on framed cardboards.

> *Klári Lakos:*
> I am a stray lamb, who went into acting by accident. I really can't say that when I went on stage, my wishful dreams came true. I was even upset, when my sister supposedly discovered qualities in me, which she had found in a relative, whom she helped to start towards a world-wide reputation. She could only change my ambition to become a gymnastics teacher, with a clothing ensemble and a pair of high-heeled shoes.
>
> *Her sister:*
> As a matter of fact, although being a senior in high school, she would only wear sailor's clothes and low heeled shoes.
>
> *Klári Lakos:*
> The Hanna Honty kind of scholarhip competition was useful for "her," because I was laughing when I participated in it, as I was sure that I wouldn't be able to win. However, it was still beneficial for me, because at least while going to the swimming meet, where I represented the FTC[19] I could wear my new outfit.
>
> *Her sister:*
> She was a swimmer since she was six. She won a lot of races since childhood. Despite being a high school student, she swam using a pseudonym. When she became an actress, she was forced to quit swimming.

[At that time, newspapers appeared that reported on how the Hanna Honty scholarship competition was organized through one of the daily papers of the capital and how the most talented ones were selected from the thousand applicants. The winners entered into one of the drama schools of the capital on scholarship. Klári Lakos, as we can read, attended Kálmán Rózsahegyi's acting school at the expense of the sponsoring newspaper. —Jenő Lévai]

Her sister:
She learned to sing from Erzsi Gervay and Mrs. Tivadar Pallós and to dance from Palotai. At the exam of the Actors' Association, she created such a stir that the rural directors were practically competing with each other for her. Kardos offered the best contract. She was very popular in Debrecen. Then she was in Kosice for a year at Andor Seregi's Company. After that, Miklós Vigh gave her a contract at the Operetta Theater of Budapest, but it was not possible anymore for her to perform there.

Klári Lakos:
The pleasant warmth of love from the audience has made me a fan of my profession. For their love and applause, I showed my gratitude by learning and giving my best. Each performance is a holy day for me. When I felt the rumbling of the iron curtain that blocked my way because of my religion, not even my despair could make me use the "back door" by leaving my religion.

Her sister:
She applied to the Chamber (Theater Guild) but was not accepted. They suggested she try to pass the acrobat exam. But she was afraid that she wouldn't be able to go back on stage again. The stage means life to her; the audience, the applause, and success are her happiness.

Klári Lakos:
The OMIKE Artistic Enterprise opened the back door for us through the iron curtain. This is how the Goldmark Hall became our temple, allowing us to rise above all petty, vain, human fallibilities. My only objective is to make people forget their problems and smile and, if I succeed, that will make me feel happy. And that I have succeeded in it is proven by every one of my performances. The applause and the encores can't be wrong, can they? I comply with my pleasant duty by using this opportunity to thank the audience of the OMIKE very much.

Béla Lénárd

Béla Lénárd's Honest Confession about His 33 Years on Stage

In 1911 at the graduation ceremony of the high school in Barcsay street, the principal gave a piece of advice to the graduating students for the journey ahead of them:

"Those who graduated now, will start life. Each of you has chosen a profession. I wish you success on the bumpy road of life."

In the evening at the graduation banquet, the graduates declared what they would do.

"And you, Béla, what are you going to be?" they asked Béla.

"Actor!"

And the following day, even if it was only in the park, he could already get on stage. He was in the choir of Kornél Sziklai's company.

In the fall, he applied to the Academy of Dramatic Arts.

"What do you want to perform?"

"A scene from *Cyrano*."

"We would like to hear a poem."

The candidate was silent.

"Whoever doesn't know any poem should not be an actor," said the examiners, as they pronounced the verdict.

Thus Béla Lénárd enrolled in Szidi Rákosi's acting school where Margit Halmi and Imre Pethes were his teachers, apart from the director. His teacher, Károly Stoll, didn't just reveal the secrets of acting to his ambitious student, but also those of directing. He found this latter knowledge very beneficial later on.

He received his first role as a student member of the *Magyar Színház* (Hungarian Theater).

"The problem was that I had a little disagreement with László Beöthy," Béla Lénárd recalls. "I asked for the leading part, to which he reacted by giving up on me very fast."

Then some adventurous years followed. Újpest and Kecskemét, here he was an actor-singer and his partner was Olga Turcsányi, the famous Merry Widow.

"The fault must be with me," he admits, "because I had to break the contract. I couldn't bear standing in front of the audience in big roles almost unprepared, following only two or three rehearsals."

Following a short contract in Budapest, he performed on the podium of the *Modern Színpad* (Modern Stage) at Timisoara. He sang songs and performed in small plays. Egon Dorn, the founder and director of the world-renowned *Simplicissimus* heard the young actor. He gave him a contract immediately. The war nullified the agreement.

Budapest again. The *Télikert* (Winter Garden) presents revues. Adolf Mérei, the writer-director, wrote songs for him. Even at the side of Márton Rátkai, Ernő Király, Nusi Somogyi, and other celebrities, Lénárd soon became a "hot shot." His songs, full of feeling, were real three-minute pieces, which the young artist didn't only sing, but also performed artistically.

At that time, a terrible caste system still reigned in the actors' world in Budapest and it caused such consternation that Béla Lénárd became member of the "Folie Caprice." In 1918, he could already be seen on the stage of the popular *Apolló kabaré* (Apollo Cabaret).

"In the following years, I performed abroad. First, I performed in Vienna, then in the cabarets of Berlin and other German cabarets as a vocal performer. I brought literature into the cabaret and maybe this is the reason why I stood out from the usual song (chanson) singers."

Tours in Switzerland and The Netherlands came next. He performed in classical comedies, operettas, cabarets, and he also directed several times. Success didn't only manifest itself in applause, but in income as well. Because of this, when he returned from abroad in 1922, he became a manager. He opened the *Faun kabaré* (Faun Cabaret). The strengths of the company were Dóra Bársony, Frigyes Tanay, Gyula Kővári, Aladár Sarkadi, and Jenő Virág. Gyula Kabos built up his "cabaret form" in the "Faun" as well.

"Today it might sound strange," Lénárd says, "but it was a reality then, that after a year of operation, my cabaret application to re-open was rejected because of security reasons. A short guest stint followed, abroad again. Then the Apollo Cabaret called me back. With Szőke Szakáll, we made the audience laugh for months in a burlesque called *Albert VIII*. After that Sándor Rott gave me a contract at the *Kis komédiá* (Little Comedy). I have to say that I owe Sándor Rott a lot. He was one of our greatest artists. As a comedy director, he was one of the best. I learned a lot from him."

In 1927 Lénárd, who gave contracts to many famous Viennese actors, went on tour with his own company. They had success in the cities of Switzerland, The Netherlands, and Romania. The next stop was Graz, where he rented a music hall.

1934. The huge posters of the Viennese *Simplicissimus* advertised the following:

Küsse im Mai (Lénárd Production).

From then on, in Vienna, Berlin, Zürich, and other world cities, it could often be read "Lénárd Production." This manager's revues had the same success as his announcements and songs.

1938. The Netherlands. On the stage of the *Theater der Prominenten,* two Hungarian actors shared in popularity: Szőke Szakáll and Béla Lénárd.

"Szőke Szakáll was about to go to America then. I directed his last European tour."

1939. Belgium. The famous actor performed in Antwerp for the first time in a Jewish theater. The *Melodie Juive* was founded with the support of the Jewish community. Soon, the company performed in front of full houses in German, French, and Yiddish languages. The female star was Henny Lehmann, about whom it must be noted that she was a young Christian woman who sang Yiddish folk songs from the age of 16.

"I got to know and came to like Jewish folk songs," Lénárd continued. "In the following programs, I already sang Jewish songs as well."

1940. Two months that could be part of a novel. While the German-French war was raging, the Hungarian artist lived in an abandoned castle on the outskirts of a town around Lille. In the fall, he performed at the most elegant little theater of Brussels called *Petit Casino*. *Le Soir* wrote the following about him: "This excellent Hungarian actor, who is the master of portrayal, has to be kept here. Everybody must get to know him."

In Brussels he was allowed by the German authorities to open his theater, called *Les Artistes Juives*. Without any official support, this theater became a refuge for Jewish actors.

1942. Lénard returned home.

1943. He presented himself on the stage of the OMIKE. He served as an announcer and since he is also a lyricist, this all-round artist sings his own songs. The fact that he became one of the most popular members of the company, after only a few performances, is the best evidence of his successes abroad.

This is how we can present the 33 years of Béla Lénárd's acting career in a nutshell. After 25 greatly successful directorial roles; countless roles in revues, operettas, classical comedies; many hundreds of fine songs; and numerous witty program announcements, now the outstanding entertainer is at the service of the audience of the OMIKE.

György Nagy and His Wife, Kató Bán

The OMIKE program advertised a happy evening. György Nagy was standing in front of the velvet curtain:

"Ladies and Gentlemen, the next performer will be Kató Bán, who will sing opera arias. While the stagehands are working industriously, let me introduce the artist in a few words.

"Kató Bán comes from a family 'infected' with acting. Her mother Elza Vajda was a famous opera singer and she had a lot of success in Vienna for years. Her uncle Frigyes Vajda is an opera singer as well, and still a member of the Metropolitan in New York. After all this, when the little girl told her mom that 'I will be a singer,' she was given full understanding and approval. However, Kató Bán was not admitted to the Music Academy for a reason that is very pleasant for ladies; she was found to be too young. Nevertheless, two years later she entered the 'promised land,' where she became Bianca Maleczky's student. She graduated in 1942 and she received an opera singer degree.

"'She is not a usual lyrical soprano,' her teachers stated during the years of her studies. Before the exam at the Academy, Vilmos Komor drew the attention of the OMIKE to the opera singer, as the great promise of the future. This is how it became possible for the new artist to present herself at this colorful evening."

Measuring the length of applause, she had an overwhelming success at her first performance. Kató Bán's artistic career started here and also something else. As we mentioned, György Nagy announced the young singer. It is just natural that the black-haired beauty caught the attention of the announcer. Certainly, György Nagy didn't go to the Music Academy coincidentally when Kató Bán was having her exam. And just one and a half months following the first time they met, they whispered to each other the promise of "till death do us apart."

Already in her first year, she played a leading role in the OMIKE, in *Varázsfuvola* (Magic Flute), *Fidelió*, *Pillangókisasszony* (Madame Butterfly), *Hegyek alján* (The Lowlands), and in *Windsori víg nök* (Merry Wives of Windsor). She soon became the favorite of the audience. She didn't disappoint her teachers, who predicted a great future for her.

After all this, it is necessary that we speak about György Nagy, as well, who got a wife after (or through) the program announcement. Following high school graduation, he enrolled in the Academy of Dramatic Arts. As a result of his acting exam, the very first, private theater, the Comedy Theater, offered him a contract. A known theater critic recalled in his individual style, in his first premiere, the following way: "A strapping, elegant young man performed in a significant role in front of the demanding audience of the Comedy Theater. This man is capable!—you must have said after he opened his mouth. He moves deftly. Of course he still needs to chisel it."

The capital city rewarded him at the beginning of his artistic career with a scholarship offered to actors.

At the time of his first successes the young artist suffered a terrible blow: he lost his beloved parents. When the heart's painful wounds started to heal, he signed a contract in Szeged. Here he excelled not only as a character actor, but as a director as well.

The audience of the capital actually got to know György Nagy following his two-year performances at Szeged. At this time, he was already the member of the *Belvárosi Színház*. In the comedy called *Helyet az ifjúságnak* (Make Room for Youth), he and Antal Páger played the leads. The young actor established himself with the highly successful comedy. Then *Szent Johanna* (Saint Johanna), *Láz* (Fever), *Ördög cimborája* (The Devil's Disciple), *Barbara őrnagy* (Major Barbara), and *Amerikai komédia* (American Comedy) raised him to stardom. Also sound film made him known nationwide. His popularity peaked with the movies *Lilac akac* (Purple Acacia), *Magdát kicsapják* (Magda is Expelled), and *Nehéz apának lenni* (It's Is Hard to Be a Father).

However, history intervened. Only the OMIKE could give György Nagy, one of the most popular members of the Artistic Enterprise, an opportunity as an actor and as a director. György Nagy achieved great success, for he is a significant factor in the field of actors' education as well.

Béla Ormos

"I wanted to be a trader"

We could see Béla Ormos for twenty years on the big stages of Pest. He played awkward characters. His typical posture, his squinting and his apologetic gestures characterized this popular entertainer, who is really a personality among the comedians.

"Tell us your career from the beginning until the stage of the OMIKE," we ask.

"I have to begin in 1920, when I graduated from Jenő Herceg and Gyula Kővári's acting school. I received my first contract at the Bonbonniere Cabaret. Soon I became a member of the Royal Music Hall. My role was as a comedian, but I was also romantic lead once. The way it happened was that Harmath-Zerkovitz's operetta, *Aranymadár* (Golden Bird) had been on the program more than three hundred times. In the evenings, I would put on the dancer-comedian's clothes and make the audience laugh in the superb role. Once, not long before the performance, it turned out that 'György Kubányi, the romantic lead, could not perform because he suddenly fell ill.'

"'Ormos! You know Kubányi's role,' the manager declared. 'This evening you will perform as a romantic lead.'

"The comedian hesitated. He even mentioned that he would need an appropriate voice and an 'alluring appearance.'

"'Only you can play the Chinese role,' they insisted, and Béla Ormos couldn't protest anymore.

"Erzsi Magyar was brilliant in the role of the prima donna at that memorable performance, too. The first scenes went smoothly. There was no problem until the duet."

"The duet started," the comedian recalls smiling. "I was trying, but in vain. A comedian cannot aspire to the honors of an actor in love. My voice faltered. I made a big mistake. Prince Odescalchi and his company happened to sit in the proscénium[20] box. They jumped up from their seats angrily and left. From then on, Erzsi Magyar 'sang the duet by herself,' until Kubányi could reappear in his role."

"I was young and in love," he continued. "I decided that I would become a serious man. I wanted to be a trader. I left the theater. For three years, I vegetated in the field of trade. However, I was not able to make a living and managed to destroy my family."

He said good-bye to trading and returned to the stage. He performed in Pesterzsébet and other rural venues. He learned, he acquired great experience, and his personality developed as well. The *Bethlen-téri Színhaz* (Bethlen Square Theater) was preparing for its first season. It gave a contract to the already reknowned comedian. However, the theater had financial difficulties before the opening and the company was transformed into a consortium. Although he only had a small role in the operetta *Csikágó* (Chicago), by Dezső Kellér, he made a success out of it with his performance. In the next piece, in the comedy *Egy óra az őrültekházában* (One Hour in the Madhouse) by Miklós László, he had already a large role and he received 'double units' of the proceeds. This is when he started to rise on the ladder of popularity. He performed in a red wig in the piece. The audience became fond of him. From then on, the ticket buyers often asked at the cashier's desk of the Bethlen Square Theater if the red-haired actor would perform. Soon they remembered his name because *Timosa*, in which he played the awkward Chajim, was performed four hundred times. Not only did the audience give great recognition to his fine acting performances, but the press did as well. He was invited to guest performances more and more often because it turned out that there were not many cabaret actors who were as good as he.

"Apart from the Bethlen Square Theater, I performed in cabarets and night-clubs. Artúr Bárdos, and then Aladár Wertheimer wanted to give me a contract. Both of them wanted me to stop cabaret roles. I had to choose. Should I go for the financial or the moral success?

"This was the question. Unfortunately I chose the financial one."

Years passed by. Béla Ormos became more and more popular. His heart was aching though. He regretted that he didn't sign a contract with Bárdos or Wertheimer. However, success is an excellent balm. He performed among the great comedians at the *Terézkörúti Színpád* (Teréz Boulevard Stage). In every role, he made the laughing muscles of the audience work hard. Later, under the direction of László Szücs, he made his name more popular as a member of the *Kamara Színház* (Chamber Theater).

"Then 1939 came. I didn't get a contract. That is when the OMIKE Artistic Enterprise was founded. I applied together with the first members. Today, I can relate the difficulties at the beginning. I prepared for the very first performance for six weeks. After six weeks of rehearsals, I stood in front of the audience. The piece presented was performed twice. Instead of salary for the second performance, we received tickets. However, the audience soon recognized the significance of the OMIKE Artistic Enterprise, and even those who had only seen one performance became fans of the Goldmark Hall. Today as well, when the OMIKE Artistic Enterprise has developed into an enormous operation, I play all my roles with the same love and enthusiasm as in the difficult days at the beginning."

Sometimes I Am Seized With Doubt

Written by Erzsi Palotai

No, my getting on stage was not opposed by my family. The only person who was opposed to it was me, myself. And the reason why? Don't think of banal stories; I didn't believe, already as a child, in the monstrosities rumored about the "painted world," which were spread with such a pleasure by fake actresses to cover up their failures. Even if it is true that the temperature is hotter by a few degrees and the air is denser than in the surrounding world, an actress gets used to this climate the same way as a man living at the equator does to heat. There are no electrical sparks from the constant heat, which could scorch and set fire to those present. This constant, so to speak "tempered heat," rather allows a sort of "casualness." Spiritually we sit in shirtsleeves, but definitely not in camisole. Concerning the other thing, the favoritism, the scrambling, elbowing: favoritism is worth much more in every other field than acting. Elsewhere weeks, months, years might pass by, by the time it turns out that the favored gentleman or lady is unworthy of the favored position. In acting, it turns out at the first role, and the bigger and more important the role is, the more it is evident. When the curtain goes up, it doesn't matter at all how strong the hand was that pushed the gentleman or lady on the stage. You have to let the patronized person go, he will stay here by himself, fighting all by himself. He or she is as alone as in the most important moments of real life: at birth and death.

So why did I protest, why didn't I want to go on stage, although the stage attracted me with a magnetic force since childhood? I expected so much, so terribly much of myself, such perfection and high level, for which I felt weak. I had come to a halt even before starting. If I cannot achieve the most, it's better to do nothing. I don't want mediocrity. I suppressed the desire inside me and I would only recite in secret if nobody could hear me. However, once I came from Kosice, where I grew up, to Pest, then my asceticism suddenly failed. My "I don't care" courage of my 17 years was overcome and one morning, bringing two scores with me, I knocked on Endre Nagy's door, who was then the manager of the of Teréz Boulevard Stage. Inside was a woman with nice legs rehearsing her singing, holding her head up, sawing the air with her hands like someone thrown into water who doesn't know how to swim. She was interrupted. "Yes, miss," Endre Nagy turned to me with a harsh voice, hands in his pockets. I went up to the stage, stumbling through all sorts of narrow, winding little corridors. I gave the score to the first conductor I saw, who didn't even know at what pace I was going to sing. It was raining. I remember that I was in a dark blue, silk raincoat. I sang in it. A song. Then hands clapped. They belonged to Endre Nagy. My acting career started with this clap. I signed my contract in the afternoon.

The following day, there was a premiere at the cabaret. They couldn't put me on the playbill, so Endre Nagy announced me. He was speaking in front of the curtain. I was listening behind the curtain with my heart beating. He was speaking about me. He called me a Hungarian Yvette Guilbert, the new Medgyaszay. He was still speaking about me. Oh my God, he spoke more about me than could a politician—I started to gather confidence. Since then, how many times has a manager, a director, an audience or the press had to prove to me with a role, applause, or criticism that—supposedly—I am talented! Because sometimes I am seized with doubt and I run away from the stage. Of course, I always had some real excuse for it: because I got married. In the meantime, although my husband was not against acting, I still had to urgently say good-bye to the stage, settle down for the strictly closed civilian life and only got enthusiastic for the theater from the audience box. When I returned to it—following a tragic event, my husband's death—I went to the Hungarian Theater as an ordinary actress. László Márkus founded at that time the *Új Thalia* (New Thalia), an enthusiastic, avant-garde theater. In the first play, I received the female lead. It was in *Bábel* by Felkay-Volkmann, and we performed it at the Hungarian Theater. I like to remember some of my roles, in *Jedermann Jótétjére* (Jedermann's Good Deed). (Lajos Gellért was an unforgettable Jedermann, what a partner!) I performed in films, in two Fejős Productions, *Tavasz záporban* (In Spring Shower) and *Annabella,* and in a Szőke Szakáll comedy. In the meantime, I was idle at the *Andrássy-úti Színház* (Andrássy Avenue Theater) until it became a theater with a full evening program. I don't have a fondness for any particular genre. I like the theater and acting and even if I prefer performing dramas, I am pleased to take part in light forms of entertainment as well; comedies, operettas, and songs. At the OMIKE I performed, most recently, in *Játék a kastélyban* (Playing in the Castle) by Ferenc Molnár.

What else should I say? On some pretext, I ran away from Pest at the end of 1934. I fled again from the theater, from the duty that I had given myself, to look for some kind of civilian occupation and solution. I went abroad to a country the language of which I didn't understand. I learned it in six months, I passed a university exam and I had already shot a movie there in the seventh month.

In December 1937, I came to Pest for a visit. I felt already homesick. Success abroad had accumulated in me. I had to take it home in my suitcase. I got married to Aladár Komlós at the end of the month.

Now should I say something funny, and typically trite about myself? Here you go: I'd like to act in a play that I wrote, the music of which I composed, whose scenery I designed, whose costumes I made, direct the play and perform the lead role. This is quite typical and—for others—maybe quite funny, too.

Judit Párdány

"My Great Love: The Stage"

The last stroke of the gong. The chandeliers closed their lit eyes. Silence descended upon the auditorium. The reflectors' beams of light were thrown onto the purple velvet curtain of the Goldmark Hall. The curtain rose. The performance started. *Rembrandt* by Sándor Bródy came to life on the stage. Oszkár Beregi was the male lead. When the first scene of the actress performing Hendrick's role started, the audience stirred. They looked at the playbill. "Who is this pretty, tall, young woman?" The cast directory revealed: Hendrick—Judit Párdány . . . The audience of the OMIKE Artistic Enterprise soon learned the young actress's name.

Now Judit Párdány is sitting opposite us without makeup, costume, and limelight in civilian clothes.

"How did you take your first step on the bumpy road of acting?"

"I was 13 years old and already in love . . . with the stage. I recited in front of Aranka Váradi, Frida Gombaszögi, and Oszkár Beregi. Their opinion was unanimous: I should go for an acting career. However, my family had a different opinion. It was out of question for me to become an actress. I didn't give up. I waited for the right time."

She got married at the age of seventeen. She had a child. Nevertheless, she was faithful to her dream. Coincidentally, His Majesty (her son) finally felt that he could also intervene. At an evening party, the guests entertained each other. They played the piano and sang. Judit Párdány recited. Andor Pünkösti, who was present, said enthusiastically: "Wonderful singing . . ."

"My family insisted on keeping to its original position. However, I remained adamant. I went to see Andor Pünkösti. I learned from him that he was already informed about my visit to him. He had been asked to throw me out. I performed the big scene from *Virágzó asszony* (Flourishing Woman).

"The excellent writer-director, who rarely undertook to teach pupils, announced his judgement immediately: 'I cannot listen to the request of your relatives. You were born to be an actress. I will undertake your education. I will make you a first-class dramatic actress.'"

Two difficult years followed. The candidate actress had to make great sacrifices in order to make her dreams come true. Pünkösti cared for his pupil, who learned fifty roles, with faith, conviction, and a lot of enthusiasm. She learned easily and fast. What characterizes this the most is the fact that she learned the lead of *Sasfiók* (Eaglet) in six days, to the greatest satisfaction of her teacher.

Following two years of learning, Andor Pünkösti thought that she could now perform before the general public. She became member of the *Belvárosi Színház* (City Center Theater). However, she couldn't perform because Patkós (the theater critic and director) took over the leadership of the theater.

She performed for a year in Mihály Sebestyén's company in Miskolc. This was in 1939.

"I undertook every role," she says. "I wanted to have a theatrical routine. I was on stage every evening. At the end of the season, I applied to the Theater Guild (Chamber). Ferenc Kiss presided over the exam.[21] I was the only Jew who passed the entrance exam."

She couldn't receive any contract to perform in the theater:

"I remember Géza Ribáry with everlasting gratitude, to whom I owe everything. Not only did he predict a great future for me, but he also gave me the opportunity to improve, to learn, to perform."

Leading roles were assigned to her in succession. Most of the time she acted in dramatic, ingenue roles on the stage of the OMIKE. Among her roles, her acting was excellent in the beautiful biblical piece by Lajos Bálint, *Tamar,* and in *Őszi szonáta* (Autumn Sonata) by Hugó Csergő, a play with poetic beauty. Ten leading roles were assigned to her in three years. Each time, she was Oszkár Beregi's partner:

"I owe Oszkár Beregi a lot," she says. "He is not only an ideal partner and helpmate, but also my infinitely benevolent teacher. I must express my gratitude to Lajos Gellért, as well."

"What would you like to perform?" asking the inevitable question.

"My real role is as a dramatic heroine. The sum of all my wishes are: Electra, Antigone, Eaglet, Hedda Gabler. I hope I will have a chance to get these roles.

"I learn with persistence and enthusiasm to be a useful worker of the stage."

Judit Párdány sacrified everything to be an actress. She doesn't have ambitions to be a star. She just wants to be a very useful worker of the stage.

Sándor Radó

His Life Story and Confession

"My parents' highest aspiration was that I obtain a diploma in higher education. However, they weren't lucky in this serious aspiration because the Budapest Children's Theater was next to the school." This was how Sándor Radó, the popular comedian, began his autobiography.

First, the little boy was an extra. Later he even got roles from Papa Feld, who saw a "little talent" in him. By contrast, the school principal held that the student had to learn and must abandon the stage. He told his opinion to the student's mother.

"At home my parents asked me," Radó recalls, "what I wanted: to go to school or to the children's theater? Naturally, I chose the theater. My father beat me and I ran away from home the following day."

When the student returned from voluntary exile, he promised that he would learn. Unfortunately, at the end of the year, his father's cane became operational to underline the fact that he failed in every subject. However, he who has artistic blood will soon forget about the beating. By the afternoon, the little Radó performed theater for his friends.

"I couldn't be saved," he admits, "they couldn't get the deep affection for theater out of me."

In the meantime, years passed by. The only child of the family begged so much, until his parents enrolled him at the acting school of the *Vígszínház* (Comedy Theater) or rather that of the Actors' Association.

However, here, Incze the teacher noticed that the students attended the rehearsal of *Tatárjárás* (Mongol Invasion) more than classes. Thus the teacher spent the lesson by asking questions about it from the students.

Radó confessed that, "From me, he asked, 'When was the Battle of Mohács?'"[22] Since there was a big difference between the real date and the one mentioned by me and because, apart from that, I also misbehaved, I was expelled from the school."

Following the expulsion, smaller roles were assigned to Radó at Faludi's *Modern Színház* (Modern Theater) and he mainly sustained himself by directing children's cabarets. Before the start of the next season, he took the admissions exam of the National Actors' Association and was enrolled as an actor.

As the artist wrote in his autobiography, he became a "choral singer" and a supernumerary (extra) at Sándor Krémer's Company. He traveled around the countryside. A year later, Uncle Réthy, whom he went to see for a contract, told him: "You can now try for yourself to become a theater member. The theater manager at Szolnok said, via a telegram to me, that he is looking for a dancer-comedian. If you manage to impress him tomorrow with a great performance in *Erdészlány* (Forester Girl), in the role of Walperl he will give you a contract with a nice salary."

The new dancer-comedian performed in the great role in Szolnok. However, his performance didn't elicit thunderous laughter from the ones sitting in the auditorium. The manager summed up his critique this way: "Look, here is 20 crowns. If you hurry up, you can still catch the train to Budapest and you can be home by morning."

After leaving the Krémer Company, he said good-bye to cabaret performances. Then Sándor Radó sang solo. He had success singing Gyárfás and Bauman's hits. Later, he performed in the cabaret by Ernő Kondor, the *Bonbonnière* in Oradea, for two seasons. Then he received his first contract in the capital, at the *Trocadero* nightclub. He went to do his military service in 1913 and the following year he was at the battlefield of Levoca. He was discharged in 1918.

1919. Radó had a contract at the *Muskátli kabaré* (Geranium Cabaret) of Imre Harmath and Gyula Gózon.

"Here I sang the first original couplet of my life, written for me. I spent two seasons there."

1924. *Apollo Cabaret.* By now everybody knew the splendid comedian, whose individual performing style and big smile were his "sex appeal."

"I sang the most successful couplets of my life at the Apollo in *Kemál* and *Hol vegyek én egy banánt?* (Where Can I Buy a Banana?)"

Andrássy-úti Színház (Andrássy Street Theater). He was already a star here. Everybody can remember the parodies of *Sonny Boy* and the parodies of Galli Curci.

Fővárosi Operettszínház (Budapest Operetta Theater). Great roles in *Zenebona,*[23] *Miss America, Csodabár* (Wonder Bar), and in other operettas. For five years the audiences of the operetta theater applauded the funny Radó, who made their laughing muscles work so hard.

He related something of interest. He was in the forefront of record-holders at large-scale New Year Eves. On a New Year's Eve, he would perform at twenty places.

After this, I worked in Budapest for shorter or longer periods of time at the *Royal Orpheum* (Royal Music Hall), *Tabarin, Terézkörúti Színpád* (Teréz Boulevard Stage), even at the *Nemzeti Színház* (National Theater). It is true that I only performed once at the National Theater, on the occasion of the jubilee of Gyula Fehér's 30 years of acting. I even said, when I went on stage: "I managed to get in here, as well, at last." There was great laughter. A colleague of mine said: "If you had been smart, you could have got in the National Theater earlier." "How?" I asked. "You could have just bought a ticket," was the funny answer.

The notable contracts of the following years were at the *New York Bár* (New York Bar), *Moulin Rouge, Márkus Park Színház* (Markus Park Theater), *A*

Komédia (The Comédy), and the *Kamara Varieté* (Variety Chamber). Then 1939 arrived. The contracts were terminated. The great comedian could only perform on the stage of the OMIKE Artistic Enterprise, where each of his performances is a new stage in his successful career.

Alíz Rajna

Who "was still there at Lepsény" (aki "Lepsénynél még megvolt")[24]

Bright-eyed girls and confident boys were chatting in the break between two classes at the Academy of Dramatic Art.

"What do you want to be?" they asked fellow student Alíz Rajna.

The young girl answered without any hesitation: "Dramatic heroine!"

"The role suits you!" her companions agreed.

Yes. At the Academy, Alíz Rajna prepared for a dramatic career with lots of enthusiasm. When she was a student, she performed many times on the stage of the National Theater. At that time, nobody guessed yet that she would be at the forefront of the most famous comediennes. As an academy student, many roles were assigned to her on the premier stage of the country. Among others, she performed with Mari Jászai, the shining star of dramatic art, in *A nagyasszony* (The Lady) by Szomory.

The day of the final exam arrived: Alíz Rajna received a lot of applause and recognition for the roles of Puck in *Szent Iván-éji álom* (Midsummer Night's Dream) and Kathleen in *Makrancos hölgy* (The Taming of the Shrew).

"A great dramatic ingenue!" the experts said.

On her first contract, in the role section, the following was written: "dramatic ingenue." Alíz Rajna performed in the countryside for a year. And what kind of success did she have? It is enough to note that she drew the attention of Arthur Bárdos and the *Belvárosi Színház* (City Center Theater) offered the actress a contract.

Now we let Alíz Rajna speak:

> I performed in a male[25] role in the capital for the first time. I was a cadet. I had hardly entered onto the stage when the audience started to laugh. I got scared. What are they laughing at? I soon realized that my funny words and my performance made them laugh. So I calmed down.

In the musical comedy, called *Kék orgonák* (Blue Lilacs), Alíz Rajna played a German governess. The warning of *Still, Pistike!* (Be Still, Little Stevie!) soon became a maxim. The two successful comedies didn't mean that the artist, who had been on contract only for two years, gave up dramatic roles. Bárdos often made her perform in dramas as well. The press and the audience were equally enthusiastic about her in drama or in comedy.

In 1920, the *Vígszínház* (Comedy Theater) gave Alíz Rajna a contract to become a member. The young actress got the role abandoned by Hermin Haraszthy.

The old, famous plays were revived. The new member of the ensemble performed Mici Haraszti's and Zsófi Csatai's roles in *Az Osztrigás Mici* (The Girl from Maxim's) and in other comedies. Other successes came as well: (Zaza) and two famous comedies by Béla Szenes, *Fizessen nagyság* (Pay, your Honor!) and *Csirkefogó* (Scoundrel). Alíz Rajna had greater and greater success at the side of Gyula Hegedűs, Irén Varsányi, Frigyes Tanai, and other notables of Hungarian acting.

In 1927 Endre Nagy and Béla Salamon were talking in the manager's office of the Teréz Boulevard Stage before the opening of the season. Endre Nagy raised the idea that "Alíz Rajna would make an excellent female lead."

This idea was soon followed by its realization. Public posters appeared, which advertised the premiere of the burlesque called *Romantika* (Romanticism), with Alíz Rajna and Béla Salamon in the leading roles. After the premiere, the artist's fate was determined for good. The audience laughed till their tears rolled out. For more than ten years, there was no program at the Teréz Boulevard Stage without Alíz Rajna.

She performed feisty women in a tilted hat, who molded the gutless men as they wished. The voluble comedienne became the number one favorite of the audience. With Béla Salamon, the master of humor, the theater had more and more success.

A few lines from the one-act play called *A motoros* (The Motorcyclist) are today still a maxim: "I am an old pro," Salamon boasted, who was soon forced to admit that "the lady was still there at Lepsény." The theater echoed with applause for minutes when Alíz Rajna, "the lady who was still there at Lepsény," raced onto the stage. Károly Nóti tailored the great roles to Salamon and Alíz Rajna's bodies. The great artistic couple continued to perform until 1938 at the Teréz Boulevard Stage.

In the silent film era, the Astra movie company gave the artist a contract for a dramatic role. She performed with Jenő Törzs in the social drama called *Elítélt* (Convicted). During the silent film era, the audience could often see their favorite artist on the silver screen. After the victory of sound film, Alíz Rajna played as Stamcsek, the bad student, in a film version of the burlesque called *Az osztály szégyene* (The Shame of the Class), eliciting thunderous laughter. The great comedienne was mentioned among the stars of *Havi 200 pengő fix* (Salary, 200 a Month) and other film comedies.

Now the actress recalls her performance on the radio:

> I can tell you that I stood in front of a microphone during the primitive age of the radio. At that time, the studio consisted of only one large and one small room at Rákóczi Road. I performed in a Nóti burlesque. That was the first attempt to broadcast a one-act play at this time. The poor late Endre Nagy was sitting in the next room in front of the radio, all excited, to hear what the comedy would sound like. I became a permanent radio performer. I often performed with the unforgettable Gyula Kabos in front of the micro-

phone. I also had numerous performances with Béla Salamon. We mostly performed Nóti pieces. I could only perform on the radio and in sound film until 1938.

We arrive at the day when she first appeared in front of an audience on the stage of the OMIKE Artistic Enterprise.

After 1938 I didn't receive any theatrical contracts. I couldn't perform on the radio, or in sound films. Then the opportunity presented itself to me to go on stage in the framework of the Jewish (OMIKE) Artistic Enterprise. I welcomed the offer. I prepare for every role with the same enthusiasm as before. I am happy that the audience receives me with the same old love, each time. Nowadays, my heart is often heavy. I am very sympathetic to those in pain. However, when I go on stage, I forget about everything. I perform comic roles. I am happy that the audience also forgets about the daily sorrows and laughs and laughs.

Imre Ráday

AKA "A Painter at the Provincial Company"

Imre Ráday once started his life story like this:

I was attending an acting school, when I signed the first contract of my life with a provincial company. I was happy to discuss with the manager what roles I would perform at the company. I picked Romeo, Peer Gynt, and Bilitzky for my first roles and I explained, enthusiastically, about the basic interpretation under which I would like to perform them. The manager agreed with a beaming face but one sentence caught my eyes: "at the manager's request you are obliged to participate in the choir." What is this? I asked. You don't think that I will perform in an operetta, what's more, in a choir? Nonetheless, my first manager gently explained to me that this is only a formality, it is not entirely compulsory. It only concerns huge revues, anyway, where I and a few new colleagues of mine will perform as elegant gentlemen in tails. So, I reluctantly signed the contract. I feverishly prepared for the journey, learned all the great roles by heart, the whole of *Az ember tragédiája* (The Tragedy of Man) and *Mit lehet tudni?* (You Can Never Know!). My father provided an outfit for me, just like for a young prince. I traveled to our first site, Veszprém. I arrived at the hotel on a four-wheeler where I changed and went down to the promenade. I also dropped by the theater to have a look at the notice board about the rehearsals. This was written on it: *Hamburgi menyasszony* (Bride from Hamburg), with choir. "Well, this doesn't apply to me," I thought and I calmly walked on. I was turning my brand new walking stick and watching

> the pretty girls. Suddenly the stage manager rushed out from the theater. He grabbed my arm and took me to the stage. The director snarled at me:
>
> "What is it, why aren't you at the rehearsal?"
>
> "What for?" I asked gently, "I don't perform in the operetta."
>
> "Sure you do, you will be in the choir."
>
> "I angrily explained that I only have to be in the choir at the manager's request."
>
> "Well, if this is the only problem," the director laughed, "we can easily fix that."
>
> He found the manager, who, to my greatest surprise, immediately "requested" that I rehearse. So I rehearsed singing. I followed the conductor's scale as falsely as possible, hoping that they could not use me. "Tenor II," the conductor said triumphantly and my fate was sealed. And the manager "requested" my choral performance for the whole season.

On another occasion, he also told us what brought him to an acting career although he wanted to be a painter:

> Yes, I wanted to be a painter. Already when I was a student, my dream was to go out in nature with a canvas, brush, and palette and capture the wonder that is, to use a gray word, simply called "nature." Later, my daydreaming as a student almost became a reality. I went to the College of Applied Arts during the day and I attended a famous painter's free school in the evening. At that time, I only lived for the fine arts. I read specialized books and admired masters' works at art exhibitions. I was especially keen on drawing caricatures. I often visited the auction market and drew caricatures of people there.
>
> Then I realized that, although I have talent for painting and drawing, I could never be as great a painter or sketch artist as are those I idolized. My friends advised me to rather become an actor. As such, it was more likely that I could work my way up to be among the greatest ones. This is why I threw away the brush and pencil.
>
> At the age of 14, I won a competition, which was organized for young drawing artists, but then I buried these dreams forever. I wanted to be an actor, a 100% actor. I felt that an acting career required a whole man. However, it still feels good to draw sometimes.

He sketched almost all the notable actors of the *Vígzsínház* (Comedy Theater) during breaks in rehearsals. When he buried the painter on the stage of the OMIKE, it seems that he buried it for good. Here, he didn't draw during the breaks in rehearsals anymore.

A Hundred Actors Look For a Stage

Told by Magda Rosty, the Winner of the Competition

The eternal rule of the interview is that the journalist asks, the subject replies. After that, there is the "material" to be shaped. Certain parts have to be emphasized, others left out.

We spoke with Magda Rosty, who jumped into the front row of dramatic heroines with two roles in the OMIKE. After her first words, we noticed that they weren't the regular "key words" we wrote down, but instead we wrote what the artist said word by word. Here is the candid confession:

> Ever since I can remember, the stage was the goal of my life. When I was in primary school in Szentes, I already played theater. I gathered the children in our house in the laundry room and organized big performances. We sold the tickets at school. And when the audience appeared in the laundry room decorated as the shelter of Muses, they found the scenery, the curtain, the installation all in place. Obviously, something was still missing. We didn't have a play. We always made it up on the spot. This way, we really performed a commedia dell'arte for our dear spectators.
>
> Later, in high school, I became the "main reciter" of the school. I performed before the general public countless times. Thus my form-master was not surprised when I replied to the great question that sounded like this: "What do you want to be?" I could only say what was burning inside me: "I have chosen an acting career." My parents dissuaded me. Finally we came to an agreement: I enrolled in the Music Academy. (This seemed to them to be a more conservative and bourgeois institution than acting school.) The die was cast: I learned to sing. I felt that this was not the real thing. Not what I longed for. I stopped singing and began to learn prose. During the first year, I really studied day and night. When the day of the exam approached, I fell seriously ill. I stayed in bed for six weeks. My willpower was paralyzed by sorrow, since my dream couldn't be realized, even at the first steps. I then heard that there was a so-called big "audition" at the *Magyar Színház* (Hungarian Theater). Recruitment of actresses. I almost staggered when I entered the gate of the theater since I had taken my first steps, following my long illness, only two days before. I learned that Oszkár Beregi, who had returned home from Vienna, was going to perform in a classical group of plays and that his female lead would be chosen that day. He and Ferenc Hont did the "recruitment" of the applicants. There was a kind of an exam on the stage. My colleagues and I, about fifteen of us, competed for the contract. I may have been the only unknown actress out of all of them. I forgot about my tiredness, weakness, and physical and mental lethargy. The theater is the most wonderful thing in the world. This is the only thing worth living for.

I gathered all my strength and knowledge. *Alice Takács* by Szomory was being performed with great success at the *Vigszínház* (Comedy Theater) then. I performed a scene from that. "Enough!" Beregi and Hont said almost at the same time. Half an hour later they "delivered their judgement." They chose me! A few days later, the rehearsals for *Romeo and Juliet* began and in a few weeks' time, I could introduce myself to the audience of Pest in the role of Juliet. A debutante cannot wish for better reviews than the ones I received.

Next year, the *Új Színház* (New Theater) gave me a contract. After the role of a dramatic heroine, I had the leading role in the French burlesque play, *Csókpirulák* (Kiss Pills). Then in Alapi's *Kamara Színház* (Chamber Theater), I performed with Ferenc Kiss in the play *Aranyásó* (Gold-Digger) by Ferenc Molnár. Then there was a long break. I got married. I stayed loyal to my profession; I only gave up the struggle for a while. When I wanted to start again, there were even more difficult and bitter obstacles before me since it was 1939.

That's when the OMIKE era started. A hundred actors looked for a stage. For two years, I watched others perform since I just "showed up" from time to time. For whom the profession means everything, that person cannot bear the pain and suffering that not performing means. She who cannot wait will leave the profession. She will be a private woman, a dressmaker or something else. I waited! I felt that something must happen. And indeed, something did happen. The OMIKE was preparing to stage *Alice Takács*. Dezső Szomory was in charge of selecting the most competent among five named actresses. And he chose the sixth one: me! I owe an inexpressible gratitude to the great writer. Not only for choosing me, but mostly because this excellent writer, whose works the greatest Hungarian actresses performed, insisted that I perform the title role in his revived play. After years of disappointments and struggles, it was my recompense that he wasn't disappointed with me. And perhaps the new audience, which got to know me in this role, may have become a little bit fond of me. This is the most that an actress can achieve today in Goldmark Hall. I played the second leading role in *Ismeretlen lány* (Unknown Girl) by Ferenc Molnár and there might be new opportunities for me.

This is what Magda Rosty, winner of the "auditions" told us, who stood out in *Alice Takács* on the stage of the OMIKE, and rose to be among the best actresses.

The "Little Rott"

Everybody knew everything about Sándor Rott, "little Rott." There was not a single theater manager in Budapest, or rather in Hungary, whom he didn't know and see, or whom he didn't make laugh in tears.

His jokes and "gags" go around by word of mouth even today. He was happy if he could make somebody smile. He, who made hundreds of thousands laugh, could also laugh so hard. He was as happy while laughing at a joke as perhaps no one else. That's why he became a comic because he really knew what laughter was. Now we relate an old story about him the way he told it to us:

> It was a different world. People and actors were more jovial, when I started. Life was carefree, happy,and charming behind the scenes and on the stage as well. In such a jovial atmosphere the jokes and teasings came naturally one after the other. In one burlesque, according to the script, I had to die and fall down. Every evening I collapsed in front of the prompt-box. Of course, my colleagues were aware of this and also knew that I couldn't stand the smell of cheese.
>
> One evening, according to the script, I was about to die again on stage and I fell down in front of the prompt-box. That day I died again. But I had only been lying on the stage for a few moments when a terrible "scent" spread around my nose. My colleagues had smeared the floor with cheese. I struggled for a few seconds, but I couldn't take it any longer and to the surprise of the audience, the dead man suddenly sat up and shouted:
>
> "Oh my god! I could pass out from this smell!"
>
> The audience laughed so hard that from then on, I had to do the cheese improvisation every evening.

Not only did the audience adore Sándor Rott, but his family did as well. Those who knew the great artist's private life talked about it with envy. His wife and children surrounded him with as much affection as the love "little Rott" showed when he spoke about them. During our conversation, he told us that when his mother saw him on stage for the first time, she rushed up to his dressing room afterwards and said in a reproachful tone: "My little Sándi, you were very good. I really liked you. I just don't understand, why you disfigure yourself. You are such a pretty, classy man."

It is not possible to write about Sándor Rott without mentioning his wife, Berta Türk, who is indeed classy and is still pretty today. We now relate from a newspaper article when she gave them an interview about her artist husband. We repeat Berta Türk's statement in its original Hungarian style, word by word:[26]

> I really like to speak about Rott. Sándi is good husband, good father and quite talented actor. If he continues like this, he will get far. Not in vain me was Sándi's ideal, our marriage be ideal. Sándi said many times that there are two famous actresses, who are never mentioned in relation to divorce. One be me, the other Shirley Temple.
>
> Nothing proves more how much I love Sándor Rott than that when once I sat in the old Gambrinus Restaurant then there, I was waiting for Rott, the headwaiter came to me and asked:

"Excuse me, are you Sándor Rott's widow?"

I faint . . . When they sprinkled water over me, it turned out that he saw in the newspaper that a man called Sándor Róth died in a railway accident. They thought he was mine husband.

We will relate another story, the one which Rott most likes to recall:

When I was in Rome, we went through one of the famous tunnels with my son. School children were coming towards us. The next moment, the children shouted in unison:

"Long live the little Rott!"

I would have never imagined that I was known in Rome, too. However, later it turned out that the cheerers were the commercial students of the Róser.

One more thing to add about Sándor Rott, the blessed artist of entertainment, is that when he had his 50-year jubilee, the Actors Chamber (Guild) refused to enroll him among its members. Since then, he had made audiences at the OMIKE Artistic Enterprise's happy evenings forget about their daily sorrows. Sándor Rott is accompanied on his last journey, which took place during the writing of this book, with the devotion of the artistic company and audience of the OMIKE.

Béla Salamon

His Presentation on His Sex Appeal

The autumn wind is creeping into the city from the Buda Hills. The yellowed leaves of trees on the boulevard are sadly falling onto the pavement. At this time, when fall is coming, it is nice to talk to people about everything that reminds one of the summer; happy days, freedom from care, tranquility.

We are walking with Béla Salamon, the uncrowned prince of comedians on Andrássy Road. An old friend is coming towards him. When he sees Salamon, his face brightens, he lifts his hat as well.

"Good afternoon, Mr. Manager!"

"Manager . . . manager . . . Those times have passed by. I slowly even cease to be Salamon."

People might think that Béla Salamon is always happy and always laughs. It is not quite true. Theater is different from life. Salamon is two persons. This doesn't mean that the smile only appears on his face when he's on stage and that he is always sad during the day in his free time. No! It is often the opposite. Since this is art, he's good at hiding his true feelings from people. Many don't want to know that he has a private life as well. We spoke about this with each other and I asked him to tell our readers why it is said that he has the biggest feet in Budapest:

"There were many jokes about Ernő Király's ears, Károly Ferenczy's nose, and Dezső Gyárfás's belly. However, the comedians made most of the jokes about my feet. Don't misunderstand me, I don't mean to complain. I'm even grateful for the jokes since they helped to popularize my name. But the truth is that I don't actually have such big feet. The newspapers only exaggerated. They wrote a thousand times about me that I have big feet, but I never got upset. The mockery might have been painful for a romantic lead, but not for a comedian, who usually plays awkward, clumsy figures. Perhaps I envied Kálmán Rózsahegyi sometimes, because it is still nicer if stories are written about somebody's pipe rather than about his feet. I also envied the handsome Imre Szirmai because of the anecdotes, which dealt with his everlasting youth. Youth is also a much nicer subject than two behemoth feet.

"I had to accept that my name was linked to my feet. Chamberlain was recognized for his umbrella, Eden for his hat, me for my feet. With a little self-irony I could say that this is my sex appeal. What a smile is for Chevalier, a small moustache is for Chaplin, eyes are for Charles Boyer, for me are feet. However, it often happens that I walk in the street and pretty women come towards me, look at me carefully and whisper to each other while laughing: 'it is not true that he has such big feet.' At these times, I am unspeakably happy and I am flattered by the compliment, which warms my heart like a spring sunshine.

"Ultimately, it's my fault as well that my feet entered the public consciousness so much. For a good joke, I am even willing to sacrifice my feet. Once Alíz Rajna asked me:

'Tell me, Béla, what size shoes do you wear, after all?'

'47,' I replied.

'47?' she asked me, horrified.

'Yes. It is better if they pinch a little.'"

Well, this is the story of Salamon's "big" feet. It is true that in describing Béla Salamon, we should have written about the wise man. About the wise man, whom the audience doesn't know, although this might not matter to the audience. The point is to have fun, to laugh, to forget about all our problems and troubles for the three hours in which we enjoy his art at the OMIKE performances.

From Kölesd until the OMIKE: Aladár Sarkadi's 50 years

When Aladár Sarkadi was asked about his age, he answered: "It is a little bit more than I look and a lot more than I confess to."

After all, Aladár Sarkadi is quite a young man. If he was not as young as he is, he wouldn't be able to recall past years so accurately:

> Not long ago, in 1881, my parents took me to Vienna to the Carl Theater. This is where I first saw a theater and decided right away to be an actor. Not much later, I was close to changing my mind. I saw the ruins of *Ring-Színház* (Ring-Theater); it had burned down eight days before. Later, when I was more mature and realized that many theaters perform without burning down, I finally went back to my first decision. Sadly, I had to later experience that theaters catching fire are not the only ones to fall prey to flames. My

parents did everything to make a "decent" man out of me. However, despite this, I was still attracted to my first love, the theater. It was not easy. I applied to the Academy of Dramatic Arts, but was not admitted. I sought patronage because at that time it still existed.

I approached Baron Frigyes Podmaniczky, Intendant (general director) of the *Nemzeti Szinház* (National Theater) and the Opera, who resigned around that time. He received me in a very friendly way and asked me how he could be of service. When I pronounced the word "theater," his face suddenly changed at that moment and he showed me the door. On the staircase, I realized that Baron Podmaniczky was probably fed up with the theater. I desperately looked for another patron. Finally, I went to see Ferenc Fenyvessy, Member of Parliament and President of the Mutual Pension Fund of the National Theater and the Opera. I managed to find out that he was going to speak at a membership meeting. There were people younger than me, who certainly didn't know that the membership hall was in the National Museum, where public affairs of the Austro-Hungarian monarchy were discussed. The session ended at 2 pm. The members left one after the other. At last, there appeared the most elegant and most handsome man in Budapest at that time, Ferenc Fenyvessy. He was not alone. He left the meeting togetherwith a rear admiral. I couldn't decide, should I approach him or not? Finally, I walked up to him and asked him when and where would he be available for a matter that is very important to me. He told me, in an extremely friendly manner, that he would be waiting for me in his flat on Mária Valéria Street, at 5 pm. I had never been as punctual as then. I quietly knocked on the door of the vestibule. A butler opened the door. The vestibule could have been a hall. There were wardrobes all around, up to the ceiling. There were clothes in them, but so many that any clothing wholesaler in Budapest would have been proud of such a stock. From the vestibule I went to the gentleman's room. I noticed a huge piano, on which there were more hats than in a factory showroom. Now I knew why it's not possible to see Fenyvessy twice in the same clothes. It is said that even if he changes clothes every day for a year, he still wouldn't wear the same clothes twice.

Finally, I got to see the member of parliament, who wrote a passionate reference letter to Béla Bercsényi, an academic professor. As a result of this patronage, I was admitted to the academy as a supernumerary (amateur character artist or extra). This is how I became an actor. Though not yet. I forgot to mention that eight weeks later at the exam, Imre Nagy, the dramatic actor of the *Nemzeti Színház* said: "It is a pity that you are so short, because you could have been a good dramatic actor." The following day, it was "recommended" that I leave. I received a letter saying: "On the basis of the poem recited at the exam, we found that your abilities are not satisfactory and for this reason, you are dismissed from our institute."

This is how I became an actor; or still didn't. I was looking to gain a contract without having graduated from an acting school. I toured in villages with the Ripacs Company. Our first stops were: Kölesd, Tab, Karád, Igal, Szil, and so on. Then villages in Transylvania followed, then Cluj (I was a chorus singer there), Gyöngyös (here already as an actor), Léva, Eperjes, Óbuda, Bratislava, Kecskemét, Debrecen, Arad, and from here to the *Vígszínház* (Comedy Theater). Here I performed before the elderly, the young, adults, and children. Only an audience can decide how I performed. Since then, I performed at all the theaters of Budapest. Once at the *Nemzeti Színház*, as well. I had a two-year contract in Vienna. I was called to Berlin and they sent the role of a Hungarian play in English from America. They asked my little brother living there to intervene so that I take the role. This happened six years ago. But who leaves Budapest, if one is not forced to? I stayed here and waited until I was invited to the OMIKE. I was motivated to go on stage here, because I hadn't performed here in Budapest. Well, from Kölesd to the OMIKE (only 50 years!). My career has been going quite well. And who knows what else will come since I am so young.

Zsuzsa Simon, the Devil's Disciple

Someone knocked modestly and quietly on the door of the manager's office in the *Belvárosi Színház* (City Center Theater).

"Come in!," came the reply from inside.

A young girl entered, wearing black framed glasses.

"I am looking for Manager Bárdos."

"On what matter, please?"

Silence.

"On what matter do you want to see the manager, please?" she was asked again.

"It's about my contract."

The secretary started to go through her notes. She checked who had an appointment and asked:

"Can I have your name again, please?"

"Zsuzsa Simon."

"I don't have an appointment for you today."

"Probably in order to let me in, out of queue and not waste my time there. Please announce me because the manager has been waiting for me."

"Here you go."

Zsuzsa Simon's heart was beating fast when she told Artúr Bárdos that she had just finished high school and that she wanted to be an actress. She didn't attend acting school, she only had ambition. Bárdos was surprised by the young girl's behavior and firmness.

"Perform something . . . Maybe recite a poem . . . by Ady, if you know one," the manager said.

The aspiring actress recited and was successful. She received a contract and in 1932, in the drama called *A térkép* (The Map), by Mózes Székely, she performed with Beregi and Páger and she achieved great success. Not much later, the *Belváros Színház* included *Az ördög cimborája* (The Devil's Disciple) by Bernard Shaw in its program and Eszter's role was assigned to Zsuzsa Simon. The young actress was also the assistant director of this play as well as of recordings of the Hungarian scenario. Actors' photos and photos taken of certain scenes were sent to Bernard Shaw. The world-renowned English writer then sent the original copy of *The Devil's Disciple* to Budapest, with his warm inscription, which he asked be forwarded to Zsuzsa Simon. Allegedly this is the only Bernard Shaw autograph to be found in Budapest.

Zsuzsa Simon has kept on studying since her high school graduation exam. She speaks several languages fluently, and she has translated plays. Her flat resembles a library, in which the finest works of world literature can be found in their original languages. All of Bernard Shaw's works are in the young actress's library. It is interesting that Zsuzsa Simon likes only to perform plays, but not to read them. She highly esteems good novels. Following her high school graduation, she had two wishes, of which the first one couldn't come true: she would have wanted to play Lady Macbeth, but—as she said—there was not a theater manager, who would assign this role to her. The other: to get married. She has already accomplished that wish. She got to know a nice young man, Lajos Mányai, who married her, at the OMIKE, the scene of her many successes in the last two years:

"I am grateful to OMIKE also for this."

Ibolya Solt

She lives together with her dad in their happy, modern home with large windows. Since her mother died, her father's only thought, only aspiration, has been to make his child forget her ordeal. "I have been her father and mother for eleven years and I'm proud of the result of her upbringing," he says.

Ibolya Solt starts her story: "I learned how to play the piano. I was Arnold Székely's student. Once I was talking with my dad and asked if it's alright to have plans requiring lengthier studies. Then I asked him what he would think if I became an actress."

"And this occurred to you just like that?"

"I inherited a willingness for it. My late mother had the same wish, but she couldn't achieve it. I applied to the Academy of Dramatic Arts. After the entrance exam, they called me down to the office and told me that the committee unanimously found me worthy, but that I could only be admitted if I abandoned my religion. I said good-bye. I graduated with honors from the acting school of the National Actors' Association. I received my degree following three years of work and study and with it several nice books as presents."

"How did you get to the OMIKE?"

"When I was a student, Sándor Forgács, a member of the National Theater in Cluj, directed *Szomorúságának énekese* (A Singer of His Own Sadness) by Osip Dymov, at the Goldmark Hall. I acted in this play. The OMIKE Artistic Enterprise started regularly a few months later and I received an invitation by mail to 'present my art.' I introduced myself and soon I received a part in a one-act play, in which Beregi had the lead role. I was his page. I sat on the ground and held a mirror. This was my first 'performance.'"

"Your first bigger role?"

"I already had the lead role in *Május* (May) by Ernő Szép. I got the role conditionally, with the stipulation that if the director preparing for the performance had anything against me, then I will give back the role without becoming offended. After the reading rehearsal, they decided that I could have the role. I achieved success. It was a great experience, not only for the role, but also because the author and my colleagues liked me."

She continued enthusiastically:

"I had my own evening with György Nagy, only the two of us. We performed in a three-act comedy. Just the two of us were on stage for the whole evening. I even acted as a mother in a play. I was the woman whose child was to be split in half according to Solomon's judgement."

"What was your greatest experience on stage?"

"In February 1943, I received notification that I would have the female lead role in *Aranyórá* (Gold Watch) by Ernő Szép. The review stated this about me: 'Young Ibolya Solt demonstrated her great talent, her lovableness. and fascinating femininity again.' I was very happy."

"Are you member of the Chamber?"

"My acting school diploma would have actually entitled me to membership in the Chamber (Guild). Since the time I received it, every season, when a Jew could be employed according to the Chamber's law, I submitted my application. It was rejected four times. In the fifth season, when the quota allowed it, I was admitted."

"Now we can talk about the future. How do you imagine it?"

"Since they said that I was 'not bad' in the past, I hope that I will be employed in the future and that they will think of me if there is a role that suits me."

"What do you think is your most important acting virtue?"

"My friends say that I speak the same way in life as on stage. The truth is that I try to be as natural and simple as in life."

Dr. Dezső Szabó

Doctor of Political Science on Stage

On our prosaic stages, there are rarely any actors with a PhD, even though we are used to this phenomenon in the Opera House. This is why it is striking to see a

PhD attached to the name of Dezső Szabó, the cheerful, funny, entertaining artist formerly of the *Magyar Színház* (Hungarian Theater) and actor in several good Hungarian movies. This blond, tall, young man has two degrees: an acting degree and a political science PhD degree. However, he begins to speak despondently since, although he has had many successes, the situation now is not too promising. He admits honestly, when it comes to this duality:

"I was asked many times: How can a talented Jew be so silly? I prepared for two careers and both are blocked to Jews today."

But let's start at the beginning!

"How did you start these two careers?" we asked.

"It was my dream in childhood," he said with a serene, passionate face, "to be an actor. I was still in primary school, when I once ran away from home to the *Újpesti Színház* (Theater of Újpest), to the performance of *Az ember tragédiája* (The Tragedy of Man). There was a big scandal at home, because I got home at midnight. That was when I decided that I would become an actor. I didn't say a word in advance at home but following high school graduation, I applied to the Academy of Dramatic Arts. I only revealed it after I had been admitted and I had enrolled.

"At the same time, I submitted my application to the university, too. I had passed the high school graduation exam remarkably well. Thus I was also admitted to the Faculty of Law and Political Sciences.

"At the academy, I first prepared to be a dramatic actor. Then the dear, late Árpád Odry and Ferenc Kiss got to know me and slowly transformed me and I went, rather, into the field of comedy. By the exams, I already performed as the traffic manager in *Süt a nap* (The Sun Shines) and as the physical education teacher in *Tündérlaki lányok* (Fairy House Girls). In my academic career, I industriously attended the university. At the same time, I passed my exams with very good grades. However, inside me, I always thought that this was of no importance. I only studied at the university to complement my general erudition. By then, I was only interested in acting. After the academy, the *Magyar Színház* (Hungarian Theater) awarded me a contract. I obtained one of my first important roles by being an understudy, taking Ferenc Pethes's role in *Méltóságos asszony* (Milady). However, for one or two years, I couldn't advance at the Hungarian Theater. They were preparing to stage *Házasság* (Marriage) by János Vaszary. However, they took away my role in it, as well. At that time, I felt that I wouldn't be able to make it. Vaszary didn't find me suitable. I am most proud that the subsequent years at the Hungarian Theater were very much linked to the two. Vaszary and I owe them everything. Altogether, I spent five years at the Hungarian Theater; out of these I count just three when I actually worked. Once it was written about me that I created a stir with great, clownish humor of high quality. About another role of mine, it was written that I had a Hollywood sense of humor.

"In the meantime, I got my PhD with honors. I learned everything very well, although perhaps, it was partly redundant. The university professors, who attended the *Andrássy-úti Színház* (Andrassy Street Theater), always said, when

I went to the university: 'I saw you in this and this play. I told my wife, "I am proud of him, he's my student."' However, I don't like the PhD title on the playbill, because it has nothing to do with the theater.

"Later I transferred to film. János Vaszary took me there, too. I performed in many films directed by him. I earned really high salaries at the movie studio and I also received contracts. At that time, I was not asked yet if I was a Jew. When the new system came, they were shocked to learn that I was a Jew and all doors closed to me. In those days, I was called to the movie studio for one of the leading roles in a new movie. They asked me to read the script. I sat down and read it in the morning. Then I answered them that I would take it. However, I knew that it was out of question and I didn't go to the movie studio anymore."

"What have you been doing since then?"

"The Artistic Enterprise of the OMIKE was launched in Goldmark Hall and I became involved in it, too. I also had a few good roles here. The main thing about this initiative is that we can perform and won't forget our professional skills."

"Have you thought of trying another profession? To make use of your other degree?"

"I can't even make a living with my PhD in political science. To be honest, I'm so much an actor that I wouldn't be able to do anything else. I feel that I wouldn't even be able to live outside the framework of acting. There are people who say that I should go abroad, but I want to be a Hungarian actor until I die."

Kálmán Szentiványi, the Announcer-Poet

There are few large theaters, small theaters, cabarets, and provincial stages in the country where Kálmán Szentiványi hasn't performed. He started as an actor and when he had his greatest successes, he switched to a "profession" that is much more difficult than acting, announcing. The reason is that it is something that you really must be good at. Announcing can be developed into an art and whoever doesn't realize this, also doesn't know how to announce. An actor says what the director tells him to say. It is only his performance which can contribute to success. An announcer must be both an actor and a writer, and even more. He has to know the audience's tastes and cannot say the same thing every day, because events always determine the content of an announcer's speech. Kálmán Szentiványi knows, perfectly, this genre. Although he didn't even want to be an actor, he became one by accident.

He came from Veszprém to Budapest in order to find some kind of a decent civilian occupation which would provide him a modest living. As youth in general, he, too, was in love. He met his true love at an amateur performance. A young girl performed well in a play called *Felhő Klári*. The printers performed this folk play at Gutenberg's Home. The play was staged at least ten times. It was performed on ten Sundays and Kálmán Szentiványi went to each performance to see and hear the "prima donna." He already knew the play by heart, all the words of each role. The destiny of the romantic young fan from Veszprém was sealed at *Felhő' Klári's* tenth performance. The male lead in the play, an amateur acting in the role of Istók Csík, became ill. The theater was full. The directors were desperately discussing what to do. That's when Kálmán Szentiványi presented himself.

"I am a provincial actor," he said, "I can perform the role."

"The directors were happy. Everybody forgot to ask whether the man who showed up had performed as an actor. After a delay of a few minutes, the curtain rose and the performance began. Kálmán Szentiványi was successful. Szidi Rákosi was a spectator at the performance. Her favorite, Berta Kornai, sang a duet with Szentiványi. At the end of the performance, Szidi Rákosi called over the country boy and she interrogated him. Szentiványi admitted that this was his first time on stage.

The following day, Szentiványi applied for admission to acting school, but when he had finished his studies, the war broke out. He was at the front for 42 months. When he returned home, the *Madách Színház* (Madách Theater) signed him to a contract. There he premiered in the title role in *Púpos* (Hunchback) by Frigyes Karinthy. Sándor Bródy wrote a critique of his performance. Afterwards, he signed a contract with the *Apolló Kabaréház* (Apollo Cabaret). He achieved his greatest successes with his rhymed improvisations. Few people know the Hungarian poets, both classical and modern, as well as Kálmán Szentiványi.

If three spectators from the audience chose one word each, the fourth spectator could then decide which poet's poem he should recite, which contained these three words. After a little bit of thought, the clever announcer recited the desired poem. If the specified poet didn't write a poem which contained the three words cited, then Szentiványi improvised a poem in a style defined by the audience. His performances were characterized by glowing patriotism.

He entertained audiences for thirty years and now, for four years, he has cheered listeners at the OMIKE Artistic Enterprise evenings.

I Wanted to Be the World's Smallest Actor

Written by Vilmos Szirmai

I am not an actor whose aristocratic family repudiated him because of this profession.

I was born the son of simple parents on September 24, 1890, in Csobaj, a small village in Szabolcs County. However, later, we moved to Budapest and I have felt like a real child of Budapest. I was naughty here. I went to school and my parents—as is usual with the youngest child—wanted me to graduate school, unlike my older brothers, who became businessmen. Nonetheless, I already had this idea that it is more important to know than to learn. Thus, their attempt failed.

When I finally blurted out at the age of sixteen-and-a-half that my latent desire for eight years had been to be an actor, my poor, late parents were very happy. Evidently, I didn't want to hear about acting school because I had this great idea, at the age of nine or ten already, that somebody should write a role for me. Since I am still short, it should be the role of a hunchback because hunchbacked adults are all short and this way I could easily perform it. In my mind's eye, I could already see large posters: "Vili, the smallest actor in the world!" (Contrary to those who dream of being the "greatest" actor in the world.)

Since I still needed some kind of preliminary training, I enrolled in Révay's variety school, which was on Király Street. Its owner and sole teacher was Conductor Révay, who accompanied programs on piano at the *Wertheimer mulatoba* (Wertheimer Nightclub). Later I had great success in front of my older colleagues when I recited my couplets (poetic verses) as Mr. Révay had taught me. Mr. Révay (poor man, he died long ago) played the piano very well, but unfortunately he didn't hear well and his teaching method reflected it. He told me that one has to gesticulate and articulate in a way that, even if there is a deaf man in the last row, he would also be able to understand each word.

I don't want to speak at great length now. My master brought me to the Wertheimer Nightclub and I began my career there as couplet singer. As I started to write couplets there, I also became a song writer. But although I was quite an insignificant couplet singer, some of the couplets, written by me and performed by others, achieved great success. I could relate so many funny incidents about my first years that they could fill a thick volume, but since I haven't written a book about myself, you will never know.

In short, I'll just relate as a fact that I spent quite a few years in café chantants and on rural cabaret tours until the late Dezső Bálint signed me to a contract at the Royal Music Hall on December 1, 1913. From there, they took me on at the newly established Blaha Lujza Theater in Újpest in 1920, where I achieved really great successes as an operetta buffoon and a character comedian. Since then, I have been to almost all the important theaters in Miskolc, Szeged, Debrecen, Kosice, and Budapest. I performed in lots of good roles, big and small, without distinction, because I never repeated any role.

I was a really enthusiastic soldier for Hungarian culture and even if they have taken the weapon from my hand, I will continue to fight as a partisan at the OMIKE.

Good Evening! Ferike Vidor Became a "Decent" Woman

She wore a checkered red blouse and a loose skirt, just like the little maids, who timidly walk Sunday afternoons in front of the Green Hunter restaurant, in case there is somebody, ready to invite them for a glass of wine and a dance. Her hair was tied in a red, polka-dotted scarf. Her face was a healthy red, like that of young little peasant girls who have just arrived in Budapest to be servants. This was how she was recognized by those who like the light genre of theatrical entertainment, and who went to cabaret at least once a month to spend two or three happy hours there.

Ferike Vidor mimicked a little girl's life, who had just arrived in Budapest from the village, and a maid's sadness and joy. The audience smiled expectantly, when they saw her enter the stage in red and white, striped, woollen stockings and say: "Good evening."

We write about this Ferike Vidor, née Fanni Wechselmann, who has been entertaining audiences for years at performances of the OMIKE Artistic Enterprise. I spoke quietly with Ferike Vidor about the past years, her great successes, her struggles, and about the present.

"I feel richer than I was," she says.

"I don't mean to boast because those who know me, know well that I've never been like that. Some time ago, I came across an extremely interesting book which gave reassurance about life. It's a novel by a Chinese writer, which teaches that all aspects and troubles of life have to be accepted not only with acquiescence but with joy, because the reward value of all evil is more than the pain and bitterness caused by it."

We talked about her plans, the future. She asked me to write about how she intends to introduce herself in a new role next season, because she has become a very decent woman. I remarked that one cannot say about oneself that one has become decent, only others can say that.

"I can also say that about myself," she replied. "I just have to look in the mirror. Since I've been eating bread, I've put on weight, so I've become a decent woman. To us, little maids, the word 'decent' means 'stout.' If I could start my life all over again, I would be a maid and I know that my goodwife (household mistress) would be really satisfied. To save money the way I can, only few are able to do so. It's true that I have learned to be economical, since even I have to budget my pennies well. I cook for myself. But how? I'll gladly tell you because certainly there are many who would happily want to learn how to economize."

Ferike Vidor, the celebrated female artist of cabaret theaters, tightens her polka-dotted scarf around her head:

"You certainly haven't heard about the ironing coal stove. How could you have? It is not you who usually cooks your lunch and dinner and it's not you who warms up your bathwater. However, I do it myself. Now I'll tell you the secret of how to warm up breakfast, cook lunch and dinner, prepare tender meat—if there is any—and to bathe on eight pennies day. For the ironing coal stove, which costs only two pengő, you have to use coal worth eight pennies per day for cooking. There will certainly be many who will say: 'I don't want ironing coal in my house, because I don't want my flat to smell and I don't need a headache either.' My message to these people is to sprinkle a little bit of salt on the ironing coal. It will take away the smell of gas."

After cooking, Ferike Vidor tells us that she plays with kids on Gugger Hill during the day. At the invitation of a girlfriend of hers, she spends sunny mornings in Buda and hoes and weeds a vegetable garden, as a little maid on her free time is supposed to do. Afterwards, she returns to the OMIKE stage to make the audience forget their troubles, which cause her many restless nights, too.

Kálmán Zátony

He is a little bit reluctant to reveal himself to the public other than on the stage. The short, quiet conversation we had with him can be characterized most aptly by his words: "One can be quiet and reticent, yet one might say more than with long sentences."

When we ask him to tell us about his life, career and the latest developments in them, he replies tersely and briefly to our questions, in his customary way. Mostly he doesn't speak in the first person, but uses the general subject in his sentences:

> Decades ago, Ferenc Rajna, who wrote reviews in *Pester Lloyd*, asked the most famous actors to write something about themselves and about acting for a book. I wrote about how I escaped back home from Russian captivity in Siberia in an adventurous way. There was not a single word about acting. I already, by then, avoided this topic. Let's not talk about it! Rajna found my article interesting, although most people wrote about which play they first performed in and mainly about their great successes. I spoke rather about life, which is, by the way, almost like theater.
>
> At that time (I don't know if one is lucky or unlucky to be an actor for such a long time) a review was written unselfishly, out of conviction, and the most valuable part in it was that a young actor didn't know that with critics and friendship, commercial concerns, personal interests, or political matters were not involved. We read the papers and saw the way others perceived what we were doing. One was internally proud of the appropriate, hard, short comments, which at the same time told us a lot.
>
> I still say today that we shouldn't talk about actors' private affairs nor, mostly, about the history of their career ("Wow, when I performed Romeo . . ."). Rather, let's see what they know now. Actors should speak about the stage, for themselves, not about themselves. There can be a generation which remembers your life; to them nothing has to be said. Meanwhile a new generation—because naturally the audience constantly changes—should get to know the actor when he performs. Otherwise the actor should keep quiet.
>
> Art belongs to the world, to the public. It can't be narrowed down. The actor's art mustn't be narrowed down when in a poor theater. He belongs to the entire public, and as of today not all of us have the opportunity to really be part of this. It is a source of great pain. If he gets inside, if he is narrowed into a tight circle, then he will contradict himself and won't bear it. But it's today's fashion.

Notes on the Translation

1. Zugliget is a section of northeastern Budapest.
2. In original text it's *krajcár*, a type of old small coin, similar to a penny.
3. *Libapezsgő* is a drink made of vinegar or tartaric acid and baking soda diluted with water. It was used for heartburn.
4. The Sixtus Affair was an attempt by Emperor Chares I of Austria to conclude a separate peace with the allies in World War I. The affair was named after his brother-in-law and intermediary Prince Sixtus of Bourbon-Parma.
5. Feri is the shorter version of Ferenc; it is like a nickname.
6. *Színkör* is a theater building with a circular auditorium and the company performing at its center.
7. Princess was probably the name of a tobacco company.
8. "Dude."
9. A ten fillér coin, now obsolete, was equal to less than an American nickel (5 cents).
10. A park near Debrecen. Its meaning is "Great Forest."
11. A famous cafe in Budapest.
12. This is a misunderstanding: Beregi is referring to the shipwreck of the French ship, the Francois Coppée, which occurred in November 1903 off the coast of California.
13. Voluntary right means in this context that even without the high school graduation (equivalent to Regents) exam one can be admitted to acting school.
14. Part of Budapest in the 12th district. It means Swabian Hill.
15. Angyalföld (meaning "Land of the Angel") is a neighborhood in Budapest. Administratively it belongs to District 13 (a traditionally working-class neighborhood).
16. Shloyme Zanvl Rappoport: "S. An-ski" is his writer's pseudonym, 1863–1920, Russian Jewish writer, playwright.
17. In the schools in Hungary, each class has a teacher who is responsible for the class.
18. Little Cumania (Kiskunság) is a historical and geographical region in Hungary situated in the current Bács-Kiskun County between Kalocsa and Szeged.
19. Ferencvárosi Torna Club (FTC), also known as Ferencváros, nicknamed Fradi, is a sports club in Hungary, founded in 1899 by Ferenc Springer and a group of local residents of Budapest's ninth district, Ferencváros.
20. Proscénium: the part of a modern theater stage between the curtain and the orchestra (i.e., in front of the curtain).
21. Kiss was president of the Theater Chamber (Guild) from 1938–1944 and in this role was instrumental in banning Jewish artists from performing on the Hungarian stage. When Ferenc Szálasi, the Hungarian Nazi leader, took control of the government in October 1944, he made Kiss the director of the *Nemzeti Színház*. After the war, Kiss was sentenced to prison till 1953 for collaboration the the fascist and Nazi governments of Hungary.
22. A battle between the Kingdom of Hungary and the Ottoman Empire in 1526, lost by the former. It was an important battle in Hungarian history since it led to the partition of Hungary for several centuries between the Ottoman Empire, the Habsburg Monarchy, and the Principality of Transylvania.
23. Uproar or riot. Also playing music in a chaotic or hurly-burly way.
24. Who hasn't got lost (yet) at Lepsény (a town).
25. In the original text it says something like "trousers role"; it is an expression in Hungarian referring to a young man's or boy's role, generally played by women.
26. In translation, the literal bad English was used because her (Berta Türk's) Hungarian was not correct either.

4

Musical Life in the OMIKE Artistic Enterprise

The List of Artists Performing in Musical Events (Opera, Concert, Operetta)

Conductors

Vilmos Komor, Dr. Ferenc Bermann, György Bondi, László Erdősi, Sándor Fischer, Károly Fraknói, János Hajdu, László Káldi, Walter Lajtai-Lazarus, Alfréd Márkus, Tivadar Pallós, Frigyes Sándor, László Somogyi, László Weiner.

Performing artists, singers

Kató Bán, Hanna Brand, Ibolya Darvas, Lili Dános, Edith Fábri, Kató Gödri, Manci Herendi, Kató Kraszner, Ilona Ladányi, Lenke Leopold, Zsuzsi Pogány, Erzsi Radnai, Gabriella Relle, Vera Róna, Vera Rózsa, Stefi Sebők, Olga Sík, Piri Somogyi, Annie Spiegel, Mária Szendrő, Viola Vera, Béla Bálint, István Basa, Miklós Bence, Dezső Ernster, Ferenc Faludi, Sándor Farkas, Pál Fehér, Ernő Garay, Oszkár Kálmán, Árpád Keleti, Miklós Kovács, György Leitner, Andor Lendvay, Dávid Ney, Jenő Pál, Ferenc Roth, Dr. Jenő Sipos, Tivadar Teszler.

Musicians, piano

Tibor Bálint, Klári Benedikt, Jenő Deutsch, György Eiser, Edith Farnadi, György Halmos, Lili Herz, Ági Jámbor, Lili Rauchwerger, Sándor Sammler, Hedvig Schneider.

Musicians, violin

Viktor Ajtai-Adler, Gábor Bánát, Alice Bárdos, József Biró, Sándor Fejér, János Gál, Róbert Gerle, Pál Lukács, György Trietsch.

Musicians, violoncello

Vera Dénes, László Horváth, Pál Hütter, János Starker.

The 45-member orchestra and 30-member choir of the OMIKE.

The Musical Direction of the OMIKE

Vilmos Komor

"The most difficult task of my life"

The pulsating musical life of the OMIKE is supervised by an enthusiastic organizer, a leader and inspired genius, possessed by extreme zeal: Vilmos Komor. Certainly the multitude of great artists available makes his task easier. However, it is his inspiration and vigor which forge together these forces, these many talents. In such a complex machinery, where, among so many sensitive people, the occasion for friction is inevitable, Vilmos Komor can say about himself that he is not only respected and appreciated, but loved as well. He told us the following about his busy life, which never pauses:

> I wanted to go into music from childhood. At the Conservatory, I simultaneously learned how to play the piano and the violin along with the appropriate minor subjects. Following the high school graduation exam, I enrolled in the University's Faculty of Philosophy. However, after one and a half years, I had to join the army. I fought through the World War. Then after it ended, I finished my musical studies at the National Conservatory as a violinist and a conductor. In 1920, based on an audition, the Opera House awarded me a contract.
>
> At the audition, I played the violin. After the audition, Izsó Fodor came to me and asked me if I was willing to play the viola. There was no problem as I could play the viola. They signed a contract with me as violist and I rehearsed all through the summer.
>
> In 1921, I became the secretary of the Philharmonic and I stayed in this position until 1927. In the meantime, in 1923, I founded a chamber orchestra with musicians from the Opera House and I constantly played concerts with them. This is how I actually began my career as a conductor. With this chamber orchestra, I signed a contract at the newly established radio station as well, the conductor of which I was until 1928. From 1925, I was the permanent conductor of concerts at the zoo and performed several times abroad as a guest conductor. I conducted opera for the first time in 1926: *Lohengrin* and *Rigoletto* at the *Volksoper*, in Vienna. This experience was memorable but a little bit painful at the same time because, as chance so ordained, I haven't had the opportunity to conduct *Lohengrin* again. In the

framework of a fourteen-day tour, I performed as a guest with the chamber orchestra in Italy in 1928. In the same year, I signed a contract with the *Városi Színház* (City Theater) as primary conductor. I was there until the 1931 season, until the winding up of the business. I worked abroad from 1931 until 1934. Then I conducted operetta for the first time at home. At the same time, I organized rural opera performances. We performed regularly in the following towns, partly with members of the Opera House, partly with members of the City Theater, with local orchestras, and local choirs: Pécs, Szeged, Miskolc, Debrecen, and Kaposvár. We primarily performed Italian works, mainly Verdi's, Puccini's, and Rossini's. I worked again in the City Theater with Aurél Földesi in 1934–1936. The rural guest performances continued during this time as well. In the following four years, I did exclusively rural and foreign guest performances in such places as Estonia and Poland among others. Also, I played concerts in Germany, including Berlin.

Since 1933 and until today, I've conducted subscription concerts at the Music Academy every year. My work has always excited great interest. Hungarian artists featured at these events and I also introduced works, even recent ones, by Hungarian composers at every concert of mine. Among these works, certain ones haven't been performed since then in any Hungarian concert hall. For instance, a composition by Béla Bartók called *Falun* (Village Scenes), composed for seventeen instruments and four alto voices, probably because it requires a lot of work and rehearsing. The two nicest memories of my past as a conductor are two concerts: I conducted the Philharmonic of Budapest in 1928 in Bratislava. The other one: I conducted the Philharmonic of Warsaw in April 1939 and it was so successful that they made me commit myself to four concerts in the following year, which, however, couldn't take place anymore.

In the first season, the OMIKE presented only concerts and parts of operas performed with piano. I joined at the end of the first season in the spring of 1940 at Géza Ribáry's request. I immediately explained to him that if we wanted to serve the audience well and provide a serious opportunity for the artists at the same time, we could only achieve it by establishing a certain standard. It is not possible to do things which are, although respectfully diligent, kind of dilettante after all, such as performing parts of operas with a piano. I managed to convince him and as a result, for the 1940–1941 season, opera performances and twelve concerts were advertised. We have gradually built up our repertoire through three seasons and now we have an ample one. With the premieres of the 1943–1944 season, the number of our operas will reach 25. We are considerably limited in that in the selection of our repertoire we must take into account the small size of the stage. Apart from that, we can only perform pieces whose scores are available in Budapest because it is not possible to import them from abroad now.

> We are in a more advantageous position concerning the company. We can choose among great singers who have previously made their name in this profession and whose names and reputations are well known within and outside the country. Furthermore, we can also choose among talented, young people, and I have already discovered several very valuable youths.
>
> The orchestra was a given. We worked together on the orchestra. In the second season, I remolded everything thoroughly according to my previously presented idea. As for myself, I conduct a maximum of one or two concerts in a whole season because I don't want to take away opportunity from others who can't work in this field elsewhere. In the second year, we switched to opera performances with scenery and we are already at the point where the audience is not even interested in opera performances anymore if there is no scenery. We had to face some administrative difficulties, too. The small, limited budget already seriously impeded us. However, in three years, we managed to bring the deficit of opera performances down (it is generally known that the opera performances are in deficit everywhere) to such a minimum that it amazes all the experts.
>
> The musical direction of the OMIKE is a more difficult task. It makes greater demands on me than anything else that I have done so far in my career.

Conductors of the OMIKE

Dr. Ferenc Bermann replaces the absent László Káldy as Chorus Master.

György Bondi is Operetta Composer and Operetta Conductor.

László Erdősi ("Erdélyi") is Operetta Composer and Operetta Conductor. A small comic opera of his has been performed at the Artistic Enterprise.

Sándor Fischer was at the *Vigszínház* (Comedy Theater) and the *Belvárosi Színház* (City Center Theater). He conducts concerts.

Károly Fraknói conducts operas and concerts. He was Chorus Master at the City Theater and Répétiteur at the Reinhardt Theater in Berlin. He's the founder of the women's chamber orchestra.

László Káldy was Chorus Master at the City Theater. He conducts oratorios, too.

Alfréd Márkus, the excellent Operetta Composer, only conducts his own works at the OMIKE.

Frigyes Sándor was also the Conductor of the woman's chamber orchestra. By the way, he started his career at the OMIKE.

László Somogyi conducted concerts in Budapest, Gothenburg and Brussels. *Don Pasquale* under his conduction had quite a great success at the OMIKE.

László Weiner graduated recently from the Music Academy. He won the 800-pengő award of the Ministry of Education and Religion with his chamber music composition with a submission under an alias. He has conducted symphonic concerts and one liturgical concert.

Pál Gergely, Répétiteur, was with Klemperer at the *Staatsoper*, in Berlin.

János Hajdu, Répétiteur.

Walter Lajtai-Lazarus, Répétiteur, was Dela Lipins's permanent accompanist.

Tivadar Pallós, Operetta Conductor, former Head of the Pallós Ladies Company.

Pál Zsigmondi was Conductor at private theaters. He conducts operettas at the Artistic Enterprise.

Hugó Kelen

Hugó Kelen lives and works in a half villa, half owlery, attached to a hill, above a rambling yard in Buda in a charming setting fitting in a Krúdy novel. He teaches voice and composes music. The most interesting part of his flat is the large terrace, from which emerges an old tree with a shady foliage. On the walls of his study are laurel wreaths, portraits by artists, Toscanini's autographed portrait, and photos of many of his students who are now established artists, autographed with gratitude and love. A wise man lives in this setting, who, while speaking about music, states impressive truths. This is not even surprising, because he has been accustomed to express his great and important messages most honestly through his fearless music.

"The task of today's artist," he emphasizes,"cannot only be to entertain and to delight, but it must be primarily an expression of the truths of current life. Today, it is not enough to create something beautiful or something interesting; one has to create something truthful. This is a hundred times more important for us Jewish artists, since from us, as creators of music, they will demand an explanation for today's situation which we must face with the armor of truth. Thus, we must express true feelings in a truthful way. Today, I only want to create music which expresses the soul of Jews and their intellectual sense of vocation. There were sometimes differing opinions about this at meetings of the OMIKE and concerning the objective of the Artistic Enterprise. This is how I received the honorable designation of representing the opposition on the cultural council."

Interviewer: We know that your compositions are always included on the program of the OMIKE Artistic Enterprise. So how does your opposition manifest itself?

Hugó Kelen: This is just a clash of principles. I, as member of the cultural council, was always in a battle with Géza Ribáry while he was still alive. I had great respect for him. I was amazed by his superhuman endurance, his unflagging work and I feel that he could have developed to be the greatest, contemporary Jewish leader if he hadn't died prematurely. This is why I dedicated my piano piece called *Concerto Grosso* to his memory, which best expresses the feelings of my soul. There might be some who don't understand, for the moment, but even they feel that it means something to them and has something to say.

Interviewer: Comment about this piece of yours that you love so much and your other compositions on the OMIKE program.

Hugó Kelen: The *Concerto Grosso* is a three-movement piano concerto, in which I incorporated Jewish-Persian fragments of melody. Its first movement is a confession-like monologue, in which I relate my feelings or practically the feelings of all of us and in which I give expression to our broken, harassed lives. The final part is so upsetting that some artists said that they couldn't sleep for days after having listened to it. My wife, Rózsi Kelen, performed it. I can tell you that, so far, I haven't found a better interpreter than her, although my works have been played many times in Hungary and abroad. Although my wife prefers classical pieces, she is in a way conservative. It was an act of heroic sacrifice on her part when she agreed to perform my *Concerto Grosso*. It had a great impact on her as well, and it called attention to her first-class piano performance.

(Let us mention here that Mrs. Hugó Kelen dropped by later during our conversation.) We read out loud to her those few sentences which her husband said about her. She kindly protested and pointed out: "Remove the word 'heroic.' This performance was a labor of love for me. It's been long since I played a piece with such joy. If you do something out of unselfishness, you are unable to make it yours as much as you should." We didn't accept the artist's request. Let the world see how deep is the clash between principles and disharmony, in a born and bred musical couple.

Hugó Kelen: My cantata called *Napsütötte földön* (On the Sunny Earth) was performed in concerts of the Artistic Enterprise. It is about people stagnating in the sun, shivering, being afraid of the future. But someone comes along (the soloist), who encourages and fills them with enthusiasm and at last, they follow him energetically and confidently. My song cycle called *Sirató* (Lament) is based on lyrics of Ady poems. It is a pessimistic-spirited, symphonic series. Actually, I meant it as an Ady requiem, but I realize now, when I think about it, that I practically don't lament Ady in it, but ourselves. The Philmarmonic once performed it. I wrote music for the poetic legend, *A gyermek és a Messiás* (The Child and the Messiah) by Jenő Mohácsi. It was first performed in youth religious circles. Then, the OMIKE also included it in its program. It's a kind of an oratorio work about the Seder Night.

Interviewer: With traditional tunes?

Hugó Kelen: No. I assumed that here I couldn't use the Haggadah melodies because Mohácsi also wrote a part of the ritual in an individual way. I'd prefer Mohácsi to speak about this. Maybe I managed to now create a tradition.

Interviewer: Your new works?

Hugó Kelen: I composed an oratorio called *Zsoltár a mindenség szeretetéről* (Psalm About the Love of the Universe), the text of which was written by Jenő Szentimrey, the Baumgarten award winner and Transylvanian writer. I am working on an oratorio about Job based on a text by György Sándor Gál. I actually would like to categorize its genre as a large-scale choral drama, the plot of which is the tragedy of Job's life and his apotheosis.

Interviewer: What is the reason for living a retired life, almost in the solitude of a hermit?

Hugó Kelen: I am not a self-advertising man. I am a vocal teacher. I make a living by training students. Only a very small circle knows about me. On the one hand, I had students who asked me surprisedly if I also compose, when they heard that one of my pieces was performed. On the other hand, there were people, who knew me a as composer, but didn't know me as a vocal instructor, although there are world-famous people among my students. However, a question excites me: will I achieve in my lifetime, without any external influence, that my works gain importance? Will I achieve something that others achieved by using connections and external influence? I never make any concessions, neither for the sake of a better meal nor for a better coat. My family doesn't expect that from me.

The conversation turned to Jewish folk songs. We asked for some information about these.

Hugó Kelen: I was one of those who first dealt with the adaptation of Hungarian Jewish folk songs. There are Hebrew folk songs and folk songs in Yiddish, the authors of which are unkown and which express psychological and spiritual manifestations of a community. These Jewish folk songs of ours are as valuable and expressive as the folk songs of any other people.

The interview lasted very long. We said good-bye to the master.

The Vocal Artists of the OMIKE Artistic Enterprise

Dezső Ernster

The Wonderful Career of the Son of the Chief Cantor of Pécs

The applause thunders. The audience at the OMIKE opera performance calls Dezső Ernster back in front of the curtain for the third time. The opera fans cannot get enough of the bass-baritone singer's voice. As if an organ boomed. Time passes, each minute of which is organized and counted, as to who can stay on stage and for how long. Official regulation allows actors only until 10:30 pm to enable audiences to forget their daily problems through their artistry. It will be Dezső Ernster's turn, again, in eleven minutes. It was during this time that we spoke with him about the path that he traversed from the Opera in Berlin, through America, to the stage of the OMIKE. He prefers to remember the *Tannhauser*, in which, in the role of the Marquis, he performed for the first time in front of an audience. He sang in operas in San Francisco, Chicago and Detroit for years. Then the biggest radio broadcaster in America, NBC in New York, signed a contract with him. He came back to Hungary in the spring of 1939 to see his father, Géza Ernster, the Chief Cantor in Pécs:

> I wanted to see my father and enjoy hearing his voice. My father is 74 years old and he still has a sonorous voice, as if preparing for a premiere, even though he had been singing for 45 years in Pécs. Sorry, I made a mistake. My father is not 74, but only 73 years old, and he is such a young man that he would certainly feel hurt if his son made him older.

We asked Ernster in which city and in which role did he reap his greatest success?

> I feel ashamed when I am asked about this, I'm not able to answer this question. Only the audience can decide if I succeeded. I feel that I'm in "form" now when I can do my best. I came home from New York with a five-year contract. However, I'm not able to comply with this obligation of mine anymore, I can't go back. I feel infinite gratitude towards the OMIKE, not only because it provides a living, but also because it gives an opportunity to develop my capabilities. I have learned a lot during the past two years, since I started performing on the stage of Goldmark Hall. With direction by great conductors, I enjoyed all roles that I was assigned.

After this, we spoke about performances on the American radio and their directing techniques:

> NBC is in contact with 1200 concert halls in the United States. They talk about it a lot in Europe that in the New World it is not art or knowledge that is important, but administration. Everything depends on advertising, they say at home. This is a false conception, because in America one has to know! Only those can make a career who are better than their predecessors. When NBC presents a new singer in its studio, it sends the artist's curriculum vitae, works, and photo to 1200 affiliates. Leaders of the artistic companies, based in different cities, listen to the artist's performance at the central location through the radio. If they like his voice, they immediately tell NBC central that they want to have the artist perform in the framework of a concert or a solo perfomance on such and such a day. Generally, the artistic directors of five or six rural cities answer. If the artist does well before an audience, then his career is established. This is the secret of why singers on American radio usually receive five-year contracts, because this is the the amount of time needed to satisfy the invitations of the North American concert halls.

Dezső Ernster, who achieved success after success on the stages of German and American operas for years, is now only on the program of the OMIKE Artistic Enterprise, but he is still happy. He likes evenings when he can sing and he is happy that with his extraordinarily beautiful voice he can dazzle music fans and make the audience forget our harsh fate even if it is just for a few hours.

Sándor Farkas

This popular and versatile baritone had been working at the Opera House for almost a quarter of a century when his contract was not renewed. We can only understand this long and pleasant past when he tells us how young he was when he began his highly successful career. As we look at his young, calm face and bright eyes, it is hard to imagine that he is a pensioner. He replies to our question on how he became a singer, in the following way:

Sándor Farkas: I was to be an economist. I went to a school of economics. However, my uncle, who raised me, as I was an orphaned child, had a good friend, a musician. He convinced him to make a singer out of me. This is how I enrolled in the Music Academy and there I became József Sik's student. In the first year, I was exempted from tuition. In the second and third years, I was sponsored by the Opera. Following the three academic years, I couldn't do two years of opera because the National Theater in Cluj urgently needed a baritone. On the recommendation of Kálmán Aszeghy, I was awarded a contract. I stayed in Cluj for six years.

Interviewer: How did you get back to Budapest?

Sándor Farkas: I was invited to be a guest performer at the Opera House in Budapest. I sang the role of old Germont in *Traviata.* I was offered a contract to be a "member on contract." I first performed in the role of Tonio in *Bajazzók* (Pagliacci). Then assignments in lyrical and heroic baritone roles came in succession. I sang 70–80 roles at the Opera: Wagner, Verdi, Puccini and Mozart, as well.

Interviewer: When were you superannuated?

Sándor Farkas: I was a member of the Opera for 23 years, until I was forced into retirement in 1940. I was told that since under the law we are unable to hire you, to our greatest regret, we cannot renew your contract. I had to accept this explanation and I asked for my pension using this justification.

Interviewer: You didn't sing abroad?

Sándor Farkas: I was the most loyal member of the Opera House. I was called to occupy very prominent positions. Knappertsbusch, the world-famous Chief Musical Director, offered me a very beneficial contract when he came to see us. He really wanted to convince me, but I didn't accept his offer. However, I often performed at concerts abroad.

Interviewer: Does your current working situation satisfy your ambitions?

Sándor Farkas: I am happy and pleased that I joined the OMIKE Artistic Enterprise, this excellent undertaking. Not only because this way I can contribute to the enthusiastic work of the community here, but also because of a selfish consideration: not to get out of practice. This year, I sang Marcell in *Bohémek* (Bohemians), the third role in *Hoffmann meséi* (Hoffmann Tales), the role of Sebastian in *Hegyek alján* (At the Bottom of the Mountains) and the role of Germont in *Traviata*.

Pál Fehér

"The Famous Hungarian Tenor"

On a spring morning, when the great aria of *Salome* by Handel could be heard through the open window of the small rehearsal room of the Opera House, a young blonde boy in shorts stopped at the side of Dalszínház Street and took an eager look in the direction from "which notes of wonderful music flew towards the sky."

The music grew quiet, but the little boy, who couldn't be more than ten, was still waiting dreamily for the continuation. In the meantime, some kind of decision was maturing in him, because he went firmly to the artist entrance, to Uncle Csepke, who was known by everybody in Budapest.

"I want to sing in the opera," he said.

"And do you have a good voice?" the receptionist asked.

"Do I have? Let me show you."

And in the next minute, the unknown boy started to sing *Sir John*. Even opera singers who were sitting on the bench, talking to each other, turned their attention to his tinkling voice. One of them got up, grabbed the child's hand and took him to Noseda, the conductor.

"Introduce yourself, please."

"I am Pál Fehér," he said, and politely bowed.

This is how ten-year-old Palika Fehér's singing career started. His voice hardly needed any polishing. He learned easily and soon he received small roles. He showed his real "greatness" when he sang solo in *A bibliás ember* (The Scripturist). He received great applause. He performed with Károly Burián and he was called in front of the curtain together with him. He was a "member" of the Opera House for four years. Then the fifteen-year-old heroic tenor was not on stage any longer. He enrolled in the Music Academy at the age of fifteen and prepared for a career with unprecedented diligence. However, he had to make a living as well. He became a clerk at the Credit Bank. He struggled with bank functions in the morning and studied in the afternoon. Once, the officers of the Credit Bank gave a banquet. Baron Adolf Ullmann, President of the Credit Bank, sat at the head of the table. Pál Fehér was requested to sing. He had such success that Baron Ullmann immediately made arrangements: the little clerk got a new post, where he only had to be busy in the morning.

After he finished at the Music Academy, it happened that Walter Bruno was visiting a friend in Budapest. Somebody recommended that he listen to Pál Fehér. That's how it happened. The young opera singer was introduced to the world-famous conductor, who listened to Pál Fehér and gave him a contract within five minutes. Fehér got to the Opera in Berlin, where he sang for six years. The public posters advertised his name this way: "The Famous Hungarian Tenor."

His contract was not renewed in 1933. This is how he got to the *Kulturbund Deutscher Juden*, the OMIKE of Berlin, the leader of which, the former director of the Opera House of Berlin, tried to save valuable people who had lost their jobs because they were Jews. Artists dismissed from the Opera House and different theaters performed in the *Berliner Theater*, the former *Reinhardt Theater*. The *Berliner Theater* held 1200 seats, which were filled each day with spectators forced into the Jewish theater. However, at the end of the season, there was a deficit of 70,000 marks.

The head of the theater, who had converted to Judaism, went to see the president of the religious community of Berlin, Stahl, the architect, and told him that the new season could not start because the previous one closed with a huge deficit. The president of the religious community reached into his pocket without thinking and covered the huge deficit with his own money.

We must also mention Pál Fehér's guest performance in Vienna, his successful tour in Austria, his opera performance in Zürich, and also about *Josephin*, which was performed in the City Theater, where he appeared with Mária Németh. Fehér played Napoleon.

He's been home since 1938 and has delighted opera friends of OMIKE with his wonderful voice for years. He doesn't complain. He is happy that he can perform on the stage of the OMIKE. As he says, he didn't prepare with more enthusiasm for the number one opera of the the world and invest more knowledge into the performance of any single role than here. Everybody here knows and feels that, nowadays, he is here to fulfill a mission.

Kató Gergely: A Hungarian Jewish Opera Singer Launches Her Career

The Inner-City Youth Group organized a vocal competition for young Jewish male and female singers, with the support of the Youth Groups of the Jewish Religious Community of Pest. The jury was composed of known leaders in Jewish musical life. The first prize was awarded to Kató Gergely. We spoke with Kató Gergely after the competition. Where did she start?

I can see pictures here in the flat of this quiet Pest citizen, which were taken somewhere in a rural town, at a performance organized for the benefit of the Red Cross.

Now, finally, every little detail makes sense and has significance: the confident prediction of "well, I told you"; the encouragement of teachers at the evangelist girls' high school; and the recognition by the mayor of the town and the notables, which were hard to notice at the time. Whether these instances were meant for the student girl flushed with success, who passes the test as in Latin classes; or for the feeling of apprehension of a future great singer; or for a young child, who captures hearts simply with the beauty of her voice; they make experts wonder: what would happen if she were trained by professionals?

This is what happened. Afterwards, practically nothing else occurred. Music Academy! Unrealizable, a never fulfilled dream. Studying and practicing meant the "artistic" life. But she is not only an artist, she is also a Jew, which means a certain fate, what's more, a difficult one. Through her events and the news in the papers, she caught the attention of the audience. She was invited by associations and youth groups to sing at their performances. I saw and read these invitations and articles. Now, every line, every note still matters. In the young opera singer's life, this is more than just a simple vanity issue. She needs this to improve her self-confidence, to increase her willpower, to cherish the hope that it's still worth studying in spite of the struggles and sacrifices. Kató Gergely, the young Jewish opera singer, lives a strange life. Whoever thinks that he or she is going to read about something like that in the theatrical papers, should put the book down because he or she will be disappointed. This opera singer doesn't live the life that clumsy journeymen make up in order to entertain their bored readers. She works really seriously: she has students and she makes arts and crafts and toys. This is how she earns the money to continue her studies.

This is how Kató Gergely, the young Jewish opera singer, who won the first prize at the vocal competition of the Youth Groups of the P. I. H.,[1] launched her career.

Manci Herendi, the "Whistling Artist"

There was a barnstorming company in Aszód, which planned to entertain the intellectuals of the small town for a week. For some reason, the people of Aszód were not interested in the wandering ambassadors of the acting muse. They were at their third performance, but in the auditorium there were still fewer people than artists on stage. The company got into a desperate situation. They were ready to leave, but they didn't even have enough money to cover the cost of train tickets. The people of Aszód were not interested in the theater. They said: "Manci Hermann is worth more than any of your performances."

The director of the barnstorming company went to see Manci Hermann's father and asked him to allow Manci to perform for a single evening. Mr. Hermann agreed. The Aszód printer, who had already printed their third poster bill on credit, exclaimed, "It's no use crying over spilled milk" and printed the playbill of *Regí szerető* (Old Lover) on credit, on which the biggest sensation, printed in bold letters was was the "guest performance" by six-year-old Manci Hermann. There was a full house, higher priced tickets sold out, the actors paid their debts, they could leave and—Manci Hermann didn't want to do without applause anymore.

"Whistling Manci"—because that's what she was called in Aszód—told her parents at the age of ten that she would be an actress. It is just natural that the parents, living with the mindset of a rural town, didn't want to agree to this plan under any circumstances. They protested, asked, begged, but nothing worked.

"Then I'll die!"—little Manci declared with great pathos.

Of course, the parents didn't want that. They brought her to Budapest, took her to the *Király Színház* (King Theater), to László Beőthy, where Manci demonstrated her knowledge the following day. She sang, whistled, recited a poem, and was successful. László Beőthy, whom the parents went to see to make their child change her mind with his help, said: It would be a sin not to let the child be taught, what's more, if Manci Hermann finished fours years of high school and the Rákosi Acting School, he will immediately give her a contract at the King Theater. Manci was still in year two at the Rákosi school, when she played the title role in *Napsugár kisasszony* (Little Miss Sunshine). There was a thunderous applause in the auditorium. Manci Hermann, who became Herendi in the meantime, was called in front of the iron curtain. Afterwards, still during that evening, she signed a three-year contract at the theater. Her real dream, however, was the opera. She learned from Rosa Papir and Kasovszka in Vienna and from Madame Caier in Berlin. At the same time, she performed in Berlin as well, as a whistling artist. Her teacher forbade her whistling, because, as she said, "it's bad for the voice." She performed on the stages of almost all the great cities of Europe.

She achieved her greatest success in Vienna in 1917, and yet she got embarrassed there on stage for the first time. She was invited as guest performer by the Apollo Theater. The young girl was escorted to Vienna by her father. Her performance was advertised by huge, public posters in the streets of the imperial city with the following text: "Manci Herendi; guest performance by the youngest female artist of the *Király Színház* (King Theater) in Budapest." She performed in front of a full house. She was a success and had to repeat her performance several times. In the first rows of the theater soldiers were sitting who welcomed Manci Herendi, known from her performances in Budapest, by shouting in Hungarian: "Long live our product from Hungary!"

"The Hungarian words came so unexpectedly in Vienna," she said, "that I was standing there fascinated for some moments and I couldn't say a word. This was the only time in my life, when the audience made me feel embarrassed."

There was a big surprise in the OMIKE when the role of Musette in *La Bohème* was assigned to her. Only insiders knew of Manci Herendi's cultivated voice. She was a success that evening, when she showed that she was not only an operetta and cabaret actress, a whistle artist and a skillful performer of imitative numbers, but also an opera singer.

Oszkár Kálmán

About the Opera Section of OMIKE

Oszkár Kálmán's every word, every movement, is as refined and elegant as his artistic individuality. He's not only full of piety on stage, but it seems as if he walks all dressed up in real life, too. Neither a single complaint leaves his lips, nor an expression of resignation, when we ask him about past and present. With fine, noble gestures, he only speaks about topics of which he can say nice and good things. About his long work at the Opera House, full of success, he only has this to say:

I was attached to the Hungarian Royal Opera House, where I worked for 25 fruitful years and which gave me lots of nice memories. Nothing can overshadow this! I created every possible, first-class, bass role and fully participated in the great artistic work of the Opera House. I sang in half of Europe and achieved real successes, especially in the great cities of Germany. I spent two beautiful years at the *Staatsoper,* in Berlin, under Klemperer's direction. Apart from that, I sang oratorios for 25 years and I like the fact that I can do it now, too. This year, as well, I have sung the Matthew Passion many times. I hope that my repertoire will not be so much narrowed down as it is now.

Interviewer: What prompted you to serve in the OMIKE Artistic Enterprise?

Oszkár Kálmán: My friend, Dr. Géza Ribáry, asked me to support his Artistic Enterprise with my artistic experience and prestige. I fulfilled his wish with the greatest pleasure. With all my heart I made my knowledge and prestige available to him without any hesitation and I will be at his service as long as the existence of this institution is necessary. This institution employs a great number of excellent artists and, in my opinion, it fulfills its most important function by providing opportunities, especially to lesser-known ones. It ensures some livelihood for a lot of artists, musicians, and choral singers, for whom even the smallest salary is vital. They are the vast majority here and because of this, it is of great importance that the best-known actors and artists support them with their prestige and contribute to the development of this institution, through which they provide a steady living to these others. It was impossible not to support such a noble goal.

Another reason why it's impossible to keep aloof, is because, for the artist, it is vital to stay in touch with the audience all the time, even if they represent only a certain class. We mustn't forget about this in our profession.

However, I have to stress that the OMIKE Artistic Enterprise should receive the greatest recognition and appreciation for the artistic work it's been doing. Of course, I only speak about the work of the opera and musical sections. I must say that there is such an excellent, combined opera and musical staff; the artistic direction is so great—I don't want to highlight names—and the opera performances are of such high quality, that this would definitely bring credit to great opera stages of any world-class city.

Ilona Ladányi

A "Courtyard" Singer's Career

In spring mornings, a song can be heard in the courtyard of gentry houses in downtown Miskolc. A little girl wearing a bright dress sings. Her voice sounds like twittering. Those who listen know the child, who goes from house to house, delighting her "audience." She likes to be applauded, but this kind of recognition is not enough for her. She makes them give her financial rewards for her moral success. She holds out her small chubby hands for pennies, which fall abundantly. She only sings one song for the pennies. However, the connoisseur audience wants more entertainment, they want her to sing again. The little artist doesn't have to be asked twice. She is happy to comply with their wishes, but she has conditions. She will only sing the second number of the program—as she says it—if she gets a white penny.[2]

Years pass by, the venturesome "courtyard" singer girl attends primary school, later high school. There are people who didn't forget about the little one's wonderfully musical voice. They have a premonition that the girl will be an artist and launch a campaign so that the little one can continue learning. The women of the Jewish Women's Association of Miskolc hold a meeting, at which they decide to give their full support for the little girl's education. The "courtyard singer," who proved her sense of reality already in childhood, didn't really trust art and that it can ensure a livelihood. Thus, she was happy when she received a clerical position at an insurance company in Miskolc, which provided a modest salary. She also continued to learn to sing.

The insurance institute organized a sports evening with entertainment in 1930, in Budapest. The employees of the rural branch were also invited, because they had heard that she had a pleasant voice. The career of the little girl from Miskolc started here, at this sports evening. She was a huge success. The directors congratulated the bright-eyed, flush-faced girl and they asked her how they could help her to continue her studies.

"If it's possible, I'd like to come to the center, to Pest," she answered.

On the first of the next month, the little typist from the rural branch received her salary in Budapest. The patrons continued to support the candidate singer and made it possible for her to develop her skills. In the morning she typed, wrote letters; in the afternoon she attended the Music Academy. The rural girl learned fast and easily. Her teachers, Béla Szabados and Frida Vadnay, predicted a great future for their student, whom they taught for three years. She introduced herself to the public in 1932, which welcomed the new star. Miklós Radnai, the manager of the Opera House, immediately gave her a contract and she was awarded an 800-pengő scholarship, with which she traveled to Italy, where she continued her studies. When she finished her studies, she went home through Salzburg, but her reputation preceded her. They celebrated Archduke Frederick's birthday in the castle of Ischl and the young singer of the Hungarian Royal Opera House was also invited to this event as the guest performer. She was a great success.

Lujza Szabó, the world famous Hungarian opera singer, was singing the lead role in *Varázsfuvola* (Magic Flute) in 1933. She became ill on stage. The curtains went down, but within minutes the performance went on. The clerk of the insurance institute stepped in. The audience rewarded her singing with great applause.

She was a member of the Opera until 1939, when the Jewish Law came into force. Her greatest roles, greatest successes were in *Rigoletto*, *Téli rege* (The Winter's Tale) and *Sevillai borbély* (Barber of Seville). She performed in maid servant and dramatic roles. Since she had to leave the stage of the Hungarian Royal Opera House, she hasn't taken a rest, hasn't retired. She's delighted the audience with her nice voice, at opera evenings of the OMIKE Artistic Enterprise for two years. This little girl from Miskolc, former clerk of an insurance company, scholar of the Hungarian Royal Opera House, former member of the Opera is: Ilona Ladányi.

Andor Lendvay

He was the factotum (all-purpose) baritone of the Hungarian Royal Opera House. We hardly have any artists with a repertoire as ample as his. Even then, when the most wishful dream of his colorful, diverse life—a contract at the Opera House—became a reality, he knew more than a hundred operatic lead roles. Most of them in more than one language. For such a great achievement, it is not enough to be born with talent and a boisterous temperament. The real artist finds himself only at the cost of difficult struggles and for this, beside commanding inspiration of the soul, tenacious will power is also needed. This process never ends, never stops, it goes on forever. This restless agitation and formation of artistic individuality cannot fill life. A ceaseless fight has to go on, which does away with inhibitory circumstances, with complexities life has to offer and with man-made difficulties. In such an obstacle race, there are also benevolent helpers, but they only help those who deserve it.

We sit at a little table in an espresso café with Andor Léndvay, who speaks about his life. Certain parts of his stories are reminiscent of the heroic age of the Hungarian theater history of the last century, starting from the time when he fatefully became engaged to the stage. How many astounding and fascinating encounters with human generosity and human pettiness, financial problems, and difficulties caused by war! Even his family circumstances are so ambiguous that sometimes they hinder, sometimes they stimulate his theatrical endeavors.

When he was a little boy, he was a cigarette vendor at a railway station. He escaped with a traveling circus. Later he was a young waiter in the coffee house of a small town. Apart from happy and sad memories about theatrical life in the countryside, at this difficult stage of his career, he also made delightfully typical discoveries. For example, he explains why members of the company have to arrive together at a new venue: "The actor alone, all by himself or herself, with a small travel bag, is a gray, little, bird man, whom nobody notices, when he or she sneaks into town. However, the company arriving as a group, makes a stir. And every provincial company needs this little stir."

Naturally, he considers the fulfillment of his varied career to be the opera, most of all, the time spent on the stage of the Opera House of Budapest. When we turn the conversation to his present work, he hurls his words vehemently, with glowing nostalgia: "Let's rather look back at my performances at the Opera House and the long way I had to go to get there."

This is the refrain after each topic.

He remembers his foreign performances, Luzern, Munich. He would have received the title of Guild Singer, after three years of working in Munich, which a key Opera official had already reserved for him. He was only weeks away from this high rank, when he was asked certain questions and was forced to leave Munich. We ask him: "Do you regret that you didn't become Guild Singer?"

Lendvay waves bitterly: "I regret only one thing: that following the nicest fulfillment of my dreams, after having spent five years in the Hungarian Royal Opera House, I have such a lengthy pause in my career. Yet, I feel that I am not finished yet. I still have to continue what I have started."

The Ney Family

It's now over one hundred years ago that the eternal pride of Hungarian singing art, Dávid Ney, was born in a low, small earthen room next to the little tanner workshop in Várpalota. His poor, industrial worker parents didn't even dare think to educate little David, who showed strong intellectual abilities at an early age. They made him a tailor's apprentice. Afterwards, the well-developed boy left to become a soldier. He was in the military for six years; he fought hard as an artillery soldier at Königgrätz in the Prussian-Austrian war, which left bad memories. However, when the din of arms died down, from time to time, a wonderful singing voice broke the silence of the camp. The officers also noticed the singing. They gathered around the private soldiers and listened as Dávid Ney sang songs he learned in secret from Hungarian boys and girls, on the slopes of transdanubian hills. They became aware of his innate talent, but couldn't do anything for the young man with the wonderful voice. When Dávid Ney was discharged, he didn't go back to the tailor's workshop anymore. He joined the choir of the Jewish synagogue in Tapolca. The people of Tapolca recognized his great future promise and they gave the young choirist the possibility to develop his talent by sending him to Vienna. Ney learned from the best masters. The world-renowned composer and conductor, Franz von Suppé himself, started to teach him. However, when he finished his vocal studies, he returned to liturgical singing again and joined the synagogue choir of Győr. He only reached the National Theater in 1874. From then on, his rising career became known to many members of today's generation as well. No one can forget him, who has once heard him sing in *Hugenották* (Huguenots) or who has enjoyed his wonderful voice and his superior art when he sang the roles of Hans Sachs, Falstaff, Wotan, and Bánk Bán. However, perhaps more of us remember when we heard his voice on our sacred holidays in the Dohány Street synagogue, where he returned on every important holiday, never forgeting that, in his youth, he used to be a Jewish synagogue singer in Tapolca and Győr.

Today's Dávid Ney (David Ney II) is the youngest member of the world-famous Ney opera singing family. His grandfather's name was the same as his. He inherited his voice and name from him, but the name brought him much discomfort. It turned out that in rural tours, there were many who had heard the singing of the grandfather, Dávid Ney. Now, when they saw the grandson on stage, they didn't want to believe newspaper articles and public posters about the grandson. They expected the appearance of the bearded Dávid Ney on the concert podium. They only calmed down when the grandson's voice cooed. Then, people were not even interested in who was singing. They were preoccupied by the artistic experience.

He wanted to become an actor. After graduation from the Academy of Dramatic Arts, he was an ordinary actor at the *Magyar Színház* (Hungarian Theater). Somehow, he didn't feel comfortable in these roles. All the members of his family sang in the Opera House. He was the only one, who went "astray." He learned roles assigned to him by the Hungarian Theater in the afternoon and he went diligently to the Music Academy in the morning. He was an ordinary actor for a year. He passed the exam of the Music Academy with honors, after which he immediately received a contract from the Opera House. He was a member of the Opera for ten years, until the Jewish Law came into force.

He was most successful in Wagner operas. His great knowledge and voice unfolded in *The Walkür*, *The Mastersingers of Nuremberg*, *The Flying Dutchman*, and *The Rhine Gold*. He never denied his Jewishness. He didn't only remember his identity when he lost his job because of his religion, but also in the years, when he was a member of the Opera, he was the soloist of the Fasor synagogue on our major holidays every year.

He would always take his papers proving his identity with him to rural concerts, to convince unbelievers: he is Dávid Ney, too. From the papers it was clear that he's the grandson of the world-famous opera singer, from whom he inherited his voice. His uncle, Bernát Ney and his soprano aunt, Hermin Ney, are the elder Dávid Ney's children.

A few years ago, the Ney family increased by one more singer, Ibolya Darvas, Dávid Ney's wife, who became the coloratura singer of the *Városi Színház* (City Theater) after finishing her studies at the Music Academy. After some minor successes, she rose from one day to the next to the height of her career.

Dubarry was on the program at the *Fővárosi Operett Színház* (Budapest Operetta Theater), the star of which was Gitta Alpár. The world-famous singer had attracted full houses for months, when one day, in the morning hours, the phone of the Manager of the Operetta Theater rang: "This is Gitta Alpár's maid. The artist is lying ill with fever and the doctor said that she mustn't perform."

This was a memorable event, not long after which, Gitta Alpár's daughter, Julika, was born. The performance series couldn't be interrupted, because *Dubarry* was the greatest success in recent decades. The management of the Operetta Theater had to think hard about who could replace Gitta Alpár. This was when Ibolya Darvas appeared, who had recently ingratiated herself with the audience in small roles at the *Városi Színház*. She was asked to play Gitta Alpár's role.

A lot of people went to see the *Fővárosi Operett Színház* twice, first with Gitta Alpár, second, just to see whether Ibolya Darvas really deserved the compliments that echoed in the theatrical press for days.

Ibolya Darvas was not only excellent as a singer, but as an actress as well. The *Fővárosi Operett Színház* finished the season after hundreds of performances. Then *Dubarry* was played on provincial stages, where Ibolya Darvas performed roles written for Gitta Alpár, 120 times. She was also successful on radio. Then following enforcement of the Jewish law, she had successive success on the stage of the OMIKE Artistic Enterprise.

Erzsi Radnai

"An opera singer also has to know this"

The water of Lake Balaton was smooth as a mirror. The tiny, little waves stroked the golden sand of the shore. It was towards the end of August. There were only a few people in the water at this evening hour. Those who were, were there only because their holiday was almost over. The following day they had to leave and they wanted to enjoy, once more, for the last time this year, the velvety caress of the wonderful water. The administration did everything to prolong the season. Their aspiration was also helped by warm days at the end of August.

The Balaton tourism managers well knew that, at this time, nice weather doesn't satisfy guests anymore. There must also be some kind of entertainment. This is why a decision was made to try to keep those who were about to leave with guest performances by known European artists.

Huge public posters appeared on the streets of Siófok, on trees of promenades and on walls of the casino, which announced that Károly Burián, the opera singer and Erzsi Radnai, the *Magyar Király Operaház* (Hungarian Royal Opera House) artist, will provide an evening performance together on the last day of the month.

The idea worked brilliantly. All seats were reserved days beforehand. The audience was waiting for the performance of the two artists with understandable interest. For that evening, there were music fans arriving even from Budapest. The audience gathered in elegant evening dresses. Nine pm, the starting time of the opera arias, was dangerously approaching. However, the artists did not reveal their whereabouts. The management anxiously looked at the clock, then at the road leading to the hotel, but in vain. They sent a car for Erzsi Radnai and Károly Burián to the hotel, which was just a few minutes away, but this didn't work either. The bath manager of the resort also ran out of patience. He ran to the Wave Hotel, where the two guests were staying.

In the hotel lobby everybody already knew that there was a problem upstairs. Shouting could be heard. The voice that most loudly came was extraordinary. The people in the hallway also caught snatches: "This is not a hostel . . . This is not a hotel . . . You want to do tourism? . . . What staff you have . . . You should be ashamed . . ."

Nobody knew what happened, but it was certain that Mr. Burian had a complaint. And now, only three minutes before the performance. The bath manager rushed upstairs, straight into the opera singer's room. A shocking picture burst before him. Four waiters and a maid stood around the opera singer, who was still dressed too slightly for performing in front of the audience in one minute.

"What happened, Sir?" the manager asked desperately.

"I am not going to perform . . . Tell them that I'm not going to sing," was the answer.

"For God's sake, tell me what's the matter?"

"Sir," Burián answered, "take note that this is a hotel where the waiters are incapable of tying a guest's white tie. Since you wanted to know what the problem was, I told you. And I also tell you that my female partner doesn't know how to tie a white tie either."

"I had to tell this story before speaking about my career," Erzsi Radnai says, "I received a contract from the Opera that summer and before my performance there, I appeared before the public for the first time that evening. I never thought that the success of a performance could depend on such episodes. I admit that since then, I've learned how to tie a white tie artistically. It seems that if one wants to be an opera singer, she also has to know this.

"Although I confess, honestly, I didn't even want to be a singer. I wanted to be a piano teacher. When I was studying, an operetta called *Leányvásár* (The Bachelor Market) was on the program in Budapest. I couldn't escape from the magic of the music of the operetta. I bought its score and I sang it at home for my own entertainment. Just like every parent with their child, my father was also delighted with my voice. He grabbed my hand and took me to the Music Academy. The audition exceeded our expectations. I studied for three years and won a scholarship and a contract from the Opera House. I was a member of the Opera for two years. Then I acted in operas at the City Theater. I performed in *Aida* for the first time. Then I acted with the greatest, such as Gigli and Lauri Volpi. The last time I performed before the public was at a Zoo concert, in *Parasztbecsület* (Rustic Chivalry) with Mária Németh, Pataki, and Sándor Svéd.

"I've been trying to use my knowledge, at the opera evenings of the OMIKE Artistic Enterprize, to forget all that I'd like to forget," said Erzsi Radnai, the sympathetic singer.

Gabriella Relle

"I almost failed singing class in primary school"

Venue: The artist's "study." (In the left corner, near the window, there is an ebony black pianino. There are scores on top of it. The walls are covered with pictures. We can see Gabriella Relle in different roles, the way famous painters and photographers immortalized her. Many world celebrities smile at us from behind glassed-enclosed picture frames. Female and male partners. On the pictures, inscriptions in commemoration. On these, it is striking that there are not the usual signatures and dates, but a lot of text. "The acting partners' rapturous accolades for the great partner." The opera singer's intimate room gives evidence that the star of stage is also a diligent housewife in her private life.)

Protagonist: The famous opera singer.
It's happening: Sometime in 1943.

Usually an opera singer's voice is already noticed in school. Gabriella Relle can't say that about herself.

"I attended primary school," she begins, "and I always got just satisfactory or good marks. However, I almost failed. The reason for this was that I didn't dare to sing. My classmates laughed and teased me because I had a "strong" voice. This is why I didn't dare to open my mouth at singing classes. I received bad marks."

However, the little girl didn't become sad because of the singing grades. Her parents sent their child, who was interested in music, to play piano. Gabriella often sang at home. Later she recited, even danced. Her mother once very cautiously spoke about this with her husband.

"Our daughter is going to be an actress," she ventured to remark.

"Never! I won't allow it!" was the father's response.

Actor Lajos Horti lived in the same house. He was a member of the *Margitszigeti Színház* (Margaret Island Theater) at the time.

"Her place is on the stage!" the artist said, and he persisted until he was allowed to introduce the little girl to his manager.

The fourteen-year-old Gabriella Relle obtained a role in the operetta called *Heje-huja báró*. Her role consisted of only a few lines, but she sang and she even danced in the piece, in which Lia Putty and Olly Szokolay were the female leads.

"This is not a place for you!" Uncle Hegedűs, the old opera singer on stage at the island would say. "I will tell your mother what to do. You have to become an opera singer. You have a wonderful range of voice."

Little Gabriella Relle soon heeded Uncle Hegedűs's advice, who convinced the girl's mother to take her child to the entrance exam of the Music Academy. Although the father was against it, the mother still took the advice.

More than 250 applicants gathered in the marble corridors on the day of the entrance exam of the Music Academy. Gabriella's turn came early in the afternoon and she sang bravely. In the evening, before the announcement of results, György Anthes, a great opera singer, one of the members of the selection committee and a teacher at the Academy, was looking for someone in the corridor.

"Where is that little girl?"

When he saw Gabriella Relle with her mother, he went to them.

"Your little girl and eight other students passed the exam. Don't think, Madam, that I exaggerate, but I have to say that I think your child is a worldwide talent. She will be my student."

The professor proved to be a good fortune-teller. At the exam performance, organized at the end of the fourth school year, Baron Gyula Wlassits, Director of the Opera House, heard the great prospect of the Academy, who still had a school year left, sing in *Bűvös vadász* (Magic Hunter). Baron Wlassits awarded a contract to Gabriella Relle, who was still a student, and made her perform in *Lohengrin*, in the role of Elsa.

The audience, just like the critics, noticed with surprise when the debutant opera singer appeared on stage. The audience didn't get excited because of her beauty, but because of her charming voice. It's worth reading the first reviews: "Only once, every hundred years, appears such a really great opera singer as Gabriella Relle."

As the saying goes, the young soprano received great press. Opera fans didn't talk about anything else than the new, outstanding talent. Indeed, every performance of the young singer was a rare success. It is true that we hardly know of any student of the Music Academy who became a paid member of the Opera House before his or her last exam.

She already had achieved great successes on the foremost stage of the country for a year, when she passed her exam at the Academy at Jenő Hubay's request. Thus, she officially finished her studies. However, Gabriella Relle took her masters' advice and further trained herself diligently. The young opera prima donna became the number one favorite of the audience and received lead roles in succession.

"All through the years," she recalls, "I played forty lead roles in the Opera. I sang the lead roles of all the Wagner and Puccini operas. Naturally, I performed in lead roles in other operas as well."

Abroad, they soon became interested in Gabriella Relle, as well. She performed at concerts and sang operatic lead roles in Germany and Italy. Reinhardt also awarded her a contract. The Hungarian artist increased her success in *Hoffmann meséi* (Tales of Hoffmann) with Baklanoff and other world celebrities at the 4000-seat theater in Berlin.

Years passed by. The time of the "greatest opportunities" arrived. However, something intervened; the management of the Opera House informed Gabriella Relle that "her contract cannot be renewed."

The audience could hear their favorite in only concerts for only a while longer. The audience showed their love and affection by hastily prepurchasing her tickets. Afterwards, a preliminary program of the OMIKE Artistic Enterprise advertised Gabriella Relle's first performance. A crowded auditorium celebrated and celebrate, even today, the artist's every performance.

"The time will come," the opera singer says, "when we will be able to evaluate the valuable activity of the OMIKE Artistic Enterprise from a certain distance. However, we can already tell today, that the Artistic Enterprise has achieved a double goal. The first is what is the most important for the artists: it provided a stage and an opportunity. For this, even the so-called leading actors are grateful. The second and equally great merit of OMIKE is that it can provide a living for poor artists."

We say good-bye. The tram jolts with us towards the city. In the journalist's memory a hot opera evening comes to life. *Turandot* was staged with Mária Jeritza's guest performance at the Opera. The world famous singer was brilliant as always. Gabriella Relle was in Liu's role. In the third act, the Hungarian soprano had sweeping success. The theater rewarded Gabriella Relle with a thunderous applause. She received greater applause than Mária Jeritza! The world celebrity wrapped her partner in her gown and kissed her in front of the curtain. She pointed at her in a way as if Gabriella Relle deserved the celebration alone. And the following day the papers wrote that "the great surprise of Mária Jeritza's guest performance was—Gabriella Relle's brilliant performance and phenomenal singing."

Vera Rózsa

The Most Splendid Performer of Yiddish Songs

We heard Vera Rózsa sing at the Music Academy for the first time. She gave a solo concert. When her tiny, fragile figure appeared on the stage, I had the feeling that she was going to have some trouble either with the high notes or the low notes. I was afraid for her. I think that not only I had this feeling, but that each person in the crowded room felt the same. After the first song, I was almost relieved of this feeling. Vera Rózsa was good. She was a huge success. Since then I've heard her a few times. Last time at the OMIKE, as she was standing confidently on the stage, she looked at the audience smiling, as if she wanted to encourage each member of the audience separately with her look: "Relax, there won't be any problem."

At the Music Academy we've seen successes and failures. However, at the OMIKE, whoever stands there in front of the audience can only be a success. Because there you have to be good, really good. In Goldmark Hall, where artists give their best, each actor has to prove that he or she deserves the publicity.

Vera Rózsa, the youngest member of the Artistic Enterprise, knows that she, in particular, has to fulfill the expectations they have of the OMIKE artists. Her humming voice didn't only impress those who heard her concerts in the capital. Vera Rózsa is known throughout the country since she has given almost a hundred concerts in different rural towns in past years. This young artist's huge merit is that she has acquainted Hungarian Jewry with Yiddish music, which they had previously known at most from hearsay.

The success of her Yiddish songs reached America as well, where she was invited to exclusively perform folk songs about Jews. Vera Rózsa prepared for her performance in the New World, full of ambition. She was to travel in May. She had received the invitation last year, in December. She wanted to learn, polish her voice and to make a name during the American tour. At the same time, with the signing of the contract for New York, she also answered an invitation in which she committed herself to a one-month guest performance in Bayruth.[3] With this income she wanted to study in Italy and to travel to America via Naples.

She didn't have success in Syria,[4] as she said. The audience, used to oriental music, didn't like the opera arias at all. Also, she couldn't go on the study trip to Italy because of the war.

Vera Rózsa says the following about her career:

> I performed in front of the "public" at the age of fifteen for the first time. The high school, where I was a student, organized a performance at the *Városi Színház* (City Theater). I sang there. I will never forget *Vorrei Morire* by Tosti. Then I performed Beethoven's Ninth Symphony, under the baton of Vilmos Komor at the Music Academy. When the doors of concert halls closed in front of me, I could then perform for the public at the OMIKE. In the summertime, I accepted rural invitations. I sang opera arias in the evenings at meetings of women's associations. My greatest success was still with Yiddish songs, which I had started to learn on my father's advice.
>
> I can't really speak about my plans. I don't think it's worth planning since I didn't even succeed in realizing those that I was sure of. I had a contract in America and yet I couldn't leave. I have no plans, at most only wishes.

This is what Vera Rózsa says. Instead of her statement, her mezzo-soprano voice says more since we enjoyed it so many times at concerts and opera performances of the OMIKE Artistic Enterprise.

Annie Spiegel

"I always start from the beginning"

If life was a university course, then Annie Spiegel, an opera singer, could be invited as a lecturer. She would tell students her life story, which shows that faith, enthusiasm, diligent study, and indestructible cheerfulness help you through all difficulties. She could teach everyone that you often have to start again, from the beginning. For example, not long ago, she started everything again for the fifth time.

She says laughingly:

> Let's start at the first performance. It was a great day! I performed on stage in Nagyvárad (Oradea) at the age of seventeen, in *Carmen*. Károly Burián

> performed as Don José. My other partner was Dezső Kovács. My father didn't dare to come to the theater. He cheered from the terrace of the Weiszlovics Café. Lili Darvas and Frigyes Karinthy cheered from behind the stage. Karinthy pronounced his verdict after the first act: "Annie dear! You are not that bad!" He also gave his opinion to my father, who ventured into the theater for the second act. It seems that the debut went really well, because Burián, the world famous opera singer, took me with him on his tour.

Her first attempt at Oradea was preceded by a lot of studying. József Gábor, her first instructor, was happy to teach Annie Spiegel, who had learned to love art in her parental home. In the house of her father, Frigyes Spiegel, the famous architect, everybody showed up, who mattered in the artistic world. The former colleague of Reinhardt[5] didn't hinder the realization of his daughter's artistic amibitions. What's more, he supported her aspirations by all means.

"The only thing that matters," her father said, "is to arm yourself with all the weapons of knowledge."

Annie Spiegel took the fatherly advice. Following her school years in Pest, she continued her studies in Vienna. Among others, Franz Steiner, the famous Schubert singer, was her master. Saleschi, the world-famous Italian opera singer, didn't only teach his student to sing, but also taught her the secrets of the profession. He also taught her how to act and "make the most" of a small role. During her school years, the young singer performed in Gratz and Linz. The now well-known Joseph Krips, present conductor of the *Staatsoper*, started his career at that time as well. As they say: Annie Spiegel tested her wings in good company. Richard Tauber, the great tenor, was also among her first partners.

"I received my first contract at the Teplitz-Schönau Theater," the artist says, "actually the contract was for a Second Alto role, but I sang First Alto all the time. I performed for the first time with Andor Lendvay at the Teplitz Theater. He was one of the best colleagues."

The practically novice singer performed the lead roles of *Trubadur, Aida and Mignon*, as well as in operas such as *Mesterdalnokok* (Mastersingers),[6] *Holt szemek* (Dead Eyes), and many other operas in her first year. If world records were noted in this field, then it would be written that, in her first year, Annie Spiegel performed in thirty roles.

Prague, Düsseldorf, Frankfurt, Augsburg, Cologne, Munich, and several other large cities in Germany were important locations in the artist's career. There were only a few who knew that the German press highly praised the Hungarian singer, who struggled to be among the best.

"I got married and my little girl was born when I came to Pest for a visit," she recalls. "I went to see my first master, József Gábor. 'It's great that you are here!' Gábor exclaimed, 'You have to sing this evening in the Opera House. You will perform instead of Erzsi Sándor.' I had to rehearse the lead role of Mignon again from morning until the evening and then I went on stage. According to the critics, I was a great success."

Following performances in Brno, Prague and Vienna, Annie Spiegel performed again on operatic stages in the great cities of Germany.

"In the meantime, I directed several operas," she continues, "allegedly well, because after my first attempt, I was often requested to do so again. I also have to admit that I prepared thoroughly before my directorial debut."

Years passed by. The opera singer four times fought afresh those battles which everyone who lives backstage must on a daily basis. World events brought about the resumption of her career.

"It is difficult to recall the events of my career in a nutshell," she remarks, "since I would have to give account of twenty years. I'm not one of those who list their world-famous partners. I only mention them if it is necessary for the sake of historical authenticity. However, I cannot keep quiet about my guest performance in Strasburg. After a long hiatus, a German opera company under the baton of Richard Strauss staged a guest performance in this great city. It was an honor for me that Strauss thought of me. Before my departure, I performed there in *Rózsalovag* (Knight of the Rose) among other pieces."

Of course, something intervened again. Annie Spiegel came home in 1940 to start everything all over again, here, where they only knew her by her reputation. The cheerful, talented, and diligent artist began her career anew. Her colleagues became fond of her because she helped everywhere where she could.

"Now we arrive at the day," she finishes, "when I could appear for the first time on the stage of the OMIKE. I was hardly known at home. I began again for the fifth time. Today, they know me and maybe also even like me at home. I have to thank the OMIKE that I had a chance to perform in front of a Budapest audience. I will never forget this. For an actor, it is a question of vital importance to have a stage. The OMIKE not only provides this, but also a chance for further development. The OMIKE Artistic Enterprise also taught us that we are strong even when in difficult times."

These were some parts of our long conversation. Annie Spiegel, who is also engaged in opera tutoring and training of actors, hasn't stopped studying, because she hopes to start all over again for the sixth time.

Known and Unknown Heroes of the Orchestra

Among the violin soloists of the OMIKE, there are many excellent people. Almost all of them graduated from the College of Music, partly Jenő Hubay's, partly Ede Zathureczky's students.

The four first cellists are equally able soloists and members of the orchestra. They occupied an important place in general Hungarian musical life, as well. Pál Hütter was a member of the Royal Opera House and László Horváth was a member of the Belgrade Opera.

Among our pianists who have traveled extensively in the world, Annie Spiegel, Ági Jámbor, and Imre Ungár performed at the OMIKE. Edit Farnadi, Lili Herz, Lili Rauschwerger, and Sándor Reschovszki have excellent reputations in Hungary.

It wouldn't be right to highlight certain persons among the artists of the orchestra to the detriment of the others. The unknown heroes of this first-class institution are significant participants in its success. The string section—according to impartial experts—consists of the most outstanding members. The performance of the winds has also increased to the highest standards. Unfortunately, the difficulties with procurement cause serious problems, because it is hardly possible to obtain certain instruments and parts.

Notes on the Translation

1. *Pesti Izraelita Hitközség* means "Jewish Religious Community of Pest."
2. *Krajcár*, in original text, is probably a silver coin worth more than a penny.
3. As in original Hungarian text; more probably Beirut.
4. As in original Hungarian text; more probably Lebanon.
5. This was probably Max Reinhardt (1873–1943), influential actor, director and producer.
6. The original German title of this Richard Wagner opera, *Mastersingers*, is *Die Meistersinger von Nürnberg*, in English *The Mastersingers of Nürnberg.*

5

The Technical Operation of the OMIKE Artistic Enterprise

Finally, we present the so-called invisible part of the theatrical operation of the OMIKE Artistic Enterprise, all of which the audience can hardly see directly, but which is as important as the visible performance.

The Auditorium

Goldmark Hall essentially consists of two rooms joined together. The larger one's length is 15 meters and its width is 12 meters. The other one, which joins the big one along its width, is 9 meters long and 7 meters wide. The distance between the rows of seats ensures such comfort that is only provided by one or two theaters in Budapest. The number of rows of seats: 3 proscenium rows, 4 orchestra seats, 4 first-class seats, and 4 second-class seats. The seating capacity is 382, as previously noted in chapter 2, and the seats rise row by row. (The cloakroom is on the second floor and holds 322 hangers.)

The big room is lighted from the ceiling by 56 sixty-watt bulbs and from the side by 32 candle-shaped bulbs of the same size. In the room, a big lamp and 10 sixty-watt bulbs give light. The hall is completely light during the day. (The darkening installation was already on the huge windows before being required by air-raid defense rules.)

One of the biggest prides of the leaders of Goldmark Hall is the cooling equipment. In the first years, the OMIKE couldn't present performances when summer arrived because the hall was so hot and its air so muggy that it was impossible to entice the audience. This mistake has been resolved and today the auditorium is being relatively cooled at a quite low cost. An exhauster is working in the attic of the building. This machinery consumes two hundred pounds of ice a day. The air is pushed through an ice holder and, from there, pushed through the grilled gaps of the ceiling into the hall. This operation begins one and a half hours before the performance starts. This way, the guests arriving first will find themselves in a cooled hall.

The Stage

The height of the stage opening is 4 meters, its width 5 meters. The width of the whole stage is 7 meters [23 feet], its whole depth is 7.5 meters, its usable depth is 6.3 meters. (A 1.2 meter zone has to be left free for fire protection purposes.) The height of the stage is 95 cm [37 inches]. The orchestra has its proper place between the stage and the rows of seats. This is where the podium is placed, which serves to expand the stage, when the orchestra is seated at the same height with the stage on the occasion of orchestra concerts.

Every part of the stage, curtains and scenery included, is impregnated with a material that prevents burning. One part of the curtain system is the drop-curtain, made of heavy blue velvet, striped with gold braids, behind it the so-called Bayrouth curtain, and inside, a blue velvet solo curtain. The drop-curtain goes to the two sides and the Bayrouth curtain is pulled away in a curve, sideways. Next to the stage manager's place, the gong hangs and the stage manager's bell is also placed there. The three buttons of this bell make the bells ring in the women's dressing room, the men's dressing room, and the auditorium to call or to signal a break.

To make a stage functional so that it can perform different pieces in succession, a really versatile, technically prepared, and specially trained staff is needed. One of the very essential parts of this technical preparedness is the lighting equipment. It is very important to solve the lighting effects of the different pieces performed. On modern stages, the once so often mentioned limelight is not there anymore. It is replaced by reflectors placed at different places in the auditorium and on the stage (they change colors). The stage of the Goldmark Hall is equipped in a completely modern way in this respect as well. The complex structure is directed by a lighting designer from a switch board built in the wall, which can be locked up.

On this stage, as on modern stages in general—it is especially true for small chamber stages—the old-fashioned big canvas scenery walls are not used anymore. Instead, the stage is surrounded by a cyclorama, and within this stylized, so-called "Versetzs" (offset), the required environment can only be indicated. The stage of Goldmark Hall has three cycloramas: one black, one red, and one blue. Which is used when? If it is about a room, the red one; if the location is an open-air place, the black; at solo performances, the blue one. When there are two scenes in one act and a fast change of colors needed, the other picture has to be ready in the back. Then the actor performs in front of the first blue curtain until the second, already decorated, is ready behind it.

The scenery at the performances of the OMIKE is either newly made according to the piece or it is combined with the already existing, appropriate scenery. In any case, it is important that the scenery used in combination (here, as at repertoire theater where different pieces are on program alternately) shouldn't be conspicuous. It shouldn't be immediately seen that it was used in this or that piece.

The scenery effect can be changed with lighting. The most common example of this is the piece called *Hajnalban, déliben, este* (At Morning, Noon, Evening). The scenery is the same in all three acts; only lighting makes it look different.

The application of these modern principles and tools makes it possible that, since the scene dock of the OMIKE stage doesn't occupy huge premises any more, there is no need to transport large scenery by carts from a remote scenery dock to the location of the performance, day by day.

In order to create a complete illusion by the performance, there is, of course, a need for other theatrical equipment, specifically for furniture and accessories. The furniture has to be selected according to the style of the piece. The OMIKE is in an advantageous position, in this regard, because it receives furniture from a big furnisher company, on loan, for free. The procurement of the accessories is done by the property man on the director's instructions. He either procures them or he makes them himself.

He procures the costumes also on the director's instructions or gets them on loan. If it is a very special outfit, which cannot be used elsewhere, he makes it himself domestically.

The Property Room

The OMIKE Artistic Enterprise is also lucky concerning the technical staff. Since it received the most outstanding artists, it didn't have to struggle with their training. Such a valuable member is Miksa Würdiger, the chief property man, who even has an assistant bustling about by his side. Würdiger was the chief property man of the *Fővárosi Operettszínház* (Budapest Operetta Theater) for fifteen years. Most of all, he has such knowledge of wares, like an appraiser with long experience. Apart from that, he perfectly knows the resources of procurement and acquisition because theaters, as we already mentioned, if possible, try to loan the accessories and furniture from traders, private individuals, and other theaters. Last, but not least, he is the live inventory of the collection entrusted to him.

Two small rooms constitute the property room of the OMIKE and—as everything in this building—is impossibly crowded. In a systematic confusion, there can be found a thousand kinds of whatnot. It is impossible to give a perfect picture of this richness, but, as we looked around, we hastily noted the following things: crutches; the key of heaven; a real hurdy-gurdy; serious and toy musical instruments; mounted instruments; a photo camera; a whistling kettle; stuffed animals; artificial flowers; medical equipment; desk equipment; champagne buckets; a telephone; and mounted fruits in large variety and quantity, among them a real, vivid orange, which they guard with solicitous care so that it won't disappear from the stage during a scene. Also there are carefully packed umbrellas, swaddling clothes, and pacifiers for babies. A section of the corridor and the hall cloakroom are filled with a stack of furniture, among which we find a medical rack as well as a Rococo sofa and school bench.

The Invisible Actors

The technical components, the whole complex device, are directed by men. Above all of them is the director. The director's scope of activities is what the French call "maître de scène." He has a dual task: artistic and technical.

The artistic part is to set and to direct the piece. There is a piece, written scene by scene. He primarily determines the style, according to the age and the environment. He sets the groups and the movements. He checks if the actors interpret the text correctly.

The technical part of the director's task: designing the scenery that will reflect the spirit and style of the piece through discussion with the stage designer, who will also prepare the scenery. In the same spirit, the selection and lighting of furniture and accessories are discussed with the stage manager because the stage manager leads the performance on the basis of the director's setting. In theatrical language, the director's authority extends from the time of rehearsals to when the curtain rises. Supreme power is then transferred to the stage manager. He replaces the director and takes care of keeping his conceptions on everything. The director gives his instructions in writing to the stage manager, scenery officer,[1] lighting designer, and property man, the person in charge of the furniture, and to the theater hair stylist. The lighting designer, who also receives the "lighting bill," works together with the stage manager: light effects are switched on at the stage manager's waving. Furthermore, one of the most important tasks of the stage manager is to call actors to the stage at the right moment. At the beginning of the performance, the person in charge draws the curtain at the stage manager's signal. By contrast, at the end of the performance, the prompter will give the sign for the lowering of the curtain. At opera performances, it is the conductor, who gives the sign for the lowering of the curtain.

Mr. Benő Csillag, the Dear, Gray-Haired Stage Manager of the OMIKE

His biggest achievement is that he can manage 43 operas by heart, without a book. He can testify to the fact that it's not a cliché at all, that it is a special gift to be a good stage manager. When he was young, he was very excited. He wanted to be an actor, although they already predicted in acting school that he would become a stage manager. He didn't listen to the advice in the beginning but then he found his real profession. He's been a stage manager for 45 years, first in the countryside and since 1911 in the theaters of Budapest. He learns all the plays during rehearsals. He "doesn't hold anything in his hands" in the evening. At the first one or two performances, he might have a look at the director's instruction, just to be sure. At the *Varázsfuvola* (Magic Flute), for instance, which is a sixteen *nyílt-változásos*[2] opera, he alone does the work which is done by five persons at the Opera House.

The Prompter

He is one of the indispensable factors of the performance and is always present, starting from the first rehearsal. When actors read their lines he provides assistance. Of course, as the rehearsals advance, his role decreases.

Here, the prompter is also a tried and tested power: József Szilágyi, the retired prompter of the *Nemzeti Színház*. He's been a prompter for 44 years. He was at the *Nemzeti Színház* for 30 years. We ask him to reveal some workshop secrets of the intimacies of the prompter vocation. He is not willing to do it:

> When I had the 25th jubilee at the *Nemzeti Színház*, an editor came to see me and he also asked about the intimacies. I refused it at that time, too, because the internal secrets of the theater shouldn't be taken out to the public. My vocation is about one thing: the actor must know his role. How the prompter leads him is a question of conscience and experience. Because the prompter, who is really a prompter, can make everything good. I grew up in this and this is why I could succeed at the *Nemzeti Színház* for so long.

The Dressers

There are only two small dressing rooms available near the stage. One belongs to the ladies, the other to the men. At the performances where there are many actors involved, one or two offices have to be opened in the building of the religious community to serve as extra dressing rooms.

The Theater Tailor and Theater Hair Stylist

They are also tried and tested old experts who work in these dressing rooms.

Endre Friedmann, theater hair stylist, worked at the *Vígszínház* for a long time in this capacity and at other theaters, such as the *Fővárosi Operettszínház*, *Pódium Kabaré*, *Városi Színház*, and at different open-air performances at Margaret Island, Opatija, and Szeged. A good hairpiece contributes greatly to the success of the character role. He elaborates conception and design with the involvement of the director and the actor. Whether it will be perfect—and the audience in the Goldmark Hall knows it—depends on the hair stylist's skills and talent.

Sándor Gárdos, theater tailor, started his career at the *Népopera* (Folk Opera) in 1910. He is responsible for the preparation of costumes. Part of his everyday's hard work is "to make the actors appear decently" and give assistance in dressing, especially when they have to change clothes fast.

There has to be perfect harmony between the two fast and open-eyed female dressers of the women's dressing room. There is nothing more harmful than rivalry and jealousy. Thus it is great that two excellent sisters were found for this vocation, Margit and Lili Reich.

The artists sit in the dressing rooms long before the beginning of the performance or their appearance and carefully put their makeup on. Everybody has to know, at the OMIKE as well, how to put makeup on. Everybody has to know his or her own face and its defects, objectively, in order to correct them with makeup. They can only ask the hair stylist's assistance if a hairpiece needs to be prepared.

The Lighting Designer

Kálmán Rosenstein, lighting designer, started working in this profession at the Opera House 18 years ago. He was the chief lighting designer at the *Fővárosi Operettszínház* for a long time. He professionally explains with pleasure about the most expensive part of the theatrical equipment of the OMIKE, the value of which today is indeed priceless:

> The reflectors changing colors (which automatically change the color of light by gelatin sheets with appropriate colors) focus on one point or one person with the support of a condenser lens. The reflecting, fill-in lights throw white light on the whole stage. The reflectors of the accompanying lamps are set for one person and this way it is possible to accompany the actor's movement. These reflectors are one or two thousand watts. If the whole equipment is switched on, and the whole stage is filled with white light, then twelve thousand kilowatts of electricity is consumed.

The Stage Designer and the Scene-Painter

The stage designer of the OMIKE is the excellent painter, István Zádor. He has to read the piece as well, so that he can enter into its spirit. Then following the discussions with the director he draws his ideas. He draws pictorial scenery as he imagines it, that is, in perspective. Then he makes detailed drawings, precisely, according to the sizes, on the basis of which sceneric painting can be realized.

The stage has quite special requirements for perspective. The stage picture has to be produced in a way that it creates illusion, in accordance with the designer's idea, in the auditorium. The very specialized expert of this task is Ferenc Horn, scenery painter. After the skilled workers put the gridiron together and roughly prepare the material of the scenery, he paints the scenery according to the designer's images.

Preparing for the Show

One Day with the Actors of the OMIKE

A piece has to go a long and complicated way in the OMIKE theater from the moment it is selected for performance until the curtains rise for the first time to present it to the audience. The milestones of this difficult way are the rehearsals.

Ordinary Pieces

First of all, the piece, read through by the dramaturgist, is then passed to the director. The management and the director together assign the roles. Then the director holds the reading rehearsal. On this occasion, the actors familiarize themselves with their parts and because of this, even the actors having the smallest part or finishing the earliest or starting the latest must be present from the beginning until the end. The director's ideas, the ones found useful for the piece, are practiced in the roles at this rehearsal.

Following this, the next rehearsal is the preparatory rehearsal, where the director sets the play in detail. Walking, moving, sitting, and so on. At the same rehearsal, he explains the style of the play, the voice, the tone.

The memorizing rehearsals come next. At these rehearsals the roles gradually have to be known by heart. It is very important, because holding and reading the text can be an obstacle in many respects for the actors while performing. After an average of fifteen memorizing rehearsals, the play is performed well enough to have the full rehearsal. At this stage, the actors appear in masks and costumes. There is already full lighting and the incidental faults of the masks and costumes are corrected. Even before the full rehearsal, the director, independently from the actors, holds a scenery and lighting test. He checks at this time, whether the scenery prepared by the stage designer is appropriate and whether the setting of the lights requires any changes.

At these rehearsals, the stage manager is also present beside the director. He executes the director's instructions concerning the scenery, the furniture, the accessories, and the lighting and supervises the technical staff as well. This is how it goes in the theater of the OMIKE, too.

Opera Rehearsals

If the opera section is preparing for a premiere, the score and the piano recitation are given to the conductor. The reading rehearsal is replaced by the conductor and the director agreeing on the structure of the piece, even before learning it.

This is followed by the solo rehearsals. The conductor and the répétiteur start teaching the roles to the performers. This is the biggest difference compared to the prose. There, the actor has to learn himself at home and only gives an account in the theater of all that he has learned. When the singers are at the point that they can sing their part from the score, then the joint rehearsals begin. Here not just one person sings, but everybody sings the whole piece together. These joint rehearsals go on until the piece is impeccable. The performers go on stage only if this happens.

At the preparatory rehearsals, the conductor and the director decide the movements and positions in accord with the singing, while always taking the music as starting point. If they already know this, as well, then the memorizing rehearsals come next with the prompter. When they know the roles by heart, the rehearsals with the group follow, since the choir started learning simultaneously with the soloists under the supervision of the choir master. When the stage is set for the soloists, the choir joins. If the whole staff know their roles by heart, it means that the time of the music correcting rehearsals has arrived. At these events, only the orchestra is present with the conductor. If this is done, even before the full rehearsals, then there is a so-called sitting rehearsal. This means that there are only chairs on the stage for the performers and the choir. They go through the piece musically from the beginning to the end so that performers of the stage get used to the orchestral sound. Up to the sitting rehearsal, only piano accompanies the singers at all the rehearsals. Beginning at the stage memorizing rehearsal, one of the répétiteurs sits at the piano and the conductor directs. They start the full rehearsals in masks after the sitting rehearsal, and finally the public or private main rehearsal.

The preparatory work for operas takes longer time than for ordinary pieces. For thorough preparation of an opera performance, an average of two to three months is needed.

The répétiteur's main task is to teach, until the soloists learn the piece. In past years, the répétiteurs were: Sándor Vándor, Walter Lajtai-Lazarus, Péter Mura (Mandl), János Hajdu, and Gabriella Bártfai.

Orchestra and choir: On the occasion of an opera performance, the number of orchestra members varies between 32–40 depending on what the piece requires. It is also determined by the fact that the area in front of the stage can actually accommodate only 39 orchestra members and it is difficult to find space for the 40th person, if needed.

At a Morning Opera Rehearsal in Goldmark Hall

On the stage, there is symbolic scenery representing rocks, a little table, and one or two chairs. In front of the stage is a piano, and in front of it, a little girl: Gabi Bártfai. The score is on top of the piano. Vilmos Komor directs from it in shirtsleeves. At the bottom of the stage, also with a score and text, is Uncle Szilágyi, the prompter. In the first row of the auditorium, we can see a young man also with a score, who zealously conducts together with the conductor.

It is hot in the hall. Everybody blows and fans himself. Oszkár Kálmán arrives first. He came from farther, from Svab Hill. However, they are together within minutes: Relle, Ladányi, Sík, Fehér, Lendvay, Ernster, and the others. Komor waves, the piano can be heard, and the great singers start with full force. There is barely anything to correct. They have to repeat only few times. Komor, himself, sings on a nice, almost wine-tasting tone the parts of those missing. There is a sheet of paper in the hands of one of the young singers. He just got his role. He doesn't know his role yet and he hasn't fit into the ensemble. The prompter goes to him. Everybody is making the same effort to help him. Who is standing closest to him corrects his movements because each time he gets the knack of it, his right hand goes back and forth like a clock pendulum. He apologizes that he doesn't know the words yet, but they shouldn't worry. After tomorrow there won't be any problem, even if he won't be able to make it to the rehearsal tomorrow.

Ernő Szabolcs moves the most on the stage. He tirelessly comes and goes and gets out of the way. At this time, he is the only scenery designer. This is not preparation for a new piece. This piece was on a program a few times, during the season. Here artists, used to each other, are repeating, rehearsing, refining.

A scene is over. The conductor says the usual:

"Cigarette break!"

I ask one of the singers, who is in a hurry to light a cigarette: "Is it allowed to smoke at this time?"

He replies: "It is not allowed, but it is a must."

Notes on the Translation

1. He is in charge of setting and storing the scenery.
2. A special term for changing scenes openly in front of the audience without closing the curtains.

6

A Few Interesting Statistical Data

The Development of the Artistic Enterprise 1939–1943

Genre	Programs	Performances	Programs	Performances	Programs	Performances	Programs	Performances
Season	1939–1940		1940–1941		1941–1942		1942–1943	
Theatrical Comedies	12	75	14	76	14	116	23	164
Musicals	26	50	34	65	35	90	33	97
Total	38	125	48	141	49	206	56	261
No. of Visitors	40,000		60,000		80,000		92,000	

In the four seasons, altogether, 733 performances were held with 191 programs in front of an audience of 272,000.

The Most Successful Opera Performances

Eugen D'Albert: *Hegyek alján* (At the Bottom of the Mountains); G. Donizetti: *Don Pasquale, Lammermoori Lucia* (Lucia di Lammermoor); Nicolai: *A Windsori víg nők* (The Merry Wives of Windsor); J. Offenbach: *Hoffmann meséi* (Tales of Hoffmann); Verdi: *Aida, Rigoletto*; Beethoven: *Fidelio*; G. Bizet: *Carmen*; K. Goldmark: *Sába királynője* (The Queen of Sheba); R. Leoncavallo: *Bajazzók* (Pagliacci); Mozart: *Szöktetés a szerájból* (The Abduction from the Seraglio), *Varázsfuvola* (Magic Flute); Puccini: *Bohémélet* (La Bohème), *Pillangókiasszony*

(Madam Butterfly); Rossini: *Sevillai borbély* (Barber of Seville); Strauss: *Denevér* (The Bat); Verdi: *Traviata*, *Trubadur* (Troubadour), *Álarcosbál* (Masquerade).

Ballet

Robert Schumann: *Karnevál* (Carneval).

The Most Successful Among the Ordinary Pieces

1940–1941: F. Hebbel: *Judit* (Judith); Imre Fazekas: *Cirkusz* (Circus); Ernő Szép: Május (May); Lajos Bíró: *Álarcok* (Masks); Ferenc Molnár: *Játék a kastélyban* (Playing in the Castle); S. An-ski: *Dybuk* (Dybbuk).

1941–1942: Dezső Szomory: *Takács Alice*; Ferenc Molnár: *Marsall* (Marshal); Hugó Csergő: *Őszi szonáta* (Autumn Sonata); Elemér Boross: A nős ember (The Married Man); Jenő Mohácsi and Hugó Kelen: *A gyermek és a Messiás* (The Child and the Messiah); Racine: *Eszter* (Esther); Lajos Bálint: *Támár* (Tamar).

1942–1943: Ferenc Molnár: *Az ismeretlen lány* (The Unknown Girl); Béla Szenes: *A gazdag lány* (The Rich Girl); Ernő Szép: *Aranyóra* (Gold Watch); Ferenc Molnár: *Liliom* (Lily); Ibsen: *Vadkacsa* (Wild Duck).

Afterword to the English Edition

Jenő Lévai's book is an unrivaled document of its era. It's a screenshot in which he ultimately immortalizes performances, artists' portraits, and memory fragments of a bygone cultural age. He does it in a period when the threat is becoming tangible for the Hungarian Jews, but the final destruction has not yet arrived. The material on the OMIKE was dormant over many decades, until Magda Horák collected and published her work of great historical value.[1] Still, the only contemporary witness of OMIKE's forgotten history is this 1943 book, which was compiled with a reporter's consistency by Jenő Lévai, perhaps subconsciously feeling its significance. Being a musician, I have been primarily interested in OMIKE's music. Although the Artistic Enterprise (*Művészakció*) was of extraordinary importance in other areas too (theater, literature, visual arts, cabaret), the music part was of straight world-class quality for me. Here are just a few examples of artists who performed regularly on OMIKE's stage—the string players mostly as members of the orchestra: Annie Fischer, pianist; Viktor Ajtai-Adler, violinist (later the concertmaster of the Chicago Symphony Orchestra); Gábor Bánát (aka Gabriel Bánát), violinist (later the concert master of the New York Philharmonic Orchestra); cellist János Starker; violinist Alice Bárdos (chamber partner of Béla Bartók and member of the Waldbauer-Kerpely String Quartet); and Róbert Gerle, violinist, conductor and music professor (immigrated to US, where he started an orchestra program at University of Maryland Baltimore County and taught there for 20 years). To understand OMIKE's significance in that contemporary environment, let's look around in the areas of Nazi-occupied Europe in the thirties and forties.

One of the most important European Jewish cultural organizations, the Berlin Jüdischer Kulturbund, originally known as the Kulturbund Deutscher Juden, started its activity in 1933 as a result of the first actions of the Hitler regime. Using prominent Jewish artists who had been made redundant,[2] the Kulturbund managed to obtain 12,500 members of the 175,000-member Jewish Community in Berlin in just the first year. The number of members increased to 18,500 and stayed like that until September 11, 1941, when the association was banned.[3]

In Poland, the Jewish leader of the Lodz ghetto, Mordechai Chaim Rumkowski, organized a special cultural institution. The four hundred-seat Cultural House regularly produced concerts, revues, dance performances, and literary evenings.

The quality of the concerts was raised by employing their own symphonic orchestra.[4] One of the largest populations of urban Jews in Europe was in Warsaw. After November 1940, approximately 400,000 Polish Jews were forced into the Warsaw Ghetto. By the end of 1940, a full symphonic orchestra was founded, but in addition to this, five theaters, choirs, coffee houses, and concerts tried to make the terrible conditions bearable.[5] This cultural system was able to function until the summer of 1942. Then in July, the first transports to Treblinka started.

The ghetto in Riga was set up in October 1941. Among the prisoners were many Jewish artists and musicians. Besides the most essential tasks like hospitals and schools, the local Jewish Council organized cultural facilities. However, a major cultural life could not really develop because, in December 1941, in a forest near Riga, the Nazis liquidated almost the entire ghetto population. Afterwards, the Riga ghetto Jews, who were deported from Europe's large cities in 1943, could still organize theater and other cultural events with the artists who survived the first wave of liquidation.[6]

In Lithuania, by 1942, the Nazis with their Lithuanian helpers had murdered most of the Jewish population. The remaining Jews were placed in three major ghettos, Vilnius, Shavli, and Kovno. The orchestras formed in the ghettos of Kovno and Vilnius functioned between 1942 and 1944.[7]

The name of Terezin (Theresienstadt), today in the Czech Republic, was deservedly added to the chapters of the history of European music. In 1941, the Germans established a "model camp" in Theresienstadt for the purpose of misleading international organizations, such as the Red Cross. The Nazi propaganda films shot here were also distributed abroad. Although the Nazis hypocritically set up a real small Jewish town, a ghetto with a library, a theater, playgrounds, shops, and cafés, with lively cultural life, Theresienstadt was actually a transition concentration camp leading to the gas chambers of Auschwitz. Concerts, opera, and theater performances went back to back.[8] The camp operated two symphony orchestras and a string quartet as well. In September 1943, the final transportation of the residents of the concentration camp began. Among the many excellent musicians in the Czech music scene were a number of composers, Hans Krasa, Gideon Klein, Viktor Ullmann, Pavel Haas, Carlo Taube, and the Hungarian-born Franz Weisz. They were deported and killed in Auschwitz.[9]

In Transylvania between 1941 and 1944, in Kolozsvár (Cluj-Napoca), next to the Concordia Jewish Theater, was the Goldmark Philharmonic Music Association.[10] It was established in 1934 with the participation of 20–25 Jewish musicians and music lovers. The ever growing ensemble had 75 members by 1942.[11]

The delayed consequence of the Holocaust in Hungary made it possible that the OMIKE Artistic Enterprise, one of the unique social and cultural rescue enterprises of Europe's twentieth century, could operate in World War II the longest—until March 19, 1944—in Budapest. In Hungary, the number of Jews in Budapest, despite impairment of living space, discriminatory regulations, and persecution, did not decrease drastically, as opposed to those Jews deported from the rural areas who were almost completely exterminated by the end of the war. The life-threatening situation of Jews in Budapest only escalated at the end of the war, from October 1944 to January 1945. According to the first postwar census, out of the 165,330 Jewish survivors, 117,363 were from Budapest.[12] The capital's rate of survival (47.69 % survived), thus significantly exceeded that of the rural Jews (21.76 % survived).[13]

In the past history of the OMIKE association, founded in 1909, from the first year, world-renowned artists performed with excellence, such as Dávid Popper, cellist; Mari Jászai, actress; and Elza Szamosi, primadonna[14] at the Opera House; later Dezső Antalffy-Zsíros, Mária Basilides, József Szigeti, and Oszkár Beregi. Among its supporters, besides the names of Manfréd Weiss, the Baumgarten family, Baron Hatvani, and Baron Mór Herczog, we can also find the names of Archduke József and Count Tisza.[15] Initially, OMIKE events were organized in Budapest; later in several other parts of the country such as Békéscsaba and Tata.[16] Then in 1928, the first rural branch of OMIKE was founded in Debrecen.[17]

Later, in 1939, the music section of the Artistic Enterprise represented an opportunity for the best Jewish musicians to perform and thereby earn some money.[18] The Artistic Enterprise also helped needy artists and their family members to obtain medical treatment and medical supplies.[19] However, the greatest significance of the Artistic Enterprise was not these activities.

The artists who fell under the effect of the Numerus Clausus regulations and later the anti-Jewish laws were deprived of human dignity and prevented from displaying their talents. The employment of musicians displaced and forced to return home from the opera houses of Vienna, Berlin, Prague, Mannheim, Belgrade, Paris, and Brno and the artists who were laid-off from the *Magyar Királyi Operaház* (Hungarian Royal Opera House), *Városi Színház* (City Theater), *Vígszínház* (Comedy Theater), *Belvárosi Színház* (City Center Theater), *Magyar Színház* (Hungarian Theater), *Király Színház* (Royal Theater), *Fővárosi Operett Színház* (Budapest Operetta Theater), *Új Színház* (New Theater), *Művész Színház* (Artist Theater), *Renaissance Színház* (Renaissance Theater), *Kamara Színház* (Chamber Theater), *Bethlen-téri Színház* (Bethlen Square Theater), *Royal Orfeum* (Royal Music Hall), *Komédia Orfeum* (Comedy Hall), *Terézkörúti Színpad* (Teréz Boulevard Stage), and *Andrássy úti Színház* (Andrássy Road Theater)[20] initiated a busy cultural life in Budapest. Thus, even in the years of repression, they were still serving a universal culture. The Artistic Enterprise had its own orchestra, opera troupe, soloists, and choir. The opera troupe was directed by Vilmos Komor, the renowned conductor of the *Magyar Állami Operaház* (Hungarian State Opera House). Under his leadership, despite the circumstances, the opera performances organized in Goldmark Hall took place at a surprisingly high level. At one of the performances, they even managed to conjure a waterfall on the tiny stage.[21]

Some excellent singers who were trapped in Budapest, such as Dezső Ernster, Oszkár Kálmán, Gabriella Relle, Dávid Ney, Pál Fehér, and Annie Spiegel, regularly performed in various roles.[22]

In addition to Artisic Enterprise, there were in 1942–1943 a number of Jewish orchestras in which the artists could make a modest living.[23] The Religious Circles Orchestra in Budapest was formed from Budapest college students by Ferenc Koltai.[24] They rehearsed and played in the hall of the Jewish Community on Ernő Hollán Street. The Hungarian Jewish University and College Students' Association Orchestra (*A Magyar Izraelita Egyetemi és Főiskolai Hallgatók Országos Egyesületének*; MIEFHOE), led by György Rajter, performed in Goldmark Hall as well.[25] The orchestra, which was named "Symphonic Orchestra" (in fact "Anonymous Orchestra"),[26] was able to work until March 1944 thanks to the courageous stance of Vilmos Komor.[27]

Komor even instituted a season's ticket to buy for the Music Academy until January 1944.[28] The Hungarian premiere of Stravinsky's *Ragtime* is also associated with Vilmos Komor and the Symphonic Orchestra led by him.[29] The cimbalom (dulcimer) solo was played by Aladár Rácz, at the concert during which they presented *Weiner III. Divertimento*.[30] In April 1944, Pál Járdányi wrote praising criticism, which was a courageous act, since the article was published just after the German occupation. On Margaret Island, salon bands played in the clubs every summer. Many Jewish musicians could still play there for a small honorarium. First violinists of the salon bands were mostly students of Hubay.[31]

The short-lived Goldmark Music School was founded in 1943 in Budapest.[32] The first concert of the new Goldmark Music School was in February 1944.[33] It was the only music school in the area of Europe occupied or influenced by Nazis, where a number of Jewish teachers were allowed to teach from 1943. Six major faculties were launched, as well as instruction in all of the compulsory minor subjects. The staff consisted mainly of teachers of Jewish descent laid off from the Fodor Music School.[34] The teaching staff was able to teach there until March 19, 1944.

We can see what incredible cultural losses Hungary has suffered if we realize that a minimum of 170 well-known musicians were killed during the Holocaust in Hungary. This figure is probably much higher, of course, since the musicians in the countryside were far less documented than the ones in Budapest.[35] In 1944, its last year, OMIKE printed a four-page flyer, in which the management succinctly summarized OMIKE's 35 years of operation, including the activities of the Artistic Enterprise between 1939 and 1944.[36] According to this flyer, they managed to provide an opportunity to perform for 430 artists in 733 performances at several locations. The total audience number at the performances was 272,000 people. The *Képzőművészeti Csoport* (Fine Arts Group) acquired 95 works of art, thus alleviating the creators' financial concerns.[37] The Press Group's Yearbook was published in 10,000 copies. They employed 325 journalists who had been laid off because of their Jewish origins, and they published the work of five Jewish writers in 12,000 copies.[38]

After the war they tried to revive the OMIKE, but the artists were happy because of the liberation and most did not want to return to an "art ghetto." Initiatives for its maintenance slowly died away and the OMIKE was slowly forgotten.

List of Participating Artists in OMIKE's Musical Events (Opera, Concerts, Operetta)

A list was compiled on the basis of books and other information: Jenő Lévai, ed., *Írók, színészek, énekesek és zenészek regényes életútja a Goldmark-teremig. Az OMIKE színháza és művészei.* (The Illustrious Careers of Writers, Artists, Musicians Associated with Goldmark Hall: The Theatre and Artists of the OMIKE), Budapest, September 1943; Magda Horák: *OMIKE* (OMIKE); György Sándor Gál: *Atlantisz harangjai* (The Bells of Atlantis), Budapest, Móra Publisher, 1982; OMIKE Orchestral and Choral lists from the National Széchenyi Library Theater Archives; and the memories of Erzsébet Soltész (Mechler). For some artists, where it was possible to obtain data on their workplace before the OMIKE, which they had been forced to leave because of their descent, the place is marked in parentheses. The names of the artists who surely are victims of the Holocaust are marked in bold. Among the composers, conductors, pianists, and tutors, some names are listed more than once if they performed in different performances in different ways. For clarity, a victim's name is written in bold only the first time it appears. If the artist's instrument is uncertain, then the artist's name is marked by a question mark. The list includes the names of OMIKE's 46-member orchestra and the 30-member choir, too. The 100-member choir of the Collegicum Musicum from Szombathely also attended certain performances, but their names are not listed.

In assembling the list, participation in OMIKE concerts was a primary consideration. So among the members of the orchestra there are names of a few artists who, given their origins, had not been subject to the anti-Jewish laws. Nevertheless, they were employed by OMIKE as outsiders, because Jewish musicians were lacking certain groups of instruments such as the winds.

Composers

György Bondi , **Pál Budai**, **László Erdősi**, Géza Falk, László Feleki , Sándor Fischer, Oszkár Garami, Tibor Harsányi, Pál Kadosa, Hugó Kelen, Leó Kondor, **Walter Lajtai-Lazarus**, Alfréd Márkus, **Mihály Nádor**, Béla Reinitz, Sándor Reschovsky, István Szelényi, **László Weiner**, Leó Weiner, **Pál Zsigmondi**

Conductors

Dr. Ferenc Bermann (Brünn), György Bondi, László Erdősi, László Feleki (revue), Sándor Fischer (Vígszínház), Károly Fraknói (Városi Színház), János Hajdú, **László Káldi** (Városi Színház), Ferenc Koltai, Vilmos Komor, **Sándor Kuti**, Walter Lajtai-Lazarus, Alfréd Márkus, **Tivadar Pallós**, Pál Riesz (jazz), Miksa Róth, Frigyes Sándor, László Somogyi, **Imre (Buli) Szamosi** (jazz), László Weiner, Pál Zsigmondi (operetta)

Singers

József Abai (member of choir), Kefró Abai (member of choir), Lili Aschenfeld (member of choir), Mária Adorján (member of choir), József Ágoston (member of choir), István Balázs (operetta), **Béla Bálint** (Városi Színház), Kató Bán, Dóra Bársony, **István Basa** (member of choir), Miklós Bence (member of choir), Gabi Baumgarten (member of choir), Imre Bodor (member of choir), Hanna Brand (Berlin), **Harry Berky (Brenner)**, Györgyné Bruszt (member of choir), Ibolya Darvas (Városi Színház), Lili Dános, Lili Danziger (member of choir), Nándor Erdész (member of choir), Pál Érdi, Dezső Ernster (Berlin), Manó Essenfeld (member of choir), Ferenc Faludi (member of choir), Alice Farkas (member of choir), Sándor Farkas (member of choir, Magyar Királyi (M. Kir.) Operaház), Edith Fábri (member of choir), Sári Fábri, Ferenc Faludi (member of choir, secretary of the choir), Erna Faludi (member of choir) Panni Faragó (operetta), Rezső Feleki, Pál Fehér (Berlin), **Árpád Fenyő** (operetta), Márta Földiák (member of choir), Rocco Francati, Károly Füredi Vogel, Zoltán Gallay (member of choir), Ervin Galsay, Ernő Garay (Zürich), **Lajos Gárdonyi** (operetta), György Gerő (member of choir), Gidaly (jazz), Kató Gödry (Mannheim), **Dr. Pál Győri**, Péter Hajós (operetta), Ferenc Halasi (member of choir), Ferenc Halmágyi, Manci Herendi (whistle artist, as well), Ferenc Hidy, Imre Kara (member of choir), Oszkár Kálmán (M. Kir. Operaház, Berlin Opera), Árpád Keleti, Árpád Kishegyi, Kató Kornis (Belvárosi Színház), Miklós Kovács, Kató Kraszner (member of choir), Ilona Ladányi (M. Kir. Operaház)*, Klári Lakos (operetta), György Leitner, Béla Lénárd (operetta), Andor Lendvay (M. Kir. Operaház), Lenke Leopold (member of choir), Dezső Ligeti, Hanna Kolos, Erzsébet Mechler (member of choir), Sári Medák, László Molnár (member of choir), Márta Molnár (member of choir), **Dávid Ney II,** (M. Kir. Operaház), Pál Ortner (Volksoper Vienna), **Jenő Pál** (Prague), Blanka Pálffy (operetta), László Pogány, Zsuzsi Pogány, Sándor Pollák (member of choir), Ottó Presser (member of choir), Erzsi Radnai (Városi Színház), Mária Rajna, Tibor Rákos (operetta), Gabriella Relle (M. Kir. Operaház), Sándor Révész (member of choir), Vera Róna (member of choir), Magda Rosthy (Rosty) (actress, Belvárosi Színház), Ferenc Róth (Milano), Dezső Rovelli, Nándor Rózsa (member of choir), Vera Rózsa, Erna Rudas (member of choir), Jenő Sajó (member of choir), Aladár Sarkadi (operetta), **Miklós Salamon** (member of choir), Irén Sándor (member of choir), **Imre Sas** (operetta), Stefi Sebők (Városi Színház), Olga Sík (member of choir), Ili Simon (member of choir), dr. Jenő Sipos, Ibolya Solt, Dezső Somogyi (member of choir), István Somogyi, Piroska Somogyi (M. Kir. Operaház), Annie Spiegel (Berlin), László Spitzer (member of choir), Pál Sugár, Hédy Szécsi (operetta), Mária Szendrő (member of choir), **Dr. Jenő Szigeti** (Belvárosi Színház), Bea Szilágyi, **Vilmos Szirmai** (Városi Színház), Márton Sztáray (jazz), Gábor Szűcs, N. Takács (member of choir), Tivadar Tessler (Brünn), Béla Ormos (operetta), Lili Vajda (member of choir), Kató Váradi (operetta), Viola Vera (member of choir, Városi Színház), Ferike Vidor (actress, Belvárosi Színház), Márk Visó (member of choir), **György Weiner**, Miklós Weinstock, Lili Willmann, Kálmán Zátony, Magda Zsolt (jazz?), Irén Zoltán

* Ilona Ladanyi returned from a concentration camp with an illness that she suffered with until she died in Budapest in1952.

Cantors

Manó Abrahamson, Rezső Feleki, Béla Herskovits, Lajos Mandel

Piano

Tibor Adler, Magda Augenfeld, **Tibor Bálint**, Klári Benedikt, Méda Dános, **Jenő Deutsch**, Ede Donáth, **György Eiser**, László Erdősi, Edith Farnadi, Vera Fehér, Annie Fischer, Sándor Fischer, Pál Gergely (was conductor in Berlin), János Hajdú, György Halmos, Árpád Hanák, Lili Herz, Ági Jámbor, Pál Kadosa, Rózsi Kelen, Ferenc Koltai, Walter Lajtai-Lazarus, Péter Mura (Mandl), Pál Merényi, István Nádas, Tivadar Pallós, Lili Rauchwerger (Rév), Béla Reinitz, Sándor Reschovszki, Dr. Géza Ribáry, Renée Sándor, **Sándor Sammler**, Hedvig Schneider, György Sebők, **Ödön Tamás (Taubner)**, Imre Ungár, Anna Varjas

Flute

Dr. Tibor Inotai, Pál Pollák, Miklós Róth, Miklós Sonnenfeld

Oboe

György Bechar, Sándor Drechsler, Tibor Szeszler

Clarinet

György Brust (Bern), János Fekete, N. Gelber, Imre Palotai

Bassoon

György Ádám (Városi Színház), Tibor Brünauer, Frigyes Keleti (M. Kir. Operaház)

French Horn

Dezső Gross, Béla Sammler, István Székely

Trumpet

N. Galambos, Dezső Jávor, Zs. Sauer, József Szegedi, Gyula Vértes, Imre Zsoldos

Trombone

Ferenc Kalmár, Sándor Klein, N. Löwinger., József Róth, Béla Sammler

Violin

Viktor Ajtai-Adler, Ferenc Ákos, Gábor Bánát (Hirsch), **Alice Bárdos**, József Biró, Kató Bíró, István Faragó (Switzerland), Sándor Fejér, Elemér Gábori, **János Gál** (Paris), Róbert Gerle, Márta Göndör, Ferenc Heisler, **József Hirsch** (concert master, Városi Színház), Sándor Hirsch, Erzsi Hoffmann, Miklós Klein, Károly Klein, Imre Kovács, Imre Korvin, Edit Lőrincz, **István Mádai** (Városi Színház), Irén Pásztóné Meitner, **László Nád (Nadelstecher)**, **György Nádor**, Sándor Pesti, Pál Reisz, István Román, Gábor Rothfeld, **Jutka Schönfeld**, Imre Steiner (Városi Színház), Dr. Pál Solt, János Stern, Imre Steiner, **Zoltán Schultz,** Ilona Térő, György Tibor, **György Trietsch** (Városi Színház), Károly Vajna, László Vámos, Ruben Varga, Miklós Waldmann, Ákos Weinberg, József Weinberger, Jenő Zeitinger (?)

Violin and Viola

Pál Berdai, Tibor Berkovits, Endre Bolgár, László Halmos, László Klein, Pál Lukács, Béla Móri, László Rákos, György Tibor

Cello

Vera Dénes, Pál Hoffmann, **László Horváth** (Belgrade), **Pál Hütter** (M. Kir. Operaház), Tibor Kálmán, Pál Kenessey, András Mihály, János Starker, János Valér

Bass

László Lengyel, Vilmos Pilitz, Imre Róth, István Weinberger

Harp

Gyula Revere

Accordion

Ottó Kállai

Percussion

N. Goldmann, Ármin Grünfeld, István Silber, László Trumen

Saxophone

Imre (Buli) Szamosi

Coaches

Gabriella Bártfai, János Hajdu, László Káldi, Ferenc Koltai, Vilmos Komor, Walter Lajtai-Lazarus, Péter Mura (Mandl), Dr. Géza Ribáry, **Sándor Vándor**

Thus, Lévai's book, written in 1943, provides unique interviews with the individual artists whom recall their early lives and the circumstances that led them to join the Artistic Enterprise. Lévai's portraits deftly involve the reader in the struggles and lives of each of the artists.

The book records the technical functioning, structure, and operation of this remarkable theater and concert venue, under conditions of duress and persecution. It gives a unique perspective on how such a theater was run more than seventy years ago, by providing fascinating details about those who worked behind the scenes, such as répétiteurs and hair stylists, as well as personnel involved with costumes, lighting, and scenery.

In addition, this expanded and supplemented English version of Lévai's classic 1943 book further presents the memorable contributions of the OMIKE Artistic Enterprise to a much larger, English-language readership of academics, art history students and theater history students, aspiring artists, and those interested in learning about the losses to culture and Hungarian Jewry due to the Holocaust. It enhances the original edition by providing the reader with the following supplemental material:

- New, additional Foreword by Magda Horák, prominent historian and writer on the OMIKE (1909–1944) and the OMIKE *Művészakció* (Artistic Enterprise) (1939–1944)
- Historical introduction by István Deák, Professor Emeritus (Columbia University), which gives an overall historical setting of Hungarian Jewry and the OMIKE *Művészakció.*
- Afterword, by Peter Barsony, which contributes further information on the musicians and singers of the OMIKE *Művészakció* and other groups of Jewish artists who functioned during the Holocaust era.
- Complete identification of OMIKE *Művészakció* orchestra musicians with their instruments
- Complete identification of OMIKE *Művészakció* choir members

- Comprehensive identification of those artists who perished in the Holocaust
- Appendix of photographs of Goldmark Hall, OMIKE *Művészakció* performances and OMIKE *Művészakció* artists. Such photos place faces to the names of the artists, their presentations, and their venue
- Appendix of reproductions of programs of the Artistic Enterprise for plays, concerts, operas, cabaret, and operettas
- Appendix of reproductions of announcements for fine arts exhibitions of painters, graphic artists, and sculptors with a full listing of one exhibition
- Glossary
- Bibliography
- Index

Hence, it is hoped that this book will provide a fitting testimony to all the devoted artists and others who were a part of this most notable OMIKE *Művészakció*.

Notes

1. *"Ősi hittel, becsülettel a hazáért!"* ("With Ancient Faith and Honor for Our Homeland!"), *OMIKE Országos Magyar Izraelita Közművelődési Egyesület* (National Hungarian Jewish Cultural Association) 1909–1944, edited by Magda Horák, (Budapest: Háttér Kiadó, 1998).
2. In the first season there were 35 actors and singers, 35 orchestra musicians, 22 choir singers and 10 dancers. See Lily E. Hirsch, *The Berlin Jüdischer Kulturbund, Music and the Holocaust*, http://holocaustmusic.ort.org.
3. Lily E. Hirsch, *The Berlin Jüdischer Kulturbund, Music and the Holocaust*, http://holocaustmusic.ort.org.
4. Gila Flam, "Songs of the Łódź Ghetto," *Music and the Holocaust*, http://holocaustmusic.ort.org/places/ghettos/lodz/.
5. "Warsaw," *Music and the Holocaust*, http://holocaustmusic.ort.org/places/ghettos/warsaw/.
6. "Riga," *Music and the Holocaust*, http://holocaustmusic.ort.org/places/ghettos/riga/.
7. "Kovno," *Music and the Holocaust*, http://holocaustmusic.ort.org/places/ghettos/kovno/.
8. Thomas Schinköth, *Jüdische Musiker in Leipzig. 1855–1945* (Altenburg: Kamprad, 1994), 256.
9. Except for Gideon Klein. He was taken to Fürstengrub and killed there a few weeks after his 25th birthday.
10. Moshe Carmilly-Weinberger, *A zsidóság története Erdélyben 1923–1944* [The History of the Jews in Transylvania 1923–1944] (Budapest: MTA Judaism Research Group, 1995), 254.
11. Jewish Symphonic Orchestra in Kolozsvar, in *Múlt és Jövő* [Past and Present] (1941), 160.

12. Viktor Karády, "Zsidóság Budapesten a 20. Század első felében" [Jews in Budapest in the First Half of the 20th Century], http://www.karadyviktor.uni.hu/.
13. Randolph Braham, *A népirtás politikája. A holokauszt Magyarországon. II. Kötet* [The Politics of Genocide: The Holocaust in Hungary], Vol. 2 (Budapest: Belvárosi Publisher, 1997), 1249.
14. *Cultur-Almanach*, 1910, 123–56, qtd. in Horák, *OMIKE,* 47.
15. Ibid., 48.
16. *Egyenlőség* [Equality], March 27–28, 1926; qtd. in Horák: *OMIKE*, 198.
17. Horák: *OMIKE*, 217.
18. See "List of Participating Artists in OMIKE's Music Events (Opera, Concerts, Operetta)," given at the end of this afterword.
19. OSZK Theatre History Collection, OMIKE documents, Laszlo Bánóczi letter, February 10, 1942.
20. *Magyar Zsidók Lapja* [Hungarian Jews' Journal], February 25, 1943, qtd. in Horák: *OMIKE,* 494–95.
21. Courtesy of Ágnes Komor, June 11, 2009.
22. Horák, *OMIKE*, 319, 287, 298, 303.
23. Courtesy of Tamás Lóránd, June 11, 2009.
24. Ibid.
25. Ibid.
26. Tibor Tallián, *László Weiner, 1916–1944* (Budapest, 1994), 11.
27. Pál Járdányi, "Koncertkritka" [Concert Critic], in *Forrás* [Source] 2, no. 4 (April, 1944): 91.
28. Tibor Tallián, *László Weiner, 1916–1944* (Budapest, 1994), 11.
29. Pál Járdányi, "Koncertkritka," 91.
30. Ibid.
31. Péter Bársony, interview with György Korányi, Budapest, June 25, 2009.
32. *Magyar Zenei Almanach* [Hungarian Music Almanac], edited by Viktor Papp (Budapest: Edition of Fráter György Cooperative Press, 1944), 257.
33. *A Magyar Zsidók Lapja* [Hungarian Jews' Journal], February 10, 1944.
34. Ernő Fodor did not dismiss all Jewish teachers during 1942–1943, as George Garai was still among the teachers (See *Hungarian Music Almanac*, edited by Viktor Papp, 257). Probably according to the percentage specified in the anti-Jewish law they could remain on the teaching staff.
35. Péter Bársony, *A vészkorszak magyar muzsikus áldozatai* [The Hungarian Holocaust Musician Victims], 2011 doctoral dissertation, Franz Liszt Academy of Music.
36. Horák, *OMIKE*, 572.
37. Through the courtesy of Magda Horák (February 3, 2010) we know that the list provided, as a disclosure, is not complete.
38. The special Jewish Yearbook was published by OMIKE's Artist Enterprise (Action) with its serious literature left out. Among them was the work of Mihály András Rónai, Antologia Coacta (Collection of Western European Poets and Writers), which he translated and compiled between his terms in the Forced Labor Services.

Péter Bársony
Franz Liszt Academy of Music, Budapest
June 2014

Acknowledgments to the English Edition

The many years that it took to compile and edit this expanded book on the OMIKE *Művészakció* has made me grateful to innumerable persons who helped me in this effort. So at the outset, I ask the forgiveness of anyone who I may have inadvertently omitted.

First of all, I thank, herein and in my prayers, my dear, recently departed wife, Joan, who graciously encouraged me and allowed me the time to pursue this project and bring it to fruition.

My extreme gratitude goes to Mr. Zvi Erenyi, Librarian at Yeshiva University, who helped me to compile and edit this book and who supplied me with his thoughtful insight and dedication since its inception. Also my gratitude goes to Ms. Anna Etawo who diligently translated both the original Lévai text and foreword from Hungarian to English and who spent many hours to faithfully followup on subsequent details.

My gratitude also goes to the staff of my publisher, Purdue University Press, who saw the worthiness of this book, and to my excellent copy-editor, Dianna Gilroy, who worked diligently on it and also helped to bring it to fruition, as well as to others for their encouragement, such as Peter Froehlich, Bryan Shaffer, Katherine Purple, and Becki Corbin. I also thank series editor Zev Garber.

None of this effort would have been possible had I not been given the permission of the four successors (copyright holders) of Jenő Lévai's 1943 book to engage in this effort. So I offer my sincere thanks to Dr. Illés Dési and his wife, Anikó; Arnold P. Krammer, History Professor at Texas A & M; and Mr. Steven L. Krammer. I also thank Dr. Péter B. Tóth and Dr. Klaudia F. Fodor, of the Artisjus Hungarian Bureau for the Protection of Authors' Rights, for supplying me with the names of the above four individuals.

My profound thanks to:

- Magda Horák, noted OMIKE historian and writer who wrote the foreword that gives further insight to the subject material. She is also the editor of the authoritative book on the OMIKE,

Ősi hittel, becsülettel a hazáért: OMIKE, Országos Magyar Izraelita Közművelődési Eyesület, 1909–1944 (With Ancient Faith and Honor for the Homeland), which contains an introduction and chronological and assorted cultural documents of the OMIKE and OMIKE *Művészakció*.

- István Deák, Seth Low Professor Emeritus of History at Columbia University, who wrote the introduction that provides the historical context of the Jews in Hungary leading up to the OMIKE *Művészakció* and to Randolph L. Braham, Distinguished Professor Emeritus of History at the City University of New York Graduate Center, for granting his permission to use certain material used in this introduction. Professor Deák and Professor Braham are renowned authors of numerous books and articles on Hungarian history and the Holocaust.
- Péter Bársony, Viola Professor at the Franz Liszt Academy of Music in Budapest, who wrote the afterword, which further elaborates on Lévai's original book and the musicians of the OMIKE *Művészakció*. Dr. Bársony is a noted violist who tours with concerts throughout the world and who performed at the major 2008 concert, "In Memoriam: Hungarian Composers, Victims of the Holocaust."

In preparing the photograph section and playbill (program) section, numerous persons associated with archives, theater collections, institutes, and museums, as well as individuals helped me to assemble this material and I offer them my thanks. Among them are Dr. Ildikó Sirató, Head of the National Széchényi Library Theater Collection and her devoted librarians, Ms. Magdolna Both and Ms. Lujza Erdéyi; Dr. Piroska Ács, Director of the Hungarian Theater Museum and Institute, and her dedicated staff, Ms. Mariann Sipőcs and Ms. Ágnes Takács, as well as Dr. Tamás Gajdó, Hungarian theater historian and noted writer, also of this institute; Ms. Nora Wellmann, Director of the Archives at the Hungarian State Opera; Dr. Beatrix Lengyel, Head of the Historical Photo Department of the Hungarian National Museum; Dr. Mária Béres of the Koszta József Museum; Dr. László Horváth and Ms. Katalin Gulyás of the Damjanich János Museum, Szolnok; Ms. Ágnes Balasi of the Petőfi Irodalmi Múzeum, Department of Fine Arts; Dr. Zsuzsanna Toronyi, Director of the Hungarian Jewish Museum and Archives; and Mr. Tom Beck, Chief Curator, and Ms. Susan Graham of the University Archives, Special Collections, University of Maryland, Baltimore County. Among individuals who kindly supplied photographs are Dr. Illés Dési, actress Zsuzsa Simon (of blessed memory), conductor Iván Fischer, Dr. Péter Bársony, Magda Horák, Ms. Anna Sándor, Ms. Éva Kuti, and Mr. Meir Szegedi. Also, a valuable source of photographs of many artists was the website of the Nonprofit *Társadalomkutató Egyesület* (NTE). Mr. László Harsányi, who was instrumental in helping to create this site, was so kind as to provide me with the provenance of a number of its photos.

On photographs, most of them over 70 years old, Mr. Ralph Guggenheim kindly spent countless hours to enhance the quality of their digital images. Mr. David Kostiner, Esq., of Counsel LLP, also spent many hours doing research and providing advice on the legal status of and my ability to use numerous photos. Mr. Geörgy Tamáska deserves thanks for contacting persons in Budapest to get their permission for me to use certain photos.

During this endeavor many persons, including university historians, authors, musicians, religious figures, and directors of theater archives, institutes, and museums have offered me moral support and encouragement through their letters testifying to the worthiness of this project. Among them, to whom I express my gratitude, are:

- Distinguished History Professor Emeritus Randolph L. Braham, City University of New York Graduate Center, New York
- Seth Low Professor Emeritus of History István Deák, Columbia University, New York
- History Professor László Karsai, University of Szeged, Hungary
- Professor Attila Pók, Deputy Director, Hungarian Academy of Sciences, Research Center for the Humanities, Institute of History, Budapest, Hungary
- History Professor Arnold P. Krammer, Texas A&M University, College Station, TX
- Former US Ambassador to Austria Ronald S. Lauder, New York
- Ms. Fruma Mohrer, Senior Archivist, YIVO Institute for Jewish Research, New York
- Medieval Hebrew Literature and Jewish Bibliography Professor Emeritus Menachem Schmelzer, The Jewish Theological Seminary, New York
- Dr. Ildikó Siratό, Head of the National Széchényi Library Theater Collection, Budapest, Hungary
- Rabbi Angela W. Buchdahl, Senior Rabbi, Central Synagogue, New York
- Rabbi Peter J. Rubinstein, Sr. Rabbi Emeritus, Central Synagogue, New York
- Maestro Iván Fischer, founder of the Budapest Festival Orchestra, Hungary
- Dr. Zahava Stessel, historian and author of *Wine and Thorns in Tokay Valley*, and other books and articles in Hungarian, Hebrew, and English pertaining to the Holocaust in Hungary, Brooklyn, NY

- Dr. Piroska Ács, Director of the Hungarian Theater Museum and Institute, Budapest, Hungary
- Dr. Gavriel Bar-Shaked, historian and editor of the series *Nevek* (Names), recording those lost or affected by the Hungarian Holocaust, Yad Vashem, Israel
- Dr. Anna Szalai, author, literary researcher and editor of *In the Land of Hagar: The Jews of Hungary: History, Society and Culture*, Kiryat Ono, Israel

Aside from the proofreading of the book done by Mr. Zvi Erenyi and me, I thank Mary Ann and Robert Gray for careful reading of the text and numerous comments. Thanks also to Ms. Judit Harsas for her translation of several pages and helping with the index. I'm grateful to Dr. Ildikó Sirató and Dr. Tamás Gajdó for their corrections and comments on the glossary. Also, I commend Richard White, Professor of Semitic Languages, at Yeshiva University, for his useful comments on text, publishing, and other areas of this book.

Frederick Bondy
New York, 2016

APPENDIX 1

Photographs of Goldmark Hall, Performances, and OMIKE Artists

The names of the artists who were victims of the Holocaust are marked in bold. In the photo credits, the Theater History Collection at the Hungarian National Széchényi Library is abbreviated as HNL ThC, the Archives of the Hungarian State Opera as AHSO, the Nonprofit *Társadalomkutató Egyesület* (www.omike.hu) as NTE, the Hungarian National Museum as HNM, the Music Collection at the Hungarian National Széchényi Library as HNL MC, and the Hungarian Theater Museum and Institute as HTMI.

Notable Figures and Images

Figure 1. Károly Goldmark (1830–1915), composer, for whom Goldmark Hall is named. Courtesy of AHSO. Photographer Carl Jagerspacher, ca. 1890.

Figure 2. OMIKE logo. Source: *Művészakció* playbills, 1939–1944. Courtesy of HNL ThC.

Figure 3. Jenő Lévai (1892–1983), journalist, historian. Editor of original 1943 OMIKE *Művészakció* book. Courtesy of his nephew, Dr. Illés Dési. Photographer and date unknown.

OMIKE *Művészakció* Leaders

Figure 4. Géza Ribáry (1889–1942), lawyer and amateur pianist. OMZSA *Évkönyv* (Yearbook) 5703 (1942–1943) (Budapest: Oszágos Magyar Zsidó Segíto Akció, 1943), frontispiece.

Figure 5. László Bánóczi (1884–1945), director, playwright. Courtesy of HNL ThC, KA 5873/1. Photographer unknown, ca. 1928.

Figure 6. Lajos Bálint (1886–1974), writer, dramaturg. Magda Horák, *Ősi hittel, becsülettel a hazáért! OMIKE 1909–1944* (Budapest: Háttér Könyvkiadó, 1998).

OMIKE *Művészakció* Conductors, Composers, and Opera Singers

Figure 7. Vilmos Komor (1895–1971), conductor. Courtesy of AHSO. Unknown photographer, ca. 1930s.

Figure 8. Oszkár Kálmán (1887–1971), opera singer. Magda Horák, *Ősi hittel, becsülettel a hazáért! OMIKE 1909–1944* (Budapest: Háttér Könyvkiadó, 1998).

Figure 9. **László Weiner** (1916–1944), composer, conductor. Courtesy of NTE.

Figure 10. **Dávid Ney II**, (1905–1945), opera singer. Courtesy of AHSO. Ney as Siegmund in *Walkure*; Budapest Opera House, 1932. Photographer Pál M. Vájda.

OMIKE *Művészakció* Starring Actors and Comedians

Figure 11. Oszkár Beregi (1876–1965), opera singer, stage manager. Sándor Hunyady, *A Vígszínház negyven éve* (Budapest: Athenaeum Irodalmi és Nyomdai Rt., 1936). 32.

Figure 12. **Lajos Gárdonyi** (1896–1945), actor, comedian. Courtesy of HNL ThC, KA IX.31. Photographer Pál Kis, ca. 1928.

Figure 13. Imre Ráday (1905–1983), actor. German postcard by Ross Verlag, no. 1907/1, Berlin 1927–28. Photo: UFA.

Figure 14. Sándor Rott (1868–1942), actor, director. *Magyar Színházművészeti Lexikon.* Budapest: Akademiai Kiadó, 1994. Photo inscribed 1923.

Figure 15. Béla Salamon (1885–1965), actor, comedian. Róbert Füzesi, *Színház az árnyékban* (Budapest: KO-LIBRI Könyvkiadó, 1990). Photo inscribed 1933.

Figure 16. Aladár Sarkadi (1874–1949), actor, comedian. Sándor Hunyady, *A Vígszínház negyven éve* (Budapest: Athenaeum Irodalmi és Nyomdai Rt., 1936). 33.

OMIKE *Művészakció* Starring Singers

Figure 17. Kató Bán (?–?), opera singer. Courtesy of HNL ThC, KA 9474/1. Photographer unknown, Jan. 13, 1962.

Figure 18. Dezső Ernster (1898–1981), opera singer. Courtesy of the Petőfi Irodalmi Múzeum, Photo Archives, Budapest, Inv. no. 11241. Photographer G. D. Hackett, date unknown.

Figure 19. Pál Fehér (1900–1959), opera singer. Courtesy of NTE. Berlin State Opera photo. Photographer Sus Byk. Berlin, ca. 1930.

Figure 20. Kató Gödry (1900–1984), opera singer. Magda Horák, *Ősi hittel, becsülettel a hazáért! OMIKE 1909–1944* (Budapest: Háttér Könyvkiadó, 1998).

Figure 21. Vera Rózsa (1917–2010), opera singer. Ilona Kovács, *Egy ismeretlen zenekritikus: Weiner László zenei jegyzetei 1934 ből* (Budapest: Zenetudmányi Konferencia, 2014). www.ztu.hu.

Figure 22. Sándor Farkas (1888–1970), opera singer. Courtesy of AHSO. Photo signed 1932. Photographer Pál M. Vájda.

OMIKE *Művészakció* Prominent Musicians

Figure 23. Annie Fischer (1914–1995), pianist. http://www.bibl.u-szeged.hu/ha/muzsika/fisher.html. 1933.

Figure 24. Róbert Gerle (1924–2005), violinist, conductor. Courtesy of University Archives, Special Collections, University of Maryland, Baltimore County, UARC. Photographer unknown, 1974.

Figure 25. Lily Herz (1909–?), pianist. Narodowy Instytut Fryderka Chopina. http://www.parlando.hu/2014/2014-3/2014-Szuletesi.htm. 1932.

Figure 26. **László Horváth** (?–1944), cellist. Miklós Szász, brochure, *Koncertdirektion: Saison 1931–32* (Budapest, 1931).

Figure 27. Pál Lukács (1919–1981), violinist, singing coach. Courtesy of NTE. Zeneakadémia Library.

Figure 28. János Starker (1924–2013), cellist. *Fényszóró* (Spotlight) 1, no. 18, Nov. 20, 1945, 16. Courtesy of HNL ThC.

OMIKE *Művészakció* Actresses, Dancers, and Ballet Masters

Figure 29. Ibolya Darvas (1910–1990), actress, opera singer. Magda Horák, *Ősi hittel, becsülettel a hazáért! OMIKE 1909–1944* (Budapest: Háttér Könyvkiadó, 1998).

Figure 30. Hédy Hidas (1915–2011), dancer, ballet master. Courtesy of NTE. Photographer unknown.

Figure 31. Anna Pallay (1890–1970), dancer, dance teacher. Courtesy of AHSO. Photographer unknown, ca. 1920s.

Figure 32. Magda Rosty (1909–1984), actress. Róbert Füzesi, *Színház az árnyékban* (Budapest: KO-LIBRI Könyvkiadó, 1990).

Figure 33. Zsuzsa Simon (1910–1996), actress, director. Róbert Füzesi, *Színház az árnyékban* (Budapest: KO-LIBRI Könyvkiadó, 1990).

Figure 34. Ferike Vidor (1889–1970), actress. Wikimedia Commons, ca. 1910.

OMIKE *Művészakció* Composers and Conductors

Figure 35. **György Bondi** (?–1944), composer, conductor. Courtesy of NTE.

Figure 36. Sándor Fischer (1900–1995), composer, conductor. Courtesy of his son, conductor Iván Fischer. Photographer and date unknown.

Figure 37. Pál Kadosa (1903–1983), composer, pianist. Courtesy of AHSO. Amateur snapshot by unknown photographer, ca. 1940s.

Figure 38. Hugó Kelen (1888–1956), composer. Imre Molnár, *A magyar muzsika könyve* (Budapest: Merkantil-nyomda, 1936). 568.

Figure 39. **Sándor Kuti** (1908–1945), composer, conductor. Courtesy of his daughter, Éva Kuti. Photographer unknown, ca. early 1940s.

Figure 40. László Somogyi (1907–1988), conductor. Courtesy of AHSO. Photographer unknown, ca. 1950s.

OMIKE *Művészakció* Directors, Writers, and Actors

Figure 41. **Artúr Lakner** (1893–1944), theater manager, writer, film dramaturg. Magda Horák, *Ősi hittel, becsülettel a hazáért! OMIKE 1909–1944* (Budapest: Háttér Könyvkiadó, 1998).

Figure 42. **Sándor Vándor** (1901–1945), répétiteur/ singing coach, composer. Courtesy of HNM, Budapest, P_77.122. Photographer unknown, ca. 1930s.

Figure 43. **György Nagy** (1905–1945), actor, writer, director. Courtesy of HNL ThC, KA 4411/19. Photographer Rudolf Iritz, Szeged, ca. 1929, dedicated 1931.

Figure 44. **Miklós Harsányi** (1894–1944/45), director, actor. Courtesy of HNL ThC, NSZ KB H130, Rutkai and Vitkay. Photo ca. 1917.

Figure 45. **Hugó Csergő** (1877–1944), writer, journalist. Benedek Marcell, ed. *Magyar Irodalmi Lexikon.* 3 vols. (Budapest: Akadémiai Kiadó, 1963–1965), 211.

Figure 46. Lajos Gellért (1885–1963), actor, director. Magda Horák, *Ősi hittel, becsülettel a hazáért! OMIKE 1909–1944* (Budapest: Háttér Könyvkiadó, 1998).

OMIKE *Művészakció* Writers, Playwrights, and Poets

Figure 47. Elemér Boross (1900–1971), poet, playwright. *Fényszóró* (Spotlight) 2, no. 4, Jan.22, 1946, 9. Archived in HNL ThC.

Figure 48. Dezső Kellér (1905–1986), writer, dramaturg, humorist. Magda Horák, *Ősi hittel, becsülettel a hazáért! OMIKE 1909–1944* (Budapest: Háttér Könyvkiadó, 1998).

Figure 49. **Jenő Mohácsi** (1886–1944), poet, writer. Courtesy of HNM, P_2627/1951fk. Photographer Pál M. Vájda, ca. early 1930s.

Figure 50. **Károly Pap** (1897–1945), playwright, writer. Courtesy of the Petőfi Irodalmi Múzeum, Photo Archives, Budapest, Inv. no. 3130. Photographer and date unknown.

Figure 51. Ernő Szép (1884–1953), writer, poet. Sándor Hunyady, *A Vígszínház negyven éve* (Budapest: Athenaeum Irodalmi és Nyomdai Rt., 1936). 67.

Figure 52. **Dezső Szomory** (1869–1944), playwright, writer. Sándor Hunyady, *A Vígszínház negyven éve* (Budapest: Athenaeum Irodalmi és Nyomdai Rt., 1936). 19.

OMIKE *Művészakció* Painters, Graphic Artists and Sculptors

Figure 53. **Imre Ámos** (1907–1945), surrealist painter. *A Magyar Nemzeti Digitális Archívum*, www.100hires.hu /cikkek/amos-imre.

Figure 54. **György Goldmann** (1904–1945), sculptor. Courtesy of HNM, P_ 76.997. Photographer Márta Rédner, 1940.

Figure 55. **Bertalan Göndör** (1908–1945), painter, graphic artist. Courtesy of HNM, P_88.871. Photographer M. Hollós, ca. late 1930s.

Figure 56. **István Örkényi-Strasszer** (1911–1944), sculptor. Courtesy of the Koszta József Múzeum, Szentes, Hungary, Inv. No. 2015.34.1.1. Photographer and date unknown.

Figure 57. Lajos Vajda (1908–1941), painter and graphic artist. *Wikipedia*. 1939.

Figure 58. István Zádor (1882–1963), painter and graphic artist. Courtesy of Damjanich János Múzeum, Szolnok, Hungary, T3052-A. Photographer Aladár Székely, ca. 1940.

OMIKE *Művészakció* Artists Murdered in the Holocaust

Figure 59. György Ádám (?–1944/45), bassoonist. Imre Molnár, *A magyar muzsika könyve* (Budapest: Merkantil-nyomda, 1936). 525.

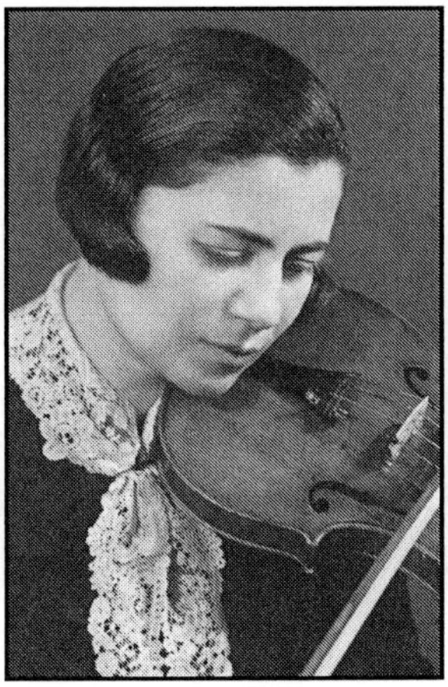

Figure 60. Alice Bárdos (1896–1944), violinist. Courtesy of HNL MC, Bárdos Alice 1/1. Photographer Juci Laub, 1935.

Figure 61. Tibor Adler (1905–1944), pianist, organist. Imre Molnár, *A magyar muzsika könyve* (Budapest: Merkantil-nyomda, 1936). 525.

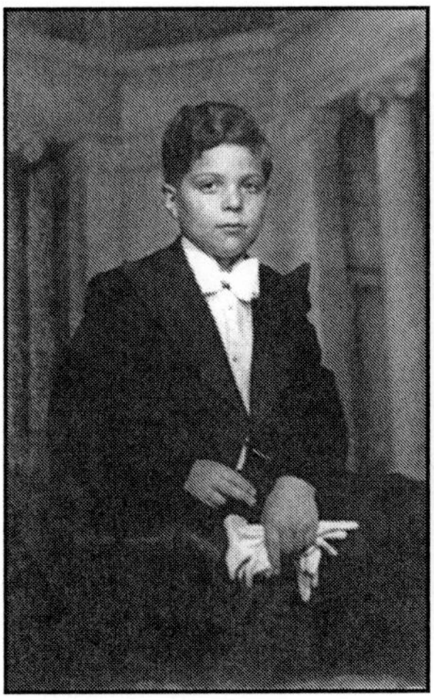

Figure 62. Harry Berky (1928–1945), child actor. Courtesy of HTMI, Photo Archive, Budapest. Photographer unknown, ca. late 1930s.

Figure 63. István Bondy (1905–1944), actor. Sándor Hunyady, *A Vígszínház negyven éve* (Budapest: Athenaeum Irodalmi és Nyomdai Rt., 1936). 58. Photographer unknown.

Figure 64. Lajos Ékes Csabai (1896–1944), painter, graphic artist. Courtesy of NTE. Photographer unknown.

OMIKE *Művészakció* Artists Murdered in the Holocaust

Figure 65. Viktor Erdei (1879–1945), painter, graphic artist, sculptor. Courtesy of NTE. Photo caption 1937.

Figure 66. Zsuzsa Földi (1924–1944), actress. Courtesy of HTMI, Photo Archive. Photographer unknown, 1942.

Figure 67. Béla Bálint (1887–1944/45), opera singer. Courtesy of HNL ThC, KA 3775/1. Photographer József Kossak, inscribed August 20, 1911.

Figure 68. József Gonda (1901–1944), actor. Courtesy of HNL ThC, KA 5211/1. Áldor Fotószalon, ca. 1930.

Figure 69. Zoltán "Zoli the Clown" Hirsch (1885–1944/45), actor, comedian, circus clown. Courtesy of NTE.

Figure 70. Dr. Pál Győri (1890–1944/45), singer. Courtesy of HNL MC, Győri Pál 101/1; Rónai photo, ca. 1920.

OMIKE *Művészakció* Artists Murdered in the Holocaust

Figure 71. Pál Hütter (?–1944), cellist. *Fényszóró* (Spotlight) 2, no. 1, Jan. 1946, 9. Archived in HNL ThC.

Figure 72. Imre Sas (1902–1944), actor. Courtesy of his son, József Sas. Photographer unknown, 1939.

Figure 73. Géza Steinhardt (1873–1944), comedian. Merkantil Ny, *Ötven Víg Esztendő* (Budapest, 1942). Frontispiece. Photographer unknown.

Figure 74. Imre "Buli" Szamosi (1908–1944), jazz altosaxaphonist. Géza Gábor Simon, *Magyar Jazztörténet* (Budapest: Jazzkutátasi Társaság, 1999). 114. Photographer unknown.

Figure 75. Hédy Szécsi (1917–1944), actress. Courtesy of HTMI, Photo Archive. Photographer M. Reményi, ca. 1930s.

Figure 76. Vilmos Szirmai (1890–1944), comedy actor. Courtesy of HTMI, Photo Archive. Photographer Veres, 1933.

OMIKE *Művészakció* Artists Who Survived the Holocaust

Figure 77. Gábor Bánát (1926–2016), violinist. *Fényszóró* (Spotlight) 1, no. 18, Nov. 20, 1945, 16. Archived in HNL ThC. Photographer unknown.

Figure 78. Gyula Bartos (1872–1954), actor. Courtesy of HNL ThC, KA 3677/8. Photographer Pál M. Vájda, ca. 1925.

Figure 79. Ági Jámbor (1907–1997), pianist. Imre Molnár, *A magyar muzsika könyve* (Budapest: Merkantil-nyomda, 1936). 563. Photographer Pecsi.

Figure 80. Gyula Justh (1887–1955), actor. Sándor Hunyady, *A Vígszínház negyven éve* (Budapest: Athenaeum Irodalmi és Nyomdai Rt., 1936). 58. Photographer unknown.

Figure 81. Ilona Ladányi (1904–1952), opera singer. Courtesy of AHSO. Photographer unknown, ca. 1930s.

Figure 82. Andor Lendvay (1901–1964), opera singer. Courtesy of AHSO. Photographer unknown.

OMIKE *Művészakció* Artists Who Survived the Holocaust

Figure 83. Béla Lénárd (1882–1960), actor. Courtesy of HTMI, Photo Archive. Photographer unknown, late 1930s.

Figure 84. Lajos Mányai (1912–1964), actor. Novó photo, ca. 1945; gift to F. Bondy from Zsuzsa Simon, Mányai's wife, 1993.

Figure 85. Erzsi Pártos (1907–2000), actress. Courtesy of HNL ThC, KA IX.65. Photographer Ibi Földiák, ca. 1927.

Figure 86. Erzsi Palotai (1907–1988), actress. *Múlt és Jövő*, July 1940, 110. Photographer unknown.

Figure 87. Sándor Peti (1898–1973), actor. Courtesy of HNL ThC, KB VII.53. Photographer unknown, ca. 1918.

Figure 88. Gabriella Relle (1902–1975), opera singer. Courtesy of HNL ThC, KA 4611/14. Photographer Angelo (Pál Funk), ca. 1925.

OMIKE *Művészakció* Artists Who Survived the Holocaust

Figure 89. Olga Sík (1911–2007), singer. Courtesy of NTE. Photographer unknown, ca. 1930s.

Figure 90. Frigyes Sándor (1905–1979), composer and violinist, with his wife Vera Dénes (1915–1970), violist, and her violoncello. Courtesy of Anna Sándor, their daughter. Photographer unknown, ca. 1960–1961.

Figure 91. Kálmán Szentiványi (1883–1950), actor. Courtesy of HNL ThC, KA 9840/001. Novafotó, ca. 1940.

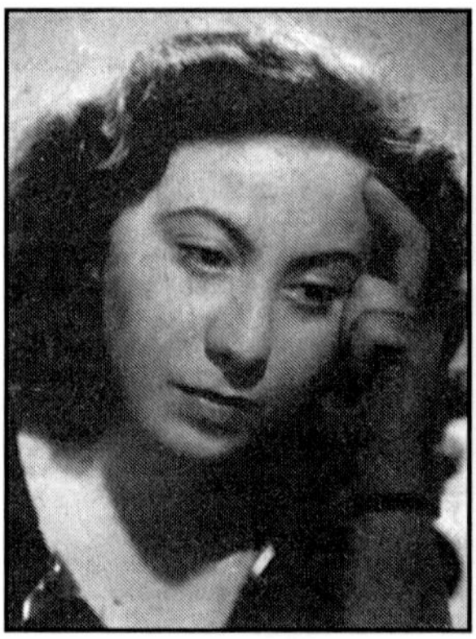

Figure 92. Anna Varjas (1929–2000), pianist. Magda Horák, *Ősi hittel, becsülettel a hazáért! OMIKE 1909–1944* (Budapest: Háttér Könyvkiadó, 1998). Photographer unknown.

Figure 93. Kálmán Zátony (1886–1957), actor. Sándor Hunyady, *A Vígszínház negyven éve* (Budapest: Athenaeum Irodalmi és Nyomdai Rt., 1936). Photographer unknown.

Figure 94. József Zsudi (1923–2013), actor, stage manager. Courtesy of HNL ThC, Ltsz: 688/1980. Photographer unknown, ca. 1975.

Goldmark Hall and OMIKE *Művészakció* Performances

Figure 95. *Judás Makkabeus*. June 1941. OMIKE orchestra and cast, Dohány Synagogue. *Music and the Holocaust: Jewish Musicians in Hungary* by Agnes Kory, photo credited to David Nordell.

Figure 96. *A denevér*. March 1941. OMIKE cast, Goldmark Hall. Courtesy of HTMI, Photo Archive. Photographer unknown.

Goldmark Hall and OMIKE *Művészakció* Performances

Figure 97. *Szulamit*. December 1941. Photographer Sándor Diskay. Courtesy of HTMI Photo Archive, B3220.1/1 (80.344).

Figure 98. *Szeretni*. 1942. Scene with L. Mányai and Z. Simon. Courtesy of Magda Horák. Photographer unknown.

Figure 99. *Őszi szonáta*. October 1942. Scene with (left to right): O. Beregi, P. Ádám, R. Füzesi, and G. Nagy. Róbert Füzesi, *Színház az árnyékban* (Budapest: KO-LIBRI Könyvkiadó, 1990).

Goldmark Hall and OMIKE *Művészakció* Performances

Figure 100. *Békebeli béke*. December 1943. Scene with D. Ney II and K. Váradi. Courtesy of HTMI Photo Archive, B3726.1/1. Photographer unknown.

Figure 101. *La Traviata*. 1941. Scene with I. Darvas and P. Érdi. Magda Horák, *Ősi hittel, becsülettel a hazáért! OMIKE 1909–1944* (Budapest: Háttér Könyvkiadó, 1998).

Figure 102. *A windsori víg nők*. 1943. Scene with I. Darvas and A. Spiegel. Courtesy of HTMI, Photo Archive. Photographer unknown.

Goldmark Hall and OMIKE *Művészakció* Performances

Figure 103a. *A varázsfuvola*. December 1941. Scene with I. Darvas and A. Lendvay. Courtesy of AHSO. Photographer unknown.

Figure 103b. *A varázsfuvola*. December 1941. Scene with K Bán, L Dános, V. Rózsa, and A. Lendvay. Courtesy of AHSO. Photographer unknown.

Goldmark Hall and OMIKE *Művészakció* Performances

Figure 104a. *Sevillai borbély*. 1941. Scene with I. Ladányi, A. Spiegel, P. Fehér, and A. Lendvay. Bequest of Andor Lendvay. Courtesy of AHSO. Photographer unknown.

Figure 104b. *Sevillai borbély*. June 1941. Scene with A. Spiegel, A. Lendvay, I. Ladányi, P. Fehér, B. Bálint, and cast. Bequest of Andor Lendvay. Courtesy of AHSO. Photographer unknown.

Goldmark Hall and OMIKE *Művészakció* Performances

Figure 105. *Rigoletto*. October 1942. Scene with I. Ladányi and A. Lendvay. Bequest of Andor Lendvay. Courtesy of AHSO. Photographer unknown.

Figure 106. *Liliom*. May 1943. Scene with Zsusza Simon. Courtesy of HTMI, Photo Archive, Album Collection, Album 126. Photographer unknown.

Figure 107. *Bohemelet*. May 1941. Scene with I. Ladányi and P. Fehér. Courtesy of AHSO. Photographer unknown.

Goldmark Hall and OMIKE *Művészakció* Performances

Figure 108. *Szeretni*. May 1942. Scene with (left to right): L. Mányai, Z. Simon, and G. Nagy. Courtesy of HTMI, Photo Archive, Album Collection, Album 125. Photographer André.

Figure 109. *Delila*. February 1944. Scene with L. Mányai and M. Rosty. Courtesy of HTMI, Photo Archive. Photographer unknown.

Figure 110. *Mózes*. January 1944. Scene with M. Róbert, L. Mányai, and D. Kelen. Courtesy of HTMI, Photo Archive, Album Collection, Album 125. Photographer unknown.

Goldmark Hall and OMIKE *Művészakció* Performances

Figure 111a. *A párbaj*. 1942. Scene with G. Justh, G. Nagy, and Z. Simon. Courtesy of HNL ThC, KA 9437/1. Photographer unknown.

Figure 111b. *A párbaj*. 1942. Scene with I. Solt, Z. Simon, G. Nagy, and G. Justh. Courtesy of HNL ThC, KA 9437/2. Photographer unknown.

Goldmark Hall and OMIKE *Művészakció* Performances

Figure 112. Goldmark Hall Building. F. Bondy photo, August 1993.

Figure 113. Goldmark Hall façade. F. Bondy photo, August 1993.

Figure 114. Goldmark Hall in ruins, 1945. Courtesy of *Magyar Zsidó Levéltár* (Hungarian Jewish Archives, Budapest). Photographer unknown.

Goldmark Hall and OMIKE *Művészakció* Performances

Figure 115. Károly Goldmark Memorial Plaque from postwar restoration of Goldmark Hall. F. Bondy photo, April 2016.

Figure 116. The OMIKE *Művészakció* Martyrs Plaque, Goldmark Hall. F. Bondy photo, August 1993.

Goldmark Hall and OMIKE *Művészakció* Performances

Figure 117. Goldmark Choir, led by Emil Ádám, Purim or Chanukah Concert, Goldmark Hall, ca. 1985. Courtesy of Meir Szegedi.

Figure 118a. Israeli Dance Performances, Goldmark Hall. Goldmark and Martyr plaques, respectively, to left and right of stage. F. Bondy photo, August 1993.

Figure 118b. Israeli Dance Performances, Goldmark Hall. Band on the stage. F. Bondy photo, August 1993.

Goldmark Hall and OMIKE *Művészakció* Performances

Figure 119a. Israeli dance performances, Goldmark Hall. OMIKE *Művészakció* Martyr plaque to right of stage. F. Bondy photo, August 1993.

Figure 119b. Israeli dance performances, Goldmark Hall. F. Bondy photo, August 1993.

Figure 119c. Israeli dance performances, Goldmark Hall. F. Bondy photo, August 1993.

Goldmark Hall and OMIKE *Művészakció* Performances

Figure 120a. Latest stage modernization of Goldmark Hall. Goldmark, Ribary, and Martyr plaques moved to rear of auditorium. Touch-video screens on Hungarian Jewish and Holocaust history in Jewish Museum in the center. F. Bondy photo, April 2016.

Figure 120b. Latest seating modernization of Goldmark Hall. F. Bondy photo, April 2016.

APPENDIX 2

Programs of *Művészakció* Plays, Concerts, Operas, Cabarets, and Operettas

Copies of programs contained in this appendix, for the years 1940–1944, were made for this book with the kind help of the museum and archival staff at the National Szechenyi Theater Collection (*Országos Széchényi Színháztár*) and at the Hungarian Jewish Archives (*Magyar Zsidó Levéltár*).

Copies of earlier programs for the year of 1939 were obtained from the website of the Nonprofit *Társadalomkutató Egyesület* (www.omike.hu), which in turn were obtained from the Hungarian National Archives (*Magyar Országos Levéltár*). A number of other programs were also obtained from this web site.

In the program image credits, the Nonprofit *Társadalomkutató Egyesület* (www.omike.hu) is abbreviated as NTE, the Hungarian National Museum in Budapest as HNM, and the Theater History Collection at Hungarian National Széchényi Library as HNL ThC.

OMIKE MŰVÉSZESTÉK

November 12-én, vasárnap este 8 órakor
a Goldmark-teremben (VII., Wesselényi-utca 7)

VIDÁM EST

MŰSOR:

Dr. RIBÁRY GÉZA, a Pesti Izr. Hitközség elnökhelyettesének megnyitója.
1. BEVEZETŐT mond: FORRÓ PÁL
2. Kóváry Gyula: EGY FÉL, AKI NEM FÉL. (Tréfa.)
Előadják: ORMOS BÉLA, FENYŐ ÁRPÁD
3. Emőd Tamás / Robindranath Tagore / Goethe } költeményeiből előad: FEHÉR LILI
4. Ерczkövi László: VALLOMÁS.
Előadja: ÉRCZKÖVI LÁSZLÓ. Zongorán kísér: FRAKNÓI KÁROLY
5. Megyery Sári: A FILMSZTÁRHOZ. Zenéjét szerezte: Váradi László.
Előadja: BÓTH KLÁRI. Zongorán kísér: FRAKNÓI KÁROLY
6. Rudnyánszky Gyula: EGY EMBER ÁLL A TÖRVÉNYSZÉK ELŐTT.
Előadja: FENYŐ EMIL
7. Tiszai Márton: OPERETTORSZÁG.
Előadja: OLGYAI OLGA. Zongorán kísér: FRAKNÓI KÁROLY
8. Nóti Károly: AZ ÓVATOS EMBER. (Bohózat.)
Személyek: SALAMON BÉLA, RAJNA ALICE, ORMOS BÉLA, FENYŐ ÁRPÁD, ÉRCZKÖVI LÁSZLÓ, HARSÁNYI MIKLÓS

SZÜNET.

9. FORRÓ PÁL konferansza.
10. KESZEG ÉS FENYŐ (Tréfa). Előadják: ORMOS BÉLA, FENYŐ ÁRPÁD
11. Karinthy Frigyes: BOXMÉRKŐZÉS. Előadja: RAJNA ALICE
12. Sziklai József: ÉLETEM NAPLÓJA.
Előadja: SZIKLAI JÓZSEF. Zongorán kísér: FRAKNÓI KÁROLY
13. Lőrincz Miklós: ÜGYVÉD ÚR KÉREM! (Tréfa.)
Előadják: PETI SÁNDOR, HARSÁNYI MIKLÓS
14. Millöcker: RÉSZLET „DUBARRY"-ból.
Kun László: SOSEM NYIT. (Dal.)
Előadja: DARVAS IBOLYA. Zongorán kísér: FRAKNÓI KÁROLY
15. Mouray: AZ AJÁNLÓ LEVÉL. (Bohózat.) Fordította: Simai Ede.
Személyek: ROTT SÁNDOR, FENYŐ ÁRPÁD, ÉRCZKÖVI LÁSZLÓ

A RUHATÁR SZEMÉLYENKINT 20 FILLÉR. A MŰSOR ÁRA 10 FILLÉR.

Figure 1a. Jolly Evening (*Vidám Est*). B. Ormos, B. Salamon, Á. Fenyő, I. Darvas, S. Peti, M. Harsányi, S. Rott, et.al. Nov. 12, 1939. Courtesy of HNM.

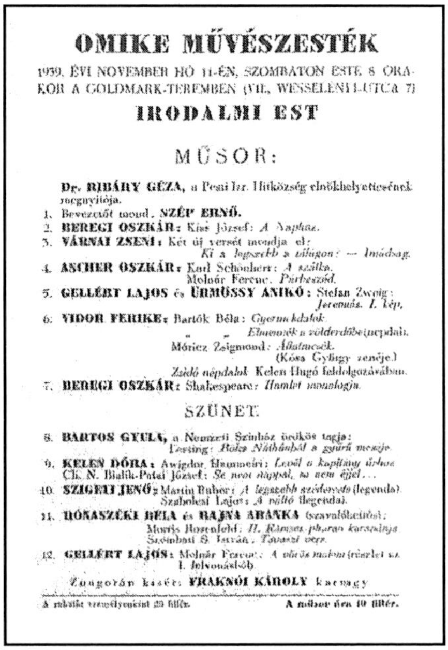

OMIKE MŰVÉSZESTÉK

1939. ÉVI NOVEMBER HÓ 11-ÉN, SZOMBATON ESTE 8 ÓRAKOR A GOLDMARK-TEREMBEN (VII., WESSELÉNYI-UTCA 7)

IRODALMI EST

MŰSOR:

Dr. RIBÁRY GÉZA, a Pesti Izr. Hitközség elnökhelyettesének megnyitója.
1. Bevezetőt mond: SZÉP ERNŐ.
2. BEREGI OSZKÁR: Kiss József: *A Napház.*
3. VÁRNAI ZSENI: Két új versét mondja el: *Ki a legszebb a világon? — Imádság.*
4. ASCHER OSZKÁR: Karl Schönherr: *A szálka.* Molnár Ferenc: *Párbeszéd.*
5. GELLÉRT LAJOS és ÜRMÖSSY ANIKÓ: Stefan Zweig: *Jeremiás. I. kép.*
6. VIDOR FERIKE: Bartók Béla: *Gyermekdalok* „ „ *Elmennék a zöld erdőbe* (népdal). Móricz Zsigmond: *Állatmesék.* (Kósa György zenéje.) *Zsidó népdalok* Kelen Hugó feldolgozásában.
7. BEREGI OSZKÁR: Shakespeare: *Hamlet monológja.*

SZÜNET.

8. BARTOS GYULA, a Nemzeti Színház örökös tagja: Lessing: *Bölcs Náthánból a gyűrű meséje.*
9. KELEN DÓRA: Awigdor Hameiri: *Levél a kapitány úrhoz.* Ch. N. Bialik-Patai József: *Se nem nappal, se nem éjjel...*
10. SZIGETI JENŐ: Martin Buber: *A legszebb szeretet* (legenda). Szabolcsi Lajos: *A [illegible]* (legenda).
11. HONASZÉKI BÉLA és RAJNA ARANKA (szavalókettős): Morris Rosenfeld: *II. Ramses pharao karavánja* [illegible] *[illegible]*
12. GELLÉRT LAJOS: Molnár Ferenc: *A vörös malom* (részlet az I. felvonásból)

Zongorán kísér: FRAKNÓI KÁROLY karnagy

A ruhatár személyenkint 20 fillér. A műsor ára 10 fillér.

Figure 1b. Literary Evening (*Irodalmi Est*). E. Szép, O. Beregi, L. Gellért, F. Vidor, G. Bartos, et al. Nov. 11, 1939. Courtesy of HNM.

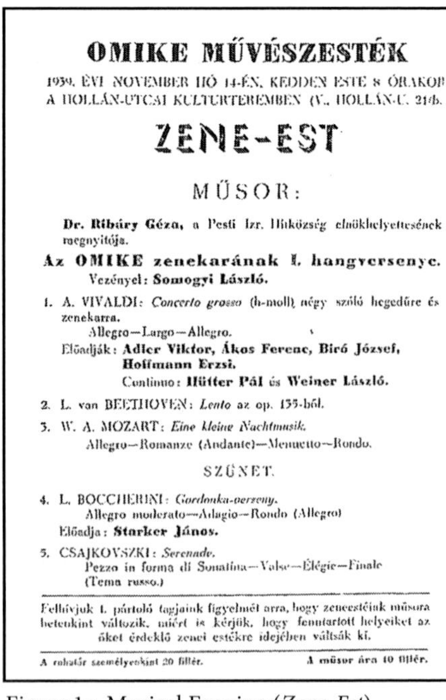

OMIKE MŰVÉSZESTÉK

1939. ÉVI NOVEMBER HÓ 14-ÉN, KEDDEN ESTE 8 ÓRAKOR A HOLLÁN-UTCAI KULTURTEREMBEN (V., HOLLÁN-U. 21/b.

ZENE-EST

MŰSOR:

Dr. Ribáry Géza, a Pesti Izr. Hitközség elnökhelyettesének megnyitója.

Az OMIKE zenekarának I. hangversenye.
Vezényel: Somogyi László.

1. A. VIVALDI: *Concerto grosso* (h-moll), négy szóló hegedűre és zenekarra.
Allegro—Largo—Allegro.
Előadják: Adler Viktor, Ákos Ferenc, Biró József, Hoffmann Erzsi.
Continuo: Hütter Pál és Weiner László.
2. L. van BEETHOVEN: *Lento* az op. 135-ből.
3. W. A. MOZART: *Eine kleine Nachtmusik.*
Allegro—Romanze (Andante)—Menuetto—Rondo.

SZÜNET.

4. L. BOCCHERINI: *Gordonka-verseny.*
Allegro moderato—Adagio—Rondo (Allegro)
Előadja: Starker János.
5. CSAJKOVSZKI: *Serenade.*
Pezzo in forma di Sonatina—Valse—Élégie—Finale (Tema russo.)

Felhívjuk t. pártoló tagjaink figyelmét arra, hogy zeneestéink műsora hetenkint változik, miért is kérjük, hogy fenntartott helyeiket az őket érdeklő zenei estékre idejében váltsák ki.

A ruhatár személyenkint 20 fillér. A műsor ára 10 fillér.

Figure 1c. Musical Evening (*Zene-Est*). L. Somogyi, V. Adler, P. Hütter, L. Weiner, J. Starker, et al. Nov.14,1939. Courtesy of HNM.

OMIKE MŰVÉSZAKCIÓ
A GOLDMARK-TEREMBEN

Január 26-án szerdán este 6 órakor (6.-szor)

Operai szelvénytöbblet fizetendő!

D'Albert

Hegyek alján

Zenedráma 3 felvonásban

Szövegét írta Lothar Rudolf

Személyek

Sebastiano	*Lendvay Andor*
Tommaso	*Kálmán Oszkár*
Moruccio	*Bálint Béla*
Márta	*Róna Vera*
Pepa	*Fábry Edith*
Antonia	*Leopold Lenke*
Rosalia	*Spiegel Annie*
Nuri	*Ladányi Ilona*
Pedro	*Ney Dávid*
Nando	*Teszler Tivadar*

Vezényel Komor Vilmos Rendező Szabolcs Ernő

Karigazgató dr. Bermann Ferenc

Kezdete pontosan 6 órakor

Az előadás megkezdése előtt a nézőtérre vezető ajtókat bezárjuk

Figure 2a. D'Albert's *At the Bottom of the Mountains* (*Hegyek Alján*). Opera. A. Lendvay, O. Kálmán, B. Bálint, V. Róna, et al. Jan. 26, 1940. Courtesy of NTE.

OMIKE MŰVÉSZESTÉK

1940. november 9-én szombaton (G/2 sorozat), 16-án szombaton (G/1 sorozat), 19-én kedden, 23-án szombaton, 26-án kedden és 30-án szombaton a Goldmark-teremben (VII., Wesselényi-utca 7.)

SZINHÁZI EST

(a Szinházi Előadások I. műsora)

HEBBEL FRIGYES:

JUDIT

Dráma 4 képben

Rendező: ***Beregi Oszkár***

Személyek:

Judit, 17 éves	*Párdány Judit*
Mirca, Judit cselédje	*Gérő Erzsi*
Holofernes, fővezér	*Beregi Oszkár*
Holofernes kamarása	*Darvas Ernő*
Holofernes kapitányai	*Kovács Imre* *Fehér Tivadar*
Libiai követ	*Somlár Zsigmond*
Mezopotámiai követ	*Várnai Jenő*
Efraim	*Róna Aladár*
Achior, a moabiták vezére	*Rónai Géza*
Asszír főpap	*Molnár József*
Hirnök	*Kornai Sándor*
Harcos	*Gonda Jenő*

Szinhely: Bethulia előtt és Bethuliában

Figure 2b. Theater Evening (*Szinházi Est*). Hebbel's *Judith* (*Judit*), drama in four scenes. J. Párdany, E. Gérő, O. Beregi, E. Darvas, et al. Nov. 9, 1940. Courtesy of NTE.

OMIKE MŰVÉSZESTÉK

1940. december 21-én szombaton (O/1 és V/2 sorozat) és 23-án hétfőn (O/2 és V/4 sorozat) a Hollán-utcai kulturteremben (V., Hollán-utca 21/b)

OPERAEST

az Operasorozat IV. műsora

OPERAÁRIÁK és EGYÜTTESEK

Karmester: ***Fraknói Károly***

Közreműködnek:

Darvas Ibolya, Radnai Erzsi, Relle Gabriella, Fehér Pál, Kálmán Oszkár, Lendvai Andor

MŰSOR:

Goldmark: **SÁBA KIRÁLYNŐJE**
a) ***Sulamit áriája*** — *Relle Gabriella*
b) ***Sába áriája*** — *Radnai Erzsi*
c) ***Assad elbeszélése*** — *Fehér Pál*

Saint-Saëns: **SÁMSON és DELILA**
a) ***Ária az I. felvonásból*** — *Radnai Erzsi*
b) ***Kettős*** — *Radnai Erzsi*, *Fehér Pál*

Mascagni: **PARASZTBECSÜLET**
a) ***Santuzza áriája*** — *Relle Gabriella*
b) ***Siciliana*** — *Fehér Pál*
c) ***Kettős*** — *Relle Gabriella*, *Lendvai Andor*

SZÜNET

Leoncavallo: **BAJAZZO**
a) ***Prolog*** — *Lendvai Andor*
b) ***Nedda áriája*** — *Relle Gabriella*
c) ***Canio áriája*** — *Fehér Pál*

Figure 2c. Opera Evening (*Opera Est*). Goldmark, Saint-Saëns, Mascagni, and Leoncavello operas. Dec. 21, 1940. Courtesy of NTE.

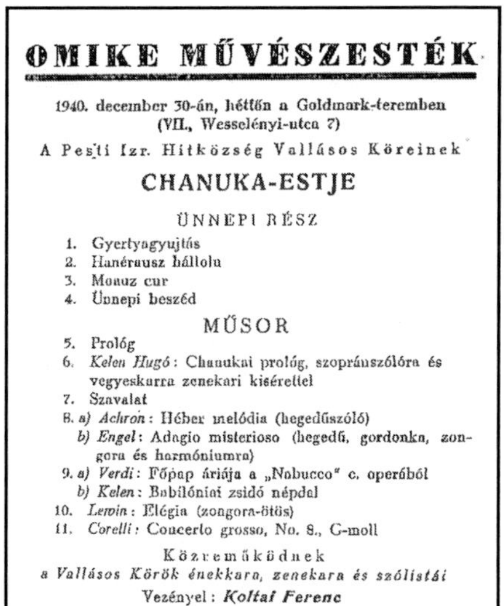

OMIKE MŰVÉSZESTÉK

1940. december 30-án, hétfőn a Goldmark-teremben (VII., Wesselényi-utca 7)

A Pesti Izr. Hitközség Vallásos Köreinek

CHANUKA-ESTJE

ÜNNEPI RÉSZ

1. Gyertyagyujtás
2. Hanérausz hállolu
3. Mauz cur
4. Ünnepi beszéd

MŰSOR

5. Prológ
6. *Kelen Hugó*: Chanukai prológ, szopránszólóra és vegyeskarra zenekari kísérettel
7. Szavalat
8. a) *Achron*: Héber melódia (hegedűszóló)
   b) *Engel*: Adagio misterioso (hegedű, gordonka, zongora és harmóniumra)
9. a) *Verdi*: Főpap áriája a „Nabucco" c. operából
   b) *Kelen*: Babilóniai zsidó népdal
10. *Lewin*: Elégia (zongora-ötös)
11. *Corelli*: Concerto grosso, No. 8., G-moll

Közreműködnek
a Vallásos Körök énekkara, zenekara és szólistái

Vezényel: ***Koltai Ferenc***

Kezdete 1/2 9 órakor

Figure 2d. Chanukah Night (*Chanuka-Estje*). Dec. 30, 1940. Courtesy of NTE.

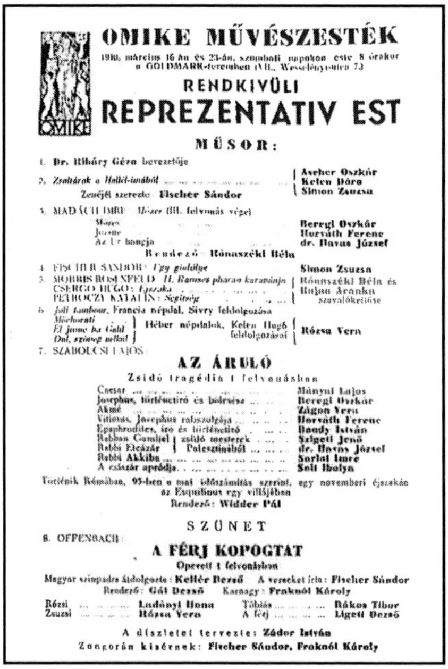

Figure 3a. Representative Evening (*Reprezentativ Est*). Szabolcsi's *The Traitor* (*Áz Áruló*), Jewish tragedy. L. Mányai, O. Beregi, V. Zágon, F. Horváth, I. Bondy,.et al.; and Offenbach's *The Husband Knocks* (*A Férj Kopogtat*), operetta. I. Ladányi, V. Rózsa, T. Rákos, and D. Ligeti. Mar. 16, 1940. Courtesy of NTE.

Figure 3b. Geraldy's *Robert and Marianne*, stage play. O. Ascher, Z. Simon, A. Spiegel, and L. Mányai. May 22, 1940. Courtesy of NTE.

Figure 3c. Musical Concert (*Zenekari Hangverseny*). Beethoven, Kodály, Reschofsky. Dec. 16, 1940. Courtesy of NTE.

Figure 3d. Cabaret Evening (*Kabaré-Est*). Lorincz's *Lady Dictator* (*Diktátornő*), comedy. K. Kornis, A. Rajna, and K. Zátony; and Gorog-Keller's *Let's Learn Languages* (*Tanuljunk Nyelveket*), farce, low comedy. B. Salamon, S. Rott, Z. Simon, K. Zátony, et al. Nov. 3, 1940. Courtesy of NTE.

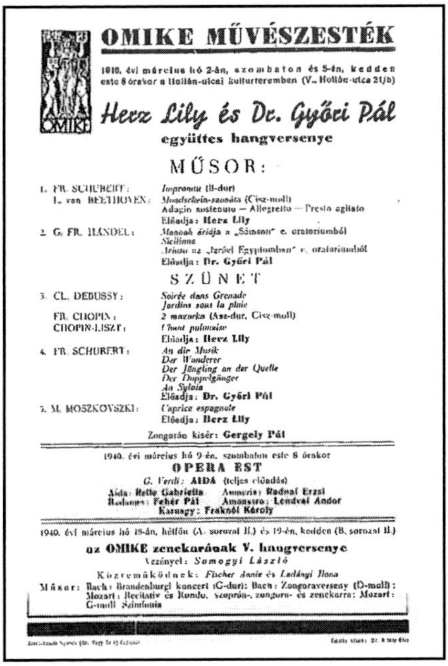

OMIKE MŰVÉSZESTÉK

1940. évi március hó 2-án, szombaton és 5-én, kedden este 8 órakor a Hollán-utcai kulturteremben (V., Hollán-utca 21/b)

Herz Lily és Dr. Győri Pál

együttes hangversenye

MŰSOR:

1. FR. SCHUBERT: Impromtu (B-dur)
L. van BEETHOVEN: Mondschein-szonáta (Cisz-moll)
Adagio sostenuto — Allegretto — Presto agitato
Előadja: Herz Lily
2. G. FR. HÄNDEL: Manoah áriája a „Sámson" c. oratoriumból
Siciliana
Ariosa az „Izráel Egyptomban" c. oratoriumból
Előadja: Dr. Győri Pál

SZÜNET

3. CL. DEBUSSY: Soirée dans Grenade
Jardins sous la pluie
FR. CHOPIN: 2 mazurka (Asz-dur, Cisz-moll)
CHOPIN-LISZT: Chant polonaise
Előadja: Herz Lily
4. FR. SCHUBERT: An die Musik
Der Wanderer
Der Jüngling an der Quelle
Der Doppelgänger
An Sylvia
Előadja: Dr. Győri Pál
5. M. MOSZKOVSZKI: Caprice espagnole
Előadja: Herz Lily

Zongorán kisér: Gergely Pál

1940. évi március hó 9-én, szombaton este 8 órakor

OPERA EST

G. Verdi: AIDA (teljes előadás)

Aida: Relle Gabriella Amneris: Radnai Erzsi
Radames: Fehér Pál Amonasro: Lendvai Andor
Karnagy: Fraknói Károly

1940. évi március hó 18-án, hétfőn (A. sorozat II.) és 19-én, kedden (B. sorozat II.)

az OMIKE zenekarának V. hangversenye

Vezényel: Somogyi László

Közreműködnek: Fischer Annie és Ladányi Ilona

Műsor: Bach: Brandenburgi koncert (G-dur); Bach: Zongoraverseny (D-moll); Mozart: Recitativ és Rondo, szoprán-, zongora- és zenekarra; Mozart: G-moll Szimfonia

Figure 4a. Lily Herz and Dr. Pál Győri, Together in Concert (*Együttes Hangversenye*). Mar. 2, 1940. Opera Evening, Concert of the OMIKE Orchestra. Courtesy of NTE.

OMIKE MŰVÉSZESTÉK

1941. január 5-én vasárnap (G/1 sorozat), 8-án szerdán, 12-én vasárnap, 19-én vasárnap, 26-án vasárnap (G/2 sorozat) és 28-án kedden este 1/28 órai kezdettel, továbbá január 19-én vasárnap délután 1/24 órai kezdettel a Goldmark-teremben (VII., Wesselényi-utca 7)

KABARÉ-EST

a Kabaré Előadások III. műsora

1. Kellér Andor konferansza
2. László Miklós:

RINGLISPIL

(Komédia)

Személyek:

Az éhes ... Szigeti Jenő
Kövér úr ... Szirmai Vilmos
Ideges úr ... Ormos Béla
A költő ... Dr. Szabó Dezső
Jellemes úr Fenyő Árpád
Kislány ... Gárdonyi Ibolya
Nevelőnő ... Győri Matild
Utcaseprő ... Major István

3. Petőfi—Huszka Jenő: Szeptember végén
Kálmán Imre—Kulinyi Ernő: My darling
Victor Herbert: Szívem édes titka
Énekli: Bibó Olga
4. Szőke Szakáll:

VONÓSNÉGYES

(Bohózat)

Személyek:

Salgó I. ... Salamon Béla
Salgó II. ... Ormos Béla
Schwartz... Fenyő Árpád
Bella ... ... Ács Rózsi
Jolán ... ... Rajna Mária
Tomi ... ... Pálfi Blanka
Margó ... Dr. Szabó Dezső
Darnai ... Szigeti Jenő
Öreg úr ... ... Major István

Rendező: Harsányi Miklós

SZÜNET

Figure 4b. Cabaret Evening (*Kabaré-Est*). Laszlo's *Carousel* (*Ringlispil*), comedy. J. Szigeti, V. Skirmai, B. Ormos, Dr. D. Szabó, et al.; and Szoke's *String Quartet* (*Vónosnégyes*), farce, low comedy. B. Salamon, B. Ormos, Á. Fenyő, R. Ács, M. Rajna, B. Pálfi, et al. Jan. 5, 1941. Courtesy of NTE.

OMIKE MŰVÉSZESTÉK

1940. november 18-án hétfőn (H/1 és V/3 sorozat) és 19-én kedden (H/2 és V/1 sorozat) a Hollán-utcai kulturteremben (V., Hollán-utca 21/b)

ZENEKARI HANGVERSENY

(a Hangversenysorozat I. műsora)

Vezényel: Fraknói Károly

Közreműködnek: Adler Viktor (hegedű), Hanák Árpád (zongora) és Hütter Pál (gordonka)

MŰSOR:

1. Mozart: Esz-dur Szimfónia (K. V. 543)
Adagio—Allegro
Andante
Menuetto
Finale (Allegro)
2. Honegger: Pastorale d'Été

SZÜNET

3. Beethoven: Hármas versenymű zongora-, hegedű- és gordonkára
Allegro — Largo — Rondo alla Polacca
4. Mozart: Hat német tánc
1. Ländler-tempo — 2. Un poco più allegro — 3. Allegro moderato — 4. Allegro (A kanári) — 5. Più moderato (A kintornás) 6. Allegro (Szánkázás)

Kezdete 8 órakor

Az előadás megkezdésekor a nézőtérre vezető ajtókat bezárjuk

Figure 4c. Musical Concert (*Zenekari Hangverseny*). Viktor Adler and Pál Hütter. Nov. 18, 1940. Courtesy of NTE.

OMIKE MŰVÉSZESTÉK

1940. december 2-án hétfőn (H/1 és V/4 sorozat) és 3-án kedden (H/2 és V/2 sorozat) a Hollán-utcai kulturteremben (V., Hollán-utca 21/b)

HERZ LILY és ERNSTER DEZSŐ

HANGVERSENYE

a Hangversenysorozat II. műsora

1. Bach: Preludium és fúga c-moll
Előadja: Herz Lily
2. Haydn: Ária a „Teremtés" című oratóriumból
Előadja: Ernster Dezső
3. Beethoven: Szonáta Esz-dur (Les Adieux)
Előadja: Herz Lily
4. Loewe:
a) Heimlichkeit
b) Meeresleuchten
c) Odins Meeresritt
Előadja: Ernster Dezső
5. a) Chopin: Variations brillantes B-dur
b) Weber: Perpetuum mobile
Előadja: Herz Lily

SZÜNET

6. Koncertetűdök
a) Chopin: E-dur
b) Scriabine: E-dur
c) Zichy: Asz-dur (balkézre)
d) Liszt: Gisz-moll (Campanella)
Előadja: Herz Lily

Figure 4d. Concert (*Hangverseny*). Concert by Lily Herz and Dezső Ernster. Dec. 2, 1940. Courtesy of NTE.

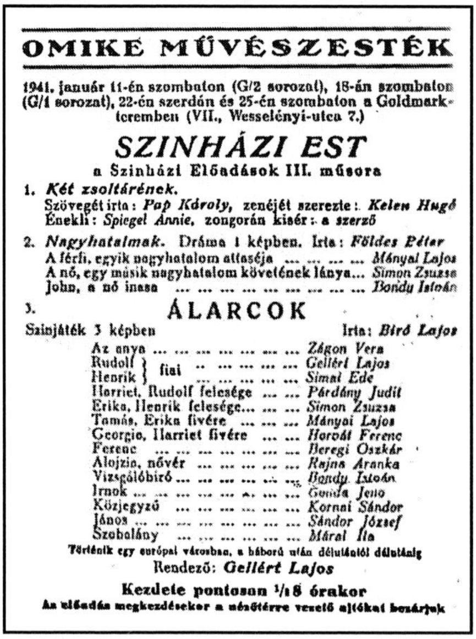

OMIKE MŰVÉSZESTÉK

1941. január 11-én szombaton (G/2 sorozat), 18-án szombaton (G/1 sorozat), 22-én szerdán és 25-én szombaton a Goldmark-teremben (VII., Wesselényi-utca 7.)

SZINHÁZI EST

a Szinházi Előadások III. műsora

1. *Két zsoltárének.*
Szövegét irta: *Pap Károly,* zenéjét szerezte: *Kelen Hugó*
Énekli: *Spiegel Annie,* zongorán kisér: *a szerző*

2. *Nagyhatalmak.* Dráma 1 képben. Irta: *Földes Péter*
A férfi, egyik nagyhatalom attaséja ... ... *Mányai Lajos*
A nő, egy másik nagyhatalom követének lánya... *Simon Zsuzsa*
John, a nő inasa ... ... *Bondy István*

3. ÁLARCOK

Szinjáték 3 képben Irta: *Biró Lajos*

Az anya ... ... *Zágon Vera*
Rudolf } fiai ... ... *Gellért Lajos*
Henrik } ... ... *Simai Ede*
Harriet, Rudolf felesége ... ... *Párdány Judit*
Erika, Henrik felesége... ... ... *Simon Zsuzsa*
Tamás, Erika fivére ... ... *Mányai Lajos*
Georgio, Harriet fivére ... ... *Horvát Ferenc*
Ferenc ... ... *Beregi Oszkár*
Alojzia, nővér ... ... *Rajna Aranka*
Vizsgálóbiró ... ... *Bondy István*
Irnok ... ... *Gonda Jenő*
Közjegyző ... ... *Kornai Sándor*
János ... ... *Sándor József*
Szobalány ... ... *Márai Ila*

Történik egy európai városban, a háború után délutántól délutánig

Rendező: *Gellért Lajos*

Kezdete pontosan 1/2 8 órakor

Az előadás megkezdésekor a nézőtérre vezető ajtókat bezárjuk

Figure 5a. Theater Evening (*Szinházi Est*). Biró's *Masks* (*Álarcok*), stage play. V. Zágon, L. Gellért, E. Simai, J. Pardányi, Z. Simon, et al. Jan. 11, 1941. Courtesy of HNL ThC.

OMIKE MŰVÉSZESTÉK

1941. február 8-án szombaton (G/2 sorozat), 15-én szombaton (G/1 sorozat), 22-én szombaton és március 1-én szombaton a Goldmark-teremben (VII., Wesselényi-utca 7)

SZINHÁZI EST

a Szinházi Előadások IV. műsora

JÁTÉK A KASTÉLYBAN

Anekdota 3 képben

Irta: *Molnár Ferenc*

Személyek:

Turai ... ... *Gellért Lajos*
Gál ... ... *Simai Ede*
Ádám ... ... *Horváth Ferenc*
Annie ... ... *Palotai Erzsi*
Almády ... ... *Mányai Lajos*
Titkár ... ... *Fabinyi István*
Lakáj ... ... *Gonda József*

Történik egy kastélyban az olasz tengerparton

Rendező: *Bálint Lajos*

Figure 5b. Theater Evening (*Szinházi Est*). Molnár's *Playing in the Castle* (*Játék A Kastélyban*). L. Gellért, E. Simai, F. Horváth, E. Palotai, et al. Feb. 8, 1941. Courtesy of HNL ThC.

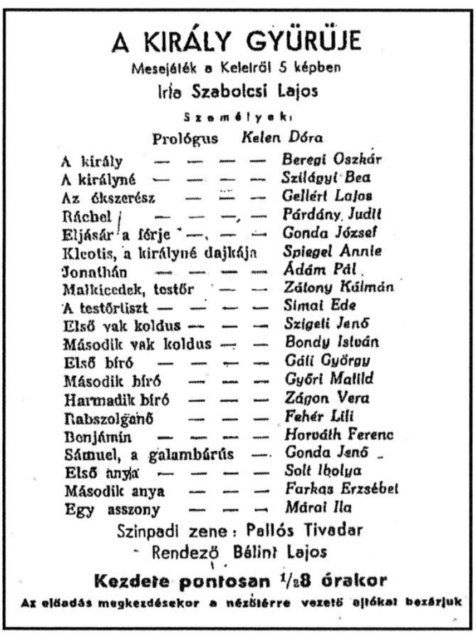

A KIRÁLY GYÜRÜJE

Mesejáték a Keletről 5 képben

Irta Szabolcsi Lajos

Személyek:

Prológus *Kelen Dóra*

A király — — — — *Beregi Oszkár*
A királyné — — — — *Szilágyi Bea*
Az ékszerész — — — *Gellért Lajos*
Ráchel — — — — *Párdány Judit*
Eljásár a férje — — — *Gonda József*
Kleotis, a királyné dajkája *Spiegel Annie*
Jonathán — — — — *Ádám Pál*
Malkicedek, testőr — — *Zálony Kálmán*
A testőrtiszt — — — — *Simai Ede*
Első vak koldus — — — *Szigeti Jenő*
Második vak koldus — — *Bondy István*
Első biró — — — — *Gáli György*
Második biró — — — *Győri Matild*
Harmadik biró — — — *Zágon Vera*
Rabszolgánő — — — *Fehér Lili*
Benjámin — — — — *Horváth Ferenc*
Sámuel, a galambárús — *Gonda Jenő*
Első anya — — — — *Solt Ibolya*
Második anya — — — *Farkas Erzsébet*
Egy asszony — — — *Márai Ila*

Szinpadi zene: Pallós Tivadar

Rendező Bálint Lajos

Kezdete pontosan 1/2 8 órakor

Az előadás megkezdésekor a nézőtérre vezető ajtókat bezárjuk

Figure 5c. Theater Evening (*Szinházi Est*). Szabolcsi's *The King's Ring* (*A Király Gyürüje*), fable play. O. Beregi, B. Szilági,L. Gellért, J. Párdányi, et al. May 6, 1941. Courtesy of HNL ThC.

AZ OMIKE MŰVÉSZAKCIÓ

rendkívüli

Templomi Hangversenye

a Dohány-utcai főtemplomban,

1941. junius 23-án hétfőn este 1/2 8 órakor a Szombathelyi Collegium Musicum énekkara (karigazgató: Gábor Albert), az OMIKE énekkara (karigazgató: Kádi László) és zenekara közreműködésével, segítségre szoruló művészeink javára.

Előadásra kerül:

Händel

Judás Makkabeus

cimü oratóriuma magánének, vegyeskar, gyermekkar és zenekarra

Bevezetőt mond:

Dr. Hevesi Simon

vezető főrabbi

Vezényel:

Weiner László

Händel remekműve első budapesti templomi előadásának magánszereplői:

Judás Makkabeus ... ... **Fehér Pál**
Simon, főpap ... ... **Ernster Dezső**
Két zsidó nő { ... ... **Pogány Zsuzsa**
... ... **Rózsa Vera**
Hirnök ... ... **Weiner György**

Continuo **Dános Méda**

180 közreműködő!

Händel monumentális alkotása a bibliai zsidó nép szabadságharcának ragyogó zenedrámai ábrázolása, a Biblia szellemében és a klasszikus zeneművészet tökéletes kifejező erejével.

Figure 5d. Synagogue Concert (*Templomi Hangverseny*) and Händel's *Judah Maccabee* (*Judás Makkabeus*). P. Fehér, D. Ernster, Z. Pogány, V. Rózsa, and L. Weiner. June 23, 1941. Courtesy of NTE.

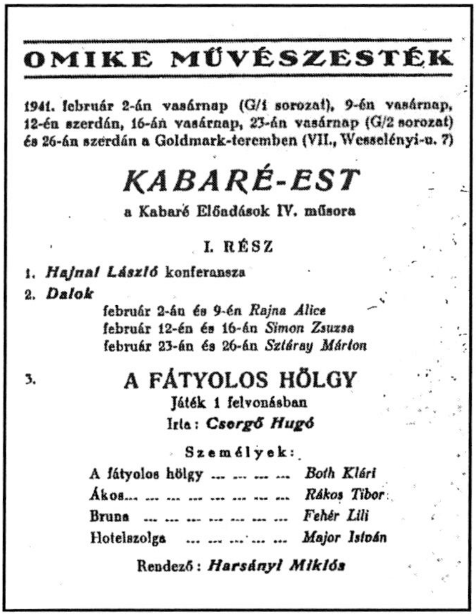

OMIKE MŰVÉSZESTÉK

1941. február 2-án vasárnap (G/1 sorozat), 9-én vasárnap, 12-én szerdán, 16-án vasárnap, 23-án vasárnap (G/2 sorozat) és 26-án szerdán a Goldmark-teremben (VII., Wesselényi-u. 7)

KABARÉ-EST

a Kabaré Előadások IV. műsora

I. RÉSZ

1. *Hajnal László* konferansza
2. *Dalok*
   február 2-án és 9-én *Rajna Alice*
   február 12-én és 16-án *Simon Zsuzsa*
   február 23-án és 26-án *Sztáray Márton*
3. A FÁTYOLOS HÖLGY
   Játék 1 felvonásban
   Irta: *Csergő Hugó*

Személyek:

A fátyolos hölgy ... *Both Klári*
Ákos ... *Rákos Tibor*
Bruna ... *Fehér Lili*
Hotelszolga ... *Major István*

Rendező: *Harsányi Miklós*

Figure 6a. Cabaret Evening (*Kabaré-Est*). Csergő's *The Veiled Lady* (*A Fátyolos Hölgy*), one-act play. K. Both, T. Rákos, L. Fehér, and I. Major. Feb. 2, 1941. Courtesy of NTE.

OMIKE MŰVÉSZESTÉK

1941. május 6-án. kedden (G/2 sorozat), 13-án kedden, 20-án kedden (G/1 sorozat) és 27-én. kedden a Goldmark-teremben (VII., Wesselényi-utca 7)

SZINHÁZI-EST

a Szinházi Előadások VI. műsora

1. Pallós-Ladies vokáltrió
   Darvas Ibolya, Somogyi Piroska, Surány Erzsébet
   a) „Kacho" (Héber dal)
   b) „Moment musical" (Schubert)
   c) „Cserebogár" (Népdalátirat)
   Az énekszámokat átirta és zongorán kisér Pallós Tivadar

Szombati előadásaink, az ünnepnek a nyári időszámítás következtében késői kimenetele folytán, elmaradnak

Közleményeinket az UJSÁG, az ESTI KURIR és a MAGYAR ZSIDÓK LAPJA rendszeresen hozzák. Sziveskedjék a lapokat figyelemmel kisérni.

Figure 6b. Theater Evening (*Szinházi-Est*). "*Pallós*–Ladies," vocal trio (*vokáltrió*). May 6, 1941. Courtesy of NTE.

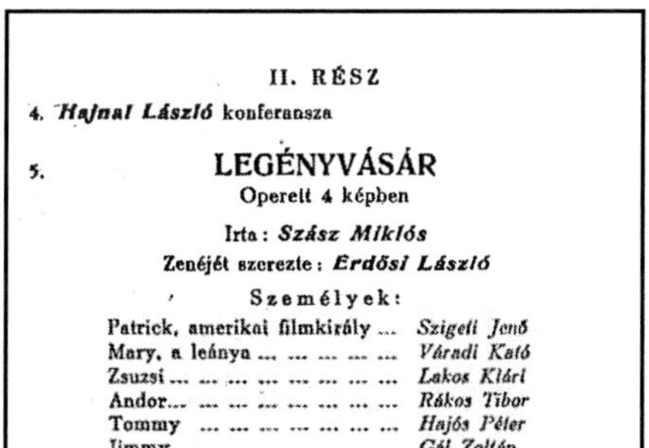

II. RÉSZ

4. *Hajnal László* konferansza
5. LEGÉNYVÁSÁR
   Operett 4 képben
   Irta: *Szász Miklós*
   Zenéjét szerezte: *Erdősi László*

Személyek:

Patrick, amerikai filmkirály ... *Szigeti Jenő*
Mary, a leánya ... *Váradi Kató*
Zsuzsi ... *Lakos Klári*
Andor ... *Rákos Tibor*
Tommy ... *Hajós Péter*
Jimmy ... *Gál Zoltán*
Titkár ... *Bondy István*
Hoteligazgató ... *Bálint Béla*
Lakáj ... *Szirmai Vilmos*
Portás ... *Major István*
Szobalány ... *Pór Irén*
Riporter ... *Spán Frigyes*

Rendező: *Gál Dezső*

A zenekart vezényli: *Erdősi László*

Kezdete pontosan 1/2 8 órakor

Az előadás megkezdésekor a nézőtérre vezető ajtókat bezárjuk

Művészakciónk közleményeit az UJSÁG-ban és az ESTI KURIR-ban tesszük közzé. Kérjük ennélfogva Pártoló Tagjainkat, hogy e két lap szinházi rovatait figyelemmel kisérni sziveskedjenek.

Figure 6c. Szász's *Bachelor Market* (*Legényvásár*), operetta. J. Szigeti, K. Váradi, K. Lakos, T. Rákos, P. Hajós, Z. Gál, I. Bondy, B. Bálint, et al. Feb. 2, 1941. Courtesy of HNL ThC.

2. ELJEGYZÉS LÁMPAFÉNYNÉL
   Operett 1 felvonásban
   Szövegét irta: *Michel Carré* és *Léon Battu*
   Magyar verseit irta: *Fischer Sándor*
   Zenéjét szerzette: *J. OFFENBACH*

Személyek:

Pierre, gazda ... *Fehér Pál*
Denise, a gyámleánya ... *Rózsa Vera*
Catherine } özvegyasszonyok ... *Spiegel Annie*
Fanchette } özvegyasszonyok ... *Darvas Ibolya*
Éjjeli őr ... *Keleti Árpád*

Karmester: *Fischer Sándor*

Rendező: *Váradi Tibor*

Kezdete pontosan 1/2 8 órakor

Az előadás megkezdésekor a nézőtérre vezető ajtókat bezárjuk

Kérjük pártoló tagjainkat, hogy előadásainkon, már a ruhatári tolongás megelőzése végett is, **lehetőleg negyedórával a hirdetett kezdés előtt** *megjelenni sziveskedjenek, mert előadásainkat a másodpercre-rendelkezésekre való tekintettel a kitűzött időpontban* **pontosan megkezdjük és kezdéskor az ajtókat bezárjuk.**

Új címünk: VII., Sip-utca 12., II. em. 33
Telefon: 423—930, 31. mellékállomás

Figure 6d. Carré and Battu's *Engagement by Lamp Light* (*Eljegyzés Lámpafénynél*), one-act operetta. P. Fehér, V. Rózsa, A. Spiegel, I. Darvas, and A. Keleti. Mar. 1, 1941. Courtesy of NTE.

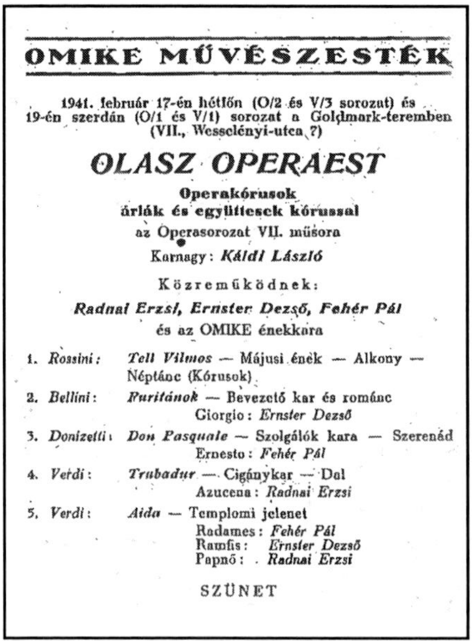

OMIKE MŰVÉSZESTÉK

1941. február 17-én hétfőn (O/2 és V/3 sorozat) és 19-én szerdán (O/1 és V/1) sorozat a Goldmark-teremben (VII., Wesselényi-utca 7)

OLASZ OPERAEST

Operakórusok
áriák és együttesek kórussal
az Operasorozat VII. műsora
Karnagy: *Káldi László*

Közreműködnek:
Radnai Erzsi, Ernster Dezső, Fehér Pál
és az OMIKE énekkara

1. *Rossini:* *Tell Vilmos* — Májusi ének — Alkony — Néptánc (Kórusok)
2. *Bellini:* *Puritánok* — Bevezető kar és románc
   Giorgio: *Ernster Dezső*
3. *Donizetti:* *Don Pasquale* — Szolgálók kara — Szerenád
   Ernesto: *Fehér Pál*
4. *Verdi:* *Trubadur* — Cigánykar — Dal
   Azucena: *Radnai Erzsi*
5. *Verdi:* *Aida* — Templomi jelenet
   Radames: *Fehér Pál*
   Ramfis: *Ernster Dezső*
   Papnő: *Radnai Erzsi*

SZÜNET

Figure 7a. Italian Opera Evening (*Olasz Opera Est*). E. Radnai, D. Ernster, and P. Fehér. Feb. 17, 1941. Courtesy of NTE.

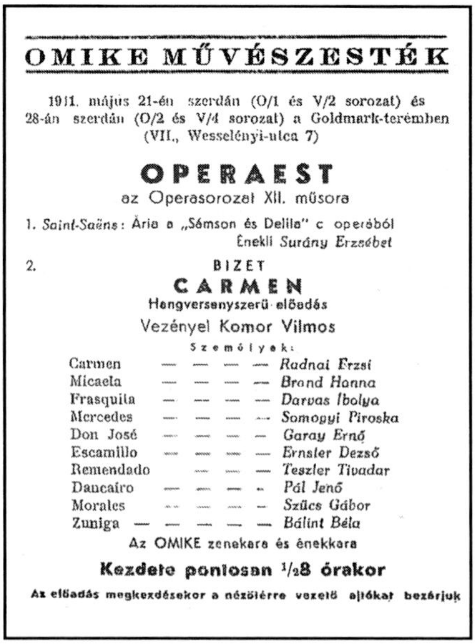

OMIKE MŰVÉSZESTÉK

1941. május 21-én szerdán (O/1 és V/2 sorozat) és 28-án szerdán (O/2 és V/4 sorozat) a Goldmark-teremben (VII., Wesselényi-utca 7)

OPERAEST
az Operasorozat XII. műsora

1. *Saint-Saëns:* Ária a „Sámson és Delila" c operából
   Énekli *Surány Erzsébet*
2. BIZET
   CARMEN
   Hangversenyszerű előadás
   Vezényel Komor Vilmos

Személyek:

Carmen — — — — *Radnai Erzsi*
Micaela — — — — *Brand Hanna*
Frasquita — — — — *Darvas Ibolya*
Mercedes — — — — *Somogyi Piroska*
Don José — — — — *Garay Ernő*
Escamillo — — — — *Ernster Dezső*
Remendado — — — *Teszler Tivadar*
Dancairo — — — — *Pál Jenő*
Morales — — — — *Szűcs Gábor*
Zuniga — — — — — *Bálint Béla*

Az OMIKE zenekara és énekkara

Kezdete pontosan 1/28 órakor

Az előadás megkezdésekor a nézőtérre vezető ajtókat bezárjuk

Figure 7b. Opera Evening (*Opera Est*). Bizet's *Carmen*, opera. E. Radnai, H. Brand, I. Darvas, P. Somogyi, E. Garay, D. Ernster, et al. Mar. 21, 1941. Courtesy of NTE.

OMIKE MŰVÉSZESTÉK

JUNIUS HAVI RENDKIVÜLI ELŐADÁSOK

1941. junius 11-én szerdán
a Goldmark-teremben (VII., Wesselényi-utca 7)

HORVÁTH LÁSZLÓ
a belgrádi opera v. magángordonkásának
GORDONKAESTJE

MŰSOR

1. *Sammartini;* Szonáta G-dur
   Allegro non troppo
   Grave con espressione
   Vivace
2. *Schubert:* Arpeggione Szonáta A-moll
   Allegro moderato
   Adagio (attacca)
   Allegretto

Szünet

3. *Kodály Zoltán:* Zongora—Gordonka szonáta
   Fantasia
   Allegro con spirito
4. a) *Bach:* Adagio
   b) *Frescobaldi:* Toccata
5. a) *Granados:* Intermezzo
   b) *Rimszky-Korzakov:* Dongó
   c) *Albeniz:* Malaguena
   d) *Musszorgszkij:* Hopak

Zongorán kisér Weiner László

Kezdete pontosan 1/28 órakor

Az előadás megkezdésekor a nézőtérre vezető ajtókat bezárjuk

Figure 7c. Laszlo Horvath's Cello Evening (*László Horváth*), musical performance. June 11, 1941. Courtesy of NTE.

OMIKE MŰVÉSZESTÉK

JUNIUS HAVI RENDKIVÜLI ELŐADÁSOK

1941. junius 16-án hétfőn
a Goldmark-teremben (VII., Wesselényi-utca 7)

LENDVAI ANDOR HANGVERSENYE
HERZ LILI közremüködésével

MÜSOR

1. *Leoncavallo:* Bajazzók — prológ
2. *Schubert;* a) Der Doppelgänger
   b) Der Tod und das Mädchen
   c) Erlkönig
3. a) *Brahms:* Scherzo
   b) *Schumann:* Traumeswirren
   c) *Chopin:* Mazurka
   d) ,, Etűd c-moll
   Előadja Herz Lili
4. *Schumann;* a) Widmung
   b) Ich grolle nicht
   c) Die beiden Grenadiere
5. a) *Löwe* Az óra
   b) *Muszorgszkij:* Bolhadal

SZÜNET

6. *Bizet:* Carmen — Escamillo belépője
7. *Verdi:* Othello — Credo
8. *Albeniz-Godowsky:* Tango
   Moniuszko-Friedmann: Tavasz
   Bartók: Rondo
   Liszt: XIII. Rapszódia
   Előadja Herz Lili
9. *Rossini:* Sevillai borbély — Figaro belépője

Zongorán kisér Hajdu János

Kezdete pontosan 1/28 órakor

Az előadás megkezdésekor a nézőtérre vezető ajtókat bezárjuk

Figure 7d. Andor Lendvay in Concert (*Andor Lendvay Hangversenye*). June 16, 1941. Courtesy of NTE.

OMIKE MŰVÉSZESTÉK
a Goldmark-teremben (VII., Wesselényi-utca 7)
11. Rendkivűli előadás
1941. december 31-én, szerdán
JOHANN STRAUSS
DENEVÉR
Operett 3 felvonásban
Vezényel Komor Vilmos
Személyek:
Rosalinda — — — — Pogány Zsuzsa
Adél — — — — Darvas Ibolya
Orlofszky — — — — Rózsa Vera
Eisenstein — — — — Rákos Tibor
Alfréd — — — — Fehér Pál
Falke — — — — — Szigeti Jenő
Frank — — — — — Ernster Dezső
Frosch — — — — — Sarkadi Aladár
Blind — — — — — Teszler Tivadar
Ida — — — — — Rajna Mária
Iván — — — — — Keleti Árpád
A második felvonás hangversenyében közreműködnek:
Ernster Dezső ének, Gál János hegedű,
Párdány Judit szavalat, Sik Olga ének, Komor Ági tánc
Az OMIKE zenekara és énekkara
Rendező Váradi Tibor
Szinpadi előadás
Kezdete pontosan 7 órakor
Az előadás megkezdésekor a nézőtérre vezető ajtókat bezárjuk.

Figure 8a. Strauss's *The Bat* (*A Denevér*), operetta. Z. Pogány, I. Darvas, V. Rózsa, T. Rákos, P. Fehér, J. Szigeti, D. Ernster, et al. Dec. 31, 1941. Courtesy of HNL ThC.

P. I. H. Terézvárosi és „Goldmark" i. csoportja Wesselényi u. 7.
1941. december 4-én, csütörtökön este 1/2 9 órakor
IRODALMI KABARÉ
MŰSOR:
1. Helyszini közvetités: Ady [illegible] Kosztolányi és [illegible] István verseiből [illegible] KORNIS KATÓ és MÁNYAI LAJOS.
2. Nagyhatalmak: [illegible] irta: Földes Péter, játszók: SIMON ZSUZSA, MÁNYAI LAJOS és BONDY ISTVÁN.
3. Az utolsó délután [illegible] irta: Molnár Ferenc, játszók: KORNIS KATÓ és BONDY ISTVÁN.
4. Kenyeres [illegible] irta: Pásztor Árpád, játszók: KORNIS KATÓ, BONDY ISTVÁN, MÁNYAI LAJOS [illegible]
SZÜNET.
5. Ridjalu törvényt mond [illegible] irta: Pogány Elza, játszók: SIMON ZSUZSA, MÁNYAI LAJOS és BONDY ISTVÁN.
6. A fekete pásztor [illegible] irta: Szini Gyula, játszók: KORNIS KATÓ és MÁNYAI LAJOS.
7. Az utolsóelőtti csata irta: Molnár Ferenc, játszók: SIMON ZSUZSA és BONDY ISTVÁN.

Figure 8b. Literary Cabaret (*Irodalmi Kabaré*). K. Kornis, L. Mányai, Z. Simon, and I. Bondy. Dec. 4, 1941. Courtesy of NTE.

OMIKE MŰVÉSZESTÉK
a Goldmark-teremben (VII., Wesselényi-utca 7)
Az Opera-sorozat III. műsora
1941 december 1-én, hétfőn A/1, december 3-án, szerdán A/2, C/1
Rendkivüli szelvényárak
Mozart halálának 150-ik évfordulója alkalmából
1. Mozart: Trauermusik K. W. 477
2. A VARÁZSFUVOLA
Dalmű 2 felvonásban, 15 képben
Zenéjét szerezte: W. A. MOZART Szövegét irta: SCHIKANEDER
Személyek:
Sarastro — — — — Ernster Dezső
Tamino — — — — dr. Sipos Jenő
Öreg pap és Második vértes Farkas Sándor
Pap és Első vértes — — Ney Dávid
Az éj királynője — — Ladányi Ilona
Pamina — — — — Pogány Zsuzsa
Első hölgy — — — Róna Vera
Második hölgy — — Somogyi Piroska
Harmadik hölgy — — Spiegel Annie
Papageno — — — Lendvay Andor
Papagena — — — Darvas Ibolya
Monostatos — — — Rovelli Dezső
Első fiu — — — Dános Lili
Második fiu — — — Bán Kató
Harmadik fiu — — Rózsa Vera
Első rabszolga — — Molnár József
Második rabszolga — — Keleti Árpád
Az OMIKE zenekara és énekkara
Vezényel Somogyi László Rendező Bálint Lajos
Karigazgató Káldi László
Szinpadi előadás
Kezdete pontosan 1/2 8 órakor

Figure 8c. *The Magic Flute* (*A Varászfuvola*), opera. D. Ernster, Dr. J. Sipos, S. Farkas, D. Ney, I. Ladányi, Z. Pogány, et al. Dec. 1, 1941. Courtesy of NTE.

2.
DYBUK
Héber kabbalista legenda három felvonásban
Irta S. An-Ski Forditotta Harsányi Zsolt
Zenéjét szerezte és összeállitotta Nádor Mihály
Személyek:
Rabbi Asriel ... Beregi Oszkár
A mesulah ... Gellért Lajos
A brinitzi reb Szender ... Simai Ede
Lea, a leánya ... Simon Zsuzsa
Fráde, Lea dajkája ... Vidor Ferike
Gitel, Lea barátnője ... Solt Ibolya
Malke, „ „ ... Szilágyi Bea
Manasse, Lea vőlegénye ... Szabó Dezső
Nahman, Manasse apja ... Fellegi István
Reb Mendel, Manasse oktatója ... Bondy István
A vendég ... Darvas Ernő
Michael, a szolgája ... Molnár József
Reb Simson ... Mányai Lajos
Első daján ... Fellegi István
Második daján ... Gonda Jenő
Özvegyasszony ... Győri Matild
Vak vénasszony ... Zágon Vera
Mayer, a brinitzi imaház szolgája ... Sándor József
Chanán, a brinitzi jesiva növendéke ... Gonda József
Enoch, „ „ „ „ ... Horváth Ferenc
Áser, „ „ „ „ ... Regős Péter
Első batlan ... Somlár Zsigmond
Második batlan ... Kallós József
Harmadik batlan ... Darvas Ernő
Első haszid ... Bondy István
Második haszid ... Sándor József
Harmadik haszid ... Fehér Tivadar
Béna koldus ... Sebestyén Jenő
Bócherek, koldusok, násznép, zenészek
Rendező Gellért Lajos
Kezdete pontosan 1/2 8 órakor
Az előadás megkezdésekor a nézőtérre vezető ajtókat bezárjuk
7

Figure 8d. An-Ski's *Dybbuk* (*Dybuk*), Hebrew kabbalistic legend. O. Beregi, L. Gellért, E. Simai, Z. Simon, F. Vidor, I. Solt, et al. Mar. 15, 1941. Courtesy of HNL ThC.

OMIKE MŰVÉSZESTÉK

a Goldmark-teremben (VII., Wesselényi-utca 7)

A Színházi est-sorozat III. műsora

1942. január hó 31-én, szombaton este Helybiztosítás : D|2, E

1. Héber dalok Énekli Sík Olga

Bemutató előadás

2. TÁMÁR

Színjáték 9 képben

Irta Bálint Lajos

Személyek:

Juda	Beregi Oszkár
Anán	Gellért Lajos
Sélah	Ujfalusi István
Rabak	Manuel Lajos
Hákán, Juda szolgája	Szigeti Jenő
Khira, Juda barátja	Simai Ede
Iráim, írástudó	Somlár Zsigmond
Támár	Párdány Judit
Ada	Spiegel Annie
Lea	Szilágyi Bea
I. bíró	Várnai Jenő
II. bíró	Darvas Ernő
III. bíró	Sándor József
IV. bíró	Molnár József
V. bíró	László Tivadar
VI. bíró	Füzesi Róbert

Rendező Gellért Lajos

A kísérőzenét szerezte Fischer Sándor

Kezdete pontosan ½8 órakor

Az előadás megkezdésekor a nézőtérre vezető ajtókat bezárjuk

Figure 9a. Balint's *Támár,* stage play. O. Beregi, L. Gellért, I. Ujfalusi, L. Mányai, J. Szigeti, E. Simai, Z. Somlár, et al. Jan. 31, 1942. Courtesy of HNL ThC.

OMIKE MŰVÉSZAKCIÓ

A GOLDMARK-TEREMBEN

Okt. 24-én szombaton este ½7 órakor (1.-ször) Helybizt.: D/2
Okt. 27-én kedden este ½7 órakor (2.-szor) —
Okt. 31-én szombaton este ½7 órakor (3.-szor) Helybizt.: D/2

Egy az Isten!

Három színjáték

Irta Szabolcsi Lajos

I.

Az ezüst serleg

Személyek:

Király	Beregi Oszkár
Felesége	Kelen Dóra
Háznagy	Dózsa István
Simon	Bondy István
Ruben	Gáti Pál
Juda	Rónai Géza
Lévi	Bársony Aladár
Benjámin	Brenner Harry
Szolga	Molnár József

Kanaáni kereskedők, földmívesek és az alkirály szolgái.

Rendező Beregi Oszkár

Folytatás a túloldalon

Figure 9b. Szabolcsi's *God is One* (*Egy az Isten!*), three stage plays: *The Silver Goblet* (*Az Ezüst Serleg*). O. Beregi, D. Kelen, I. Dózsa, I. Bondy, et al. Oct. 21, 1942. Courtesy of HNL ThC.

OMIKE MŰVÉSZAKCIÓ

A GOLDMARK-TEREMBEN

II.

A párbaj

Személyek:

Saul	Nagy György
Michál	Solt Ibolya
Abner	Justh Gyula
Dávid	Simon Zsuzsa
Eliáb	Balázs István
Abinádab	Poprádi Ernő
Góliát hangja	Rónai Géza

Rendező Nagy György

III.

Legenda

Személyek:

A Rabbi	Gellért Lajos
Az idegen	Szigeti Jenő
I. virrasztó	Simai Ede
II. virrasztó	Darvas Ernő
III. virrasztó	Sándor József
IV. virrasztó	Ádám Pál

A kísérőzenét szerezte és a szólókat énekli Herskovits Béla főkántor, az Omike énekkarának közreműködésével

Rendező Gellért Lajos

Vezényel: Fischer Sándor

Kezdete pontosan ½7 órakor

Az előadás megkezdésekor a nézőtérre vezető ajtókat bezárjuk

Figure 9c. Szabolcsi's *The Duel* (*A Párbaj*). G. Nagy, I. Solt, G. Justh, Z. Simon, et al.; and *Legend* (*Legenda*). L. Gellért, J. Szigeti, E. Simai, E. Darvas, J. Sándor, and P. Ádám. Oct. 21, 1942. Courtesy of HNL ThC.

OMIKE MŰVÉSZAKCIÓ

A GOLDMARK-TEREMBEN

Nov. 11-én, szerdán este 6 órakor (3.-szor)

Operai szelvénytöbblet fizetendő!

Verdi

Traviata

Opera 4 felvonásban

Személyek:

Valery Violetta	Darvas Ibolya
Flora	Spiegel Annie
Germont György	Lendvay Andor
Germont Alfréd	Fehér Pál
Orvos	Ernster Dezső
Báró Douphol	Bálint Béla
Márki	Pogány László
Gaston	Teszler Tivadar
Annina	Vera Viola

Az Omike zene- és énekkara

Vezényel Fraknói Károly

Rendező Szabolcs Ernő

Színpadi előadás

Kezdete pontosan 6 órakor

Az előadás megkezdése előtt a nézőtérre vezető ajtókat bezárjuk

Figure 9d. Verdi's *Traviata*, opera. I. Darvas, A. Spiegel, A. Lendvay, P. Fehér, D. Ernster, B. Bálint, L. Pogány, T. Teszler, and V. Viola. Nov. 11, 1942. Courtesy of the Hungarian Jewish Archives, Budapest.

OMIKE MŰVÉSZESTÉK
a Goldmark-teremben (VII., Wesselényi-utca 7)
A Szinházi est-sorozat II. műsora
Prolongálva ! Prolongálva !
1942. január 3-án, szombaton este
1942. január 6-án, kedden délután
1942. január 10-én, szombaton este
1942. január 18-án, vasárnap este
1942. január 24-én, szombaton este

1. A NŐS EMBER
Vigjáték 3 felvonásban
Irta Boross Elemér
Személyek:

A lány	*Simon Zsuzsa*	Apa	*Justh Gyula*
A fiu	*Ráday Imre*	Anya	*Zágon Vera*
A jelölt	*Mányai Lajos*	Nagynéni	*Pártos Erzsi*
Az egyik asszony	*Somogyi Juci*	Házmester	*Bondy István*
A másik asszony	*Kelen Dóra*		

Történik ma, Budapesten
Rendező Nagy György

2. MARSALL
Szinmű 1 felvonásban — Irta Molnár Ferenc
Személyek:

San-Friano báró	*Mányai Lajos*	Litvay	*Nagy György*
Edith	*Kornis Kató*	Orvos	*Bondy István*

Inas *László Tivadar*
Rendező Nagy György

Kezdete pontosan 1/2 8 órakor
Az előadás megkezdésekor a nézőtérre vezető ajtókat bezárjuk

Figure 10a. Boross's *The Married Man* (*A Nős Ember*), comedy. Z. Simon, I. Ráday, L. Mányai, J. Somogyi, et al.; and Molnár's *Marshal* (*Marsall*), stage play. L. Mányai, K. Kornis, G. Nagy, I. Bondy, and T. László. Jan. 3, 1942. Courtesy of HNL ThC.

OMIKE MŰVÉSZESTÉK
a Goldmark-teremben (VII., Wesselényi-utca 7)
Prolongálva ! Prolongálva !
A Vidám est-sorozat I. műsora
1942. február 8-án, vasárnap délelőtt (16)

I. RÉSZ
1. *Ormós Béla* bevezetője
2. *Nádasi László*: Keszeg és Fenyő, tréfa. Játsszák: *Ormós Béla és Fenyő Árpád*
3. *Simon Zsuzsa* költeményeket ad elő

SZÜNET

II. RÉSZ
4. CSÖPI
Márkus Alfréd uj operettje 2 felvonásban
Irta Hajós Péter. Versek: Nádasi László
Személyek:

Dénes Dániel	*Gárdonyi Lajos*	Prof. Darius	*Fenyő Árpád*
Dénesné	*Rajna Alice*	Bob	*Bondy István*
Csöpi	*Váradi Kató*	Vica	*Boros Ida*
Gereben István	*Rákos Tibor*	Ica	*Igaz Luci*
Frigyes Frigyes	*Hajós Péter*	Inas	*Tábori Ernő*
Tamara	*Lakos Klári*	Egyik soffőr	*Popráds Ernő*
Kazal Kázmér	*Szirmai Vilmos*	Másik soffőr	*Major István*

Házmester *Kürti Károly*
Karmester Márkus Alfréd — Rendező Gál Dezső
A táncokat Tábori Ernő tanitotta be
Kezdete pontosan 1/2 11 órakor
Az előadás megkezdésekor a nézőtérre vezető ajtókat lezárjuk

Figure 10b. Hajos's *Csöpi*, operetta. L. Gárdonyi, A. Rajna, and K. Váradi. Feb. 8, 1942. Courtesy of HNL ThC.

OMIKE MŰVÉSZESTÉK
a Goldmark-teremben (VII., Wesselényi-utca 7)
1942. február 18-án, szerdán este
1942. február 23-án, hétfőn este
Ünnepi előadás Goldmark Károly emlékére
Az Opera-sorozat VI. műsora

1. Megemlékezés Goldmark Károlyról
Irta és elmondja *dr. Ribáry Géza*
2. GOLDMARK:
SÁBA KIRÁLYNŐJE
Dalmű 4 felvonásban
Személyek:

Sába királynője	*Radnai Erzsi*
Sulamith	*Kraszner Kató*
Astaroth	*Ladányi Ilona*
Assad	*Garay Ernő*
Főpap	*Ernszter Dezső*
Salamon	*Farkas Sándor*
Baal Hanan	*Szücs Gábor*

Vezényel Komor Vilmos
Karigazgató Káldi László
Az OMIKE zenekara és énekkara
Hangversenyszerű előadás

Figure 10c. Goldmark's *The Queen of Sheba* (*Saba Királynője*), opera. E. Radnai, K. Kraszner, I. Ladányi, E. Garay, D. Ernster, S. Farkas, and G. Szücs. Feb. 18, 1942. Courtesy of HNL Th C.

OMIKE MŰVÉSZAKCIÓ
A GOLDMARK-TEREMBEN.
Szelvények érvényesek!
Február 11-én, csütörtökön este (14.-szer)
a Pesti Izraelita Hitközség Goldmark- és Terézvárosi Ifjúsági Csoportjai részére
Őszi szonáta
Szelvények érvényesek! — Szinmű 3 felvonásban — Irta Csergő Hugó — Szelvények érvényesek!
Személyek

Thibolt mester, nagyhirű komponista	*Beregi Oszkár*
Báró Thibolt-Martin Albert bankelnök, a sógora	*Gellért Lajos*
Konrád ujságiró, a mester titkára	*Nagy György*
Mimóza	*Párdány Judit*
Kümmer, az apja	*Molnár József*
Kümmerné, az anyja	*Győry Matild*
Anna, házvezetőnő	*Vidor Ferike*
Doktor	*Ádám Pál*
Doktorné	*Vécsey Ilona*
Lénárt, nagy kiadóvállalat főnöke	*Justh Gyula*
Lénártné, a felesége	*Ács Rózsi*
Kamilla, operaénekesnő	*Bóth Klári*
Dolorosa, költőnő	*Pártos Erzsi*
Delmár, kritikus	*Simai Ede*
Morelli, festőművész	*dr. Szabó Dezső*
Ulrik, festőművész	*Gonda Jenő*
Professzor	*Zátony Kálmán*
Riporter	*Karmos József*
Manfréd herceg	*Brust Péter*
Theodora hercegnő	*Kolos Évi*
Szárnysegéd	*Simon Lajos*
Udvarhölgy	*Szilágyi Bea*
Kristóf komornyik	*Rónai Géza*

Történik békében, a nagyhercegségi székvárosban, Thibolt mester lakásán. A második felvonás nyolc hónappal az első utáni
Kezdete pontosan 1/2 7 órakor

Figure 10d. Csergo's *Autumn Sonata* (*Őszi Szonáta*), stage play. O. Beregi, L. Gellért, G. Nagy, R. Füzesi, P. Ádám, et al. Feb. 11, 1942. Courtesy of HNL ThC.

OMIKE MŰVÉSZESTÉK

a Goldmark-teremben (VII., Wesselényi-utca 7)

A Vidám est-sorozat II. műsora

Prolongálva! *Prolongálva!*

1942. febr. 1, vasárnap este *(9)* 1942. febr. 17, kedden este *(11)*
1942. febr. 8, vasárnap este *(10)* 1942. febr. 25, szerdán délután *(12)*

I. RÉSZ

1. *Tordai Judit* költeményeket ad elő
2. *Pénteken, 13-án.* Komédia egy felvonásban. Irta: *László Miklós*; Játsszák: *Gárdonyi Lajos, Fenyő Árpád, Szigeti Jenő, Fabiny István, Dózsa István, Rajna Mária.* Rendező: *Harsányi M.*

SZÜNET

II. RÉSZ

3. **SZULAMIT**

Daljáték 6 képben

Szövegét Kövessy Albert átdolgozásából irták

Beöthy László és Makai Emil

Zenéjét eredeti héber motivumokból részben összeállitotta, részben szerezte **Donáth Ede**

Monoah	*Bálint Béla*	Cipóra	*Bán Kató*
Szulamit	*Szendrő Mária*	Eszter	*Dános Lili*
Absolon	*Balázs István*	Jeremiás	*Szigeti Jenő*
Cingitang	*Gárdonyi Lajos*	Avisono	*Dózsa István*
Áron	*Bencse Miklós*	Beliczar	*Fenyő Árpád*
Abigail	*Palotai Erzsi*	Eziel	*Fabinyi István*
Rebeka	*Bártfai Gabi*	Papok, lányok, ifjak	

A darabban előforduló „Kol Nidrê"-t *Ney Dávid* énekli

Karmester **Fraknói Károly** Rendező **Gál Dezső**

Kezdete pontosan 1/2 8 órakor, a délutáni előadásé 1/2 4 órakor

Az előadás megkezdésekor a nézőtérre vezető ajtókat lezárjuk

Figure 11a. Kovessy's *Shulamith* (*Szulamit*), opera. B. Bálint, M. Szendrő, K. Bán, I. Balázs, L. Gárdonyi, L. Dános, et al. Feb. 1, 1942. Courtesy of NTE.

Simon Zsuzsa, Nagy György, Mányai Lajos

saját rendezése

az OMIKE művészakció keretében

a Goldmark-teremben (VII., Wesselényi-utca 7.)

1942. május 3-án, vasárnap

délelőtt 11 órakor

1. Bernáth Júlia magánszáma

2. **SZERETNI...**

Szinmű 3 felvonásban

Irta: PAUL GÉRALDY

Személyek:

Henri	**Nagy György**
Helèn	**Simon Zsuzsa**
Challange	**Mányai Lajos**

Kezdete pontosan 11 órakor

Ehrenfeld Miksa Budapest. F. k. Mányai Lajos

Figure 11b. Geraldy's *To Love* (*Szeretni*), stage play. G. Nagy, Z. Simon, and L. Mányai. May 3, 1942. Courtesy of NTE.

OMIKE MŰVÉSZAKCIÓ

A GOLDMARK-TEREMBEN

Nov. 1-én, vasárnap este 1/2 7 órakor (6.-szor)
Nov. 8-án, vasárnap este 1/2 7 órakor (7.-szer)
Nov. 15-én, vasárnap este 1/2 7 órakor (8.-szor)
Nov. 22-én, vasárnap d. u. 1/2 3 órakor (9.-szer)

Három a kislány

Énekes játék 3 felvonásban

Zenéjét **Schubert** műveiből összeállította **Berté**

Személyek:

Schubert F.	*Fehér Pál, Ney Dávid, Sas Imre*	Médi	*Ladányi Ilona, Bán Kató*
Schober báró	*Lenduay Andor, Rákos Tibor*	Grisi Lucia	*Faragó Panni, Pálfi Blanka*
Schwind	*Sas Imre*	Bruneder	*Gáli György*
Kupelwieser	*Pogány László*	Binder	*dr. Szabó D.*
Vogl	*Szirmai Vilmos*		
Schantorff gr.	*Zátony Kálmán*	Novotny	*Ormos Béla, Szigeti Jenő*
Tschöll	*Sarkadi A., Szigeti Jenő*	Sáni pikkoló	*Brenner H.*
Tschöllné	*Spiegel Annie, Vidor Ferike*	Róza	*Pór Irén*
Édi, Hédi	*Bán Kató, Bártfai Gaby, Fábry Edit, Dános Lili, Somogyi Piri*	Rézi	*Horváth Mädy*
		Házmesterné	*Győry Matild*
		Wéberné	*Ács Rózsi*
		I. utcai énekes	*Pollák Sándor*
		II. utcai énekes	*Erdész Nándor*

Történik Bécsben, 1826-ban

Karmester **Fischer Sándor** Rendező **Gál Dezső**

A táncokat betanította **Szilágyi Bea**

Az egyes előadások szereposztását a pénztár és a szokott lapok közlik

Figure 11c. Schubert's *The Little Girl Is Three* (*Három A Kislány*), singing play. P. Fehér, D. Ney II, I. Sas, I. Ladány, K. Bán, et al. Nov. 1, 1942. Courtesy of NTE.

OMIKE MŰVÉSZAKCIÓ

A GOLDMARK-TEREMBEN

Dec. 7-én, hétfőn este 1/2 7 órakor

Kodály-est

a mester 60. születésnapja alkalmából

Közreműködnek

Rózsa Vera, Weinstock Miklós (ének)
Weiner László (zongora)
Starker János (gordonka)
Ákos Ferenc—Lőrincz Edith—
Lukács Pál—Horváth László-vonósnégyes

Műsor:

1. I. Vonósnégyes Op. 10.
   Allegro—Andante, Quasi recitativo—Allegro giocoso
2. *a) Kádár István*
   b) Árva madár
   c) A csitári hegyek alatt *(Weinstock Miklós)*
3. Hegedű-gordonka kettes *(Ákos Ferenc, Starker János)*

Szünet

4. *a)* Nausikaa
   b) Rossz feleség
   c) Szegény vagyok. Dal a Háry János c. daljátékból
   d) Hej, két tikom. Dal a Háry János c. daljátékból *(Rózsa Vera)*
5. Szonáta gordonkára és zongorára Op. 4.
   Fantasia. Adagio di molto — Allegro con spirito
   (Starker János, Weiner László)

Kezdete pontosan 1/2 7 órakor

Az előadás megkezdése előtt a nézőtérre vezető ajtókat lezárjuk

Figure 11d. Kodaly Evening (*Kodály-Est*). V. Rózsa, L.Weiner, J. Starker, F. Akos, E. Lőrincz, P. Lukács, L. Horváth, and M. Weinstock. Dec. 7, 1942. Courtesy of NTE.

OMIKE MŰVÉSZESTÉK
a Goldmark-teremben (VII., Wesselényi-utca 7)
Rendkivüli előadások XV. müsora
1942. március 8-án, vasárnap délelőtt

FEHÉR PÁL II. HANGVERSENYE

Közremüködnek
Horváth László (gordonka), *Halmos György* (zongora)

MŰSOR

1. a. *Händel:* Largo b. *Mozart:* Alleluja — *Fehér Pál*
2. a. *Caporale:* Largo amoroso b. *Frescobaldi:* Toccata c. *Beethoven:* Sonatina — *Horváth László*
3. a. *Schubert:* Ständchen b. *Schubert:* Ungeduld c. *Schubert:* Du bist wie eine Blume d. *Schumann:* Mondnacht — *Fehér Pál*
4. a. *Bach:* C-dur adagio b. *Busoni:* Toccata és Fuga — *Halmos György*
5. a. *Donizetti:* Szerelmi bájital b. *Cilea:* Arlesienne — *Fehér Pál*

SZÜNET

6. a. *Fauré:* Apres un réve b. *Debussy:* Menuette c. *Chopin:* Nocturne d. *Rimszky-Korsakov:* Dongó — *Horváth László*
7. a. *Meyerbeer:* Afrikai nő b. *Bizet:* Gyöngyhalász — *Fehér Pál*
8. a. *Liszt:* Les Funerailles b. *Chopin:* Asz-dur Etude c. *Chopin:* Cisz-moll Etude — *Halmos György*
9. Olasz dalok — *Fehér Pál*

Zongorán kisér *Weiner László*

Kezdete pontosan 1/2 11 órakor
Az előadás megkezdésekor a nézőtérre vezető ajtókat bezárjuk

Figure 12a. Pál Fehér's 2nd Concert (*Pál Fehér II. Hangversenye*), accompanied by L. Horváth and G. Halmos. Mar. 8, 1942. Courtesy of NTE.

OMIKE MŰVÉSZAKCIÓ
A GOLDMARK-TEREMBEN

Nov. 9-én, hétfőn este 6 órakor (1.-ször) Helybizt.: O/2, Z/1
Nov. 16-án, hétfőn este 6 órakor (2.-szor) Helybizt.: O/3
Nov. 18-án, szerdán este 6 órakor (3.-szor) Helybizt.: O/4, Z/2

Operai szelvénytöbblet fizetendő!

Offenbach
Hoffmann meséi
Dalmű 3 felvonásban (4 képben)

Személyek:

	nov. 9-én és 16-án	nov. 18-án
Olympia	*Darvas Ibolya*	*Ladányi Ilona*
Giulietta, Antonia	*Relle Gabriella*	*Gödry Kató*, *Pogány Zsuzsi*
Lindorf, Coppelius, Dapertutto, Mirakel	*Farkas Sándor*	*Lendvay Andor*
Hoffmann	*Fehér Pál*	*Teszler Tivadar*
Miklós	*Spiegel Annie*	*Somogyi Piri*
András, Pitichinaccio, Cochenille	*Teszler Tivadar*	*Rózsa Nándor*
Anya hangja	*Sík Olga*	*Spiegel Annie*
Spalanzani	*Somogyi Dezső*	*Somogyi Dezső*
Nathaniel	*Ney Dávid*	*Ney Dávid*
Crespel	*Bálint Béla*	*Bálint Béla*
Luther	*Molnár László*	*Molnár László*
Hermann	*Galsay Ervin*	*Galsay Ervin*
Schlemil	*Roth Ferenc*	*Roth Ferenc*

Vezényel **Komor Vilmos** rendező **Szabolcs Ernő**
Karigazgató **dr. Bermann Ferenc**
Színpadi előadás Az Omike zene- és énekkara

Kezdete pontosan 6 órakor

Figure 12b. Offenbach's *Hoffmann Tales* (*Hoffmann Meséi*), opera. I. Darvas, G. Relle, I. Ladányi, K. Gödry, A. Lendvay, S. Farkas, P. Fehér, et al. Nov. 9, 1942. Courtesy of the Hungarian Jewish Archives, Budapest.

OMIKE MŰVÉSZAKCIÓ
A GOLDMARK-TEREMBEN

Dec. 17-én, csütörtökön este 1/2 7 órakor

Ernster Dezső
hangversenye

Közremüködik **Gergely Pál** (zongora)

Műsor:

1. a) *Händel:* Recitativ és ária a Juda Makkabi c. oratóriumból. b) *Haydn:* Recitativ és ária a Teremtés c. oratóriumból.
2. *Schubert:* a) Wanderer's Nachtlied. b) Der Neugierige. c) Ungeduld.
3. *Cornelius:* Ária a Bagdadi borbély c. operából.

Szünet

4. *Mozart:* Ária a Figaro lakodalma c. operából.
5. *Wolff:* a) Alles endet, was entstehet. b) Fühlt meine Seele.
6. *Kodály:* a) Magányosság (Berzsenyi). b) A farsang búcsúszavai (Csokonai)
7. *Verdi:* Ária a Nabucodonosor c. operából.

Kezdete pontosan 1/2 7 órakor

Az előadás megkezdése előtt a nézőtérre vezető ajtókat bezárjuk

Figure 12c. Concert (*Hangversenye*). D. Ernster. Dec. 17, 1942. Courtesy of NTE.

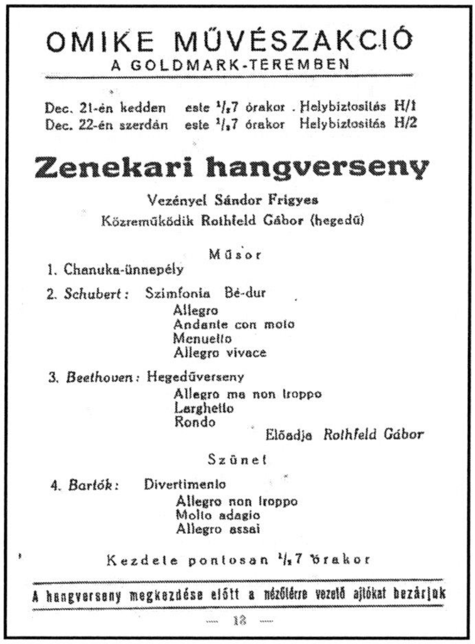

OMIKE MŰVÉSZAKCIÓ
A GOLDMARK-TEREMBEN

Dec. 21-én kedden este 1/2 7 órakor. Helybiztositás H/1
Dec. 22-én szerdán este 1/2 7 órakor Helybiztositás H/2

Zenekari hangverseny

Vezényel Sándor Frigyes
Közremüködik Rothfeld Gábor (hegedű)

Műsor

1. Chanuka-ünnepély
2. *Schubert:* Szimfonia Bé-dur
   Allegro
   Andante con moto
   Menuetto
   Allegro vivace
3. *Beethoven:* Hegedűverseny
   Allegro ma non troppo
   Larghetto
   Rondo
   Előadja *Rothfeld Gábor*

Szünet

4. *Bartók:* Divertimento
   Allegro non troppo
   Molto adagio
   Allegro assai

Kezdete pontosan 1/2 7 órakor

A hangverseny megkezdése előtt a nézőtérre vezető ajtókat bezárjuk

— 18 —

Figure 12d. Musical Concert (*Zenekari Hangverseny*). Schubert, Beethoven, and Bartók. Dec. 21, 1942. Courtesy of HNL ThC.

OMIKE MŰVÉSZAKCIÓ
A GOLDMARK-TEREMBEN

Jan. 4-én, hétfőn este ½7 órakor

Gödry Kató (ének) Herz Lili (zongora)
és
Horváth László (gordonka)
hangversenye

Műsor

1. Chopin: Ballada F-dur, Mazurka F-moll, Etude C-moll — Herz Lili
2. Haydn: Recitativ és ária a „Teremtés"-ből
Schubert: Du bist die Ruh', Gretchen am Spinnrad, Das Lied im Grünen — Gödry Kató
3. Vivaldi: D-dur koncert
Händel—Weiner László: Siciliano
Boccherini: A-dur szonáta — Horváth László

Szünet

4. Josef Marx: Hat dich die Liebe berührt, Venetianisches Wiegenlied, Waldseligkeit
Verdi: Ária a Lombardok c. operából — Gödry Kató
5. Schubert: Allegretto grazioso
De Falla: Jota
Debussy: Reverie
Rachmaninoff: Cigánytánc — Horváth László
6. Schubert—Grünfeld: Fantázia
Balakirew: Islamey — Herz Lili

Kísér Sebők György

Figure 13a. Concert (*Hangversenye*). K. Gödry, L. Herz, and L. Horváth. Jan. 4, 1943. Courtesy of HNL ThC.

OMIKE MŰVÉSZAKCIÓ
A GOLDMARK-TEREMBEN

Jan 13-án, szerdán este ½7 órakor

W. Rózsa Vera (ének)
és
S. Dénes Vera (gordonka)
hangversenye
Kísér Weiner László

Műsor

1. Schubert: Frühlingstraum, Die Stadt, Die Forelle, Das Mädchens Klage, Der Müller und der Bach, Der Musensohn — W. Rózsa Vera
2. Bach: Adagio
Locatelli: D dur szonata — S. Dénes Vera

Szünet

3. Bartók: I. Rapszódia — S. Dénes Vera
4. Mussorgszky: A halál dalai és táncai — W. Rózsa Vera
5. Chopin: Nocturne
Weber: Rondo
Paganini-Silva: Mózes-változatok — S. Dénes Vera
6. Kodály: Búsan csörög a lomb, Ballada a Székelyfonó c. daljátékból
Debussy: Nuit d'etoiles, Fantoches
Ravel: Habanera
W. Pohl: La fête champêtre — W. Rózsa Vera

Kezdete pontosan ½7 órakor

Figure 13b. Concert (*Hangversenye*). V. Rózsa and V. Dénes. Jan. 13, 1943. Courtesy of HNL ThC.

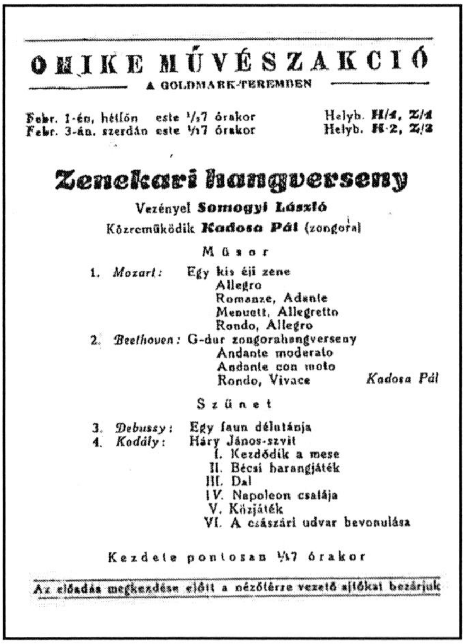

OMIKE MŰVÉSZAKCIÓ
A GOLDMARK-TEREMBEN

Febr. 1-én, hétfőn este ½7 órakor
Febr. 3-án, szerdán este ½7 órakor

Zenekari hangverseny
Vezényel Somogyi László
Közreműködik Kadosa Pál (zongora)

Műsor

1. Mozart: Egy kis éji zene: Allegro, Romanze, Adante, Menuett, Allegretto, Rondo, Allegro
2. Beethoven: G-dur zongorahangverseny: Andante moderato, Andante con moto, Rondo, Vivace — Kadosa Pál

Szünet

3. Debussy: Egy faun délutánja
4. Kodály: Háry János-szvit: I. Kezdődik a mese, II. Bécsi harangjáték, III. Dal, IV. Napoleon csatája, V. Közjáték, VI. A császári udvar bevonulása

Kezdete pontosan ½7 órakor

Az előadás megkezdése előtt a nézőtérre vezető ajtókat bezárjuk

Figure 13c. Musical Concert (*Zenekari Hangverseny*). Mozart, Beethoven, Debussy, and Kodály. Feb.1, 1942. Courtesy of HNL ThC.

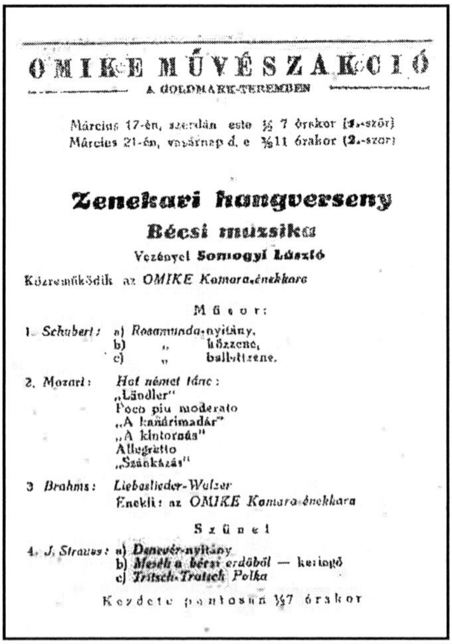

OMIKE MŰVÉSZAKCIÓ
A GOLDMARK-TEREMBEN

Március 17-én, szerdán este ½ 7 órakor (1.-ször)
Március 21-én, vasárnap d. e. ½11 órakor (2.-szor)

Zenekari hangverseny
Bécsi muzsika
Vezényel Somogyi László
Közreműködik az OMIKE Kamara-énekkara

Műsor:

1. Schubert: a) Rosamunda-nyitány, b) „ közzene, c) „ balletzene.
2. Mozart: Hat német tánc: „Ländler", Poco piu moderato, „A kandírimadár", „A kintornás", Allegretto, „Szánkázás"
3. Brahms: Liebeslieder-Walzer. Énekli: az OMIKE Kamara-énekkara

Szünet

4. J. Strauss: a) Denevér-nyitány, b) Mesék a bécsi erdőből — keringő, c) Tritsch-Tratsch Polka

Kezdete pontosan ½7 órakor

Figure 13d. Musical Concert, Viennese Music (*Zenekari Hangverseny, Bécsi Muzsika*), led by L. Somogyi. Schubert, Mozart, Brahms, and J. Strauss. Mar. 17, 1942. Courtesy of NTE.

OMIKE MŰVÉSZAKCIÓ
A GOLDMARK-TEREMBEN

Október 25-én hétfőn este 6 órakor (7.-szer)

Operai szelvénytöbblet fizetendő !

Beethoven

FIDELIO

Opera 2 felvonásban

Személyek

Don Fernando	*Farkas Sándor*
Don Pizarro	*Ernster Dezső*
Florestan	*Fehér Pál*
Leonora	*Róna Vera*
Rocco	*Kálmán Oszkár*
Jaquino	*dr. Sipos Jenő*
Marcellina	*Bán Kató*
Első fogoly	*Gallai Márton*
Második fogoly	*Molnár László*
Tiszt	*Csillag István*

Beethoven : III. Leonora-nyitány

Előadásra kerül az utolsó kép előtt

Vezényel Komor Vilmos — Rendező Bálint Lajos

Karigazgató dr. Bermann Ferenc

Kezdete pontosan 6 órakor

Az előadás megkezdése előtt a nézőtérre vezető ajtókat bezárjuk

— 6 —

Figure 14a. Beethoven's *Fidelio*, opera. S. Farkas, D. Ernster, P. Fehér, V. Róna, O. Kálmán, et al. Oct. 25, 1943. Courtesy of HNL ThC.

OMIKE MŰVÉSZAKCIÓ
A GOLDMARK-TEREMBEN

Január 31-én vasárnap délután ½3-kor (11.-szer)

Operai szelvénytöbblet fizetendő !

Puccini

Pillangókisasszony

Dalmű 3 felvonásban

Személyek:

Cso-Cso-Szan	*Gödry Kató*
Szuzuki	*Spiegel Annie*
Kate	*Leopold Lenke*
Pinkerton	*Fehér Pál*
Sharpless	*Lendvay Andor*
Goro	*Teszler Tivadar*
Yamadori	*Ney Dávid*
Bonzo	*Pogány László*
Császári biztos	*Galsay Ervin*
Cso-Cso-Szan anyja	*Rudas Erna*

Vezényel **Komor Vilmos**

Rendező **Harsányi Miklós**

Az Omike zene- és énekkara

Karigazgató **dr. Bermann Ferenc**

Színpadi előadás

Kezdete pontosan ½3 órakor

Az előadás megkezdése előtt a nézőtérre vezető ajtókat bezárjuk

Figure 14b. Puccini's *Madame Butterfly* (*Pillangókisasszony*), opera. K. Gödry, A. Spiegel, L. Lenke, P. Fehér, T. Teszler, et al. Jan. 31, 1943. Courtesy of HNL ThC.

OMIKE MŰVÉSZAKCIÓ
A GOLDMARK-TEREMBEN

Nov. 24-én szerdán este 6 órakor (1.-ször) Helybiztositás 0/1
Nov. 29-én hétfőn este 6 órakor (2.-szor) Helybiztositás 0/2

Operai szelvénytöbblet fizetendő !

Mozart

Figaro lakodalma

Vígopera 4 felvonásban

Személyek

Almaviva gróf	*Farkas Sándor*
A grófnő	*Gödry Kató*
Susanne, komornája	*Szendrő Mária*
Cherubin, a gróf apródja	*Darvas Ibolya*
Figaro, a gróf komornyikja	*Ernster Dezső*
Marcellina, házvezetőnő	*Spiegel Annie*
Bartolo, orvos	*Récsész Imre*
Basilio, énekmester	*dr. Sipos Jenő*
Don Cursio, bíró	*Gallai Márton*
Antonio, kertész, Suzanne nagybátyja	*Galsay Ervin*
Barbarina, a leánya	*Kolos Hanna*

Történik a gróf kastélyában és kertjében, a XVIII. század végén

Vezényel Komor Vilmos — Rendező Szabolcs Ernő

Kezdete pontosan 6 órakor

Az előadás megkezdése előtt a nézőtérre vezető ajtókat bezárjuk

— 12 —

Figure 14c. Mozart's *Figaro's Wedding* (*Figaro Lakodalma*), comic opera. S. Farkas, K. Gödry, M. Szendrő, I. Darvas, et al. Nov. 24, 1943. Courtesy of HNL ThC.

OMIKE MŰVÉSZAKCIÓ
A GOLDMARK-TEREMBEN

November 28-án délután ½3 órakor (7.-szer)

Operai szelvénytöbblet fizetendő !

Verdi

RIGOLETTO

Opera 4 felvonásban

Személyek

A herceg	*Fehér Pál*
Rigoletto	*Lendvay Andor*
Gilda	*Sebők Steli*
Sparafucile	*Kálmán Oszkár*
Maddalena	*Spiegel Annie*
Borsa	*Ney Dávid*
Monterone	*Ernster Dezső*
Marullo	*Molnár László*
Ceprano	*Galsay Ervin*
Ceprano grófnő	*Danziger Lili*
Giovanna	*Földiák Márta*
Apród	*Rudas Erna*

Vezényel Komor Vilmos — Rendező Szabolcs Ernő

Kezdete pontosan ½3 órakor

Az előadás megkezdése előtt a nézőtérre vezető ajtókat bezárjuk

— 13 —

Figure 14d. Verdi's *Rigoletto*, opera. P. Fehér, A. Lendvay, O. Kálmán, A. Spiegel, D. Ney II, D. Ernster, et al. Nov. 28, 1943. Courtesy of HNL ThC.

OMIKE MŰVÉSZAKCIÓ
A GOLDMARK-TEREMBEN
Február 27-én, szombaton este 6 órakor (1.-ször) Helyb.: B/2
Shakespeare
Hamlet, dán királyfi
Tragédia 5 felvonásban
Fordította Arany János
Személyek
Claudius, Dánia királya — Gellért Lajos
Hamlet, az előbbi király fia, a mostaninak unokaöccse — Beregi Oszkár
Horatio, Hamlet barátja — Fenyő Emil
Polonius főkamarás — Szigeti Jenő
Laertes, fia — Simon Lajos
Voltimand — Aczél Pál
Cornelius } udvarlék — Kis Aladár
Rosencrantz — Bondy István
Guildenstern — Kormos József
Marcellus — Simai Ede
Bernardo — Rónai Géza
Francisco, katona — Ádám Pál
Rajnáld, Polonius embere — Csillag István
Hamlet atyja szelleme — Zátony Kálmán
Első sírásó — Sarkadi Aladár
Második sírásó — Ujfalusi István
Gertrud dán királyné, Hamlet anyja — Kelen Dóra
Ophelia, Polonius leánya — Párdány Judit
Színészkirály — Nagy György
Színészkirályné — Szilágyi Bea
Fortinbras — Boros Béla
Rendező Gellért Lajos
Kezdete pontosan 6 órakor
Az előadás megkezdése előtt a nézőtérre vezető ajtókat bezárjuk

Figure 15a. Shakespeare's *Hamlet, Prince of Denmark* (*Hamlet, Dán Királyfi*), tragedy. L. Gellért, O. Beregi, E. Fenyő, J. Szigeti, P. Aczél, A. Kis, I. Bondy, et al. Feb. 27, 1943. Courtesy of HNL ThC.

OMIKE MŰVÉSZAKCIÓ
A GOLDMARK-TEREMBEN
Április 29-én, csütörtökön este 1/2 7 órakor (11.-szer)
Szelvények érvényesek!
A Goldmark és Terézvárosi Ifjúsági Csoportok részére
Molnár Ferenc
Az ismeretlen lány
Drámai történet 3 felvonásban (7 képben)
Személyek:
Gróf Armaila ... Gárdonyi Lajos
Anni ... Rosty Magda
Főorvos ... Justh Gyula
Rudolf ... Nagy György
Pálné ... Zágon Vera
Mici ... Pártos Erzsi
Tengernagy ... Zátony Kálmán
Postatiszt ... Bondy István
Georgi ... Fenyő Emil
Eliza nővér ... Simon Zsuzsa
Bárfulajdonos ... Simai Ede
Steif ... Balázs István
Carlo ... Rózsa Nándor
Postai főtiszt ... Darvas Ernő
Segédorvos ... Gonda Jenő
Műszerész ... Szigeti Jenő
Pincér ... dr. Szabó Dezső
Csendőr ... Dózsa István
Táncosnő ... Szilágyi Bea
Rendező Bálint Lajos
Szünet az 1. és 4. kép után
Kezdete pontosan 1/2 7 órakor
Az előadás megkezdése előtt a nézőtérre vezető ajtókat bezárjuk

Figure 15b. Molnar's *The Unknown Girl* (*Az Ismeretlen Lány*), drama. L. Gárdonyi, M. Rosty, G. Justh, G. Nagy, I. Dózsa, et al. April 29, 1943. Courtesy of HNL ThC.

OMIKE MŰVÉSZAKCIÓ
A GOLDMARK-TEREMBEN
Március 16-án, kedden este 1/2 7 órakor (9.-szer)
Vidám műsor
1. Sarkadi Aladár magánszáma
2. Tordai Judit szaval
3. Kezeket fel!
Zenés komédia 2 részben (4 képben)
Írták Erdősi László és Szécsén Mihály
Zenéjét szerezte Erdősi László
Személyek:
Fred Pixton — Gárdonyi Lajos
Jonny Bood — Balázs István
Joe Smith, a betörő — Szirmai Vilmos
Dorothy, a felesége — Ács Rózsi
Lilian — Váradi Kató
James — Lénárd Béla
Steve Bolter — Sas Imre
Olga — Faragó Panni
Big Bill — Ormos Béla
Szobaleány — Győri Matild
Detektívfelügyelő — Sándor József
Stills felügyelő — Bondy István
Mills detektív — Ádám Pál
Rendőr — Barna Lajos
Bártulajdonos — Kovács Imre
Jim — Békeffi Róbert
Karmester Lajtai-Lazarus Walter · Rendező Gál Dezső
A táncokat betanította Erdős László
Szünet a 2. kép után
Kezdete pontosan 1/2 7 órakor

Figure 15c. Gaity Program (*Vidám Műsor*). A. Sarkadi and J. Tordai; along with Erdősi and Szécsén's *Hands Up!* (*Kezeket Fel!*), musical comedy. L. Gárdonyi, I. Balázs, V. Skirmai, R. Ács, K. Váradi, B. Lénárd, I. Sas, et al. March 16, 1943. Courtesy of HNL ThC.

OMIKE MŰVÉSZAKCIÓ
A GOLDMARK-TEREMBEN
Május 31-én, hétfőn este 1/2 7 órakor (1.-szőr)
Molnár Ferenc
Liliom
Külvárosi legenda 7 képben
Személyek
Liliom ... Ráday Imre
Julika ... Simon Zsuzsa
Mari ... Pártos Erzsi
Ficsur ... Simon Lajos
Hugó ... Gárdonyi Lajos
Linzmann ... Justh Gyula
Lujza ... Földi Zsuzsa
Hollunderné ... Vidor Ferike
A Hollunder fiú ... dr. Szabó Dezső
Orvos ... Szirmai Vilmos
Fogalmazó ... Zátony Kálmán
Az ezredorvos ... Dózsa István
Kapitány ... Balázs István
Öreg rendőr ... Rónai Géza
Budai rendőr ... Kürti Károly
Dr. Reich ... Bondy István
Kádár István ... Sarkadi Aladár
I. detektív ... Poprádi Ernő
II. detektív ... Ádám Pál
I. lovasrendőr ... Sas Imre
II. lovasrendőr ... Sándor József
Történik a városligetben és a másvilágon
Rendező Ráday Imre
A prologust írta Szép Ernő
Kezdete pontosan 1/2 7 órakor
Az előadás megkezdése előtt a nézőtérre vezető ajtókat bezárjuk

Figure 15d. Molnar's *Lily* (*Liliom*), stage play. I. Ráday, Z. Simon, E. Pártos, L. Simon, L. Gárdonyi, G. Justh, I. Bondy, A. Sarkadi, et al. May 31, 1943. Courtesy of HNL ThC.

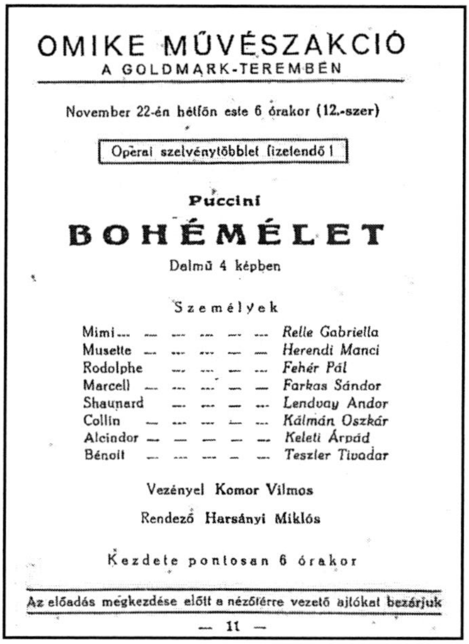

OMIKE MŰVÉSZAKCIÓ
A GOLDMARK-TEREMBEN

November 22-én hétfőn este 6 órakor (12.-szer)

Operai szelvénytöbblet fizetendő!

Puccini

BOHÉMÉLET

Dalmű 4 képben

Személyek

Mimi	Relle Gabriella
Musette	Herendi Manci
Rodolphe	Fehér Pál
Marcell	Farkas Sándor
Shaunard	Lendvay Andor
Collin	Kálmán Oszkár
Alcindor	Keleti Árpád
Bénoit	Teszler Tivadar

Vezényel Komor Vilmos

Rendező Harsányi Miklós

Kezdete pontosan 6 órakor

Az előadás megkezdése előtt a nézőtérre vezető ajtókat bezárjuk

— 11 —

Figure 16a. Puccini's *La Boheme* (*Bohémélet*), opera. G. Relle, M. Herendi, P. Fehér, S. Farkas, A. Lendvay, O. Kálmán, et al. Nov. 22, 1943. Courtesy of HNL ThC.

OMIKE MŰVÉSZAKCIÓ
A GOLDMARK-TEREMBEN

Június 6-án, vasárnap este 6 órakor (7.-szer) Helyb. 0/2, Z/4

Mindkét előadásra operai szelvénytöbblet fizetendő!

Új betanulással

1. *Mozart*: Török induló (Előadásra kerül a 4. kép előtt)

Mozart

2. Szöktetés a szerályból

Személyek

Constanza	*Ladányi Ilona*	Pedrillo	*Ney Dávid*
Blonde	*Darvas Ibolya*	Osmin	*Kálmán Oszkár*
Belmonte	*Fehér Pál*	Szelim	*Zátony Kálmán*

Vezényel Komor Vilmos — Rendező Szabolcs Ernő

Szinpadi előadás

Június 15-én kedden este 6 órakor (16.-szor)

Rossini

Sevillai borbély

Dalmű 3 felvonásban

Személyek

Rosina	*Ladányi Ilona*	Bartolo	*Bálint Béla*
Marcellina	*Spiegel Annie*	Basilio	*Kálmán Oszkár*
Almaviva	*Fehér Pál*	Fiorillo	*Teszler Tivadar*
Figaro	*Lendvay Andor*	Egy tiszt	*Keleti Árpád*

Jegyző ... *Major István*

Vezényel Komor Vilmos — Rendező Gál Dezső

Az Omike zene- és énekkara — Szinpadi előadás

Kezdete pontosan 6 órakor

Jegyváltásnál gondoljon az önkéntes áremelésre!

Figure 16b. Mozart's *The Abduction from the Seraglio* (*Szöktetés A Szerályból*), opera. I. Ladányi, I. Darvas, P. Fehér, D. Ney, et al. June 8, 1943; and Rossini's *Barber of Seville* (*Sevillai Borbély*), opera. I. Ladányi, A. Spiegel, P. Fehér, A. Lendvay, B. Bálint, O. Kálmán, et al. June 15, 1943. Courtesy of HNL ThC.

OMIKE MŰVÉSZAKCIÓ
A GOLDMARK-TEREMBEN

Február 4-én, csütörtökön este 6 órakor (2.-szor)
Február 14-én, vasárnap d. u. ½3 órakor (3.-szor)

Verdi

Trubadur

Opera 4 felvonásban (8 képben)

Személyek:

	II/4-én	II/14-én
Leonora	*Relle Gabriella*	*Róna Vera*
Azucena	*Spiegel Annie*	*Sík Olga*
Inez	*Rudas Erna*	*Rudas Erna*
Manrico	*Garay Ernő*	*Garay Ernő*
Luna	*Lendvay Andor*	*Lendvay Andor*
Fernando	*Kálmán Oszkár*	*Pogány László*
Ruiz	*Ney Dávid*	*Ney Dávid*
Hirnök	*Somogyi Dezső*	*Keleti Árpád*
Öreg cigány	*Faludi Ferenc*	*Faludi Ferenc*

Vezényel Fruhnói Károly — Rendező Várnai Tibor

Karigazgató dr. Bermann Ferenc

Szinpadi előadás

Február 15-én, hétfőn este 6 órakor (6.-szor)

Donizetti

Don Pasquale

Fordította Fischer Sándor — Vígopera 4 felvonásban

Személyek:

Don Pasquale	*Kálmán Oszkár*
Malatesta orvos	*Lendvay Andor*
Norina	*Darvas Ibolya*
Ernesto	*Fehér Pál*
A jegyző	*Ney Dávid*

Vezényel Somogyi László — Rendező Bálint Lajos

Karigazgató dr. Bermann Ferenc

Szinpadi előadás — Az Omike zene- és énekkara

Mindkét előadásra operai szelvénytöbblet fizetendő!

Figure 16c. Verdi's *Troubadour* (*Trubadur*), opera. G. Relle, A. Spiegel, E. Rudas, V. Róna, O. Sík, et al.; and Donizetti's *Don Pasquale*, comic opera. O. Kálmán, A. Lendvay, I. Darvas, P. Fehér and D. Ney. Feb. 4 & 15, 1943, respectively. Courtesy of HNL ThC.

OMIKE MŰVÉSZAKCIÓ
A GOLDMARK-TEREMBEN

Febr. 22-én, hétfőn este 6 órakor (1.-ször) Helybizt.: O 2, Z 3
Febr. 24-én, szerdán este 6 órakor (2.-szor) Helybizt.: O 1, Z 1
Márc. 1-én, hétfőn este 6 órakor (3.-szor) Helybizt.: O 3

Operai szelvénytöbblet fizetendő!

Verdi

Aida

Dalmű 4 felvonásban

Személyek:

	II/22 és III/1-én	II/24-én
Aida	*Relle Gabriella*	*Róna Vera*
Amneris	*Radnai Erzsi*	*Spiegel Annie*
Radames	*Fehér Pál*	*Füredi Károly*
Amonasro	*Lendvay Andor*	*Lendvay Andor*
Főpap	*Ernster Dezső*	*Kálmán Oszkár*
Király	*Kálmán Oszkár*	*Ernster Dezső*
Főpapnő	*Somogyi Piri*	*Somogyi Piri*
Hirnök	*Ney Dávid*	*Ney Dávid*

Vezényel Komor Vilmos

Az Omike zene- és énekkara

Hangversenyszerű előadás

Kezdete pontosan 6 órakor

Az előadás megkezdésekor a nézőtérre vezető ajtókat bezárjuk

Figure 16d. Verdi's *Aida*, opera. G. Relle, E. Radnai, P. Fehér, A. Lendvay, V. Róna, A. Spiegel, K. Füredi, D. Ernster, et al. Feb. 22, 1943. Courtesy of NTE.

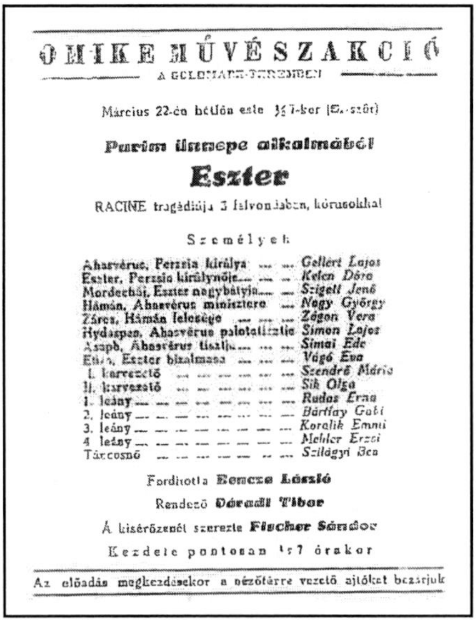

Figure 17a. Racine's *Esther* (*Eszter*) for Purim holiday, biblical drama. L. Gellért, D. Kelen, J. Szigeti, G. Nagy, V. Zágon, L. Simon, et al. Mar. 22, 1943. Courtesy of HNL ThC.

Figure 17b. Pap's *Moses* (*Mózes*), biblical drama. K. Zátony, M. Róbert, M. Rosty, G. Nagy, L. Simon, I. Bondy, et al. Mar. 10, 1943. Courtesy of HNL ThC.

Figure 17c. Spring Cabaret (*Tavaszi Kabaré*). B. Ormos, E. Pártos, Á. Fenyő, et al.; *The Bride of the Company* (*A Cég Arája*). B. Salamon, B. Ormos, A. Rajna, et al.; *With Carmen in the Opera, It's No Use Going to the Opera* (*Carmen-ni az operába*). E. Pártos, S. Radó, K. Lakos, et al.; and *The Abduction of Mrs. Sabin* (*Szabinné Elrablása*). B. Salamon, A. Rajna, P. Faragó, et al. Mar. 7, 1943. Courtesy of HNL ThC.

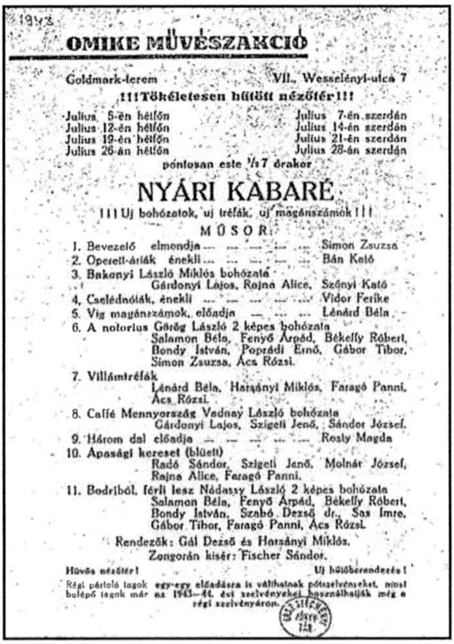

Figure 17d. Summer Cabaret (*Nyári Kabaré*). Z. Simon, K. Bán, F. Vidor, B. Lénárd, M. Harsányi, M. Rosty, J. Szigeti, B. Salamon, R. Bekeffy, I. Bondy, I. Sas, et al. July 5, 1943. Courtesy of HNL ThC.

OMIKE MŰVÉSZAKCIÓ
A GOLDMARK-TEREMBEN

Március 24-én, szerdán este 6-kor (1.-szór) Helybizt D 1, Z 1
Március 29-én, hétfőn este 6 kor (2.-szor) Helybizt D 2, Z 4

Operai szelvénytöbblet fizetendő!

Donizetti
Lammermoori Lucia
Opera 3 felvonásban (6 kép)

Személyek

Lord Asthon ... Farkas Sándor
Lucia, a huga ... Ladányi Ilona
Sir Edgard di Rawenswood ... Fehér Pál
Lord Bucklaw Arthur ... Teszler Tivadar
Raimond, Lucia bizalmasa ... Ernster Dezső
Alisa, Lucia komornája ... Sík Olga
Normann, várkapitány ... Ney Dávid

Történik 1700 körül Skóciában
Vezényel **Fraknói Károly**
Rendező **Szabolcs Ernő**
Karigazgató **dr. Bermann Ferenc**
Az Omike zene- és énekkara
Színpadi előadás

Az előadás megkezdése előtt a nézőtérre vezető ajtókat bezárjuk

Figure 18a. Donizetti's *Lucia of Lammermoor* (*Lammermoori Lucia*), opera. S. Farkas, I. Ladányi, P. Fehér, T. Teszler, D. Ernster, O. Sík, and D. Ney. Mar. 24, 1943. Courtesy of HNL ThC.

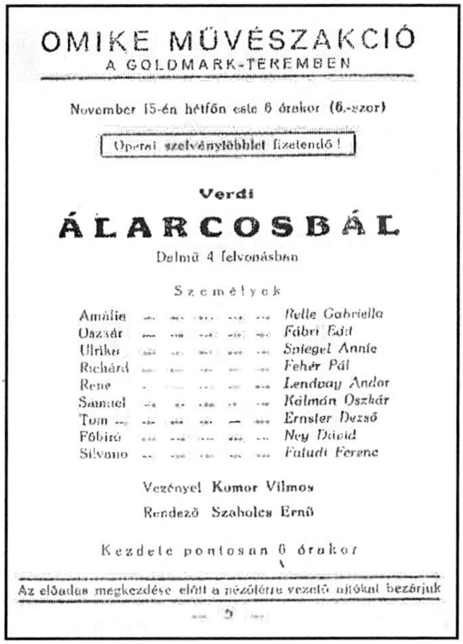

OMIKE MŰVÉSZAKCIÓ
A GOLDMARK-TEREMBEN

November 15-én hétfőn este 6 órakor (6.-szor)

Operai szelvénytöbblet fizetendő!

Verdi
ÁLARCOSBÁL
Dalmű 4 felvonásban

Személyek

Amália ... *Relle Gabriella*
Oszkár ... *Fábri Edit*
Ulrika ... *Spiegel Annie*
Richárd ... *Fehér Pál*
Rene ... *Lendvay Andor*
Samuel ... *Kálmán Oszkár*
Tom ... *Ernster Dezső*
Főbíró ... *Ney Dávid*
Silvano ... *Faludi Ferenc*

Vezényel Komor Vilmos
Rendező Szabolcs Ernő

Kezdete pontosan 6 órakor

Az előadás megkezdése előtt a nézőtérre vezető ajtókat bezárjuk

— 9 —

Figure 18b. Verdi's *Masquerade* (*Álarcosbál*), opera. G. Relle, E. Fabri, A. Spiegel, P. Fehér, A. Lendvay, O. Kálmán, et al. Nov. 15, 1943. Courtesy of HNL ThC.

OMIKE MŰVÉSZAKCIÓ
A GOLDMARK-TEREMBEN

December 20-án hétfőn este 6 órakor (7.-szer)

Operai szelvénytöbblet fizetendő!

1. **Hangverseny**
Közreműködnek *Gődry Kató, Rózsa Vera, Sík Olga dr. Sipos Jenő, Leitner György* és az OMIKE zenekar
Vezényel dr. Bermann Ferenc

Leoncavallo
2. **BAJAZZÓK**
Dalmű 2 képben

Személyek

Nedda ... *Relle Gabriella*
Canio ... *Ney Dávid*
Tonio ... *Lendvay Andor*
Silvio ... *Érdy Pál*
Beppo ... *Teszler Tivadar*
1. pór ... *Galsay Ervin*
2. pór ... *Gallai Márton*

Vezényel Fraknói Károly
Rendező Harsányi Miklós

Kezdete pontosan 6 órakor

Az előadás megkezdése előtt a nézőtérre vezető ajtókat bezárjuk

— 11 —

Figure 18c. Concert (*Hangverseny*). K. Gödry, V. Rózsa, O. Sík, Dr. J. Sipos, G. Leitner, and the OMIKE Orchestra; and Leoncavallo's *Pagliacci* (*Bajazzók*), opera. G. Relle, D. Ney, A. Lendvay, P. Erdy, T. Teszler, E. Galsay, and M. Gallai. Dec. 20, 1943. Courtesy of HNL ThC.

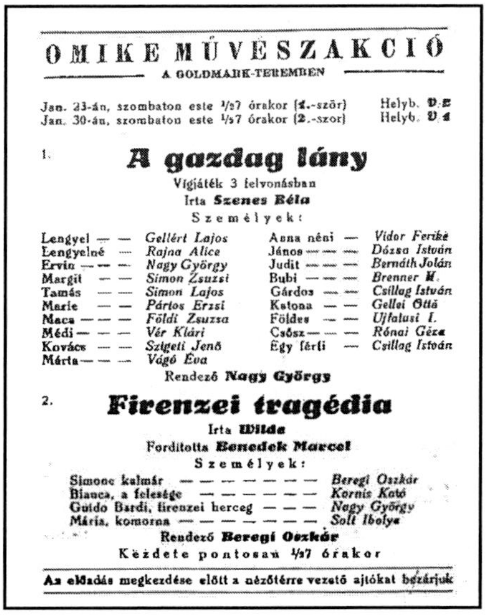

OMIKE MŰVÉSZAKCIÓ
A GOLDMARK-TEREMBEN

Jan. 23-án, szombaton este 1/2 7 órakor (1.-ször) Helyb. D 2
Jan. 30-án, szombaton este 1/2 7 órakor (2.-szor) Helyb. D 4

1. **A gazdag lány**
Vígjáték 3 felvonásban
Irta **Szenes Béla**
Személyek:

Lengyel — —	*Gellért Lajos*	Anna néni —	*Vidor Ferike*
Lengyelné —	*Rajna Alice*	János — — —	*Dózsa István*
Ervin — — —	*Nagy György*	Judit — — —	*Bernáth Jolán*
Margit — —	*Simon Zsuzsi*	Bubi — — —	*Brenner H.*
Tamás — —	*Simon Lajos*	Gárdos — —	*Csillag István*
Marie — —	*Pártos Erzsi*	Katona — —	*Gellei Ottó*
Maca — — —	*Földi Zsuzsa*	Földes — —	*Ujfalusi I.*
Médi — — —	*Vér Klári*	Csősz — — —	*Rónai Géza*
Kovács — —	*Szigeti Jenő*	Egy férfi —	*Csillag István*
Márta — — —	*Vágó Éva*		

Rendező **Nagy György**

2. **Firenzei tragédia**
Irta **Wilde**
Fordította **Benedek Marcel**
Személyek:

Simone kalmár — — — *Beregi Oszkár*
Bianca, a felesége — — — *Kornis Kató*
Guido Bardi, firenzei herceg — — — *Nagy György*
Mária, komorna — — — *Solt Ibolya*

Rendező **Beregi Oszkár**
Kezdete pontosan 1/2 7 órakor

Az előadás megkezdése előtt a nézőtérre vezető ajtókat bezárjuk

Figure 18d. Szenes's *The Rich Girl* (*A Gazdag Lány*), comedy. L. Gellért, A. Rajna, G. Nagy, Z. Simon, et al.; and Wilde's *A Florentine Tragedy* (*Firenzei Tragédia*), theater play. O. Beregi, K. Kornis, G. Nagy and I. Solt. Jan. 23 & 30, 1943, respectively. Courtesy of NTE.

OMIKE MŰVÉSZAKCIÓ
A GOLDMARK-TEREMBEN

Október 24-én vasárnap este $1/2$ 7 órakor (1.-ször)
Október 27-én szerdán este $1/2$ 7 órakor (2.-szor)
November 4-én csütörtökön este $1/2$ 7 órakor (3.-szor)
November 11-én csütörtökön este $1/2$ 7 órakor (4.-szer)
November 23-án kedden este $1/2$ 7 órakor (5.-ször)

ANYASZIV

Szinmű 4 képben

Irta Gordin — Forditotta Gellért Lajos

Személyek

Mirele	*Róbert Mária*
Joszele	*Márk István*
Donya	*Gellei Ottó*
Machle	*Vidor Ferike*
Reb Salmejn	*Szigeti Jenő*
Reb Nochumcse	*Simai Ede*
Chane Dvejre	*Faragó Panni*
Sejndele	*Solt Ibolya*
Slejmele	*Berky Harry*
Első munkás	*Bondy István*
Második munkás	*Ádám Pál*

Muzsikusok, vendégek

Rendező Szigeti Jenő

A darabban előforduló zeneszámokat Fischer Sándor állította össze

Szünet az 1. és 3. kép után

Kezdete pontosan $1/2$ 7 órakor

Az előadás megkezdése előtt a nézőtérre vezető ajtókat bezárjuk

— 3 —

Figure 19a. Gordin's *Mother's Heart* (*Anyasziv*), stage play. M. Róbert, I. Márk, O. Gellei, F. Vidor, J. Szigeti, H. Berky, I. Bondy, P. Ádám, et al. Oct. 24, 1943. Courtesy of HNL ThC.

OMIKE MŰVÉSZAKCIÓ
A GOLDMARK-TEREMBEN

Október 30-én szombaton este $1/2$ 7 órakor

26.-szor

Takáts Alice

Szinmű 3 felvonásban

Irta Szomory Dezső

Személyek

Tardy-Koós Géza	*Beregi Oszkár*
Tardy-Koós György	*Nagy György*
Takáts Alice	*Rosty Magda*
Takáts Zuárd	*Simai Ede*
Markovitsné	*Vidor Ferike*
Markovits László	*Gellért Lajos*
Hóreb Homér	*Szigeti Jenő*
Helvét Cica	*Solt Ibolya*
Ferenc	*Dózsa István*
Gazdasszony	*Győri Matild*
Pongrác	*Darvas Ernő*

Rendező Gellért Lajos

Kezdete pontosan $1/2$ 7 órakor

Az előadás megkezdése előtt a nézőtérre vezető ajtókat bezárjuk

— 4 —

Figure 19b. Szomory's *Takáts Alice*, stage play. O. Beregi, G. Nagy, M. Rosty, E. Simai, F. Vidor, L. Gellért, J. Szigeti, et al. Oct. 30, 1943. Courtesy of HNL ThC.

OMIKE MŰVÉSZAKCIÓ
A GOLDMARK-TEREMBEN

November 13-án szombaton este $1/2$ 7 órakor (1.-ször)
November 16-án kedden este $1/2$ 7 órakor (2.-szor)
November 18-án csütörtökön este $1/2$ 7 órakor (3.-szor)
November 20-án szombaton este $1/2$ 7 órakor (4.-szer)
November 25-én csütörtökön este $1/2$ 7 órakor (5.-ször)
November 30-án kedden este $1/2$ 7 órakor (6.-szor)

Asszonyok egymás között

Játék 3 felvonásban, 10 képben

Jane	*Vágó Éva*
Nancy	*Szilágyi Bea*
Peggy	*Rózsa Marika*
Sylvia	*Palotai Erzsi*
Edith	*Torday Judit*
Mary	*Rosty Magda*
Mrs. Wagstaff	*Ács Rózsi*
Fodrásznő	*Bánfi Edith*
Olga	*Földi Zsuzsa*
Euphie	*Vándor Valéria*
Iszapálarcos	*Márai Ila*
A kis Mary	*Vas Ida*
Mrs. Morehead	*Zágon Vera*
Üzletvezetőnő	*Vecsey Ilona*
1. kiszolgálólány	*Ferenczi Ágnes*
2. kiszolgálólány	*Poór Irén*
Crystal Allan	*Kornis Kató*
Tornatanárnő	*Gáspár Éva*
Betty	*Győri Matild*
De Lage grófnő	*Rajna Alice*
Miriam Aarens	*Faragó Panni*
Sadie	*Vidor Ferike*
Ruhatároslány	*Szőnyi Kató*
Watts	*Simon Zsuzsa*
Trimmerback	*Kenedi Katalin*

Rendező Simon Zsuzsa — Karmester Fischer Sándor

Kezdete pontosan $1/2$ 7 órakor

— 5 —

Figure 19c. *Married Women Among Each Other* (*Asszonyok Egymás Között*), comedy. E. Vagó, B. Szilágyi, M. Rózsa, E. Palotai, et al. Nov. 13, 1943. Courtesy of HNL ThC.

OMIKE MŰVÉSZAKCIÓ
A GOLDMARK-TEREMBEN

December 23-án csütörtökön este $1/2$ 7 órakor (8.-szor)

Ibsen

A VADKACSA

Szinmű 5 felvonásban

Személyek

Werle nagykereskedő, gyáros	*Zátony Kálmán*
Werle Gregers, a fia	*Gellért Lajos*
Az öreg Ekdal	*Sándor József*
Ekdal Hjalmar, az öreg fia, fényképész	*Nagy György*
Ekdal Gina, Hjalmar felesége	*Kelen Dóra*
Hedvig leányuk, 14 éves	*Simon Zsuzsa*
Sörbyné, a nagykereskedő házvezetőnője	*Zágon Vera*
Relling orvos	*Simai Ede*
Molvik, volt teologus	*Márk István*
Graaberg, könyvelő	*Várnai Jenő*
Pettersen, a nagykereskedő komornyikja	*Darvas Ernő*
Jensen, inas	*Gellei Ottó*
Egy puffadt úr	*Keleti Árpád*
Egy kopasz úr	*Ádám Pál*
Egy rövidlátó úr	*Sas Imre*

Rendező Gellért Lajos

Szünet az 1. és 3. felvonás után

Kezdete pontosan $1/2$ 7 órakor

Az előadás megkezdése előtt a nézőtérre vezető ajtókat bezárjuk

— 6 —

Figure 19d. Ibsen's *The Wild Duck* (*A Vadkacsa*), stage play. K. Zátony, L. Gellért, J. Sándor, G. Nagy, D. Kelen, Z. Simon, V. Zágon, et al. Dec. 23, 1943. Courtesy of HNL ThC.

OMIKE MŰVÉSZAKCIÓ
A GOLDMARK-TEREMBEN

Nov. 2-án kedden este $^1/_2$7 órakor Helybiztosítás H/1
Nov. 3-án szerdán este $^1/_2$7 órakor Helybiztosítás H/2

Zenekari hangverseny

Vezényel Komor Vilmos
Közreműködnek Farnadi Edith (zongora)
Medák Sári (ének)

Műsor

1. *Haydn:* Szimfonia G-dur 88. szám
2. *Mozart:* a) Susanne áriája
   b) Cherubin áriája
   a Figaro lakodalma c. operából
   Énekli *Medák Sári*
3. *Weiner:* Preludium, fantazia és fuga vonószenekarra
4. *Saint-Saëns:* Zongoraverseny G-moll Op. 22.
   Andante sostenuto—Allegro scherzando—Stretto
   Előadja *Farnadi Edith*

Szünet

5. *Mendelssohn:* „Halljad Izráel" Ária az Éliás c. oratóriumból
   Énekli *Medák Sári*
6. *Beethoven:* VII. szimfonia

Kezdete pontosan $^1/_2$7 órakor

A hangverseny megkezdése előtt a nézőtérre vezető ajtókat bezárjuk

— 14 —

Figure 20a. Musical Concert (*Zenekari Hangverseny*). Hayden, Mozart, Weiner, Saint-Saëns, Mendelssohn, and Beethoven. Nov. 2, 1943. Courtesy of HNL ThC.

OMIKE MŰVÉSZAKCIÓ
A GOLDMARK-TEREMBEN

December 8-án szerdán délután $^1/_2$3 órakor (3.-szor)
December 19-én vasárnap délelőtt $^1/_2$11 órakor (4.-szer)

Lakner bácsi gyermekelőadása

1. GYERTYALÁNGOK. Chanukai vers
   Irta Csergő Mária Elmondja Hegedűs Éva
2. Lakner bácsi és Inasa meg a szigorú Zebra úr
3. **JANIKA**
   Regényes gyermekoperett 3 felvonásban
   Játszák *Felhő Magda, Pethő Erika, Bér Zsuska, Márk Ági, Ács Rózsi, Mátrai Judit, Székely Ági, Sarkadi Aladár, Ormos Béla, Dózsa István, Molnár József, Rónai András*
   Karmester Feleki László A táncokat betanította Igaz Lucy

December 12-én vasárnap délelőtt $^1/_2$11 órakor (7.-szer)
December 26-án vasárnap délelőtt $^1/_2$11 órakor (8.-szor)

1. GYERTYALÁNGOK. Chanukai vers
   Irta Csergő Mária Elmondja Hegedűs Éva
2. **HAMUPIPŐKE**
   Grimm meséje 3 felvonásban Feleky László zenéjével
   Játszák *Váradi Kató, Szécsi Hédy, Ács Rózsi, Igaz Lucy, Sarkadi Aladár, Rákos Tibor, Bálint Béla, Ormos Béla*

A délelőtti előadások pontosan $^1/_2$11 órakor,
a délutáni előadás pontosan $^1/_2$3 órakor kezdődnek

— 18 —

Figure 20b. Lakner's *Little Johnny* (*Janika*), children's play. M. Felhő, E. Pethő, Z. Bér, et al. Dec. 8, 1943; and Grimm's *Cinderella* (*Hamupipőke*), fairy tale. K. Váradi, H. Szécsi, R. Ács, L.Igaz, A . Sarkadi, et al. Dec. 12, 1943. Courtesy of HNL ThC.

OMIKE MŰVÉSZAKCIÓ
A GOLDMARK-TEREMBEN

November 8-án hétfőn este $^1/_2$7 órakor

Kamarazene-est

Közreműködnek Hütter Pál (gordonka)
Nádas István (zongora)
Tibor György (hegedű)

Műsor

1. *Mozart:* A-dur szonáta hegedű—zongorára K. V. 526
   Előadják *Tibor György* és *Nádas István*
2. *Beethoven:* B-dur zongoratrio Op. 97.
   Előadják *Hütter Pál, Tibor György, Nádas István*

Szünet

3. *Brahms:* D-moll hegedű-zongora szonáta Op. 108
   Előadják *Tibor György* és *Nádas István*
4. *Mendelssohn:* D-moll zongoratrio Op. 49.
   Előadják *Hütter Pál, Nádas István, Tibor György*

Kezdete pontosan $^1/_2$7 órakor

A hangverseny megkezdése előtt a nézőtérre vezető ajtókat bezárjuk

— 15 —

Figure 20c. Chamber Music Evening (*Kamarazene-Est*). Mozart, Beethoven, Brahms, and Mendelssohn. Nov. 8, 1943. Courtesy of HNL ThC.

OMIKE MŰVÉSZAKCIÓ
A GOLDMARK-TEREMBEN

December 18-án szombaton este $^1/_2$7 órakor (1.-ször)
December 19-én vasárnap este $^1/_2$7 órakor (2.-szor)
December 26-án vasárnap este $^1/_2$7 órakor (3.-szor)
December 29-én szerdán este $^1/_2$7 órakor (4.-szer)

Vera vagy Veronika?

Buda—Pesti szerelem 3 felvonásban
Szövegét és verseit írta Lakner Artur
Zenéjét szerezte Feleky László

Személyek

Dr. Bihari Bencze Zoltán tanár	*Mányai Lajos*
Vághelyi Flóra operaénekesnő	*Herendi Manci*
Veronika	*Váradi Kató*
Dr. Radványi Tibor belgyógyász	*Rákos Tibor*
Dr. Strucc Szilárd állatorvos ...	*Gárdonyi Lajos*
Dinamit Dodó dizőz	*Wojticzky Elvira*
Rózsa Rezső zongoratanár ...	*Ormos Béla*
Tövis Tódor meteorologus ...	*Szigeti Jenő*
Picula Péterné házvezetőnő ...	*Pártos Erzsi*
Pesti Panna szobaleány	*Igaz Lucy*

Rendező Gál Dezső Karmester Feleky László

Váradi Kató ruháit az Orbán-szalon (VI. Paulay Ede-u. 58) készítette

Kezdete pontosan $^1/_2$7 órakor

Az előadás megkezdése előtt a nézőtérre vezető ajtókat bezárjuk

— 16 —

Figure 20d. Lakner's *Vera or Veronica?* (*Vera Vagy Veronika?*). L. Mányai, M. Herendi, K. Váradi,T. Rákos, L. Gárdonyi, et al. Dec. 18, 1943. Courtesy of HNL ThC.

OMIKE MŰVÉSZAKCIÓ
A GOLDMARK-TEREMBEN

December 2-án csütörtökön este ½7 órakor (12.-szer)

VIDÁM MÜSOR

(A „Tavaszi kabaré" és „Nyári kabaré" számai)

1. *Nádassy László* nézőtéri tréfája
Játszák *Pártos Erzsi, Lakos Klári, Káldor, Sík Rezső*
2. *Operettáriák*, énekli *Bán Kató*
3. **Caffé Menyország**
Vadnay László bohózata
Játszák *Gárdonyi Lajos, Szigeti, Sándor*
4. *Lénárd Béla* magánszámai
5. **Bodriból férfi Tesz**
Nádassy bohózata két képben
Játszák *Salamon Béla, Fenyő, Sík Rezső, Kürti Károly, dr. Szabó, Sas, Gábor, Faragó Panni, Ács Rózsi*
6. **ROCOCO**
Táncjelenet. Írta *Csergő Mária*. Zenéjét összeállította *Fischer Sándor*. Előadják *Szilágyi Bea* és *Komor Ági*
7. *Gellért Kató* szavel.
8. **Carmen-ni az Operába**
Operásított rémdráma. Írta *Nádassy*. Zenéjét szerezte *Puccini, Verdi* stb. Játszák *Radó Sándor, Pártos Erzsi, Lakos Klári, Ormos, Fenyő, Faragó Panni, Keleti*
9. *Herendi Manci* magánszámai
10. **A cég arája**
Nóti Károly bohózata egy felvonásban
Játszák *Salamon Béla, Rajna Alice, Ormos, Sík Rezső, Molnár József, Ferenczi Ági, Pór Irén*

Rendezők *Gál Dezső* és *Harsányi Miklós*

Zongorán kísér *Fischer Sándor*

— 17 —

Figure 21a. Gaiety Program (*Vidám Müsor*). E. Pártos, K. Lakos, et al.; *Café Menyorsag* (*Caffé Menyország*). L. Gárdonyi, J. Szigeti, and J. Sándor; *Bodriból Férfi Tesz*. B. Salamon, Á. Fenyő, et al.; *Rococo* (*Rococo*). B. Szilágyi and Á. Komor; *With Carmen in the Opera, It's No Use Going to the Opera* (*Carmen–ni az Operába*). S. Radó, E. Pártos, K. Lakos, et al.; *The Bride of the Company* (*A Cég Arája*). B. Salamon, A.Rajna, B. Ormos, et al. Dec. 2, 1943. Courtesy of HNL ThC.

OMIKE MŰVÉSZAKCIÓ
A GOLDMARK-TEREMBEN

December 4-én szombaton este ½7 órakor (5.-ször)
December 9-én csütörtökön este ½7 órakor (6.-szor)
December 14-én kedden este ½7 órakor (7.-szer)
December 26-án vasárnap délután ½3 órakor (8.-szor)

Az elvált asszony

Fall Leó operettje 3 felvonásban

Személyek

Lisseweghe Karel	*Lendvay Andor*
Jana, a felesége	*Gábor Magda*
Bakkenskeyl Péter, Jana atyja	*Sarkadi Aladár*
Wander Loo Gonda	*Lakos Klári*
Leve, ügyvéd	*Sas Imre*
Deesteldonk Lukács törvényszéki elnök	*Justh Gyula*
Ruitersplat } szavazó bírák	*Szirmai Vilmos*
Dender } szavazó bírák	*Harsányi Miklós*
Scroop, hálókocsi kalauz	*Gárdonyi Lajos*
Kromwevleit Willem, halász	*Keleti Árpád*
Martje, a felesége	*Bán Kató*
Adél, Scroop menyasszonya	*Márkus Ági*
Tjonger } szakértő professzorok	*Fenyő Árpád*
Wiesum } szakértő professzorok	*Sándor József*
Inas	*Sebestyén Jenő*
1. hölgy	*Bártfai Gaby*
2. hölgy	*Danziger Lili*

Ujságírók, közönség, törvénysz. szolgák, vendégek, holland nép

Rendező **Szabolcs Ernő** Karmester **Zsigmondi Pál**

Kezdete pontosan ½7 órakor,
a délutáni előadásé pontosan ½3 órakor

Az előadás megkezdése előtt a nézőtérre vezető ajtókat bezárjuk

— 14 —

Figure 21b. Fall's *The Divorced Woman* (*Az Elvált Asszony*), operetta. A. Lendvay, M. Gábor, A. Sarkadi, K. Lakos, et al. Dec. 4, 1943. Courtesy of HNL ThC.

OMIKE MŰVÉSZAKCIÓ
A GOLDMARK-TEREMBEN

December 7-én kedden este ½7 órakor (13.-szor)
December 27-én hétfőn este ½7 órakor (14.-szer)

Békebeli béke

Mintha 1901 óta semmisem történt volna . . . . .

Harmath Imre 3 felvonásos operettje

Zenéjét összeállította **Feleky László** és **Pallós Tivadar**

Személyek

Schneider Fáni	*Darvas Ibolya*
Schneider Kató	*Váradi Kató*
Báró Fodor	*Ney Dávid*
Dr. Berger Zsiga	*Gárdonyi Lajos*
Liliom Pepi	*Szirmai Vilmos*
Ficsur Peti	*Ormos Béla*
Házmesterné	*Spiegel Annie*
Táncosnő	*Szilágyi Bea*
Julcsa	*Pór Irén*
Arturka	*Székely Ági*

Történik 1901 májusában a Városligetben

Konferál **Kellér Dezső**

Rendező **Szabolcs Ernő** Karmester **Pallós Tivadar**

Kezdete pontosan ½7 órakor

Az előadás megkezdése előtt a nézőtérre vezető ajtókat bezárjuk

— 15 —

Figure 21c. Harmath's *Peaceful Era* (*Békebeli Béke*), operetta. I. Darvas, K. Váradi, D. Ney, L. Gárdonyi, V. Szirmai, B. Ormos, et al. Dec. 7, 1943. Courtesy of HNL ThC.

OMIKE MŰVÉSZAKCIÓ
A GOLDMARK-TEREMBEN

December 8-án szerdán este 6 órakor (6.-szor)

Operai szelvénytöbblet fizetendő !

Nicolai

A windsori víg nők

Víg dalmű 3 felvonásban

Fordította **Fischer Sándor**

Személyek

Sir John Falstaff	*Ernster Dezső*
Víg	*Erdy Pál*
Vígné } windsori víg nők	*Darvas Ibolya*
Dusné } windsori víg nők	*Spiegel Annie*
Anna } windsori víg nők	*Bán Kató*
Dus	*Gulsay Ervin*
Fenton	*dr. Sipos Jenő*
Vánnyadt lovag	*Sas Imre*
dr. Cajus	*Somogyi István*
1. } polgár	*Gallai Márton*
2. } polgár	*Erdész Nándor*
3. } polgár	*Somogyi Dezső*
4. } polgár	*Visó Márk*
Pincér	*Eszenyi Manó*
Hobgoblin	*Szilágyi Bea*
1. } tündér	*Komor Ági*
2. } tündér	*Igaz Lucy*

Vezényel **Komor Vilmos** Rendező **Bálint Lajos**

Karigazgató dr. Bermann Ferenc

Kezdete pontosan 6 órakor

Az előadás megkezdése előtt a nézőtérre vezető ajtókat bezárjuk

— 9 —

Figure 21d. Nicolai's *The Merry Wives of Windsor* (*A Windsori Víg Nők*), comedy. D. Ernster, P. Erdy, I. Darvas, A. Spiegel, K. Bán, et al. Dec. 8, 1943. Courtesy of HNL ThC.

OMIKE MŰVÉSZAKCIÓ
A GOLDMARK-TEREMBEN

Január 2-án vasárnap délelőtt ½11 órakor

Jazz-matiné

Közreműködnek

Szamosi Buli

és

15 tagu szimfonikus jazz-zenekara

Váradi Kató — Simon Zsuzsa
Ernster Dezső — Gárdonyi Lajos
Lénárd Béla — Fenyő Árpád
(magánszámok)

Szénási Lili
(akrobatikus táncok)

Corodini
(bűvész)

Kezdete pontosan ½11 órakor

Az előadás megkezdése előtt a nézőtérre vezető ajtókat bezárjuk

— 21 —

Figure 22a. Jazz Matinee (*Jazz-Matiné*) with Imre "Buli" Szamosi and jazz musicians. Jan. 2, 1944. Courtesy of HNL ThC.

OMIKE MŰVÉSZAKCIÓ
A GOLDMARK-TEREMBEN

Január 30-án vasárnap este ½7 órakor (I.-ször)

Téli kabaré

Műsoron
két bohózat, több tréfa és blüett, magánszámok és táncok

Fellépnek

Salamon Béla — Gárdonyi Lajos — Sarkadi Aladár
Radó Sándor — Ormos Béla — Fenyő Árpád
Szentiványi Kálmán — Sándor József — Békeffi Róbert
Rajna Alice, Lakos Klári stb.

Lénárd Béla mint konferánsz és magánszámokkal
Rózsa Vera Reinitz Béla dalaival
Faragó Panni Szász Miklós verseire írt Erdősi László-szerzeményekkel
Szénási Lili táncokkal

Rendezők Gál Dezső és Harsányi Miklós
Karmester Lajtai-Lazarus Walter

Kezdete pontosan ½7 órakor

Az előadás megkezdése előtt a nézőtérre vezető ajtókat bezárjuk

— 20 —

Figure 22b. Winter Cabaret (*Téli Kabaré*). B. Salamon, L. Gárdonyi, A. Sarkadi, S. Radó, B. Ormos, Á. Fenyő, K. Szentiványi, et al. Jan. 30, 1943. Courtesy of HNL ThC.

OMIKE MŰVÉSZAKCIÓ
A GOLDMARK-TEREMBEN

Február 9-én szerdán este ¾6 órakor (3-szor) Helyb. O/3
Február 23-án szerdán este ¾6 órakor (4.-szer)

Operai szelvénytöbblet fizetendő!

GOUNOD

FAUST

Opera 5 felvonásban

Személyek

	Febr. 9-én	Febr. 23-án
Faust	*Fehér Pál*	*Fehér Pál*
Margaréta	*Róna Vera*	*Medák Sári*
Mefisztó	*Lendvay Andor*	*Kálmán Oszkár*
Valentin	*Erdy Pál*	*Erdy Pál*
Márta	*Sík Olga*	*Spiegel Annie*
Siebel	*Darvas Ibolya*	*Darvas Ibolya*
Wagner	*Faludi Ferenc*	*Faludi Ferenc*

Vezényel Fraknói Károly — Rendező Szabolcs Ernő

Karigazgató dr. Bermann Ferenc

A darabban előforduló táncokat előadják *Komor Ági, Szilágyi Bea, Nemes Éva, Nemes Hédy, P. Komlós Adrienne és Szőnyi Éva*

A táncok koreográfiáját szerezte és betanította Pallay Anna, a magy. kir. Operaház v. primaballerinája

Kezdete pontosan ¾6 órakor

Az előadás megkezdése előtt a nézőtérre vezető ajtókat bezárjuk

— 11 —

Figure 22c. Gounod's *Faust*, opera. P. Fehér, V. Róna, A. Lendvay, O. Kálmán, S. Medák, P. Erdy, O. Sík, et al. Feb. 9, 1944. Courtesy of NTE.

OMIKE MŰVÉSZAKCIÓ
A GOLDMARK-TEREMBEN

Március 15-én szerdán este ½7 órakor Helyb. H/1
Március 16-án csütörtökön este ½7 órakor Helyb. H/2

Zenekari hangverseny

Vezényel Sándor Frigyes

Közreműködnek
Dénes Vera (gordonka), Gődry Kató (ének), Horvai-(Hoffmann) Erzsi (hegedű), Rózsa Vera (ének), Ernster Dezső (ének), Lukács Pál (ének), dr Sipos Jenő (ének)

Műsor

1. *Mendelssohn*: „Heimkehr aus der Ferne" (nyitány)
2. *Schubert-Cassado*: Gordonkaverseny Allegro moderato — Adagio — Allegretto Előadja *Dénes Vera*
3. *Kadosa*: „De amore fatale" (első előadás) Kantáta József Attila verseire vegyeskarra, zenekarra és négy szólóhangra A szólókat éneklik *Gődry Kató, Rózsa Vera, Ernster Dezső, dr Sipos Jenő*

Szünet

4. *Mozart*: „Symphonia concertante (K. V. 364) hegedű és mélyhegedűre Allegro maestoso — Andante — Presto Előadják *Horvai (Hoffmann) Erzsi és Lukács Pál*
5. *Haydn*: Szimfonia D-dur Adagio. Allegro spirituoso — Capriccio. Largo. — Menuetto — Allegro con spirito

Kezdete pontosan ½7 órakor

A hangverseny megkezdése előtt a nézőtérre vezető ajtókat bezárjuk

— 18 —

Figure 22d. Musical Concert (*Zenekari Hangverseny*). Mendelssohn, Schubert-Cassado, Kadosa, Mozart, and Haydn. Mar. 15, 1944. Courtesy of NTE.

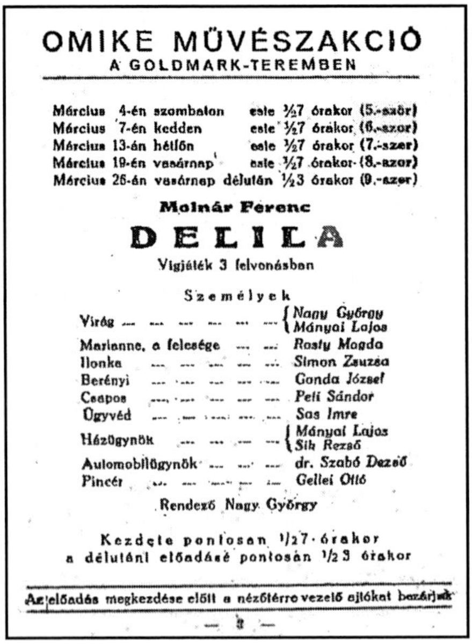

OMIKE MÜVÉSZAKCIÓ
A GOLDMARK-TEREMBEN

Március 4-én szombaton este ½7 órakor (5.-ször)
Március 7-én kedden este ½7 órakor (6.-szor)
Március 13-án hétfőn este ½7 órakor (7.-szer)
Március 19-én vasárnap este ½7 órakor (8.-szor)
Március 26-án vasárnap délután ½3 órakor (9.-szer)

Molnár Ferenc

DELILA

Vigjáték 3 felvonásban

Személyek

Virág — Nagy György / Mányai Lajos
Marianne, a felesége — Rosty Magda
Ilonka — Simon Zsuzsa
Berényi — Gonda József
Csapos — Peti Sándor
Ügyvéd — Sas Imre
Házügynök — Mányai Lajos / Sík Rezső
Automobilügynök — dr. Szabó Dezső
Pincér — Gellei Ottó

Rendező Nagy György

Kezdete pontosan ½7 órakor
a délutáni előadásé pontosan ½3 órakor

Az előadás megkezdése előtt a nézőtérre vezető ajtókat bezárjuk

— 8 —

Figure 23a. Molnár's *Delila*, comedy. G. Nagy, L. Mányai, M. Rosty, Z. Simon, J. Gonda, S. Peti, I. Sas, et al. Mar. 4-26, 1944. Courtesy of HNL ThC. The March 19th and 26th performances never occurred due to Nazi Army entry into Hungary on March 19, 1944.

OMIKE MŰVÉSZAKCIÓ
A GOLDMARK-TEREMBEN

Március 25-én szombaton este ½7 órakor (1.-ször)
Március 26-án vasárnap este ½7 órakor (2.-szor)

Molière

Kénytelen házasság

Komédia 1 felvonásban — Forditotta Hevesi Sándor

Sganarelle — Szigeti Jenő
Gèronimo — Zátony Kálmán
Dorimène, Sganarelle jegyese — Palotai Erzsi
Alcantor, Dorimène atyja — Sík Rezső
Lycaste, Dorimène imádója — Gellei Ottó
Alcidas, Dorimène bátyja — Gonda József
Pancratius, az aristotelesi bölcs. dokt. — Mányai Lajos
Marphurius, a pyrrhoni bölcs. doktora — dr Szabó Dezső
Két cigánynő — Komor Ági, Szilágyi Bea

A darabban előforduló zeneszámokat Fischer Sándor állitotta össze

A botcsinálta doktor

Komédia 3 felvonásban — Forditotta Kolozs Jenő

Géronte — Szigeti Jenő
Lucinde, Géronte leánya — Simon Zsuzsa
Léandre, Lucinde szerelmese — Gonda József
Sganarelle — Peti Sándor
Martine, Sganarelle felesége — Pártos Erzsi
Robert ur — dr. Szabó Dezső
Valère, Géronte titkára — Ormos Béla
Lucas, Jacqueline férje — Fellegi István
Jacqueline, dajka — Ács Rózsi
Thibaut, Perrin } parasztok — Sándor József, Rozgonyi Andor

Rendező Halmos István — Diszlettervező Éber György

Kezdete pontosan ½7 órakor

— 9 —

Figure 23b. Molière's *The Forced Marriage* (*Kénytelen Házasság*) and *The Doctor in Spite of Himself* (*A Botcsinálta Doktor*), comedies. J. Szigeti, R. Sík, O. Gellei, J. Gonda, J. Sándor, Dr. D. Szábo, et al. Mar. 25 & 26, 1944. Courtesy of HNL ThC. Never performed due to Nazi Army entry into Hungary on March 19, 1944.

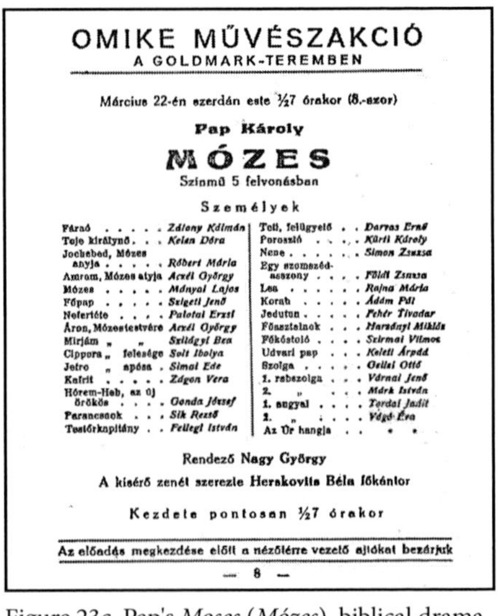

OMIKE MŰVÉSZAKCIÓ
A GOLDMARK-TEREMBEN

Március 22-én szerdán este ½7 órakor (8.-szor)

Pap Károly

MÓZES

Szinmű 5 felvonásban

Személyek

Fáraó — Zátony Kálmán
Teje királynő — Kelen Dóra
Jochebed, Mózes anyja — Róbert Mária
Amram, Mózes atyja — Aczél György
Mózes — Mányai Lajos
Főpap — Szigeti Jenő
Nefertéte — Palotai Erzsi
Áron, Mózes testvére — Aczél György
Mirjám „ „ — Szilágyi Bea
Cippora „ felesége — Solt Ibolya
Jetro „ apósa — Simai Ede
Kafrit — Zágon Vera
Hórem-Heb, az új örökös — Gonda József
Parancsnok — Sík Rezső
Testőrkapitány — Fellegi István
Teti, felügyelő — Darvas Ernő
Porosztó — Kürti Károly
Nene — Simon Zsuzsa
Egy szomszédasszony — Földi Zsuzsa
Lea — Rajna Mária
Korah — Ádám Pál
Jedutun — Fehér Tivadar
Főasztalnok — Harsányi Miklós
Főkóstoló — Szirmai Vilmos
Udvari pap — Keleti Árpád
Szolga — Gellei Ottó
1. rabszolga — Várnai Jenő
2. „ — Márk István
1. angyal — Tordai Judit
2. „ — Végh Éva
Az Úr hangja — * *

Rendező Nagy György

A kisérő zenét szerezte Herskovits Béla főkántor

Kezdete pontosan ½7 órakor

Az előadás megkezdése előtt a nézőtérre vezető ajtókat bezárjuk

— 8 —

Figure 23c. Pap's *Moses* (*Mózes*), biblical drama. J. Szigeti, J. Gonda, R. Sik, Z. Földi, P. Ádám, M. Harsányi, O. Gellei, I. Márk, et al. Mar. 22, 1944. Courtesy of HNL ThC. This performance never occurred due to Nazi closing of the OMIKE theater on Sunday morning, March 19, 1944.

APPENDIX 3

Announcements of Fine Arts Exhibitions for Painters, Graphic Artists, and Sculptors

Copies of announcements, catalog covers, and tickets contained in this appendix, for the years 1942–1944, were made with the kind help of the archival staffs at the National Szechenyi Theater Collection (*Országos Széchényi Színháztár*) and at the National Theater History Museum and Institute (*Országos Színháztörténeti Múzeum és Intézet*). Another source was the website of the Nonprofit *Társadalomkutató Egyesület*, www.omike.hu.

There were a total of six fine arts exhibitions held under the aegis of the OMIKE Muveszakcio from 1939 through 1944:

Exhibit I, Dec. 16, 1939
Exhibit. II, Feb. 2, 1941
Exhibit III, Jan. 11, 1942
Exhibit IV, Apr. 11, 1943
Exhibit V, Sept. 24, 1943
Exhibit VI, Feb. 21, 1944

A complete catalogue for the 5th OMIKE Fine Arts Exhibition, listing the artists and sculptors with their respective works and prices, has been reproduced and given herein, courtesy of Eva Kuti (daughter of martyred composer, Sandor Kuti and exhibiting painter Amy Kuti).

For a complete listing of the participating artists at these exhibitions, please consult the website www.omike.hu.

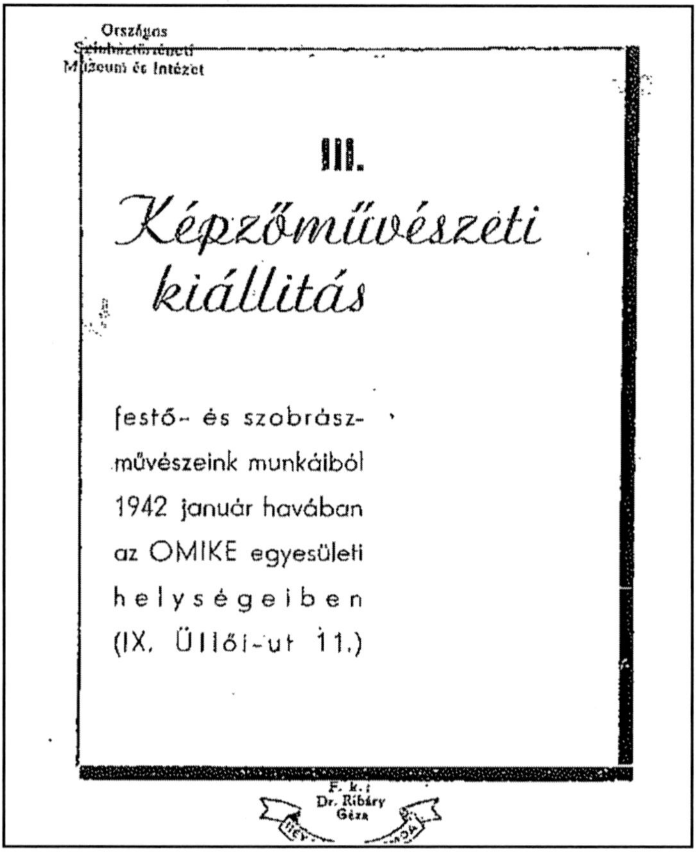
Országos Színháztörténeti Múzeum és Intézet

III.

Képzőművészeti kiállítás

festő- és szobrász-
művészeink munkáiból
1942 január havában
az OMIKE egyesületi
helységeiben
(IX. Üllői-ut 11.)

F. k.: Dr. Ribáry Géza

Figure 1. Announcement for Third Fine Arts Exhibition for painters and sculptors, January 1942. Courtesy of the Hungarian Theater Museum and Institute, Budapest.

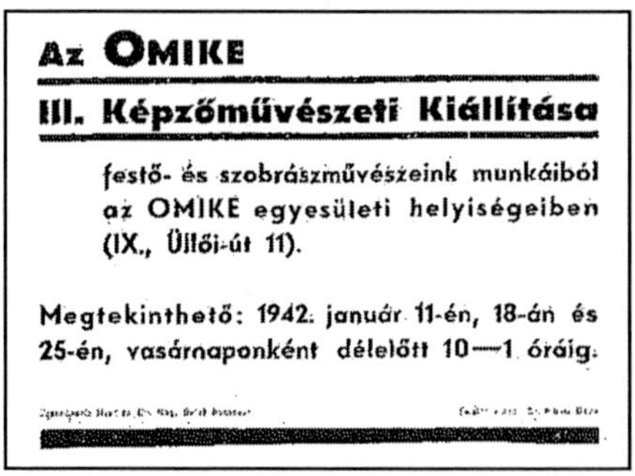
Az OMIKE
III. Képzőművészeti Kiállítása

festő- és szobrászművészeink munkáiból
az OMIKE egyesületi helyiségeiben
(IX., Üllői-út 11).

Megtekinthető: 1942. január 11-én, 18-án és 25-én, vasárnaponként délelőtt 10—1 óráig.

Figure 2. Ticket for Third Fine Arts Exhibition, held at no. 11 Ullői Road, Budapest. Courtesy of the Theatre History Collection at Hungarian National Széchényi Library, Budapest.

OMIKE
KÉPZŐMŰVÉSZETI CSOPORT
IV. KIÁLLITÁS
(FESTMÉNYEK, RAJZOK, SZOBROK)
Az ORSZÁGOS MAGYAR ZSIDÓMÚZEUM TERMEIBEN
(VII., Dohány-utca 2.)
MEGTEKINTHETŐ:
Április 11, 15, 17, 18, 22, 24 és 25-én (vasárnap, csütörtök, szombat) d. e. 10—½2 óráig.

Figure 3. Ticket for Fourth Fine Arts Exhibition, held at no. 2 Dohany Street, Budapest. Courtesy of the Nonprofit *Társadalomkutató Egyesület*, Budapest. www.omike.hu.

OMIKE
KÉPZŐMŰVÉSZETI CSOPORT
TÉLI KIÁLLITÁS
A BUDAI IZR. NŐEGYLET
HELYISÉGEIBEN
(II., KELETI KÁROLY-UTCA 22.)
1944. FEBRUÁR 21-TŐL MÁRCIUS 19-IG
NAPONTA DÉLELŐTT 9–2-IG
TÁRGYMUTATÓ

Figure 4. Catalogue cover for the Winter Fine Arts Exhibition, February 21 through March 19, 1944. Courtesy of Magda Horák.

OMIKE KÉPZŐMŰVÉSZETI CSOPORT
Téli kiállitás
a Budai Izr. Nőegylet helyiségeiben
(II. Keleti Károly u. 22.)
1944. február 21 — március 19
naponta 9—2 óráig

Figure 5. Ticket for Winter Fine Arts Exhibition, February 21 through March 19, 1944, held at no. 22 Keleti Károly Street, Budapest. Courtesy of the Nonprofit *Társadalomkutató Egyesület*, Budapest. www.omike.hu.

OMIKE
KÉPZŐMŰVÉSZETI CSOPORT

V. KIÁLLITÁS

AZ ORSZÁGOS MAGYAR ZSIDÓ MUZEUM TERMEIBEN
(VII., DOHÁNY-UTCA 2.
WESSELÉNYI-UTCA SAROK)
1943. SZEPTEMBER 24-TŐL OKTÓBER 17-IG
MINDEN SZOMBAT, VASÁRNAP, CSÜTÖRTÖK
DÉLELŐTT 10—½2-IG,
(OKTÓBER 9 KIVÉTELÉVEL)

TÁRGYMUTATÓ

FESTMÉNYEK ÉS RAJZOK:

Pengő

1. Adler Magda: Szőlődomb, olajfestmény ... 400.—
2. Adler Magda: Kislány, olajfestmény ... ... 400.—
3. Adler Magda: Zebegényi táj, akvarell ... 200.—
4. Adler Magda: Domboldal, akvarell ... ... 200.—
5. Ámos Imre: Grafikák, akvarellek, tussok, darabja ... ... 200.—
6. Ámos Imre: Szentendrei ősz, olajfestmény 600.—
7. Ámos Imre: Szobor madárral, olajfestmény 450.—
8. Ámos Imre: Csendélet, olajfestmény ... ... 500.—
9. Anna Margit: Öltözőben, tempera ... ... 450.—
10. Anna Margit: Akvarellek, darabja ... ... 200.—
11. Anna Margit: Hajnali séta, tempera ... ... 800.—
12. Aszódi Weil Erzsébet: Hajóraszállás, rézkarc ... ... 140.—
13. Aszódi Weil Erzsébet: Dante háza előtt Firenzében, rézkarc ... ... 180.—
14. Aszódi Weil Erzsébet: Kunsági tanya, rézkarc ... ... 140.—
15. Aszódi Weil Erzsébet: Falusiak Pesten, rézkarc ... ... 160.—
16. Barna Pál: Kilátás a Vár mögé, olajf. ... 300.—
17. Bálint Endre: Fiú, akvarell ... ... 250.—
18. Bálint Endre: Egy festő arcképe, tempera 300.—
19. Beck S. Elza: Falusi ház, szines rajz ... 400.—
20. Beck S. Elza: Margitrakpart, szines rajz ... 350.—
21. Beck S. Elza: Falusi udvar, szines rajz ... 850.—
22. Beck S. Elza: Budai részlet, szines rajz ... 800.—
23. Bihari Ari: Pestkörnyéki dombok, olajfestm. 400.—
24. Bihari Ari: Óbudai hegyvidék, olajfestmény 500.—
25. Bolmányi Ferenc: Tájkép, olajfestmény ... 600.—
26. Bolmányi Ferenc: Tavaszi virágok, olajf. ... 700.—
27. Bolmányi Ferenc: Szentendrei táj, olajf. ... 600.—
28. Csabai Ékes Lajos: Csendélet macskával, tempera ... ... 900.—

Figures 6a–h. Cover and complete catalogue pages for the 5th Fine Arts Exhibition, September 24, 1943. Courtesy of Éva Kuti.

Pengő

29. Csabai Ékes Lajos: Lellei táj, pasztell ... 400.—
30. Csabai Ékes Lajos: Virágos asztal, tempera 1200.—
31. Csalány Béla: Mesemondó kislány, olajf. ... 800.—
32. Csalány Béla: Marcsa néni udvara, olajf. ... 800.—
33. Csalány Béla: Kisvárosi utca, olajfestmény 800.—
34. Dános Dezső: Palotai táj, akvarell ... ... 300.—
35. Dános Dezső: Szilaspatak, akvarell ... ... 400.—
36. Dános Dezső: Malom, akvarell, ... 300.—
37. Diener-Dénes Rudolf: Tájkép, pasztell ... 600.—
38. Diener-Dénes Rudolf: Tanyai részlet, olajf. 1000.—
39. Diener-Dénes Rudolf: Kislány, pasztell ... 600.—
40. Diener-Dénes Rudolf: Zsófi, pasztell ... 600.—
41. Eisler Györgyi: Csendélet, akvarell ... ... 80.—
42. Eisler Györgyi: Bányászok, akvarell ... ... 80.—
43. Erdei Viktor: Imaház lépcsőjén, vörös kréta 350.—
44. Erdei Viktor: Szent könyvek, vörös kréta ... 400.—
45. Erdei Viktor: Férfifej, vörös kréta ... ... 400.—
46. Erdős Lajos: Csendélet piros vázával, olajf. 700.—
47. Erdős Lajos: Csendélet zöldséggel, olajf. ... 600.—
48. Erdős Lajos: Rebekka a kútnál, olajfestmény 700.—
49. Farkas László: Profil, kréta ... ... 300.—
50. Farkas László: Esti hangulat, kréta ... ... 260.—
51. Farkas László: Modellek, kréta ... ... 260.—
52. Farkas László: Tanulmányfej, kréta ... ... 250.—
53. Farkasházy Miklós: Dunapart, pasztell ... 500.—
54. Farkasházy Miklós: Virágok, pasztell ... 500.—
55. Földes Péter Mihály: Gondok, olajf. ... 2000.—
56. Friedbauer Béla: Menekülő anya, rajz ... 250.—
57. Friedbauer Béla: Ünnep bejövetele, rajz ... 150.—
58. Friedbauer Béla: Önarckép, olajfestmény 1000.—
59. Füri S. József: Zebegényi táj, akvarell ... 200.—
60. Füri S. József: Botús táj, olajfestmény ... 450.—
61. Füri S. József: Dunapart, tempera ... ... 350.—
62. Füri S. József: Gyász, akvarell ... ... 200.—

Pengő

63. Gábor Marianne: Édesapám, olajfestmény 2000.—
64. Gábor Marianne: Zebegényi utca, olajf. ... 800.—
65. Gábor Marianne: Önarckép, olajfestmény 1600.—
66. Gárdonyi Ella: Emlék, akvarell, magántul.
67. Gárdonyi Ella: Parkrészlet, akvarell ... ... 220.—
68. Gárdonyi Ella: Váci táj, akvarell, magántul.
69. Gedő Ilka: Kovácsok, kréta ... ... 200.—
70. Gedő Ilka: Falu végén, pasztell ... ... 200.—
71. Gedő Ilka: Kertben, pasztell ... ... 300.—
72. Gedő Ilka: Öregasszonyok, rajz ... ... 150.—
73. Gimes Lajos: Nyári alkony, olajfestmény 800.—
74. Gimes Lajos: Árnyas út, olajfestmény ... 1000.—
75. Gimes Lajos: Kitzbüheli táj, olajfestmény 1000.—
76. Glück Félix: Ex libris tervek, rendelésre
77. Glück Félix: Zebegényi táj, pasztell ... 250.—
78. Glück Félix: Virágcsendélet, pasztell ... 350.—
79. Göndör Bertalan: Fény, tus ... ... 160.—
80. Göndör Bertalan: Vakok, linoleum ... ... 90.—
81. Göndör Bertalan: Talmudisták, tus ... ... 160.—
82. Göndör Bertalan: A „Vándorlás könyvéből", tus ... ... 160.—
83. Gráber Margit: Festőnő, pasztell ... ... 300.—
84. Gráber Margit: Téli udvar, pasztell ... 300.—
85. Gyenes Gitta: Erdő mélye, tempera ... 450.—
86. Gyenes Gitta: Pihenő, tempera ... ... 450.—
87. Hatvani Perlusz Gyula: Részlet a Békásszorosból, pasztell, magántulajdon
88. Hellmann Márton: Önarckép, olajfest. 250.—
89. Hellmann Márton: Ablakomból, olajfest. 250.—
90. Herman Lipót: Harangvirág és nárcisz, olajfestmény ... ... 900.—
91. Herman Lipót: Ábrahám feláldozza Izsákot, olajfestmény ... ... 700.—
92. Hevesi E. Margit: Téli táj, olajfestmény 300.—
93. Hevesi E. Margit: Ősz a parkban, olajf. 400.—

Pengő

94. Horovitz Iván : Zsidó leány, pasztell 250.—
95. Horovitz Lukács Stefi : Első csalódás, tus 200.—
96. Horovitz Lukács Stefi : Katica néni, akv. 200.—
97. Horovitz Lukács Stefi : Régi históriák, akvarell 200.—
98. Horovitz Lukács Stefi : Mit hoztál ?, akv. 200.—
99. Jankai Tibor : Komp, olajfestm. 400.—
100. Jankai Tibor : Várakozók, olajfestm. 400.—
101. Jándi Dávid : Nagybányai részlet, pasztell 300.—
102. Jándi Dávid : Nagybányai szénapiac, paszt. 280.—
103. Jándi Dávid : Borús napsütés, pasztell 280.—
104. Karczag Zoltán : Vidéki utca, tempera 400.—
105. Karczag Zoltán : Fenyves szélén, tempera 400.—
106. Karinthy E. Ada : A pillangó, akvarell 200.—
107. Karinthy E. Ada : Hucul menyecske, akv. 180.—
108. Karinthy E. Ada : A dombtetőn, akvarell 180.—
109. Kazár László : Pihenés, tus 250.—
110. Kazár László : Bibliás kezek, tus 300.—
111. Kazár László : Evő paraszt, tus 200.—
112. Kazár László : Sütő asszony, szén 250.—
113. Kádár Béla : Vasárnap, tempera 300.—
114. Kádár Béla : Hollandi leány, tempera 300.—
115. Kun Sándor : Fák, olajfestmény 500.—
116. Kuti Amy : Krumpliföld, akvarell 400.—
117. Lakos Alfréd : Valahol Oroszországban olajfestmény 950.—
118. Lakos Alfréd : Munkaszolgálatos, olajfest. 700.—
119. Lakos Alfréd : Interieur, olajfestmény 500.—
120. Lázár Éva : Út, amely hozzá vezet, olajf. 700.—
121. Lázár Éva : A mi kertünk, olajfestm. 400.—
122. Lukács Ágnes : Utcarészlet, akvarell 180.—
123. Lukács Ágnes : Csendes váradi utca, olajf. 500.—
124. Lukács Ágnes : Ablakomból, olajf. 500.—
125. Lukács Ágnes : Budai kémények, olajfestm. 500.—

Pengő

126. Lusztig János : Parkrészlet, kréta 200.—
127. Lusztig János : Bérházudvar, pasztell 130.—
128. Lusztig János : Interieuer, pasztell 150.—
129. Magyar Mannheimer Nelly : Tájkép, olajfestmény 1000.—
130. Magyar Mannheimer Nelly : Vihar előtt, olajfestmény (keret nélkül) 800.—
131. Márkus Imre : Újságolvasók, pasztell 600.—
132. Márkus Imre : A szonáta, pasztell 600.—
133. Márkus Imre : A festő, pasztell 800.—
134. Mészáros Mihály : Tájkép, olajfestm. 700.—
135. Mészáros Mihály : Fák, akvarell 350.—
136. Mészáros Mihály : Szalonkaúti részlet, akv. 350.—
137. Mészáros Mihály : Tájkép, akvarell 350.—
138. Pán Márta : Ló, akvarell 200.—
139. Pán Márta : Tehén, akvarell 200.—
140. Pán Márta : Komp, akvarell 200.—
141. Pán Márta : Halászok, akvarell 200.—
142. Pásztor György : Csendélet, pasztell 300.—
143. Pásztor György : Merengés, pasztell 350.—
144. Perlrott-Csaba Vilmos : Utcarészlet, tempera 600.—
145. Perlrott-Csaba Vilmos : Kertrészlet, olajf. 1200.—
146. Pogány Margit : Falu végén, olajfestmény, magántulajdon
147. Porter Paula : Télutó, olajfestmény 700.—
148. Porter Paula : Kilátás a Rózsadombról, olajfestmény 600.—
149. Porter Paula : Barcs Károly arcképe, olajf. 600.—
150. Rasofszky H. Anna : V. E. arcképe, pasztell 600.—
151. Reichental Ferenc : Kékruhás leány, olajf. 700.—
152. Reichental Ferenc : Csallóközi táj, olajf. 600.—
153. Reichental Ferenc : Nyár, olajfestmény 500.—
154. Reichental Ferenc : Kislány virággal, olajf. 500.—
155. Rónai Géza : Mély út Nógrádverőcén, pasztell 1000.—

Pengő

156. Rónai Géza : Téli táj, pasztell 800.—
157. Rónai Géza : Március végén, pasztell 1000.—
158. Roszner Károly : Péntek este, akvarell 380.—
159. Somogyi Jolán : Szomorúság, olajfestmény 200.—
160. Somogyi Jolán : Férfifej, olajfestmény 400.—
161. Schalk László : Romantikus táj, olajfestm. 500.—
162. Schalk László : Műterem piros kendővel, olajfestmény 1000.—
163. Schalk László : Nagybányai táj, olajf. 1000.—
164. Schalk László : Sárga könyv fekete vázával, olajfestmény 1000.—
165. Scheiber Hugó : Imádkozó, tus 300.—
166. Scheiber Hugó : Kézimunkázó nő, pasztell 250.—
167. Scheiber Hugó : Talmudista, színes tus 250.—
168. Schönberger György : Munkásfiú, tus 50.—
169. Schönberger György : Gyárudvar, tempera 150.—
170. Schönberger György : Városrészlet, olajf. 120.—
171. Szatmári Markovits István : Kiscelli kastély, olajfestmény 400.—
172. Szenes Fülöp : Dr. Földesné Ribáry Edit, olajfestmény, magántulajdon
173. Szenes Fülöp : Semler Eleméré, olajfestmény, magántulajdon
174. Szécsi Armand : Műteremsarok, olajfestm. 500.—
175. Szécsi Armand : Parkrészlet, olajfestmény 500.—
176. Szigeti Jenő : Parasztudvar, pasztell 500.—
177. Szigeti Jenő : Boglya, pasztell 500.—
178. Szigeti Jenő : Faluvége, pasztell 600.—
179. Ungvári-Rosenberg Miklós : Parkban, olajfestmény 400.—
180. Ungvári-Rosenberg Miklós : Tükör előtt, olajfestmény 600.—
181. Ungvári-Rosenberg Miklós : Imádkozó, olajfestmény 400.—
182. Vadász Endre : Tél, tempera 500.—

Pengő

183. Vadász Endre : Olasz város, tempera 500.—
184. Vadász Endre : Páris, tempera 500.—
185. Vadász Endre : Zuzmara, tempera 500.—
186. Vajda Julia : Tájkép, tempera 300.—
187. Vajda Julia : Tájkép, pasztell 300.—
188. Vajda Julia : Interieur, olajfestmény 300.—
189. Vajda Livia : Vásár, akvarell 60.—
190. Vajda Livia : Piacrészlet, pasztell 150.—
191. Vajda Livia : Vízpart, tempera 200.—
192. Veszprémi Rózsi : Fésülködő leány, olajf. 700.—
193. Virág H. Tera : Tavasz, pasztell 150.—
194. Virág H. Tera : Fiatal fák, olajfestmény 200.—
195. Virág H. Tera : Csendélet, olajfestmény 300.—
196. Zádor István : Önarckép, tempera 1800.—
197. Zádor István : Anya és gyermeke, kettős arckép, olajfestmény, magántulajdon

SZOBROK:

198. Csillag István : Mózes, gipsz 1000.—
199. Csillag István : Kerner István, relief 400.—
200. Csillag István : Hunyadi Sándor, plakett 400.—
201. Kunvári Lilla : Salamon Henrik dr., gipsz 1000.—
202. Kunvári Lilla : Miku, gipsz 600.—
203. Örkényi Strasser István : Beatrice, gipsz 400.—
204. Örkényi Strasser István : Merengő, gipsz 150.—
205. Örkényi Strasser István : Mózes, gipsz 50.—
206. Setét Julia : Önarckép, terrakotta 380.—
207. Setét Julia : Nővérem, terrakotta 450.—

Műtárosok : Schalk László, Reichental Ferenc

OMIKE IX., Üllői-út 11. Telefon : 187-711

APPENDIX 4

OMIKE *Művészakció* Victims of the Holocaust

In less than one year, after the German Army entered Hungary on Sunday morning, March 19, 1944, an additional 500,000 Hungarian Jews would perish in the Holocaust. (Some 65,000 Hungarian Jews had already perished due to abuses in the Forced Labor System and in massacres by some units of the Hungarian Army.) This would be the largest, mass extermination of human beings in the shortest period of time in all of history.

Among them were approximately 750 theatrical staff and artists, composed of actors, singers, musicians, dancers, composers, writers, directors, poets, painters, graphic artists, sculptors, and others such as newsmen. An excellent, biographical listing, covering most of them, written in Hungarian, can be found in Magda Horák, *A magyar értelmiség veszteségei az 1940-es években* (The Losses of the Hungarian Intelligentsia 1940), edited by Simonyi Pálné, Budapest, 1995.

The cultural loss to the Hungarian nation and its Jewry is immense, since many of them were stars or leading, creative professionals within their respective fields of endeavor.

Within these murdered artists, there were at least 168 identifiable members of the OMIKE *Művészakció*. (A few dozen others simply disappeared and so it's safe to assume that over 170 of them perished.) The following table contains their names, in what is believed to be a most comprehensive list, and is drawn from a number of sources in addition to the above Horák book:

- The OMIKE *Művészakció* Martyrs Plaque, Goldmark Hall (see appendix 1, figure 116).
- Bársony Péter, *A vészkorszak magyar muzsikus áldozatai* (Hungarian Musician Victims of the Holocaust) (Doctoral Dissertation, Franz Liszt University of Music, Budapest, 2010).
- "A Magyar Holokauszt Színházi Áldozatai," pamphlet by *A Magyar Színházi Társaság, Országos Színháztörténeti Múzeum*

és Intezét and the Nonprofit *Társadalomkutató Egyesület kiallitasa.*

- Website (www.omike.hu) of the Nonprofit *Társadalomkutató Egyesület.*
- M. Horak email to F. Bondy, dated October 2, 2016.

Hopefully their names and contributions to entertainment and culture will be remembered by future generations.

OMIKE *Művészakció* Members Who Fell During the Holocaust

Gyorgy Ádám
Pál Ádám
Tibor Adler
Sándor Alpár
Imre Ámos
Emil Balassa
Béla Bálint
Tibor Bálint
Lóránd Barabás
Alice Bárdos
Lajos Barna
István Basa
Róbert Békefi
László Berend
Harry Berky (Brenner)
Dr. Ferenc Bermann
László Bóka
Dr. Endre Bokor
Gyorgy Bondi
István Bondy
Sándorné Braun
Pál Budai
Lajos Ékes Csabai
Dr. Hugó Csergő
Mária Csergő
Benő Csillag
Ernő Deutsch
Jenő Deutsch
György Eiser
Viktor Erdei
László Erdősi
Imre Éri-Halász
Jenő Erődi
István Fabinyi
Sári Faragó
Árpád Fenyő
László Fenyő
Zsuzsa Földi
Béla Friedbauer
Tibor Gábor
János Gál
Sándor Garam
Andor Garami
Lajos Gárdonyi
Aladár Gárdos
Ottó Gelei
Andor Endre Gelléri
Sándor Gelléri
Kató Gergely
Lajos Gimes
Géza Glass
György Goldmann
Dezső Gömöri
Jenő Gonda
József Gonda
Bertalan Göndör
Dr. Pál Györi
László Hajnal
Sándor Hajó
Imre Harmath
Miklós Harsányi
Gyula Perlusz Hatvani
Endre Hegedüs
József Hirsch
Zoltán (Zoli) Hirsch
József Holder
László Horváth
Pál Hütter
Dávid Jándi
András Janovics
Pál B. Juhász
László Káldi
Imre Kára/Krausz
Zoltán Karczag
Ida Kohner
Jenő Komlós
Imre Kőműves
György Kondor
Emil Koralik
Miklós Kósa
Miklós Kovács
Sándor Kun
Sándor Kuti
Walter Lajtai-Lazarus
Artúr Lakner
Éva Lázár
Károly György Lendvai
Ernő Lengyel
Dr. Géza Lengyel-Csendes
Miklós Lőrincz
István Lukács
István Mádai
István Major
István Márk
István Mihály
Dr. Jenő Mohácsi

Ákos Molnár
László Nád (Nadelstecher)
Pál Nádai
László Nádasi
György Nádor
Mihály Nádor
György Nagy
Károly Nagy
Dávid Ney Jr.
István Örkényi-Strasszer
Béla Ormos
Jenő Pál
János Pallós
Károly Pap
Béla Pásztor
Ernő Poprádi
Paula Porter
Endre Quittner
István Rab
Sándor Radó
László Reiter
Jenő Rejtő
Rózsika Révai
Gyula Revere
Béla Révész
Pál Révész
Péter Pál Révész
Géza Rónai
Sándor Rott
Miklós Salamon
Sándor Sammler
József Sándor
Imre Sas
László Schnabel
János Schnitzler
Jutka Schöenfeld
Zoltán Schultz
Rezső Sík
Emil Stein
Géza Steinhardt
Gyula Sugár
Dr. Dezső Szabó
Oszkár Szalai
Imre (Buli) Szamosi
Jenő Szántó
Hédi Szécsi
Ernő Szenes
Fülöp Szenes
Jenő Szigeti
György Szín
Vilmos Szirmai
Dezső Szomory
Ödön Tamás (Taubner)
Ernő Tibor
György Trietsch
István Ujfalusi
Endre Vadász
Éva Vágó
Lilly Vajda
Sándor Vándor
Lajos Váradi
Tibor Váradi
Jenő Várnai
Andor Villányi
Jenő Wallesz
Dr. Ernő Weiller
Gyorgy Weiner
László Weiner
György Weisz/Fehér
Imre Wessel
Ede Zsigmond
Pál Zsigmondi

Glossary to the English Edition

The compiler wishes to acknowledge the use of the following sources in compiling the glossary:

Special thanks to Tamás Gajdó for his comments and references.

Borsos, Zsuzsanna. *A Madách Színház Pünkösti Andor igazgatása idején.* Budapest: Magyar Szinhazi Intezet, 1979.

Braham, Randolph L. *The Politics of Genocide.* 2nd ed. New York: Columbia University Press, 1994.

Flugel, Felix, Immanuel Schmidt, and Gustav Tanger. *Worterbuch englischen und deutschen Sprache fur Hand- und Schulgebrauch.* 7th ed. Braunschweig: G. Westermann, 1904.

Friedländer, Saul. *The Years of Extermination: Nazi Germany and the Jews, 1939–1945.* New York: Harper Collins, 2007.

Hundert, Gershon David, ed. *YIVO Encyclopedia of Jews in Eastern Europe.* New Haven: Yale University Press, 2008.

Komoroczy, Geza, ed. *Jewish Budapest: Monuments, Rites, History.* Budapest: Central European University Press, 1999.

Magyar Nemzeti Leveltar Archivum. mnl.gov.hu/bal_menusor/hasznalat/kiadvanyok/segedletek.repertoriumok.

Magyar Szín Ház. magyarszinhaz.hu.

Magyar Szinhazmuveszeti Lexikon. mek.oszk.hu/02100/02139/html.

Magyar zsidó adatbázis (Hungarian Jew Database). zsido.hu.

National Committee for Attending Deportees (DEGOB). degob.org.

Otte, Marline. *Jewish Identities in German Popular Entertainment, 1890–1933.* Cambridge: Cambridge University Press, 2006.

Scheiber, Sandor. *Magyar zsido hiralpok es folyoiratok bibliografiaja, 1847–1954.* Budapest: MTA Judaiszikai Kutatócsoport, 1993.

Wikipedia: English, German, and Hungarian.

Zvi Erenyi

Academy of Dramatic Arts (*Színművészeti Akadémia*)
Also known as the Primary Theater and Film Arts School (*Színház és Filmművészeti Főiskola*), the academy was founded in 1865 for the purpose of training Hungarian actors. The period of study was three to four years. Its curriculum included classics of Hungarian and world theater.

Actors Association (*Országos Színészegyesület*)
The association functioned from 1871–1938. It was founded for the purpose of defending the values and social and material interests of actors (including retired actors). A guild (*színészkamara*) replaced it in 1938.

Alapi's Chamber Theater (*Alapi Kamaraszínház*)
Nándor Alapi (b. 1885) was an actor and theatrical director. Between 1924–1931 he directed the National Chamber Theater (*Országos Kamaraszínház*) and between 1932–1934 he headed the Budapest Chamber Theater (*Budapesti Kamaraszínház*). He joined the Arrow Cross party and left Hungary in 1944.

Albert Kövessy Company (*Kövesy Albert Társulata*)
Kovessy's company recruited talented actors and primarily staged musical farces and folk plays but also classical pieces.

Andrássy Road Theater (*Andrássy úti Színház*)
It was originally located at 69 Andrássy út and opened in 1907. It was headed in turn by Sándor Faludi, Artúr Bárdos, and Pál Bródy. Between 1926–1937 its main focus was the staging of cabarets. In 1937 it moved to 35 Paulay Ede utca (street, hereafter abbreviated as u.), where it continued to operate until 1944.

Apollo Cabaret (*Apolló Kabaré*)
It opened in 1915 at 1–3 Népszínház u. and in 1918 adopted the name Apollo Theater (*Apolló Színpad*). It changed location several times in the 1920s.

Artist Theater (*Művész Színház*)
Artúr Bárdos founded two theaters under this name. He staged two shows at 18 Révay u. and led another Művész Színház, between the years 1936–1938, in the building of the *Fővárosi Operette Színház.*

Bethlen Square synagogue (*Bethlen téri zsinagóga*)
Located at 2 Bethlen Gábor tér, the building was originally erected in the neo-Renaissance style in 1876 for the National Deaf and Dumb Society. The architect Lipót Baumhorn expanded its prayer room in 1931 into a synagogue. Prior to WWII there were also here a communal kitchen and hall, and a Chevra Kadisha operated from these premises as well.

Blaha Lujza Theater (*Blaha Lujza Színház*)
This cabaret theater operated between 1921–1925. In 1921 it came within the orbit of the Revü Theater (*Revü Színház*) on Unio Rt. It was renovated according to the plans of László Vágó and it opened its doors in 1921 under the name of Blaha Lujza Theater. It was then led by Imre Szirmai. Until May 1925 its program consisted exclusively of operettas.

Bonbonniere Cabaret (*Bonbonniere Kabaré*)
This was the first true cabaret in Budapest. It opened its doors in 1907 at no. 28 Teréz körút under the direction of Ernő Kondor. It closed in 1910. In 1920, Gyula Kővári opened a cabaret under this name at the Royal Orfeum.

Buda Round Theater (*Budai Színkör*)
This theater functioned from 1843–1937 in what was originally a wooden structure in Horváth kert (Horváth Garden). While at different times it had a variety of names, it was known as the *Budai Színkör* from 1915–1937. Originally a venue for plays by Hungarian authors, it later mounted non-Hungarian classical plays as well.

Budapest Children's Theater (*Fővárosi Gyermekszínház*)
This was one of the children's theaters run by the Feld family and was also known as the Feld Type Children's Theater (*Feld-féle Gyermekszínház*).

***Budapest Journal* (*Budapesti Napló*)**
This was a paper which appeared between 1896–1918 and represented liberal interests.

Budapest Operetta Theater (*Fővárosi Operett Színház*)
This theater opened in 1922 on the premises of the renovated Budapest Orpheum (*Fővárosi Orfeum*) at no. 17 Nagymező u.

Chamber Theater (*Kamara Színház*)
This theater functioned between the years 1932–1937, renting quarters at the Wertheimer Orfeum. It was first headed by Nándor Alapi. It featured mostly popular musical comedies.

Chamber Varieté (*Kamara Varieté*)
György Sallay founded this institution in 1939 on the site of the former Teréz-körúti Színpad. He remained at its head until its nationalization in 1949.

City Center Theater (*Belvárosi Színház*)
From 1918–1949 this theater was located at no. 6 Koronaherceg (today: Petőfi Sándor) u. During the post-WWI period it was intermittently led by Artúr Bárdos.

City Park (*Városliget*)
This is a very large Budapest park located between the 6th and 14th districts in Pest. It was and is a favorite playground, boating, and cultural center.

City Theater (*Városi Színház*)
The capital's largest capacity theater was built in 1911 at Tisza Kálmán tér (Tisza Kálmán Square). Its program included plays, operas, operettas, ballets, and musical recitals. It changed its name from the Folk Opera (*Népopera*) to City Theater in 1917–1918. For three years, beginning in 1921, the program consisted of operettas and folkloristic plays. Beginning in 1927, the building was leased to a variety of theater companies but in 1940 it was handed back to the city for lack of funds and it functioned as an educational institution until 1945.

College of Applied Arts (*Iparművészeti Főiskola*)
This college was founded in 1880 as the National Hungarian Royal Applied Arts School (*Országos Magyar Királyi Iparművészeti Tanoda*) and designated as a college only in 1948. In 1896 it moved to the *Iparművészeti Palota* (Applied Arts Palace) on Üllői út.

Comedy Theater (*Vígszínház*)
This building was originally erected in 1896 on Lipót körút (presently: Szent István körút), in the Lipótváros district of Pest. It presented Hungarian, American, and European plays, ranging in type from realism to symbolism. The building was heavily damaged during WWII but later restored.

***Country-World* (*Ország-Világ*)**
A literary paper founded as a bi-weekly in 1879 by Gyula Somogyi for middle-class readers with wide interests. By the end of the 1920s it had come to focus on economics and urban politics. It ceased publication in 1938.

Cyclorama (*körkép*)
This theatrical device consisted of a panoramic painting on the inside of a cylindrical platform which was designed to provide the audience with a 360 degree view of the painting in order to provide the illusion of being in the midst of an event or place.

Faun Cabaret (*Faun Kabaré*)
This cabaret was opened by Béla Lénárd in 1922 in the Drechsler kávéház at 23 Andrássy út. Four programs played during its period of operation of less than a year.

First Jewish Law (*Első zsidótörvény*)
This law was passed by the Hungarian Parliament in May 1938 (no. 15/1938). It limited the number of Jews in the intellectual professions and in commercial enterprises of more than 10 employees to no more than 20%.

Folies Caprice
This was a German cabaret, located in Berlin and founded in 1905 by Felix Berg, which presented programs of crude Jewish humor in imitation of classical theater. It appealed to certain sections of the middle class, both Jewish and gentile.

Franz Joseph Bridge (*Ferenc József híd*)
This is the present day Freedom Bridge (*Szabadság híd*), which connects Szent Gellért tér (Szent Gellért Square) in Buda's 11th district with Fővám tér (Fővám Square) in Pest's 5th–9th districts across the Danube.

Geranium Cabaret (*Muskátli kabaré*)
The cabaret was formed in 1918 and located at 39 Csengery u. It first operated as the Modern Cabaret (*Modern kabaré*) and then was replaced by the Geranium Cabaret. It apparently lasted for only a short period of time.

Goldmark Hall (*Goldmark terem*)
This hall served as the venue for the OMIKE theater. It is located at 7 Wesselényi u., near the Dohány Street synagogue, and is named after Károly Goldmark, the famous Hungarian Jewish composer.

Gugger Hill (*Gugger hegy*)
Gugger Hill was one of the hills overlooking Buda, about 400–500 meters high. It was and is a tourist and hikers' destination.

Heroes' Temple (*Hősök temploma*)
This small synagogue was located next to the Dohány Street great synagogue on Wesselényi Street. Here, daily prayers took place, attended by the Dohány Street and Rumbach Street synagogue worshippers. It was built to commemorate the Hungarian Jewish soldiers who fell in WWI.

Hollán Street Cultural Hall (*Hitközségi körzetek kultúrterem*)
This hall was building owned by the Jewish community and located at 21/B Hollán u., where several OMIKE *Művészakció* concerts and operas were initially staged between Nov. 1939–Dec. 1940, while other events took place at the Goldmark Hall. At this time it was known as the OMIKE *Kamara Színház.*

Home Circle (*Otthon Kör*)
Founded by Hugo Solder, this was a society for Hungarian writers, journalists, and artists which functioned between the years 1891–1948. It was first located in the Fiume Hotel in Buda and then on Múzeum körút. It was dedicated to the improvement of the social life of artists.

***Hungarian Genius* (*Magyar Géniusz*)**
This was a periodical devoted to fine literature and founded in 1892.

***Hungarian Jews' Paper* (*Magyar Zsidók Lapja*)**
The Jewish Council (*Judenrat*), appointed by the Nazis following their occupation of Hungary in March 1944, published its announcements in this paper

Hungarian Law of Reception of the Jews (*Recepció*)
This law (42/1895) granted the legal status of a "received" religion to Judaism, thus placing it on an equal footing with Christian denominations. So, for example, the formal representative bodies of Judaism could receive state financial support and Jews could enter the upper house of Parliament.

Hungarian Theater
See *Magyar Színház*.

Jewish Museum (*Zsidó Múzeum*)
This museum is located on the corner of Wesselényi and Dohány Streets, next to the Dohány Street Synagogue. It opened at this location in 1931. Theodor (Tivadar) Herzl, founder of modern Zionism, was born at this site on May 2, 1860.

Jewish Religious Community of Pest (*Pesti Izraelita Hitközség*)
The community formed the overall Jewish communal organization of the city and was headed, during the period covered by this book, by Samu Stern. It was abolished by the Nazis in March 1944 to be replaced by a Jewish Council (*Judenrat*).

Kisfaludy Society (*Kisfaludy Társaság*)
This society was founded in Pest in 1836 with the aim of publishing the works of Károly Kisfaludy but then adopted the wider goal of encouraging public taste for fine literature. In the nineteenth century it hosted monthly readings which were considered important literary events.

Komédia
Komédia was a cabaret located at 10 Jókai tér (Jókai Square) that functioned between the years 1927–1944. During the years 1928–1932, it was known as *Komédia Orfeum*.

Kornél Sziklay Little Theater (*Kis Színkör*)
Kornél Sziklay founded this theater in 1904 in the City Park (Városliget), but it functioned for only one or two seasons. He refounded it in 1917 and led it until his death in 1919, at which point his son assumed its direction.

***Kulturbund Deutscher Juden* (Cultural Association of German Jews)**
This was a cultural federation of German Jews which was founded in 1933 in Berlin for the purpose of providing employment to the hundreds of German Jewish artists, musicians, and actors dismissed because they were Jews. Membership grew to perhaps 70,000 or even 180,000.

***Lebanon* (*Libanon*)**
This was a Jewish paper which appeared in Budapest between the years 1936–1943. It was edited by József Grózinger and others and published between 1940–1943 by the Scientific and Artistic Association of the National Hungarian Jewish Museum (*Országos Magyar Zsidó Múzeum Tudományos és Művészeti Egyesülete*).

Madách Theater (*Madách Színház*)
This theater operated between 1940–1944. It opened in September 1940 at no. 6 Madách tér as a studio theater (*kamaraszínház*). It was supported by Count István Károlyi and led in 1940–1941 by Géza Földessy and from September 1941 until the end of March 1944 by Andor Pünkösti. This latter period was marked by the literary quality of its program and its antiwar stance. This underwent a marked change under the leadership of the right-leaning Lajos Cselle, who led the theater from April 1944 until the end of the year.

***Magyar Színház* (Hungarian Theater)**
This theater functioned between the years 1897–1948 on Hevesi Sándor tér (Hevesi Sándor Square), earlier known as Izabella tér (Izabella Square). Initially, French and English plays were programmed, later to be followed by a mix of dramas and a variety of operettas.

Margaret Island Theater (*Margitszigeti Színház*)
This theater opened on this island in 1918 as a summer theater. It closed and its building was demolished in 1919.

Markó Street High School (*Markó-utcai gimnázium*)
Founded as early as 1858, when its name was the Budapest Imperial and Royal Catholic High School (*Pesti császári és királyi katolikus főgimnázium*). It was considered an elite school and moved to the building at no. 35 Markó utcai in 1876, where it continued to operate until 1952.

Markus Park Theater (*Márkus Park Színház*)
The Markus Park Cinema was converted to a covered theater which functioned between the years 1938–1946. Its programs included operettas and musical comedies and it starred some of the period's popular actors.

Metropolitan Papers (*Fővárosi Lapok*)
This was a daily literary paper which appeared between 1864–1903 in Pest. It was a leading publication in its class, under the editorship of Károly Vadnai (1876–1902).

Modern Theater (*Modern Színház*)
The theater's full name was *Modern Színház kabaré*. It was founded by Sándor Faludi and located at 69 Andrássy út on the site of the former *Műcsarnok* (Art Gallery). Its period of operation, 1907–1913, fell within the golden age of cabaret, and the genre of literary cabaret, with bold caricatures of political and social events, was innovated here.

Morgenzeitung
Probably refers to the *Östrauer Morgenzeitung* published in Ostrava, Czech Republic, in the 1920s and1930s.

Moulin Rouge
Founded in 1889 by Charles Zidler and Joseph Oller and located close to Montmartre in Paris's 18th arrondissement, the site was marked by a real windmill on its roof. It was best known for the cancan dance. The revue which was based on it evolved and led to the development of cabarets in Europe.

Music Academy (*Zeneakadémia*)
The Hungarian Parliament appointed Franz Liszt as President of the Music Academy in 1875 and it soon began to function. In 1879 it received its own building at 67 Andrássy út and a new building in 1907 which opened onto both Liszt Ferenc tér and Király u. in the 6th district of Budapest.

Nation (*Nemzet*)
A political paper which represented the ruling party and appeared between 1882–1899.

National Conservatory (*Nemzeti Zenede*)
It was founded in 1840 and was the highest level institution of musical instruction until the founding of the Music Academy in 1875. Today it is known as the *Bartók Béla Zeneművészeti Szakközépiskola és Gimnázium* (Béla Bartók Musical Arts Vocational High School).

National Hungarian Jewish Aid Organization (OMZSA, *Országos Magyar Zsidó Segítő Akció*)
At the urging of the American Joint Distribution Committee, the main Hungarian Jewish communal organizations established in 1939 a unified fund-raising body to collect monies to help care for the many newly arriving Jewish refugees, to aid emigration, to relieve Jewish poverty, and so on. It was first headed by Géza Ribáry. It also provided food to Jewish prisoners in the Horthyliget Internment Camp and in other Csepel Island camps after the arrival of the German Army in March 1944.

National Theater (*Nemzeti Színház*)
This is the main theater in Budapest. It opened in 1837 and frequently presented Shakespeare's plays and other dramas. (This theater is not to be confused with either the old or current Hungarian National Theater, *Magyar Színház*.)

New Theater (*Új Színház*)
During 1927–1932 the New Theater was located at 18 Révay u. and began with cabaret, which later evolved into full evening programs.

New York Café (New York *Kávéház*)
A meeting place over a long period for those interested in Hungarian poetry and literature. It opened in 1894 at 9–11 Erzsébet körút, a building constructed as the local headquarters of the New York Life Insurance Company.

November-Anniversary (*November-Évforduló*)
This was a short-lived Jewish paper, of which two issues appeared in Budapest in 1941. It was a publication of the OMIKE Cultural Council (OMIKE *Kultúrtanács*).

Numerus Clausus
This was the appellation of the first anti-Jewish law to be passed in post-WWI Europe. It was enacted in Hungary (law 25/1920) and it placed a limit (without mentioning Jews by name) on the number of Jewish students to be admitted to institutions of higher learning in Hungary commensurate with the percentage of Jews in Hungary (6%).

***Nyílt-változásos* opera**
A term to describe a quick change of scenery, effected without the lowering of the theater's curtains.

OMIKE (*Országos Magyar Izraelita Közművelődési Egyesület*)
OMIKE was established in 1909 at the initiative of Chief Rabbi Simon Hevesi to bring traditional Jewish values to Jews in the modern world and promote the

amalgamation of Hungarian and Jewish modes of life. It founded and promoted many cultural and welfare initiatives, including the Artistic Enterprise.

OMIKE Artistic Enterprise (OMIKE *Művészakció*)
Jews were mostly excluded from the Theater and Film Guild established in 1938; their livelihoods thus were threatened. The OMIKE, therefore, with state permission, established the Artistic Enterprise to provide employment for the excluded artists. It also provided a venue for the artists to perform at cultural events for the enjoyment of the ostracized Jewish community of Budapest.

Opera House (*Operaház*)
Known formally as the Hungarian National Opera (*Magyar Állami Operaház*), the opera house was located at 22 Andrássy út and dedicated to the performance of operas and ballets. It opened in 1884 and was headed for a time by Gustav Mahler, the great Czech composer of Jewish origin. It experienced golden periods in the late nineteenth century and also between the two world wars. Today it exists as the Hungarian State Opera.

Operetta Theater of Budapest (*Fővárosi Operettszínház*)
This theater opened its doors in 1922 at the then refurbished *Fővárosi Orfeum* (17 Nagymező u.) with programs of light comedies.

Pallós Ladies Company (*Pallós Ladies társulat*)
This company was probably connected with Tivadar Pallós (1887–1950), composer and conductor, who served as the conductor of the OMIKE orchestra, 1940–1944. He composed opera parodies and comic opera revues and set many of the period's songs to music.

***Past and Future* (*Múlt és Jövő*)**
Past and Future was a periodical founded in 1911 and edited by József Patai until March 1944. It served as an important means for the dissemination of cultural and artistic values. It had a distinctly Zionist and national bent and achieved a wide circulation within Hungary and abroad.

Pester Lloyd
Pester Lloyd was a German-language newspaper which appeared during 1854–1945. It was an independent publication which represented the interests of Hungarian speakers to German speakers and defended Hungarian cultural and national values.

Petőfi Society (*Petőfi Társaság*)
This society was active from 1876–1944 with the goal of spreading knowledge about the Hungarian national poet, Sándor Petőfi, and Hungarian fine liter-

ature. It held widely attended public readings and saw to the publications of Petőfi's works.

Pódium Cabaret (*Pódium Kabaré*)
Known as the Cabaret of the Pódium Writers (*Pódium Írók Kabaréja*), it functioned between the years 1936–1942 at 2 Mérleg u. at the Gresham Palace. It mounted political cabaret shows, notably courageous considering the circumstances of the time.

Popular Theater (*Népszínház*)
The Popular Theater operated between 1875–1908 on Blaha Lujza tér with the aim of staging folk plays and operettas.

Press Chamber (*Országos Magyar Sajtókamara*)
The Second Jewish Law limited the number of Jews in professional guilds to 6%. Legally, one had to belong to the Press Chamber in order to work as a journalist, but well over half of Jewish applicants were rejected on account of their religion or race. The law also prohibited Jews from working as editors or publishers.

Renaissance Theater (*Renaissance Színház*)
The Thália Theater was located at Nagymező u. 22–24, along with a number of other theaters, including the Renaissance Theater, between 1920–1926.

Royal Music Hall (*Royal Orfeum*)
This music hall was founded in 1908 and located at 31 Erzsébet körút. It was the outstanding Budapest music hall in its time (1908–1933). After 1933 it functioned as a musical operetta theater and then as a cabaret. From 1935 it was named Royal Theater (*Royal Színház*), and this was followed by a number of other name changes.

Royal Theater (*Király Színház*)
László Beöthy founded this theater in 1903 at 71 Király u. Until 1925 it was the city's most popular and successful operetta theater, due to its founder's artistic talent and business acumen. Afterward, it slowly declined and finally closed in 1936.

Sándor Krémer's Company (*Krémer Sándor társulata*)
Krémer (1859–1918) was an outstanding actor and director. Following an acting career in provincial towns, he established his own actors' company in 1901.

Second Jewish Law (*Második zsidótörvény*)
This law (no. 4/1939) defined "Jewish" on the basis of mostly racial terms and restricted the number of Jews in the intellectual professions to 6% and banned

them from holding positions in the state apparatus and from teaching in high schools. They could not fill positions in commerce or industry which required licenses, and existing licenses were to be withdrawn.

Simplicissimus
Simplicissimus was founded by Egon Dorn and functioned from 1922 to 1923, initially as a comedy club (*mulatóhely*) on Dohány Street. It then briefly served as a cabaret, closed again and re-opened as a literary cabaret but soon closed for good. (It is not to be confused with the German satirical weekly magazine of the same name.)

Synagogue on Öntőház Street (*Öntőház utcai zsinagóga*)
The synagogue was located at 5–7 Öntőház u. in Buda. It was designed in the Moorish style by the architect Ignác Knabe and built in 1865 (consecrated in 1867). It stood beneath Buda Castle facing the Danube. It suffered damage during WWII and was later demolished, together with rest of the houses on the street.

Teplitz-Schönau Theater (*Teplitz-Schönau Színház*)
This institution was known as the *Stadttheater Teplitz-Schönau* or Erzgebirgisches Theater. It was constructed during 1921–1924 and displayed the influence of expressionism and art deco in its architecture. At the time, it was the second largest theater in Czechoslovakia. The town is known today as Teplice.

Teréz Boulevard Stage (*Terézkörúti Színpad*)
From 1923–1938 the building was located at no. 46 Teréz körút. It was Budapest's leading cabaret, one with the best acts and personnel.

Thália Society (*Thália Társaság*)
The society functioned from 1904–1908 in imitation of the German Freie Bühne and the French Theatre Libre theatrical societies. It aimed to stage contemporary plays which may have been overlooked by other, more mainstream theaters.

Theater and Film Chamber (*Színművészeti és Filmművészeti Kamara*)
As a consequence of the First Jewish law of 1938, no artist of Jewish origin could become a full member of this chamber (or guild). Theaters could not employ anyone not a member of the chamber and this effectively forced Jewish artists into unemployment. The chamber ceased to exist in the beginning of 1945.

Theater at Bethlen Square (*Bethlen téri Színház*)
A theater opened at 3 Bethlen tér (7th district) in 1929 with the original name of *Bethlen téri Színpad* (the name changed in 1934). It was home to many cabaret programs, many of which had Jewish themes. It ceased to exist in 1937.

Versatz (*Versatzstück*)
This is the term for movable scenery in a theater.

***The Week* (*A Hét*)**
The Week was a periodical originally devoted to fine literature, culture, and art which appeared between 1890–1924. From 1894 it also covered political affairs. It aimed at a progressive readership but was eclipsed by *Nyugat*.

Wertheimer Nightclub (*Wertheimer Mulató*)
This was a music café located on Népszínház u. It was founded in 1886 and for many years its programs featured Polish-Jewish companies, with the singer Pepi Littmann at their head.

Young Hungary (*Fiatal Magyarország*)
This is the name which radical, democratic youth (e.g., Sándor Petőfi, János Vajda, Mór Jókai, Mihály Tompa, Pál Vasvári) gave to their movement in the 1840s.

Contributors to the Hungarian Edition

Some of the articles in this book were written by the following former colleagues of mine:

Tibor Benczés

Péter Földes

Sándor Gervai

Ernő Lőb

Aladár Ritter

Miklós Weisz

Jenő Lévai

About Jenő Lévai

Jenő Lévai (1892–1983) was a noted journalist and editor, born in Budapest, who became the foremost Hungarian Holocaust historian, immediately after WWII.

In his youth, he earned an engineering degree from the Technical University of Budapest. However, he became interested in journalism and worked as a sports reporter soon after his graduation.

In WWI, he served as a battery commander on the Russian front until his capture. When he came home in 1921, he returned to journalism and was very active in the fight against Hungarian antisemitism. He wrote numerous articles against László Endre, the constable of Godollo, a leading antisemite, who later orchestrated the 1944 deportation of the vast majority of Hungarian Jewry in concert with Adolf Eichmann.

In 1943, he edited and published a book titled, *Írók, színészek, énekesek és zenészek regényes életútja a Goldmark-teremig: Az OMIKE színháza és művészei*

(The Illustrious Careers of Writers, Artists, Singers and Musicians Associated with Goldmark Hall: The Theater and Artists of the OMIKE). The book is notable because it captured interviews with numerous Hungarian Jewish artists, many of whom subsequently perished in the Holocaust. It also detailed the remarkable operation of this theater that had to function under the adverse conditions of the Horthy fascist regime.

Among his numerous books which detailed and documented the Holocaust in Hungary are:

A pesti gettó csodálatos megmenekülésének hiteles története (1946)
The Black Book on the Martyrdom of Hungarian Jewry (1948)
Zsidósors Magyarországon (1948)
Eichmann in Hungary (1961)

This distinguished historian died in Budapest at the age of 91, in 1983.

Contributors to the English Edition

Frederick Bondy

Fred lives in New York City, where his three children and their families, composed of seven grandchildren, live. He has a bachelors degree in chemical engineering from the City College of New York and a masters degree in chemical engineering from the University of Akron. He has over 45 years leading process (chemical) engineering designs, with up to 15 chemical engineers, for over 80 refinery, gasification, petrochemical, specialty chemical, and polymer projects. He has been fortunate to be able to travel worldwide to execute these designs.

His patents and publications include:

"Agitated Vessel Heat Transfer Design." *Carmagen Engineering Newsletter*, July 2010.

"Phenolic Wastewater Treatment with Ethers for Removal and Recovery of Phenolics." (USP No. 6,071,409, June 6, 2000).

"Steam Tracing," *Encyclopedia of Chemical Processing and Design* 54. New York: Marcel Dekker, 1996. 66–78.

"Heat Transfer, Agitated Vessels." *Encyclopedia of Chemical Processing and Design* 25. New York: Marcel Dekker, 1987. 341–453.

"Easy Way to Design Steam Tracing For Pipes." *Chemical Engineering*, Aug. 4, 1986, 65–70.

"Heat Transfer in Agitated Vessels." *Chemical Engineering*, April 4, 1983, 62–71.

He has also written an unpublished biography, *István Bondy, Hungarian Actor (1905–1944)*, located in the Széchényi National Hungarian Library, Budapest, and in the Hungarian Theater Museum and Institute, Budapest, August 2013.

For enjoyment, he reads history, spends time with his family, jogs, goes to the gym, and collects postage stamps. For many years, he was a marathon runner, having completed 43 of them.

István Deák

István Deák, who is an emeritus professor of history at Columbia University, was born in in 1926 in Hungary. Having survived the war there, he studied European history in Budapest, Paris, Munich, and at Columbia University, where he obtained his PhD in 1964. He taught at Smith College and then at Columbia University.

Following his retirement in 1997, he taught at Stanford University. His publications include *Weimar Germany's Left-Wing Intellectuals* (1968); *The Lawful Revolution: Louis Kossuth and the Hungarians, 1848–1849* (1979), which also appeared in Hungarian and German; *Beyond Nationalism: A Social and Political History of the Habsburg Officer Corps, 1848–1918* (1990), which also appeared in Hungarian, German, Italian, and Romanian; *Essays on Hitler's Europe* (2001),which also appeared in Hungarian; and *Europe on Trial: The Story of Collaboration, Resistance, and Retribution during World War II* (2015), which also appeared in Hungarian and Slovene, with the German and Chinese editions in preparation.

István edited and with Jan T. Gross and Tony Judt partly wrote *The Politics of Retribution in Europe: World War II and Its Aftermath* (2000). He has been a frequent contributor to *The New York Review of Books* and *The New Republic*. He is an external member of the Hungarian Academy of Sciences and has received several other honors.

Péter Bársony

Péter Bársony, a renowned violist, was born in Budapest. He is currently professor at Franz Liszt Academy of Music, Budapest, head of the Viola Faculty, and graduated from there in 2000. His masters were Ferenc Rados, György Konrád, Dénes Kovács, György Kurtág, Dénes Zsigmondy, Pinchas Zukerman, Zoltán Tóth, and Gerard Caussé.

Mr. Bársony gives regularly concerts all over the world. His chamber partners include Márta Gulyás, Péter Csaba, Péter Frankl, Zoltán Kocsis, Rivka Golani, Kristóf Baráti, Barnabás Kelemen, Liza Ferschtman, Dezső Ránki, Guy Ben-Ziony, Alisa Weilerstein, András Adorján, Gergely Ittzés, Miklós Perényi, István Várdai, and David Grimal, among others, and has collaborated with reknown string quartets, like the Miró, Ying, Brentano, Kelemen and Kodály string quartets. He participates in many prestigious internatonal chamber music festivals.

In 2012 Mr. Bársony was awarded the prestigious Liszt Ferenc Prize by the Hungarian government.

As a soloist he has been invited to well known orchestras like Franz Liszt Chamber Orchestra, American Symphony Orchestra, Erkel Chamber Orchestra, Hungarian Radio Orchestra or Hungarian Symphony Orchestra.

In 2013 he made his debut in Carnegie Hall, Stern auditorium, with the American Symphony Orchestra, conducted by Leon Botstein.

He earned his doctorate in 2011. His field, Hungarian musicians victims of the Holocaust, has received international interest. Recently, he published it with the world renowned historian, Randolph Braham.

Magda Horák

Magda Horák's interests are varied but predominantly lie in the artistic fields of theater, music, and the fine arts. She has worked for various publishers and museums, including the Ethnographic Museum of Budapest.

She is a noted historian and author of numerous articles and books dealing with Hungarian and Jewish-Hungarian culture. She is considered to be the expert on the *Országos Magyar Izraelita Közművelődési Egyesület* (OMIKE), The National Hungarian Jewish Cultural Society which functioned from 1909–1944, as well as on its unique theater, the *OMIKE Művészakció,* which functioned during 1939–1944, when Jewish artists were banned from performing in public venues by the fascist Hungarian regime. Some of her many publications are listed below.

Színház a gettóban (Theater in the Ghetto). In *MIOK Évkönyv 1983/84* (MIOK Year Book, 1983/1984), edited by Rabbi Scheiber Sándor, 167–99.

Kirekesztetten is előítélet nékűl: az OMIKE Művészakció (Excluded but without Prejudice: The OMIKE Artistic Enterprise). In *Múlt és jövő* (Past and Present) 5, no. 2 (1994): 105–13.

Ősi hittel, becsülettel a hazáért!: OMIKE, Országos Magyar Izraelita Közművelődési Egyesület, 1909–1944 (With Ancient Faith and Honor for the Homeland, OMIKE: National Hungarian Jewish Cultural Society, 1909–1944). Budapest: Háttér Kiadó, 1998. Contains chronological and assorted cultural documents of the OMIKE and the OMIKE Művészakció.

A magyar értelmiség veszteségei az 1940-es években (The Losses of the Hungarian Intelligentsia 1940), edited by Simonyi Pálné. Budapest, 1995.

Ms. Horák is also the editor of a lexicon of famous, world-wide Jews, titled *Kik voltak ők?* (Who Were They?), Budapest, 1995.

In April 2014, she was awarded the prestigious Wiesenthal Prize in Budapest, for her voluntary work and writing with regard to the memory and cultural losses due to the Holocaust in Hungary.

Zvi Erenyi

Zvi Erenyi lives in New York and is a librarian with Yeshiva University, located in Mahattan.

Bibliography

A holokauszt magyar zeneszerző áldozatai [In Memoriam: Hungarian Composer Victims of the Holocaust]. Budapest: B'nai B'rith, 2008.

Alpár, Ágnes. *Az OMIKE Művészakciójának műsora* [The Programs of the OMIKE Artistic Enterprise. *Színháztörténeti Füzetek* [History of Theater Booklets] 56. Budapest: Magyar Színházi Intézet, 1974.

Bálint, Lajos. *A száműzöttek színháza* [Theater of the Outcasts]. In *Művészbejáró* [Stage Door]. Budapest: Szépirodalmi Könyvkiadó, 1964. 242–48.

Bársony, Péter. *A vészkorszak magyar muzsikus áldozatai* [Hungarian Musician Victims of the Holocaust]. Doctoral Dissertation, Franz Liszt University of Music, Budapest, 2010.

———. *A vészkorszak Magyar muzsikus áldozatai* [Hungarian Musician Victims of the Holocaust]. *Tanumányok a Holokaustról* [Studies on the Holocaust] 6. Edited by Braham Randolph. Budapest: Múlt és Jövő [Past and Present], 2014. 233–92.

Braham, Randolph. *The Politics of Genocide: The Holocaust in Hungary*. Vol. 1. New York: Columbia University Press, 1981. 89, 419.

Cenner, Mihály. *Én a komédiát lejátsztam, mulattattam, de nem mulattam* [I Performed Comedy, I Amused, but I Didn't Feel Amused]. In *A száműzöttek színháza* [Theater of the Outcasts]. In guidebook to the exhibit at the Bajor Gizi Museum, *Magyar Színházi Intézet* [Institute of Hungarian Theater], edited by Gobbi Hilda. Budapest: Magyar Színházi Intézet, 1981.

Gajdó, Tamás. *In the Service of Thalia*. In *The Land of Hagar: The Jews of Hungary: History, Society and Culture*, edited by Szalai Anna, 235–41. Tel Aviv: Beth Hatefutsoth. the Nahum Goldmann Museum of the Jewish Diaspora/Ministry of Defense Publishing House, 2002.

Gál, György Sándor. *Atlantisz harangjai* [Bells of Atlantis]. Budapest: Móra Kiadó, 1982.

Horák, Magda. *A magyar értelmiség veszteségei az 1940-es években* [The Losses of the Hungarian Intelligentsia 1940]. Budapest: Simonyi Pálné, 1995.

———. "Kirekesztetten is előítélet nékűl: az OMIKE Művészakció" [Excluded but Without Prejudice: the OMIKE Artistic Enterprise]. *Múlt és Jövő* [Past and Present] 5, no. 2 (1994): 105–13.

———. *Ősi hittel, becsülettel a hazáért!: OMIKE, Országos Magyar Izraelita Közművelődési Egyesület, 1909–1944* [With Ancient Faith and Honor for the Homeland, OMIKE: National Hungarian Jewish Cultural Society, 1909–1944]. Budapest: Háttér Kiadó, 1998. Contains chronological and assorted cultural documents of the OMIKE and the OMIKE *Művészakció.*

———. *Színház a gettóban* [Theater in the Ghetto]. In *MIOK Évkönyv 1983/84* [MIOK Year Book, 1983/1984], edited by Rabbi Scheiber Sándor, 167–99.

Komor, Ágnes. *Apám, Komor Vilmos* [My Father, Vilmos Komor]. Budapest: Balassi Kiadó, 2009.

Komoroczy, Geza, ed. *Jewish Budapest: Monuments, Rites, History.* Budapest: Central European University Press, 1999. 364–69.

Kory, Agnes. "Jewish Musicians in Hungary." *Music and the Holocaust.* N.d. http://holocaustmusic.ort.org/places/hungary/.

Lévai, Jenő, ed. *Írók, színészek, énekesek és zenészek regényes életútja a Goldmark-teremig. Az Omike színháza és művészei* [The Illustrious Careers of Writers, Artists, Singers, and Musicians Associated with Goldmark Hall: The Theater and Artists of the OMIKE]. Budapest: Jenő Lévai, 1943.

"Martyred Artists of the OMIKE." *Uj Elet* [*New Life*, newspaper]. Feb. 10, 1949, 7.

P. G. "Az OMIKE Mártirak" [The OMIKE Martyrs]. *Képes Figyelő,* no. 18, May 3, 1947.

Palásti, László. "Akik véresen buktak le a színpadról" [Those Who Fell Bloodied from the Stage]. *Képes Figyelő,* no. 51, December 21, 1946.

Rózsa Vera—Mother of Stars. Directed by Lehtonen Tiina-Maija. Finnish Broadcasting Co. (YLE), 1997.

Tallián, Tibor. *Egyéb opera együttesek Budapesten* [Other Opera Orchestras in Budapest]. In *A Magyar Állami Operház és a hazai operajátszás története, A magyar színháztörténeti örökség 1920–1949* [The Hungarian State Opera House and the History of Domestic Opera 1920–1949], edited by Bécsy Tamás, Székely György, and Gajdó Tamás, section 3, para. 1–8.

———. *Weiner László, 1916–1944: A zeneszerző halálának 50 év fordulójára rendezett emlékhangverseny műsorfüzete* [Program Guide of the Memorial Concert Organized for the 50th Anniversary of the Death Composer László Weiner, 1916–1944]. Concert held in Goldmark Hall, May 2, 1994.

For additional bibliographic references on historical, musical and other background material, please see those given in the foreword, introduction and afterword sections of this book.

Index

This index covers the names of persons such as OMIKE *Művészakció* members, performers, fine artists, and others engaged in its activities; names of plays and other performances; theaters; theatrical terminology; historical events and figures; Hungarian colloquialisms; and a few other miscellaneous items. Consult the appendices for playbills, programs, fine arts exhibitions, and photographs.

Abai, József, 142
Abai, Kefro, 142
Abrahamson, Manó, 143
Academy of Dramatic Art, 61, 63, 66, 69, 77, 86, 88, 90, 114
accessories, 127, 128, 131
Ács, Rózsi, 53
Actors' Alliance, 30
Actors' Association, 58, 60, 65, 75, 88
Aczél, György, 53
Ádam, György, 143
Ádám, Pál, 53
Ádler, Tibor, 143
Ágoston, József, 142
Aida, 116, 121, 135
Ajtai-Adler, Viktor, 97, 137, 144
Ákos, Ferenc, 144
Álarcok (Masks), 136
Álarcosbál (Masked Ball), 136
Alice Takács, 82, 136
Allied successes in Normandy, 11
Altatómese (Lullaby Tale), 49
America, 48, 51, 55, 65, 87, 104, 120
American War Refugee Board, 13
Ámos, Imre, xv
Andrássy úti Színház (Andrássy Avenue Theater), 37, 73, 76, 90, 139
An-ski, S., 62, 96, 136
Antalffy-Zsíros, Dezső, 139
anti-Jewish Laws, xii, xiv, 6, 7, 11, 18, 139, 141, 147
antisemitism, 2, 3, 4
Antoine's Theatre Libre, 30
Antologia Coacta-Nyugateurópai költők és irok gyűjteménye-t, xiv, 147
Apollo Kabaré (Apollo Cabaret), 66, 67, 76, 92
apostate artists, xiii
Arany, János, 52, 60
Aranyóra (Gold Watch), 89, 136
Argentina, 15
Arrow Cross Party, xii, 5, 9, 12, 13, 14, 15, 19
Artist of Merit (1953), xvi

artistic director, the, 37, 38, 39, 104
artistic duties of the director, 31, 32
Aschenfeld, Lili, 142,
assimilation of Jews, 2
Aszeghy, Kálmán, 105
Atlantisz harangjai (The Bells of Atlantis), 141
auditorium, the (OMIKE), 73, 125, 126, 130
Augenfeld, Magda, 143
Auschwitz Reports and the Holocaust in Hungary (Randolph Braham), 1
Austro-Hungarian, 4, 16, 86

Babits, Mihály, 56
Bajazzók (Pagliacci), 105, 135
Baky, László, 9
Balázs, István, 55, 142
Bálint, Lajos, xiii, xvi, 32, 35, 37, 38, 39, 74, 136
Bálint, Marcell, 53
Bálint, Tibor, 97, 143
ballet, 136
Bán, Kató, 68, 97, 142
Bánát, Gábor (Gabriel), 97, 137, 144
Bánóczi, Dr. László, 30, 37, 147
baptized Jews, 10, 14
Bárdos, Alice, 97, 137, 144
Bárdos, Artúr, 50, 71, 77, 87, 97
Bárdossy, László, 16
Bársony, Dóra, 67, 142
Bártfai, Gabriella, 132, 145
Bartók, Béla, xii, xiii, 99, 137
Bartos, Gyula, 53, 57
Basa, István, 97, 142
Basilides, Mária, 139
Baumgarten family, 139
Baumgarten, Gabi, 142
Bechar, György, 143
Beethoven, xiii, xvi, 26, 27, 120, 135
Békeffy, Róbert, 53
Belvárosi Színház (City Center Theater), 60, 63, 69, 74, 77, 87, 100, 139, 142, 143, 147
Bence, Miklós, 97, 142
Benedikt, Klári, 97, 143
Beöthy, László, 55, 66, 109
Berdai, Pál, 144
Beregi, Oszkár, xvi, 35, 53, 54, 73, 74, 81, 82, 88, 89
Berkovits, Tibor, 144
Berky (Brenner), Harry, 142
Berlin, xiii, 49, 55, 67, 87, 99, 100, 101, 104, 107, 109, 110, 118, 139, 142, 143
Berlin Jüdischer Kulturbund, 107, 137, 146
Berliner Theater, 107
Bermann, Ferenc, 97, 100, 142
Bernáth, Jolán, 53
Bethlen, Count István, 5, 11, 18
Bethlen Square Synagogue, xiii
Bethlen-téri Színház (Bethlen Square Theater), 70, 71, 139
Bible, 55, 56
Biró, József, 97, 144
Biró, Kató, 144
Biró, Lajos, 136
Bizet, 135
Blaha Lujza Theater, Ujpest, 93
Bodor, Imre, 142
Bohémek (Bohemians), 106
Bohémélet (La Boheme), 109, 135
Bolgár, Endre, 144
Bonbonniere Cabaret, 70, 76
Bondy, István, xv, 53
Born, Friedrich, 13
Boross, Elemér, 136
Boross, Ida, 53
Bóth, Klári, 53
Brahm, Ottó, 30
Brand, Hanna, 97, 142
Braun, Sándor, 48
Bródy, Sándor, 43, 72, 92
Brünauer, Tibor, 143
Brust, György, 143
Bruszt, Györgyné, 142
Budai, Pál, 59
Budai Színkör, 59

Budapest Children's Theater, 75
Budapesti Napló (Budapest Journal), 41, 42, 48
Burián, Károly, 106, 115, 116, 120, 121

cabaret, xiii, xv, 31, 33, 35, 61, 67, 71, 72, 75, 76, 91, 93, 94, 109, 137, 146
Carmen, 120, 135
casting, 31, 32, 34, 39, 58
Catholic press, xii
Central Powers, 3
Chamber (Guild) (*Kamara*), xii, xiii, 63, 65, 74, 84, 89, 96
Chicago Symphony Orchestra, 137
chief property man, 127, 128
choir, 31, 34, 66, 79, 80, 98, 99, 113, 132, 138, 139, 141, 142, 143, 146
choir master, 132
Christian musicians, xiv
Cirkusz (Circus), 136
classical plays, 32, 33
cloakroom, 31, 125, 127
College of Applied Arts, 80
College of Music, 122
Concerto Grosso, 102
Concordia Jewish Theater, 138
conductors of the OMIKE, 38, 100
cooling equipment, 125
costumes, xiii, 3, 17, 73, 127, 129, 131, 145
counterrevolution, 4, 5, 12
couplet, 76, 93
Cross of the Legion of Honor, 51
Csathó, Kálmán, 49
Csergő, Hugó, xv, 25, 29, 32, 33, 39–45, 74, 136
Csergő, Mária, 45
Csíki, Gergely, 58
Csillag, Benő, 53, 128
Cultural Committee of the OMIKE, (Cultural Council), 29, 31, 101, 146
Cultural Hall on Hollán Street, xiii, 140
curtains and scenery, 38, 81, 100, 126, 127, 128, 130, 131, 132, 133
cyclorama, 25, 126

Dachau, 15
Dános, Lili, 97, 142
Dános, Méda, 143
Danube River, 14
Danziger, Lili, 142
Darvas, Ernő, 53
Darvas, Ibolya, 97, 114, 115, 142
Darvas, Lili, 121
Dayka, Margit, 50
Dénes, Vera, 98, 144
Denevér, A (The Bat), 136
deportation, 8–11, 13–14, 15, 18
Deutsch, Jenő, 97, 143
director of the OMIKE, 30–32, 35, 49
directors, xi, xii, xvi, 7, 33, 35, 37, 38, 39, 44, 48, 49, 50, 53, 54, 56, 62, 65, 66, 67, 69, 74, 80, 86, 88, 89, 96, 105, 107, 118, 123, 127, 128–131, 150, 151, 152
Ditrói, Mór, 54, 58–59
Divertimento, The, xiii, 140
Dohány Utcai (Street) Synagogue, xiii, 3, 21, 33, 55, 114
Don Pasquale, 33, 100, 135
Don River, 7
Donáth, Ede, 143
Donizetti, 135
Dorn, Egon, 66
Dózsa, István, 53
drama company, the, 37, 54, 56
dramaturgist (playwright), xiii, xv, xvi, 7, 30, 37, 38, 43, 45, 46, 49, 51, 96, 131
Drechsler, Sándor, 143
dressers, 129
dressing rooms, xiii, 46, 59, 61, 83, 126, 129, 130
Dual Monarchy, 3
duties of the director, 30, 31
Dybuk (Dybbuk), 61, 63, 136

economic structure of the Artistic Enterprise, 31

Edit, Lőrincz, 144
Eichmann, Adolf, 8, 10–11, 13, 18
Eiser, György, 97, 143
Elek, Zsuzsa, 53
Első Hajnal (The First Dawn), 44
Emperor-King Francis Joseph, 2, 40
Endre, László, 9, 72, 144
Erdész, Nándor, 142
Érdi, Pál, 142
Erdősi, László, 97, 100, 141–143
Ernster, Dezső, 97, 103–105, 140, 142
Essenfeld, Manó, 142
Eszter (Esther), 32, 136
Évforduló November (November Anniversary), xiv

Fabinyi, István, 53
Fabri, Edith, 97, 142
Fabri, Sári, 142
Falk, Géza, 141
Faludi, Erna, 142
Faludi, Ferenc, 97, 142
Faludi, Miklós, 43
Faragó, Erzsébet, 53
Faragó, István, 144
Faragó, Panni, 53, 142
Farkas, Alice, 97, 142
Farkas, Sándor, 97, 105–106, 142
Farnadi, Edith, 97, 143
Fasor Temple (Synagogue), 114
Faun kabare (Faun Cabaret), 67
Fazekas, Imre, 136
Fehér, György, 53
Fehér, Pál, 97, 106–107, 140, 142
Fehér, Tivadar, 53, 97, 142–143
Feher, Vera, 143
Fejér, Sándor, 97, 144
Fekete, János, 143
Feleki, László, 141–142
Feleki, Rezső, 142–143
Fellegi, István, 53
Fenyő, Árpád, 53, 142
Fenyvessy, Ferenc, 86
Ferenczi, Ágnes, 53
Festetich, Count, 54
Fidelio, 135
Final Solution (Hungarian), 8–10
Fine Arts Exhibition, xiv, 146
Fine Arts Group (*Kepzomuveszeti Csoport*), 141
First Jewish Law (1938), xii
Fischer, Annie, xvi, 137, 143
Fischer, Sándor, 33, 97, 100, 141–143
Fodor, Erno, 140
Fodor Music School, 140
Földes, Péter, 53
Földi, Zsuzsa, 53
Foldiák, Márta, 142
folk songs (Jewish, Yiddish), 67, 103, 120
Fővárosi Operett Színház (Budapest Operetta Theater), 114, 127, 139
Fraknói, Károly, 97, 100, 142
Francati, Rocco, 142
Francis Joseph I, Emperor-King, 2, 40
Franz Liszt Prize-winner (1963), xvi
Freie Buhne Movement, 30
Friedmann, Endre, 129
full rehearsals, 132
Füredi , Károly Vogel, 142
furniture, 46, 127, 128, 131
Füzesi, Róbert, 53

Gábori, Elemér, 144
Gál, Dezső, 35, 53
Gál, György Sándor, 103, 141
Gál, János, 97, 144
Galambos, N., 144
Galicia, 8
Gallay, Zoltán, 142
Galsay, Ervin, 142
Garay, Ernő, 97, 142
Gárdonyi, Lajos, 53, 59–61, 142
Gárdos, Sándor, 129
Gáti, György, 53
Gáti, Pál, 53
Gazdag lány (Rich Girl), 60, 136

Gelber, N., 143
Gelléri, Sándor, 53
Gellért, Lajos, 61–62,
gendarmes, 8–9, 11, 15
Gergely, Kató, 107–108
Gergely, Pál, 101, 143
Gerle, Róbert, 137, 144
Gerő, Erzsi, 53, 142
Gerő, György, 53, 142
Gervay, Erzsi, 65
Gestapo, 8, 10–11
Ghetto (Budapest), 8, 13–14, 15
Gidaly, 142
Goldmann, György, xv
Goldmann, N., 145
Goldmark Hall, 146
Goldmark Music School, 140
Goldmark Philharmonic Music Association, 138–139
Goldmark, Károly, 21
Gonda, Jenő, 53
Gonda, József, 53, 63–64
Göndör, Bertalan, xv
Göndör, Márta, 144
Görgey, Arthur, 42–43
Goth, Sándor, 48
Gőzgép (Steam-engine), 51
Gross, Dezső, 144
Grunfeld, Ármin, 145
Gyermek és a Messiás, A (The Child and the Messiah), 46–47, 102, 136
Győri, Matild, 53

Haas, Pavel, 138
Haggadah, 102
hair stylist, theater, 129–130
Hajdu, János, 97, 101, 132, 145
Hajós, Péter, 53, 142
Halasi, Ferenc, 142
half-Jews, xii
Halmagyi, Ferenc, 142
Halmos, György, 97, 143
Halmos, László, 144
Hanak, Árpád, 143
Harmath, Imre,70, 76
Harsányi, Miklós, 35
Harsányi, Tibor, 141
Hatvani, Baron, 139
Havi 200 pengő fix (salary, 200 a month), 78
Hebbel, Friedrich, 30, 32, 136
Hegedü es koldusbot (Violin and Misery), 47
Hegyek alján (The Lowlands), 69, 135
Heisler, Ferenc, 144
Heltai, Jenő, 42
Henny Lehmann, 67
Herczog, Baron Mór, 139
Herendi, Manci, "Whistling Manci," 109, 142
Hermann, Manci, "Whistling Manci," 109, 142
Herskovits, Béla, 143
Herz, Lili, 97, 123, 143
Herzl, Theodor (Tivadar), 2–3
Hét, A (The Week), 40, 42
Hevesi, Sándor, 30, 61–62
Hevesi, Simon, xi
Hidas, Hedy, 53
Hidy, Ferenc, 142
Hirsch, József, 144
Hirsch, Sándor, 144
Hirsch, Zoltán (aka "Zoli the Clown"), xv
Hitler, Adolf, 5–7, 9, 17–18, 137
Hoffmann meséi (Hoffmann Tales), 106
Hoffmann, Erzsi, 144
Hoffmann, Pál, 144
Holocaust history in Hungary, 6–15
Holocaust of Hungarian Jewry, 6–15
Hóman, Bálint, 22
Honorary Citizen of London (1999), xvi
Honty, Hanna, 64–65
Horn, Ferenc, 130
Horthy, Miklós, xii, 4, 12
Horti, Lajos, 117
Horváth, Ferenc, 53

Horváth, László, 98, 122, 144, 150
Horváth, Mady, 53
Hubay, Jenő, 118, 122
Hungarian army, 6–7
Hungarian Bibliophile Society, xv
Hungarian Final Solution, 9
Hungarian Jewish Theater, xvii
Hungarian Jewish University and College Students' Association Orchestra (*A Magyar Izraelita Egyetemi es Főiskolai Hallgatók Országos Egyesületének*) (MIEFHOE), 140
Hungarian Kingdom, 2
Hungarian Law of Reception of Judaism, xi
Hungarian Royal Opera House, 110
Hungarian Second Army, 7
Hungarian soldiers, 7
Hungarian Theater (*Magyar Színház*), 30, 37, 63, 66, 72–73
Hungarian-Jewish historical context (1848–1945), 1–16
Hungarian-Jewish patriotism, 2, 9
Hunyadi, Sándor, 50
Hütter, Pál, 98, 122, 144

Ibsen, Henrik, 30, 32–33, 61–62, 136
Igaz, Luci, 53
Inner City Religious Community (Budapest), 47
Inner City Youth Group, 107–108
Inotai, Tibor, 143
Interwar Hungary, 4–6
invisible actors of the OMIKE, 128
Ismeretlen lány (Unknown Girl), 51, 82, 136

Jámbor, Ági, 97, 123, 143
Járdányi, Pál, 140, 147
Jaross, Andor, 9
Jászai, Mari,xi, 77, 139
Játék a kastélyban (Playing in the Castle), 51, 73, 136
Jávor, Dezső, 144
Jávor, Pál, xii
Jászai, Mari, xi, 77, 139
Jedermann, 61–62
Jedermann Jotetjere (Jedermann's Good Deed), 73
Jewish community, 137–138, 140
Jewish Community, Hollan Street, 140
Jewish community in Berlin, 107, 137
Jewish Councils, 8, 10, 138
Jewish Hungarian Poets of a Hundred Years, xv
Jewish Laws, 1938,1939, xix, 6, 7, 11
Jewish Museum, xiv, 21
Jewish Question, xiv, 4, 5, 9
Jewish Religious Community of Pest, 21
Jewish survivors, 139
Jewish survivors, Budapest, 139
Jewish survivors, total, 139
Jewish synagogue (Tapolca), 113–114
Jewish theater, xiii, 138–139
Jewish victims of SS and Ukrainian militia, 8
Jewish victims, musicians, 7
Job, Daniel, 61
joint rehearsals, 131–132
Jókai, Mór, 41
journalists, xiii, xiv, 4, 29, 41, 141
József, Archduke, 139
Judit (Judith), 136
Justh, Gyula, 53

Kabos, Gyula, 60, 67, 78
Káldy, László, 100
Kadosa, Pál, 141, 143
Kállai, Ottó, 144
Kállay, Miklós, 7, 8
Kálmán, Oszkár, xvi, 97, 110, 132, 140, 142
Kálmán, Tibor, 144
Kalmár, Ferenc, 144
Kamara Variete (Variety Chamber), 77
Kamera Színház (Chamber Theater), 71, 82, 139

Kara, Imre, 142
Karinthy, Frigyes, 92, 121
Karnevál (Carneval), 136
Kárpáti, Aurel, 44
Kárpáti, Gyula, 53
Karsai, Laszlo, 19, 20, 151
Kasztner, Rudolf (Rezso), 19
Kelen, Dóra, 53
Kelen, Hugó, 46, 47, 101, 102, 103, 136, 141
Kelen, Rózsi, 102, 143
Keleti, Árpád, 97, 142
Keleti, Frigyes, 143
Keller, Dezső, 45, 70
Kemény, Baron Gábor, 13
Kenessey, Pál, 144
Képzőművészeti Csoport (Fine Arts Group), 141
Keresztes-Fischer, Ferenc, 6, 22
King Gustav VII, 11
Király, Ernő, 66, 84
Király Színház (King Theater), 109, 139
Kis komedia (Small Comedy), 67
Kisfaludy Society, 39, 51
Kishegyi, Árpád, 142
Kiss, Ferenc, 74, 82, 90, 96
Klári Felhő, 91, 92
Klein, Gideon, 138, 146
Klein, Károly, 144
Klein, László, 144
Klein, Miklós, 144
Klein, Sándor, 144
Klemperer, Ottó, xvi, 101, 110
Knappertsbusch, 105
known and unknown heroes of the orchestra, 122
Kodály, Zoltán, xii, xiii
Kohn, Dr. Zoltán, 47
Kolos, Hanna, 142
Kolosváry-Borcsa, Miklós, xiv
Kolozsvar, 54, 58, 138, 146
Komédia Orfeum (Comedy Hall), 139
Komor, Ági, 53, 147
Komor, Gyula, 49
Komor, Vilmos, xvi, 32, 68, 97, 98, 120, 132, 140, 142, 145
Kondor, Leo, 141
Kornel Sziklay Kis Színházköre, 45
Kornis, Kató, 53, 142
Korvin, Imre, 144
Kovács, Imre, 144
Kovács, Miklós, 97, 142
Kovno ghetto, 138
Krasa, Hans, 138
Kraszner, Kató, 97, 142
Kulturbund Deutscher Juden, 107, 137
Kurti, Károly, 53
Kuti, Sándor, xv, 142, 150

La Boheme, 109, 135
labor service, xiii, xiv, 6,7, 9, 11, 13, 14, 18, 146, 147
labor servicemen, 7
Ladányi, Ilona, 97, 111, 112,132, 142, 143
Lajtai-Lazarus, Walter, 97, 101, 141, 142, 143
Lakner, Artúr, xv
Lakos, Klári, 53, 64, 65, 142
Lammermoori Lucia (Lucia of Lammermoor), 135
Lányi, Dezső, 53
László, Tivadar, 53
Le Soir, 68
leadership, the, xiii, 21, 29, 37, 39, 57, 74
Leányvásár (The Marriage Market), 116
Legenda (Legend), 47
Lendvay, Andor, 97, 112, 113, 121, 132, 142
Lengyel, László, 141
Lengyel, Menyhért, 30
Lenke, Leopold, 97, 142
Leoncavallo, 135
Libanon (Lebanon), xiv
life member of *Nemzeti Színház* (1946), xvi
life member of the Opera House in Budapest (1947), xvi

Ligeti, Dezső, 142
light opera, 33, 35, 43, 45
lighting designer, 126, 128, 130
lighting effects, 126
Liliom, egy csirkefogó élete es halála (Lily, a Scoundrel's Life and Death), 49
Lodz Ghetto, 138, 146
Lőrincz, Miklós, xv
lovag úr, A (Mr. Knight), 43
Low, Lipót, xi
Lowinger, N., 144
Lukács, Pál, 97, 144
Lutz, Carl, 13, 19

Madách Színház (Madach Theater), 92
Mádai, István, 144
Madam Caier, 109
Magyar Állami Operaház (Hungarian State Opera House), 140
Magyar Királyi Operaház, 139
Magyar Színház (Hungarian Theater), xv, 30, 37, 63, 66, 81, 90, 114, 139
Magyar Zsidók Lapja (Hungarian Jews' Paper), xiv, 147
Majom Színház (Monkey Theater), 61
Major, István, 53
Május (May), 89, 136
Mandel, Lajos, 143
Mányai, Lajos, 54, 88
Margitszigeti Színház (Margaret Island Theater), 117
Márkus Park Színház (Markus Park Theater), 76
Márkus, Alfréd, xvi, 97, 100, 141, 142
Márkus, László, xii, 72
Marsall (Marshal), 136
Mauthausen, 15
Medák, Sári, 142
Meitner, Irén Pásztóné, 144
Melodie Juive, 67
memorizing rehearsals, 131
Mérei, Adolf, 66
Mérenyi, Pál, 143
Metropolitan Opera, New York, xvi, 68
Mihály, András, xiv, 144, 147
militant Christian ideology, 5
Miss America, 76
Missa Solemnis (Solemn Mass), 61, 62
Modern Színház (Modern Theater), 75
Modern Színpad (Modern Stage), 66
Mohácsi, Jenő, 102, 136
Moliére, xi, 32
Molnár, Ferenc, 32, 41, 42, 43, 44, 48, 49, 50, 51, 73, 82, 136
Molnár, József, 54
Molnár, László, 142
Molnár, Márta, 142
Mori, Béla, 144
Moulin Rouge, 76
Mozart, xiii, 26, 32, 76, 105
Múlt es Jövő (Past and Present), xiv, 146
Mura (Mandl), Péter, 132, 143, 145
Music Academy, 68, 81, 99, 101, 105, 106, 107, 108, 111, 114, 116, 117, 118, 119, 120, 140
music correcting rehearsals, 132
musicals, 135
Muskátli kabaré (Geranium Cabaret), 76
Művész Színház (Artist Theater), 49, 139

Nad (Nadelstecher), László, 144
Nádas, István, 143
Nádor, György, 144
Nádor, Mihály, 141
nagy riport, A (The Big Report), 62
Nagy, Endre, 72, 78
Nagy, György, xv, 35, 53, 54, 68, 69, 89
Napsütötte földön (On a Sunny Day), 102
National Actors' Association, 75, 88
National Conservatory, 98
National Széchenyi Library Theatre Archives, 141, 150, 151
National Theater in Cluj, 87, 89, 105, 138
nationalist revolutions (1848–1849), 2
Nazi Germany, xiii, 5, 18
NBC, New York, 104

Nemzet (Nation), 41
Nemzeti Színház (National Theater), Budapest, xii, xvi, 37, 54, 55, 57, 59,76, 86, 87, 96, 129, 130
Népopera (Folk Opera), 129
NépSzínház (Popular Theater), 40
New York, xv, xvi, 16, 17, 18,19, 20, 43, 50, 68, 76, 104, 120, 137, 150
New York Bár (New York Bar), 76
New York Café, 43
New York Philharmonic, 137
Ney, Dávid, xv, 97, 113, 114, 140, 142,
Ney II, Dávid, 19, 114, 142
Nicolai, 135
nős ember, A (The Married Man), 136
Noti, Karoly, 78–79
Numerus Clausus, xii, 4, 139

Odry, Árpád, 40, 90
Offenbach, J., xiii, 26, 32, 135
official duties and regulations of the Artistic Enterprise, 31
OMIKE Művészakció (OMIKE Artistic Enterprise), xi, xvi, 1, 6, 7, 16, 145, 146, 149, 150
OMIKE Orchestra, 141
OMIKE orchestral and choral lists, 141
OMIKE's company, 33
OMZSA (Országos Magyar Zsidó Segítő Akció) (Hungarian Jewish Aid Organization), 26, 27
Öntőház Street Synagogue, xiii
Opera House (*Operaház*), xvi, 23, 89, 98, 99, 105, 106, 107, 110, 111, 112, 113, 114, 115, 116, 118, 121, 122, 128, 130, 139, 140,
opera performances, the most successful, 135
opera rehearsals, 131
opera section of OMIKE, 110
Operetta Theater of Budapest, 65
Oradea, 76, 120, 120
orchestral concerts, xiv
Order of the British Empire (1991), xvi
ordinary pieces, rehearsals of, 131, 132, 136
Ördög (Devil), 48, 49
ördög cimboráját, Az (The Devil's Disciple), 69, 88
Ormos, Béla, 54, 69,70, 71
Ortner, Pál, 142
Őszi szonáta (Autumn Sonata), 45, 74, 136
osztály szégyene, Az (The Shame of the Class), 78, 142
Osztrigás Mici, Az (The Girl from Maxim's), 78

P. I. H., 108
Páger, Antal, 69, 88
painters, xii, xiii, xiv, 7, 27, 52, 117, 146
Pál, Jenő, 97, 142
Pálffy, Blanka, 53, 146
Pállay, Anna, xvi, 17
Pállos Ladies Company, 101
Pallós, Tivadar, 65, 97, 101, 142, 143
Palotai, Erzsi, 53, 65, 71
Palotai, Imre, 143
Pál-utcai fiúk, A (The Paul Street Boys), 51
Pap, Károly, xv
Párdány, Judith, 53, 73, 74, 76
Pártos, Erzsi, 53
performances, 41, 45, 49
Perlasca, Giorgio (Jorge), 13
Pester Lloyd, 41, 95
Pesti Napló, 41, 43
Pesti, Sándor, 144
Petit Casino, 68
Petőfi Society, 51
Petschauer, Attila, 6
Philharmonic of Budapest, 99
Philharmonic of Warsaw, 99
Pilitz, Vilmos, 144
Pillangókisasszony (Madame Buttertfly), 69
Pódium Kabaré, 129
Pogány, László, 142

Pogány, Zsuzsa, 97
Pollák, Pál, 143
Pollák, Sándor, 142
Pope Pius XII, 11
Popper, David, 139
Poprádi, Ernő, 54
Por, Irén, 53
Portuguese consulate, 11
post-World War I, 4, 20
POWs, 6, 18
preparatory rehearsal, 131
preparing for the show, 130
President Roosevelt, 11
Press Chamber (Guild), xiv
press group of the OMIKE, xiv
pre-World War I population, 2
prima ballerina, xvi
program booklets, xiv
programming, xiii, 31, 32
programs, xii, xiii, 16, 32, 33, 34, 38, 67, 93, 135, 146
prompter, 128, 129, 131, 132
property man, 127, 128
property room, 31, 127
protected buildings, 13, 14, 15
Puccini, 26, 99, 105, 118, 135
Pünkösti, Andor, 50, 74

Rab, István, 54
Racine, 32, 136
Rácz Aladár, 140
Ráday (Radai), Imre, 50, 54
rádió, 8, 62, 78, 79, 98, 104
Radnai, Erzsi, 97, 115, 116, 117, 142
Radnai, Miklós, 111
Rajna, Alice, 53, 77, 78, 85
Rajna, Mária, 53, 142
Rajter, György, 140
Rákos, László, 144
Rákos, Tibor, 54, 142
Rákosi, Szidi, 60, 66, 92
Rátkai, Márton, 50, 60, 66
Rauchwerger (Rev), Lili, 97, 143
reading rehearsal, 89, 131
Red Army, 7, 10, 12, 13, 14, 15
Red Cross, 13, 107, 138
reflectors, 62, 73, 126, 130
rehearsal, xi, 49, 50, 62, 66, 71, 75, 79, 80, 82, 89, 106, 128, 129
Reich, Lili, 129
Reich, Margit,
Reinhardt Theater, 100, 107
Reinitz, Béla, 141, 143
Reisz, Pál, 144
Reiter, László, xiv, xv
Religious Circles Orchestra, Budapest, 140
Relle, Gabriella, 97, 117, 118, 119, 132, 140, 142
Renaissance Theater (*Renaissance Színház*), 139
repetiteur, 100, 101, 131, 132
Reschovszki, Sándor, 123, 143
Revere, Gyula, 144
Révész, Sándor, 142
Rhine Gold, The, 114
Ribary, Géza, xiii, 6, 21, 24, 25, 26, 27, 29, 37, 74, 99, 101, 110, 143, 145
Richard III (Richard III), 63
Riesz, Pál, 142
Riga Ghetto, 138
righteous gentiles, 15
Rigoletto, 98, 112, 115
Robert, Mária, 53
Roboz, Imre, 61
Rokoko (Rococo), 45
Román, István, 144
Róna, Vera, 97, 142
Rónai, Géza, 54
Rónai, Mihály András, xiv, 147
Rosenstein, Kálmán, 130
Rossini, 99, 136
Rosthy (Rosty), Magda, 53, 142
Rota, Angelo,
Róth, Ferenc, 97, 142
Róth, Imre, 144
Róth, József, 144

Róth, Miklós, 143
Róth, Miksa, 142
Rothfeld, Gábor, 144
Rott, Sándor "Little Rott," 84
Rotta, Angelo, 13
Rovelli, Dezső, 142
Royal Festival Hall, London, xvi
Royal Orfeum (Royal Music Hall), Budapest, 139
Rózsa, Mária, 53
Rózsa, Nándor, 142
Rózsa, Vera, xvi, 97, 119, 120, 142
Rózsahegyi Kálmán acting school, 65
Rózsavölgyi, Márk, 47
Rudas, Erna, 142
Rumkowski, Mordechai Chaim, 138

Sába királynője (Queen of Sheba), 135
Sajó, Jenő, 142
Salamon, Béla, 54, 61, 78, 79, 84, 85
Salamon, Miklós, 142
Sammler, Béla, 144
Sammler, Sándor, 97, 143
Sándor Kremer's Company, 75
Sándor, Frigyes, xiii, 97, 100, 142
Sándor, Irén, 143
Sándor, József, 54
Sándor, Renee, 143
Sarkadi, Aladar, 54, 67, 85, 142
Sas, Imre, 54, 143
Sasfiók (Eaglet), 74
Sauer, Zs., 144
scenery and lighting test, 131
scenery officer, 128
scenery painter, 130
Schlachta, Margit, 14
Schneider, Hedvig, 97, 143
Schönfeld, Jutka, 144
Schultz, Zoltán, 144
Schumann, 136
sculptors, xiii, xiv, 7, 27
Sebők, György, 143
Sebők, Stefi, 97, 143
second alto, 121
Second Jewish Law (1939), xiii
Sevillai borbély (Barber of Seville), 112, 136
Shakespeare, 30, 32
Shaw, George Bernard, 88
Sík, Olga, 97, 143
Silber, István,145
Simai, Ede, 54
Simon, Ili, 143
Simon, Zsuzsa, 53, 87, 88, 150
Simplicissimus, 66, 67
Sipos, Dr. Jenő, 97, 143
Sirató (Lament), 102
sitting rehearsals, 132
Social Working Committee, 21
solo rehearsals, 131
Solt, Dr. Pál, 144
Solt, Ibolya, 53, 88, 89, 143
Soltész (Mechler), Erzsébet, 141
Somlár, Zsigmond, 54
Somló, Sándor, 55, 59
Somogyi, Dezső, 143
Somogyi, István, 143
Somogyi, László, 97, 100, 142
Somogyi, Nusi, 66,
Somogyi, Piroska, 97, 143
Sonnenfeld, Miklós, 143
Soviet POW camps, 7, 8
Spiegel, Annie, 97, 120, 121, 122, 123, 140, 143
Spitzer, László, 143
Staatsoper, in Berlin, 101, 110, 121
stage designer, 128, 130, 131
stage manager, xvi, 30, 46, 53, 54, 80, 126, 128, 131
stage of Goldmark Hall, 126
Stalin, 16
Stalingrad, 7
Starker, János, xvi, 98, 137, 144
statistical data, 135
Steiner, Imre, 144
Steinhardt, Géza, xv

Stern, János, 144
Stern, Samu, 22, 25, 29
Stollár, Béla, 14
Strauss, Richárd, 122, 136
Stravinsky's *Ragtime,* 140
Sugár, Pál, 143
Suppé, Franz von, 113
Süt a nap (Sun Shines), 90
Svábhegy, 57
Swedish consulate, 11
Swiss consulate, 11, 14
Szabó, Dezső, Dr., 54, 89
Szabó, Gábor, 58
Szabolcs, Ernő, 35, 53, 56, 92, 133
Szakáll, Szőke, 67, 73
Szálasi, Ferenc, xii, 12, 13, 14, 16, 19, 54
Szamosi, Elza, 139
Szamosi, Imre "Buli," 142, 145
Szántó, Klára, 53
Szécsi, Hédy, 53, 143
Székely, István, 144
Székely, Mózes, 88
Szelényi, István, 141
Szemere, György, 30
Szendrő, Mária, 97, 143
Szenes, Béla, 60, 78, 136
Szentiványi, Kálmán, 54, 91, 92
Szép, Ernő, 32, 50, 52, 53, 89, 136
Szeszler, Tibor, 143
Szidi Rákosi's school, 60, 66, 92
Szigeti, Jenő, 54, 143
Szigeti, József, 139
Szilágyi, Bea, 53, 143
Szilágyi, József, 129
Szilárd, Ágnes, 53
Szirmai, Vilmos, 54, 92, 143
Szöktetés a szerájból (The Abduction from the Seraglio), 135
Sztehló, Gábor, 14
Sztójay, Döme, 8, 9, 16, 19

Tamar (Tamar), 74, 136
Tamás (Taubner), Ödön, 143
Taube, Carlo, 138
technical part of the director's task, the, 128
Télikert, (Winter Garden), 66
Temple of Heroes, 21
Terezin (Theresienstadt), 138
Terézkörúti Színpad (Terez Boulevard Stage), 139
Térő, Ilona, 144
Teszler, Tivadar, 97
Thalia Society (Company), 30
Theater and Film Chamber (Actors' Guild), xii
theater hair stylist, 128, 129–130
theater tailor, 129–130
theatrical comedies, 135
Tibor, György, 144
Timosa, 61–62
Tisza, Count, 139
Tiszaeszlar blood-libel trial, 2
Tordai, Judith, 53
Traviata, 105
Treblinka, 138
Trietsch, György, 97, 144
Trubadúr, 121
Trumen, László, 145
Turk, Berta, 83
Tüzek az éjszakában (Fires in the Night), 63

U.S., 6, 44, 51, 104
U.S. Army, 15, 16
Új Színház (New Theater), 30
Új Thalia (New Thalia), 72
Újfalusi, István, 54
Újházi, György, 62
Újpesti Színház (Theater of Ujpest), 90
Ukraine, 6, 15
Ullmann, Viktor, 138
Ungár, Imre, 123, 143
University of Maryland, Baltimore County, xvi, 137, 150

Vadász, Endre, xv
Vadkacsa (Wild Duck), 136
Vágó, Éva, 53
Vajda, Elza, 68
Vajda, Frigyes, 68, 143
Vajda, Lili, 68, 143
Vajna, Károly, 144
Valaki (Somebody), 51
Valer, Janos, 144
Vámos, László, 144
Vándor, Sándor, 132, 145
Vándor, Valéria, 53
Váradi, Aranka, 73
Váradi, Kató, 53, 143
Váradi, Tibor, 53–54, 143
Varázsfuvola (Magic Flute), 69, 112, 128, 135
Varga, Ruben, 144
Varjas, Anna, 143
Várnai, Jenő, 54
Városi Színház (City Theater), 30, 45, 99, 114, 115, 120, 129, 139, 142–144
Vass, József, 63
Vatican consulate, 11
Vecsey, Ilona, 53
Verdi, xiii, 26, 99, 105, 135–136
Vertes, Gyula, 144
Vidor, Ferike, 53, 93–94, 143
Vígh, Miklós, 65
Vígszínház (Comedy Theater), 82, 100
Vilnius Ghetto, 138
Virág, Jenő, 67
Virágzó asszony (Flourishing Woman), 74
visitors, number of, 135
Viso, Márk, 143
vocal artists of the OMIKE Artistic Enterprise, 103

Waldmann, Miklós, 144
Walkur, The, 114
Wallenberg, Raoul, 13, 19
war criminals, 12, 15–16
Warsaw Ghetto, 138, 146
Wechselmann, Fanni, 94
Weinberg, Ákos, 144
Weinberger, István, 144
Weinberger, József, 144
Weiner, György, 143
Weiner, László, xv, 97, 101, 141, 142
Weiner, Leo, xiii, 141
Weiner's "Number III. Divertimento," 140
Weinstock, Miklós, 143
Weiss, Manfred, 139
Weisz, Franz, 138
Wertheimer-mulatóba (Wertheimer Nightclub), 93
Willmann, Lili, 143
Windsori Vig Nők (Merry Wives of Windsor), 33, 69, 135
Wlassits, Baron Gyula, 118
World War I, 2–5
writers, the, 7, 22, 37–40, 141
Würdiger, Miksa, 127, 142

Yad Vashem, 15
Yearbook, Press Group, 141
yellow star, 8
Yellow Star houses, 11
Yiddish music, 103, 119–120
Yiddish songs, 119–120
Youth Groups of the Jewish Religious Community of Pest, 107–108
Yugoslavia, 8, 15

Zádor, István, 130
Zágon, Vera, 53
Zathureczky, Ede, 122
Zátony, Kálmán, 54, 95, 143
Zeitinger, Jenő, 144
Zionism, 3, 17
Zionist nationalism, 17
Zionists, 3, 14, 19
Zoltán, Irén, xii, xv, 19, 30, 47–48, 54–55, 142–144
Zsigmondi, Pál, 101, 141, 142
Zsoldos, Imre, 144

Zsolt, Béla, 44
Zsolt, Magda, 143
Zsoltár a mindenség szeretetéről (Psalm about the Love of the Universe), 103